DISCARD

One Islam, Many Muslim Worlds

RELIGION AND GLOBAL POLITICS

SERIES EDITOR
John L. Esposito
University Professor and Director
Prince Alwaleed Bin Talal Center for Muslim-Christian Understanding
Georgetown University

RACHID GHANNOUCHI
A Democrat Within Islamism
Azzam S. Tamimi

BALKAN IDOLS
Religion and Nationalism in Yugoslav States
Vjekoslav Perica

ISLAMIC POLITICAL IDENTITY IN TURKEY
M. Hakan Yavuz

RELIGION AND POLITICS IN POST-COMMUNIST ROMANIA
Lavinia Stan and Lucian Turcescu

PIETY AND POLITICS
Islamism in Contemporary Malaysia
Joseph Chinyong Liow

TERROR IN THE LAND OF THE HOLY SPIRIT
Guatemala under General Efrain Rios Montt, 1982–1983
Virginia Garrard-Burnett

IN THE HOUSE OF WAR
Dutch Islam Observed
Sam Cherribi

BEING YOUNG AND MUSLIM
New Cultural Politics in the Global South and North
Asef Bayat and Linda Herrera

CHURCH, STATE, AND DEMOCRACY IN EXPANDING EUROPE
Lavinia Stan and Lucian Turcescu

THE HEADSCARF CONTROVERSY
Secularism and Freedom of Religion
Hilal Elver

THE HOUSE OF SERVICE
The Gülen Movement and Islam's Third Way
David Tittensor

MAPPING THE LEGAL BOUNDARIES OF BELONGING
Religion and Multiculturalism from Israel to Canada
Edited by René Provost

RELIGIOUS SECULARITY
A Theological Challenge to the Islamic State
Naser Ghobadzadeh

THE MIDDLE PATH OF MODERATION IN ISLAM
The Qur'ānic Principle of Wasaṭiyyah
Mohammad Hashim Kamali

ONE ISLAM, MANY MUSLIM WORLDS
Spirituality, Identity, and Resistance across Islamic Lands
Raymond William Baker

One Islam, Many Muslim Worlds

Spirituality, Identity, and Resistance across Islamic Lands

RAYMOND WILLIAM BAKER

OXFORD
UNIVERSITY PRESS

OXFORD
UNIVERSITY PRESS

Oxford University Press is a department of the University of Oxford.
It furthers the University's objective of excellence in research, scholarship,
and education by publishing worldwide. Oxford is a registered trade mark
of Oxford University Press in the UK and in certain other countries

Published in the United States of America by
Oxford University Press
198 Madison Avenue, New York, NY 10016,
United States of America

Library of Congress Cataloging-in-Publication Data
Baker, Raymond William, 1942–
One Islam, many Muslim worlds : spirituality, identity, and resistance
across Islamic lands / Raymond William Baker.
p.   cm. — (Religion and global politics)
Includes bibliographical references and index.
ISBN 978–0–19–984647–4 (cloth : alk. paper) 1. Islam—21st century. 2. Muslims.
3. Islamic sociology. 4. Islam and politics—21st century. I. Title.
BP161.3.B344 2015
297.09'051—dc23
2014048242

1   3   5   7   9   8   6   4   2

Typeset in Scala Pro

Printed on 45# Glatt offset 400 ppi

Printed by Edwards Brothers, North Carolina

To Laila, Suad, Muhammad, and the numerous other ordinary Muslims encountered in Islamic lands who somehow create small miracles of kindness and courage, as they wage everyday battles to live good and productive lives in often extraordinary and, far too often, cruel circumstances.

How splendid is the wisdom of God in revealing the nature of Islam. Islam appeared as a River of Life, welling up in the barren desert of Arabia.

MUHAMMAD ABDUH

Contents

Acknowledgments

TWO CIRCLES OF special people have made this book possible. The first arose from decades of interaction with friends, colleagues, and a multitude of strangers in the Islamic lands where I have lived and traveled for some four decades. Always to my great delight, they have very often been more than willing to share with an American student of their religion, culture, and political life their experiences and their feelings—not to mention whatever they were eating or drinking as I passed by. Endless acts of generosity have marked those encounters. Relationships of all kinds emerged, and those relationships inform the observations offered here. The second circle has taken shape from the generations of students, especially in Egypt and the United States, who have struggled with me to better understand and appreciate one of the world's great civilizations and the astonishingly diverse personal and collective lives it has made possible.

Only living in communities of Muslims can provide the indispensable experiential grounding for an interpretive essay on contemporary Islam like this one. Islam is about acting in the world. For believers, faith is very much about the struggle to live personally and in community as God intended for his creations. I am grateful for the wonderful opportunities I have received from the Muslims among whom I have lived to share joys and sorrows through the years. Without my designation as a Carnegie Islam Scholar and the generous support from the Carnegie Corporation of New York that came with it, travel to these far-flung places to meet and discuss with scholars, public intellectuals, and ordinary people would not have been possible, although Carnegie bears no responsibility for what I imagined I learned from those encounters.

Academic colleagues across the disciplines and around the globe, most notably those in Egypt, Lebanon, Jordan, Cyprus, Syria, Tunisia, and Iraq as well as the United States, have reacted continuously to my earlier published work on Islam. I have greatly appreciated their kindnesses in pointing out shortcomings and misinterpretations. I like to imagine that their efforts have improved this latest effort. It is impossible to list all of those colleagues. However, I simply cannot fail to mention three: Tareq Ismael of the University of Calgary, Manar Shorbagy of the American University in Cairo, and John Esposito of Georgetown.

Of the hundreds of students who have studied things Islamic with me, two Americans have been especially helpful on this project: Alex Henry over the course of several years, including a summer in Cairo, and Alex Hermsen, most recently, for assisting in the very final stages of the manuscript. Of former Egyptian and Arab students, allow me to celebrate Karen Aboul Kheir and Omar Mahmoud, two of the most brilliant who very early made the teacher–student role a reversible one and taught me a great deal about Islam, the many Muslim worlds, and the world beyond. They are now lifelong friends and professional peers in very different fields. I have learned most when our disagreements on issues have been sharpest and the discussions most animated. I have reveled in those friendships. Miraculously, both Karen and Omar still respond to calls for help from a former teacher. Lively discussions with both of them have proceeded apace as I have worked for a very long time to finish this manuscript. Omar, I should also add, has read every line in this book. He helped me reconsider and rewrite more sections than I can count. He corrected errors and offered suggestions for important improvements all along the way. Omar deserves considerable credit for any strength the book may have and no blame at all for the weaknesses and misinterpretations that remain, since I did not always take his advice.

In Cairo, I am indebted to Mostafa Mohamed, my lead research assistant for the book and for a myriad of other research projects. We have worked together for years now, and I still marvel at his prodigious memory and impressive analytical skills. To Ramadan Abd el Aziz I owe deep gratitude for managing my research office and great affection for decades of close friendship. Finally, I appreciate the support and assistance of Muhammad Ismail who found smart ways to overcome the everyday challenges of life in Cairo and Alexandria to make sure I had time to revel in the endless adventures possible in those wonderful cities.

Big projects never go forward without the support of family and friends. My sister-in-law Jan Baker and her mother, Joyce Townsend Garrod, rival my Muslim friends in their Methodist version of generosity of spirit and hospitality, while my endlessly talented brother Don repeatedly offers support in matters large and small. When I took breaks from the writing, my nephew Huan Ngoyen and I had great discussions on life chances and choices, across the generations and in out-of-the-way locations. Many ideas and concerns from this book found their way into those talks.

Tareq Ismail and Jack Waggett have been a part of my life for years that we have stopped counting but have never ceased to enjoy. Shafiq Badan has managed over some ten years of friendship to meld together the roles of father, brother, and son. I have no idea how he accomplishes this improbable feat; the mystery only increases the pleasure of our deep friendship. Only the Persian mystic poets Rumi and Hafez rival the standing of these three personal friends as life companions and sources of support.

I have lost my beloved wife, Elaine, with whom I began the adventures recorded here. Our four children, Sarah, Dorian, Madalyn, and Pamela, are all sources of unabashed pride, not least for the ways they cherish and live the humane values and perspectives of citizens of the world that Elaine and I strived to impart. Elaine's unbounded goodness, ease of forgiveness, and compassionate caring for the most wounded among us survive through their presence and their acts of kindness in the world.

Note on Style and Conventions

THIS BOOK IS not intended to be a work of social science. It offers an interpretation of midstream Islam today. It is written in essay style. This approach has made the avoidance of jargon possible. It has produced a text as unburdened by notes as possible. In addition, the essay style has also allowed a streamlined approach to problems encountered going from Arabic sources to an English text.

All Arabic-language materials are listed only with English translations of titles and without cumbersome transliterations of the Arabic titles. The translations will make the Arabic original obvious to Arabic readers while sparing English readers distracting and meaningless transliterations. Arabic newspaper articles are cited in streamlined fashion by author, source, and date only. However, important Arabic terms used in the text have been transliterated in a simplified way that avoids hyphens and diacritics, except for the *ain* and the *hamza*, both represented by (ʻ). Readers of Arabic will immediately recognize the original, while non-Arabic readers will be spared the cumbersome symbols necessary to render Arabic letters in English. For plurals, I have simply added an "s" to singular forms rather than introduce complicated Arabic forms, unless they have already become somewhat familiar. I hope that the relief afforded general readers will mollify the rightful objections of purists to these deviations. All citations in the notes are complete, allowing the omission of a separate bibliography while still enabling interested readers to locate sources used.

There are no absolute equivalents in English for many of the important Islamic concepts and phrases used throughout the book. The translations provided should be viewed as only rough approximations to the Arabic terms. They are offered with the practical aim of helping non-Arabic readers to overcome initial discomfort with important Islamic concepts with which they are unfamiliar. In all cases, the translations follow as closely as possible the meaning given to these terms in their works by the centrist

Islamic thinkers and activists who are the subjects of this study. Readers should understand that other Islamic scholars might well contest these meanings. Indeed, even among the centrists there are disagreements about the precise ways in which particular terms are to be understood. A fuller sense of the meaning of all of these phrases will come with attention to the actual contexts in which they are used. The format for the Arabic terms used in the text generally will be that the first time the expression is used in a given chapter it will appear in italicized Arabic transliteration followed by English equivalent in parentheses. However, for a small group of terms for which an adequate and relatively standardized translation is available, the English translation may also be used after the term has been introduced with the transliteration. A handful of Arabic words, now widely used and understood in English, will be treated as English words. Throughout, I avoid the adjective "Islamist" and substitute "Islamic" for it. In Arabic, the phrase is *"Islami"* and it is simply the adjective "Islamic." In the Western press the translation of the term as "Islamist" has in recent years become a term of opprobrium and condemnation when applied to politicized Islam. It is now too negatively freighted in English to be useful, and I have therefore reverted to the literal and neutral translation.

One Islam, Many Muslim Worlds

I

The Mystery of Islam's Strength

It is God Who created you in a state of helpless weakness,
Then gave (you) strength after weakness . . .
He creates as He wills, and it is He Who has all knowledge and power.

QUR'AN 30:54

ISLAM TODAY PRESENTS itself wrapped in a conundrum. By all economic and political measures, the late twentieth century was a time of terrible decline for the Islamic world, particularly its Arab heartland. The deterioration continues in the first decades of the twenty-first century, accelerated by the American shattering of Iraq and Afghanistan, the disintegration of Syria, and the resurgence of virulent extremisms. Sober voices from the Islamic world regularly and accurately describe the condition of *Dar al Islam* (the Islamic world) as the worst in the 1,400-year-old history of Islam.[1]

Yet, precisely at this time of unprecedented material vulnerability, Islam emerged as the only transnational force to create a galvanizing identity strong enough to challenge America's homogenizing global power. At the same time, Islam inspired the most successful of the Arab resistances to the expansion of the Israeli state. In the spring of 2011 the extraordinary popular uprisings in Arab lands, although not led by Islamic groups, evinced a distinctive Islamic coloration. The ordinary Muslims who made these revolutions, notably in Egypt and Tunisia, framed their mobilizing calls for freedom and justice in an Islamic idiom rarely appreciated or even understood in Western commentary. Calls celebrating the greatness of God were as loud as or louder than those demanding the fall of the regime. Such invocations of Islam should not be regarded as the exclusive property of political groupings. They are expressions of faith of all Muslims, including those who explicitly oppose any particular Islamic political party or movement. Ordinary Muslims quite naturally differentiate between Muslims and Islam. The unexpected assertiveness of Islam should not be obscured by the deadly distortions of extremist forces like al Qaeda and the Islamic State of Iraq and Syria (ISIS) or the failings of particular Islamic parties like the Muslim Brothers in Egypt. This assertiveness of Islam itself, in so many ways, is the central and little-understood paradox of today: How, at a time of such unprecedented weakness, did midstream Islam make itself such a powerful transnational force with so promising a future?

Islam's Unlikely Strength

Two things are clear. Islam's unexpected strength does not originate from official political, economic, or religious systems and institutions, all of which are in decline. Nor can it be explained by focusing exclusively, as we in the West do obsessively, on the often-criminal assertions of violent minorities who rationalize their crimes in Islamic terms. Nor does the explanation lie with political parties that define themselves in Islamic terms, whether ruling or in opposition. The source of Islam's power derives from the far broader *al Tagdid al Islami* (Islamic Renewal). First stirring in the late 1960s and early 1970s, the Renewal has swept across Islamic lands. Those who respond call for revitalizing and rethinking the heritage. At the same time, they resist Western intrusions, challenge established authoritarian systems, and counter criminal Islamic extremists. The Renewal takes multiple forms, ranging from quietism and compliant withdrawal to radical reform (*islah*) and revolutionary agendas. The values and higher purposes of Islam, the historian Tareq al Bishri argues, shine through the differences explained by time and place. He adds emphatically that Islam, wherever found and however expressed, is inherently political.[2] The most important source of Western confusion about the meaning of the Renewal is the insistence on distinguishing between Islam as religion and so-called political Islam. Neither of these characterizations is in fact applicable. Islam is far more than a religion, and its political dimensions have no such autonomy. Islam is a pluralistic way of life that in all its varieties is insistently holistic and therefore unavoidably political. The notion of political Islam is an alien construct whose fortunes have little bearing on Islam's development. Only Marxism rivals "political Islam" in the number of times it has been pronounced dead or dying or in some obscure "post" state. Meanwhile, Islam itself appears to magically reassert itself in new and more energetic forms, providing inspiration for yet another generation of believers. In the wake of the overthrow of the

Muslim Brotherhood in Egypt, assessments once again announced the end of the Islamic wave of renewal. The premature obituaries for a failed political Islam miss a simple but fundamental point: Islam as lived faith refuses any division between the religious experience and human efforts to act in this world. In short, there is no such thing as political Islam. There is only Islam, although it is subject to adaptations and a wide variety of human interpretations.

No effort will be made here to pronounce one or another of these many human understandings of Islam authentic, while discrediting all others. The salience of one or another interpretation flows from the aims and purposes of the observer rather than any inherent character of one or another form of Islam. Depending on time and place, all human understandings of Islam draw inspiration from the sacred Islamic texts, no matter how unpersuasive or distorted particular interpretations of those texts might be. All have made contributions, for better or worse, to the development of Islamic civilization at one time and place or another.

The Islamic Midstream and the Renewal

The many incarnations of Islam, however, do not have equal importance for an inquiry like this one that seeks to understand Islam's unexpected contemporary strength. This book argues that the motivating force of the broad and varied Islamic Renewal is the contemporary *Wassatteyya* (Islamic midstream) that emerged in complex and adaptive forms as the guiding force of the Renewal. The *Wassatteyya* is neither myth nor meaningless slogan. It is rather a manifest historical tradition, whose evolution and importance are subject to analysis, documentation, and critical assessment. In the view of its adherents, the *Wassatteyya* functions as a vital yet flexible midstream, a centrist river out of Islam. Today, the *Wassatteyya* has made itself a presence everywhere Muslims are found. It connects, but does not unify, all parts of the Islamic world or *ummah*. It plays an important role even in those parts of the globe where Muslims are a minority.

The midstream defines Islam for the vast majority of Muslims, even as it acts as a wellspring for all manner of tributaries that allow Islam to renew itself in the most diverse ways. The Islamic midstream draws, as no other force, on the inherent strengths of the revelation. It is the world of midstream Islam that is safeguarding the faith in these difficult times. It is the world of the midstream that will ultimately shape the future of

Islam and Islamic societies. The obsessive focus of the West on contemporary Islamic extremism has obscured and, at times, even obstructed and delayed this outcome. The horrific violence used to combat extremism has had the effect only of augmenting its role at the expense of the midstream. Military invasions, occupations, and bombings radicalize the Islamic world in destructive ways. They temporarily crowd out the midstream. In the end, when calm returns to Islamic lands, midstream Islam of the *Wassatteyya* will prevail and, consistent with well-established historical patterns, reabsorb the extremists into a recentered and inclusive Islamic body.

What exactly is the Islamic *Wassatteyya*, and how does it work these effects? It is most useful to *start* with the provisional definition that the *Wassatteyya* is what its adherents say it is. We can then follow their self-descriptions to discover what supporters take to be its essential elements. At their heart these self-definitions identify the *Wassatteyya* as a cultural/institutional configuration, which emerges from a unique Islamic historical tradition that has gained new life as part of the much broader Islamic Awakening of the 1970s. The transnational midstream tradition comprises a complex of elements, both intellectual and organizational, linked by shared commitments and a "network of networks" of interaction. These elements form a composite conceptual unit, a "difficult" whole, with a common centrist orientation to Islamic reform, resistance, and a constructive global role, expressed in a shared vocabulary. As a manifest historical tradition, the *Wassatteyya* can be critically evaluated, measuring pronouncements against actions, with all the usual tools of historical and social scientific analysis. It is, however, impossible to elaborate the comprehensive meaning of such a unique historical phenomenon in advance. A concept of this kind must be constructed gradually from its individual elements, identified and empirically verified as the analysis unfolds. The "final and definitive concept" in such analyses, as Max Weber has pointed out, "cannot stand at the beginning of the investigation, but must come at the end."[3]

The most violent and vociferous of these offshoots, with their clamorous claims and deadly disruptions, have inevitably captured the lion's share of attention around the world, as ISIS does today. Proponents of criminal versions of Islam have been successful in making themselves available to the Western media and policy elites for interested manipulations that advance the interests of extremists in both the West and the Islamic world. However, they have not captured the hearts and minds of the vast majority of Muslims, whose faith continues to find its most compelling and durable expression in the Islamic midstream. Muslims of the center, this book argues, are writing Islam's epoch-defining story.

This substantive thesis on the centrality of the midstream to the strength of the Renewal raises a large question: What are the prospects of Islamic centrists with democratic and social justice commitments participating in the antisystemic struggles of global civil society for political freedom and more just social orders? This question, let me be clear, originates in my own commitments. However, I find it perfectly appropriate to ask it of the Islamic world, and so would many of the Islamic activists and thinkers of the center with whom I have interacted over the years. It is as much their question as mine. In itself, the question leans against the grain of prevailing Western views of Islamic exceptionalism that rule out any serious prospects for democracy in the Islamic world. In my view, neither the historical record nor the present landscape is as bleak for democratic prospects as such views assume. On the contrary, I will argue explicitly that the most promising advocates of democratic development in the Islamic world are, in fact, Islamic centrists. In a variety of sites and most often in alliance with centrists of other trends, they are seriously engaged in theorizing and acting on democratic experiments to advance the goals of freedom and justice. By nature, real experiments are as open to failure as they are to success. The difficulties of democratically elected parties in both Egypt and Tunisia do not signal the end of all such experiments. They offer lessons that, in the end, are more likely to advance the aims of the Renewal. Thanks to the reality of these reforming experiences, discussion must now move from airy speculations about the compatibility of Islam and democracy to far more meaningful assessments of the actual struggles of democrats in Islam. I am quite aware of the standard arguments that Islamic centrists merely adopt democratic rhetoric as a screen for theocratic ambitions. I am familiar as well with the view that moderate forces, even if genuine, will easily be swept aside by the more powerful militants who lurk in the shadows. However, I am not persuaded by these cautions on the basis of long observation and careful analysis of the real histories of events on the ground. There are, of course, no absolute guarantees. Still, the chapters that follow will show that the historical record speaks clearly and reassuringly enough to encourage us to proceed with an exploration of possible forms of cooperation with Islamic centrists on behalf of common democratic and social justice goals.

This prospect of cooperation in common projects raises its own intellectual challenges, for which we are quite unprepared. The Western literature on the Islamic world is an overgrown jungle. Yet very little of that work is of much use to the purposes of this study. For cooperation with others, what we need is practical knowledge of the actors in whom we are interested and of the contexts in which they live their lives and act on their commitments. Such knowledge of others is never complete, although it can be rigorous and verifiable. The measure of such knowledge is its usefulness for effective interaction in pursuit of common ends.

Western Scholarship: Absolutism, Relativism, and Ethnocentrism

The bulk of Western writings on the Islamic world has a quite different aim that is far more extravagant but ultimately debilitating. Western scholarship on Islam, for the most part, has a representational rather than a practical purpose. It seeks to present a true and complete picture of the Islamic world, or various aspects of it. The aim is to make Islam and all things Islamic transparent to us. Despite this shared general understanding of truth as accurate representation, there is of course great variety in the dominant literature. One way to sort it out is to recognize absolutist, relativist, and ethnocentric attitudes toward the common, but misplaced, goal of truthful representation.

From an absolutist point of view, there is an objective reality and sure knowledge of it is possible. Absolutists offer their work as embodiments, or at least approximations, of that ideal. The Arab mind, for example, exhibits certain invariable qualities that can be accurately catalogued. Islam has a determinate, unchanging character that can be faithfully portrayed. The political economy of the Islamic world responds to the laws of liberal or neoliberal economic theory and can be fully understood in its terms. These economic regularities about the Islamic world are knowable in an objective sense, whatever our motivations and whatever the subjects of our work may think of our findings. By these lights, one should envision cooperation only with those who accept the objective character of these truths. Such an inflated truth claim builds a high barrier to shared projects with others.

Those with a relativist bent, in sharp contrast, reject any such notion of absolute truth. However, for contrary reasons, this approach also rules out cooperation. All truth is relative to one's own experience, its advocates argue. Our truth will be about ourselves, our world, and perhaps the way we see others. We can know very little, if anything at all, of a cultural or social world other than our own. Despite our best efforts, it remains mysterious and unfathomable. Since we cannot know this world, however much we might want to, it is impossible to form any coherent, evaluative judgments about it or about the behavior of the persons who act in it. All we can do is record the strange goings-on as we see them. Implicitly, conversation, let alone cooperation, is rendered unthinkable with people whom we cannot know and whose behavior is ultimately incomprehensible. Others are knowable only to the extent that they remake themselves in our image. In such cases, of course, they are not really "other" but pale, inadequate imitations of ourselves. The Western literature on the Islamic world is littered with such invidious, demeaning characterizations. They are hardly an invitation to joint action.

The ethnocentric stance essentially agrees with the relativist position but without the slightest hint of regret at the loss of potential partners. The ethnocentrist believes, quite insistently, that our way of doing things is the best way and, really, the only way. Our truths, objective or not, are the only truths that matter. Others must either conform to our way of thinking and acting or any joint action is completely ruled out.

The representational notion of truth, no matter whether given absolutist, relativist, or ethnocentric shading, has done enough damage to our relations with others. The intolerable arrogance of both the absolutist and the ethnocentrist dictates that dialogue on their terms will really be monologues about their own truths and the agendas for action that those truths unilaterally define. The relativist will give us truths about ourselves, including our understandings of those different from ourselves, but abandons the quest for genuine knowledge of others. None of these prevailing approaches opens to genuine cooperation.

Pragmatic Humanism and Understanding the Islamic Renewal

In contrast, humanistic scholarship should aim for the kind of mutual understanding that makes possible conversation and working together to achieve some common purpose. What we need is a pragmatic notion of truth, geared to those practical ends, rather than the tyrannical demands of some unattainable aim.

My intellectual and personal journey toward this goal started with a remarkably generous grant, over multiple years, from the Foreign Area

Fellowship program while I was a graduate student. With that support, I traveled widely throughout the Islamic cultural continent stretching from Spain, across North Africa, through the Middle East and Central Asia to the borders of China. I eventually settled in Cairo for two years from 1968 to 1970. I went as a student of language and culture, a painter, and an art history major who had wandered, not quite innocently, into international studies. From my studies in the arts and French culture, it seemed elemental that you needed to know the language of a culture to hope to make any sense at all of its arts, literature, and customs. My love of conversation, with all manner of people, made it imperative that the language I studied be a spoken language. I didn't realize at the time what a fateful choice that was between an emphasis on the sacred language of the Qur'an and its modern written derivatives, where my studies of Arabic began, or the ordinary spoken language of everyday life. I do recall thinking about the relative merits of Lebanese, Moroccan, and Egyptian dialects and deciding that only Egyptian made any real sense. Thanks to the Voice of Cairo radio broadcasts, popular songs, and especially films, Egyptian Arabic established itself as something of a *lingua franca* throughout the Arab world. I confess that I agree with the Egyptian poet Ahmed Fuad Negm, who argued forcefully that the Egyptian dialect has a quite special, much loved role in the life of Arabs everywhere.[4] To this day, however, I sometimes regret that I did not stay focused on the starkly beautiful Qur'anic Arabic with which I began at Harvard. But the regret fades when I see one of the early films of Salah Abou Seif or Yusuf Chahine, read or hear Ahmed Negm recite one of his poems, or just chat with friends or, for that matter, with Muhammad, my local grocery man, about the state of the world or our children's prospects.

So, my first paradigm for what it meant to study Arab and then Islamic culture, more broadly, was that of the language student. That approach tipped things in decisive favor of the native speaker, who is the only real expert. The danger, of course, is "going native," or sliding into that compliant cultural relativism that, with language as a model, takes culture as a consistent whole with self-generated and self-regulating grammars for speaking and acting that can only be understood from within. In the end, "going native," even if it were a desirable goal, can never be attained. It simply leads to the dead end of one's indelibly foreign identity.

With this danger in mind, I have modified that approach in fundamental ways, both in my life in Cairo and in my scholarship. The special challenges and opportunities of choosing to spend so much of my life in

Cairo and other Arab cities have forced a more practical stance. I learned to put emphasis on that most surprising of inalienable rights, "the pursuit of happiness," both personal and professional, in novel surroundings. In these settings, I share my life and work with others quite different from myself, rather than just observing and recording. I seek to know them just well enough to cooperate in all manner of shared projects to make our lives fuller and richer. In this way, I have become something of a practical interpreter, trying to make myself and my family at home and happy in societies into which we were not born, with the exception of my son, who was in fact born in Cairo.

The Strange Loops of Personal, Philosophical, and Islamic Pragmatism

In fact, a pragmatic thread runs throughout this book, woven into strange loops that merit an explanation. The habits of heart and mind of pragmatism, as a way of knowing the world and the people who move through it, came naturally to me as one of the gifts of my childhood. That background shaped my reaction to studies in pragmatism as social theory at Harvard. The pragmatists, especially John Dewey, captured my imagination when everyone around me was beguiled by European social theory, Marxism of course but also the French poststructuralists such as Foucault and Derrida. Strangest of all, in pragmatism I had found, without quite knowing it, a bridge to midstream Islam. On that bridge, I would encounter quite unexpectedly some of the great theorists and activists who animated the contemporary Islamic Renewal that has been a worldwide force since the early 1970s. But all of that lay ahead.

My mother embodied the pragmatic spirit, and from her I learned to make it my way of being in the world. Her version was a lived rather than an academic one, as my mother had only minimal elementary education. At Harvard I encountered pragmatism as a formal philosophy. To my surprise, this quintessential American philosophical school gave names to the concepts and vocabulary that I had already absorbed, as naturally as the air I breathed. Pragmatism, as systematic philosophy, also tied life lessons to grander quests for knowledge and the betterment of the human condition, although if the truth be told these larger purposes lurked just below the surface of the lessons my mother taught as well. However, it is the third loop in the pragmatic thread woven into the texture of this book that is most unexpected of all. A good deal of my academic work has dealt with Islam, particularly midstream Islam, and its remarkable capacity for adaptation and absorption. In retrospect, my attraction to the neglected Islamic midstream tradition clearly has a great deal to do with how centrist movements interpret the heritage in order to accommodate and make the best of an astonishing variety of times and places, while preserving a recognizable core of higher purposes and values. Midstream Islam cultivates habits of heart and mind with which I have been familiar all of my life. Still, it was an unexpected revelation for me to discover in the course of wide reading in the Islamic literature of the Renewal that influential centrist Islamic intellectuals explicitly recognized and embraced American pragmatism as "the Islam of the Western world."[5] A connection that I felt intuitively, in fact, had an external and independent reality that others had noted and acted on.

In these ways, the skills of interpreting others and making the best of my situation were honed long before my formal studies, although I have not until recently given the matter much thought. One thing, however, was always clear to me from the time of my graduate studies. The cultural barriers entailed in making sense of another culture are no more difficult to breach than the social minefields through which I had made my way as a working-class boy who eventually got his doctorate from Harvard. Such social mobility is, of course, very much part of what Americans believe distinguishes their country and the opportunities it offers from more stratified societies around the world. Millions of Americans have had my experience, with individual variation to be sure, although today we are witnessing the erosion of those possibilities. Whether the context was a middle- or upper-class academic setting, or a cultural environment formed of Arab and Islamic elements, the fundamental challenges, I found, were fairly constant. Always there was a new language to learn and a prevailing pattern of practical and moral reasoning to apprehend just well enough to talk with people and join with them in common endeavors. In whatever setting I land, I aim to make myself feel as much at home as I can and available to potential partners in my new environment for the adventures open to us. This personal quality of adaptability is again not at all unique nor particularly American. In fact, Arab culture reserves a special place for such legendary travelers as Ibn Battuta, the fourteenth-century figure who traversed the length and breadth of the *ummah* and beyond. Ibn Battuta had a remarkable capacity to find his footing in the most diverse settings and to find the words to convey something of what he learned.[6]

Contemporary American society is more fast-paced than most, with not only social but also geographic mobility. I can almost always locate my Egyptian and Arab friends in the same neighborhoods where I left them, even a decade or more before. In contrast, we Americans are always on the move, it seems, and perhaps for that reason we need more than others to tap into the skills of landing on our feet and adapting to new settings, skipping only a beat or two. So my journey to a practical method of understanding others and their contexts did not begin with encounters in the Islamic world at all, but much earlier. Later it was my good fortune to study and then work collaboratively with some of the great American, Canadian, Arab, and European scholars of the Islamic world, who collectively represent a wide variety of disciplines and just about all the approaches under the academic sun. It is, therefore, somewhat surprising to me that the most fundamental methods that underlie my work today derive more from the practical sensibility that I first absorbed as a child from my mother, the first of that series of remarkable teachers. The lessons she imparted to her seven children, always by her own steady practices, showed us who we were, or rather should be, and what our environment demanded of us. These practical lessons, learned early, opened my mind to the critical values and reformist aims that marked the work of the pragmatists. More importantly, such acquired pragmatic attitudes of mind and spirit brought what should have been an alien tradition within comfortable reach. Islam of the midstream, from the first, made intuitive good sense to me.

Our neighborhood in Jersey City was not the best, and neither was our five-room, one-bath apartment for such a large family. My mother's trick was to make the best of what it was. Not all the problems were outside. They never are. My father was often either between jobs or laid off. When things weren't going well, he drank, and so my mother always put her wallet under her pillow when she slept. She let us know that by her action, with no comments about my father or visible embarrassment about the matter. We kids understood why she guarded what money there was. My mother coped.

Coping was an active thing, and it demanded some imaginative thinking and maneuvering to make the most of what was at hand. We kids had a red wagon that I can still picture. Family legend had it that my mother would take my older brothers to gather coal that spilled from the coal car alongside the railroad tracks at the end of our street. The oil burners might be empty in our living room, but the old iron kitchen furnace would heat the apartment. I loved that large kitchen with its wonderful metal ceiling. So did my mother. It had to be beautiful. Our side of the duplex house had been condemned and both apartments abandoned for a while, before we moved in on the second floor. Among other challenges, all the kitchen cabinet doors had been stolen. My mother found the solution in a deep reddish-maroon material, cut to size for each missing door, perfectly hemmed, and then mounted with wide loops on spring-set curtain rods. We all helped paint and wallpaper the kitchen. The cloth panels were the finishing touch. I have yet to see a kitchen I liked more. Resilience, my mother taught, need not be grim nor white knuckled. The pragmatists projected this same insight. Years later I was to discover that it was the Islamic centrists who really owned that concept.

Dealing with the world outside was a taller order in our Jersey City neighborhood. The first priority was the way we presented ourselves. We were "the Baker Boys" and the way my mother said that meant something very important, although to be honest I never thought through exactly what that might be. My brothers and I all look a good deal alike, but that's where the similarities end. Our interests and personalities are all over the board. The complexities of dealing with such a diverse lot went off the charts when my twin sisters, the youngest of my siblings, arrived late and to an adoring if somewhat bewildered welcome. I think that living in such a small space with such diverse human beings taught me more about the challenges of understanding people different from me than any other life experience. My mother never wavered in her insistence that we recognize, respect, and make the effort to understand or at least live peacefully with the differences. At the same time, whatever our differences, to the neighborhood we were to present a united front.

How you presented yourself to the world outside mattered greatly, but what you thought of yourself mattered more. Clothes were a problem, but a needle and thread and soap and water were the solution. Every time I later saw my Muslim friends thoroughly wash both hands and feet before prayer, I could not help but think that my mother would approve. Cleanliness in Islam is not a minor matter, nor was it for my mother. Although my mother did the bulk of the wash, we all learned to clean and mend our own things. When the clothes wore out, handed down from one brother to the next, my mother would organize a trip to Burns, the used clothes store. In retrospect, I think that should have been a humiliating experience. It wasn't. I am still not quite sure why. The one thing I do remember clearly is the shoes. That should have been the biggest problem, wearing other kids' discarded shoes. It wasn't. What I remember most clearly are the huge shoe bins that I could barely see into. My mother would lift me up and I would plunge into the shoes. A first victory was always finding that first shoe in good shape and the right size, but the real triumph came from rummaging through the piles to find the mate. Holding it up was sheer joy. My mother made it possible to feel like a hero under her affirming gaze. I never thought much about what other people might be thinking. I still don't. What mattered then was her gaze and how it made me feel.

My mother encoded guidelines for dealing with the neighborhood in her own behavior. We were not to look for trouble, but to stick together, all five of us boys, if trouble came our way. You never hit first, but you always defended yourself and your brothers and sisters, whatever it took. My mother was not a pacifist and neither am I, although I abhor violence in all its forms. The scene I remember best occurred somewhat later, when my mother was working as a waitress at a lunch counter, attached to a bar. There, she encountered all types. I was visiting one day and saw one smart ass take the spoon out of his hot coffee and jokingly put it on the back of my mother's hand. My mother didn't flinch. She simply picked up a cut-glass bowl of sugar, rose to her full four feet eleven inches to look him right in the face, and told him that he would be wearing the sugar bowl if he dared do any such thing again. Much later, I never found mysterious or repugnant the spirit of resistance, even against improbable odds, that is at the very heart of the Islamic Awakening. That resistance emerges naturally from the pragmatic way of being in the world that midstream Islam cultivates. Pragmatism means that you are moved by higher purposes but use the weapons at hand, even if all you have is personal dignity, an indomitable spirit, and a sugar bowl.

We needed to see such things. To make it from one end of our street to another without being hassled was often a challenge. Luckily, at the upper end of the street on the way home from school, my mother's friend Rita, with her elaborate hairdos and strong perfume, had a ground-floor apartment. If there was a problem on the street, we were to go there if we couldn't get to our place. But if her husband, Dave, came home, we were to leave immediately. Dave drank heavily and was not to be trusted. He could be violent and worse. It was important to keep things real. There really are no completely safe havens, so sometimes you just have to keep moving.

We very rarely saw a doctor. My mother believed in cleanliness of body and home as the major antidote to illness. It was also one we could afford.

Pepto-Bismol, peroxide, and aspirin were household staples; they could be trusted based on long experience. Burns were treated with tea leaves, high fevers with cool baths. Doctors did stitches only when the tightly taped bandages could not bridge a wound. Hospital emergency rooms and clinics were avoided. My mother believed that there was nothing for free. When my brothers were in the military, a stern warning was issued against volunteering to test anything, whatever the incentive offered. They experiment on people in those free clinics and in the army, she warned. And of course she was right.

As a graduate student I was delighted to discover many of these realistic, practical, and self-reliant habits of mind and heart in John Dewey, the great American pragmatist philosopher and social reformer. John Dewey, I am convinced, would have liked my mother, just as I am convinced my mother would have understood my choice to live so much of my life in contexts shaped by Islam. There is a great deal of my mother's spirit and of her ways in Dewey's championing of the practical improvement of human well-being and in the pragmatic approach he took to the great issues of education, social justice, and democratic reform. I suspect as well that he would have liked the way she taught us to deal with others, especially those who are different in one way or another—which means, in effect, just about everyone. I find it unhelpful to single out the difficulty of understanding those from another culture. It may be a longer walk from home, but the journey through cultural barriers in its essentials is no more daunting than working through individual, gender, or class differences. I will refer to Dewey and the other pragmatists as guides for my interpretive efforts to understand midstream Islam throughout this book, but I thought it only fair to let my readers know that he was not my most influential teacher of the ways of pragmatism. The pragmatic philosophers provided generalized insights. My mother had prepared me to understand them in personal terms. In the Islamic world, I was to discover those same insights expressed in Arabic and articulated in wonderfully expressive Islamic forms.

The core of Dewey's work is the notion that doing is at the heart of knowing and doing always takes place in value-laden human interactions within a specific environment. Theories that make sense of the world are always, in this sense, grounded theories of particular situations in which identifiable people find themselves and discern the possibilities for action that their situations offer. There is no substitute for such textured, local knowledge, even for a project as ambitious in geographic scope as the one raised in this book—that is, for the daunting task of developing an understanding of midstream, transnational Islam. The Islamic Renewal unavoidably is about a broadly shared human religious and cultural experience. It is distinctive, but not incomprehensible to others. Dewey reminds us that, when our subject is religion, we should bring into view not only religions in general but also particular religions and the actual religious experiences that religion makes possible for specific human beings. We must pay attention to Islam's distinctive message to humanity, while not losing sight of the fact that there is nothing exotic or alien about the religious experience itself. But we also need to remind ourselves that access to the meaning of a particular religious experience can only come through our interactions with the men and women for whom it represents *their* religious experience. They are the ones who seek to make it a force in the world in ways that make it available to us. Precisely for that reason, the religious experience should not be regarded as totally interior and unavailable for engagement.

These pragmatic attitudes mark all of the engagements with the Islamic centrists who are the primary actors in this book. I am not sure that Goethe is exactly right when he pronounces that to understand something you must love it, but there is surely something to his observation.[7] To be frank, although not uncritical, I do find much that is admirable in the thinking and actions of the main figures and movements of the *Wassatteyya* on both intellectual and moral grounds. For that reason I have found it easy to sustain my interest in their work for decades as successive generations have renewed the centrist project in a wide variety of settings, almost all of which I have visited. Shared affinities must surely facilitate understanding, although the inclination to airbrush shortcomings must be actively resisted. After all, those who love us most have the obligation to be our sharpest and most incisive critics—at least that is what my mother taught. Moreover, when we are interacting with those to whom we are drawn, it is important to be clear about precisely what is shared and what is not.

Few intellectual blunders are as irritating to me as the very common misuse of the term "pragmatism" as a synonym for opportunism. This misusage runs through the Western literature on Islamic movements. The pragmatists, of course, strongly objected to thought and action voided of its moral implications. As a school, pragmatists stood firmly for progressive reform against the rigidities of conservatism and the excesses of ideological extremism. At the core of their thinking is a positive faith in human beings, all human beings, and their shared potential to do good things with their lives, however depressing the clear-headed record of actual behavior can be. Doing is, for the pragmatists, both an intellectual and moral activity of the highest order. None of these attitudes would be foreign to the centrist Islamic groups, as subsequent chapters will make clear. They share the focus on actions rather than simply words, on the inclusive rather than the exclusionary, and on rescuing the best of past efforts rather than destroying and building anew. The explicit acknowledgment of the reflexive loop in the exchanges means that the midstream current has an awareness of both American pragmatism, or at least of the basic concepts, ideas, and values that define it. Moreover, they recognize in this way of knowing and being in the world a good deal that is Islamic.[8]

There is for Islamic centrist Muslims great promise in the Qur'anic advisement that God created a diverse humanity so that they might "know one another" and in the Qur'anic injunction to a righteous humanity to "build the world."[9] Both themes echo clearly in pragmatism. Centrist Islamic groups, like the best of global civil society bodies in non-Islamic societies, are working actively to lessen the violence of our shared world, the damage to our lonely planet, and the miseries that plague our human race. Practical knowledge of these shared aspirations to improve the human condition can be the grounding for acting together. Such joint projects, so important on their own terms, are also needed in the task of containing the deadly mischief of fundamentalists and extremists of all stripes. These extremist elements, particularly destructive in our Western world because of our exorbitant power but no less murderous in theirs, routinely attack the center and undermine those who work to build a world with a modicum of justice and freedom. It is perfectly reasonable to think that we should at least remain open to the possibility of finding among the centrists and democrats in Islam partners for works, large and small, that advance the human interest.

The responsive openness of this approach expresses a degree of optimism that is not fully justified by the facts of human experience, particularly the record of Western violence toward the Islamic world and the criminality of extremist Islamic groups. It is rooted ultimately in faith in a human nature with the potential for good. That faith assumes a human love of justice and freedom, a human capacity for science and learning, and an always unwarranted human willingness to reconcile and forgive. The contradictory record of human history makes such assumptions just as reasonable as their opposites. Dewey's responsive openness to others suffuses his practical drive to ameliorate the human condition and his search for partners in that endeavor. It finds its grounding in the idea that all human beings, given the right circumstances, could contribute to the development of sound science and just democracy, the highest human attainments and the most promising means of human advancement. To think otherwise, he believes, is racism. So do I and, more importantly, so do major Islamic thinkers of the center who are major players in the stories of the *Wassatteyya* told here. To be sure, American pragmatists and Islamic centrists arrive at these conclusions from very different starting points. But what matters is that they do arrive.

For those with direct knowledge and lived experience in the Islamic world, it will seem self-evident to comment that the vast majority of Muslims live rather ordinary and decent lives, concerned with the health and well-being of their families while quietly entertaining moderate hopes of making a positive difference, however small, in their city or village, society, and the world. It will seem unnecessary as well to comment that ordinary Muslims often do so in the quite extraordinary circumstances of domestic tyrannies, foreign incursions, and local extremisms. Muslims do look to Islam for balance and moderation in their everyday lives. At the same time, without contradiction, they also find in Islam a source of practical inspiration for resistance to foreign incursions and domestic tyrannies, whether of ruling regimes or extremist minorities that distort the faith for criminal ends. Today, however, we need to say these things out loud to a broader Western public and to identify the sources and trends in the Islamic world that speak for this longstanding and pragmatic centrism.

The Fourth Wave of Renewal in a Global Age

The contemporary Islamic Renewal has deep roots and clear historical precedents. The efforts of the Islamic midstream to renew Islamic thought and provide foundations for actions for reform have come in three successive historical waves, at the end of the nineteenth century, after World War I, and after World War II, each responsive to the felt need for the tradition to speak more effectively to changed conditions. In the period beginning in the late 1960s and early 1970s, a fourth wave of renewal swept through the Islamic world. It continues to work its effects today. Intellectuals of the Islamic center, from Morocco to Malaysia, began articulating their assessments of the radical transformations that were reshaping the world in these critical years. They advanced their visions of how Islamic reform should proceed in the startling new conditions created by the collapse of the Soviet Union, American hegemonic claims as the sole superpower, and the combined impact of the Information Revolution and the unified global market. These several factors combined to sweep away the order of the Cold War international system and create a new global context to which Islamic groups had to respond. In their writings, centrist Islamic groups identified core concepts from the heritage that would allow Muslims to understand and overcome the chaos of a world falling apart, while also invoking the Qur'anic values that could be the basis for repair. Self-consciously, they announced their projects with the hope that they would be recognized and understood by similar-minded intellectuals elsewhere in the Islamic world.

In the late 1970s and early 1980s such independent Islamic intellectuals, connected to social groups and movements of reform rather than official religious institutions or radical movements of violent opposition, responded most effectively to this historical moment. These disparate, centrist assertions all had a principled yet pragmatic character, suffused with a worldview that sought out a middle way. They eschewed stagnation, on the one hand, and radical excesses, on the other. They argued that the validation of their ideas would come with their implementation. All of their manifestos were calls to action, tied to particular local circumstances, but informed by a broader vision of happenings elsewhere in the *ummah*. They were soon connected in a loose network, facilitated by the improved means of communication and transportation. These networks made it possible to share ideas and experiences in order to define the *Wassatteyya* for a global age.

In its decentralized form, the centrist Islamic web has more in common with computer networks and their systems of parallel processing and distributed intelligence than with traditional political movements that depended on the secret cells of underground systems. In the Western literature, these movements are more often than not mischaracterized as social movements. Yet the *Wassatteyya* is clearly distinguished from the new social movements that are for the most part characterized by a singular focus. In contrast, the Islamic midstream has a comprehensive orientation toward social change. In the new conditions created by the Information Revolution, new relationships have emerged among dispersed intellectual leaders and between the attentive publics that responded to them. These relationships have an organic character in ways made possible by the personal computer and the Internet. The lifelike character of this flexible web of groups and movements of the center does not escape notice and quite vivid commentary within the Islamic world. Alert intellectuals of the center have found in updated versions of the organic imagery that suffused the inherited Islamic tradition a perfectly suitable vocabulary to describe the new kinds of "living" systems that the *Wassatteyya* is spontaneously generating. These familiar organic vocabularies help Muslims understand how the thinking and action of those moved by the Islamic Renewal are undergoing profound transformations.

These radical changes of the fourth wave of renewal enabled the unprecedented forms of spontaneous coordination and cooperation on a transnational level that is the subject matter of this study. The revitalized *Wassatteyya* addresses the major issues of reform and resistance, as they present themselves in the late twentieth and early twenty-first centuries. The *Wassatteyya* insistently sets its own agenda, adamantly refusing that imposed by the West. It formulates its own models to respond to the challenges of the new age. It does so most often as much in opposition to existing regimes in the Islamic world as to the West. Inherited tradition is made to speak to the new age. The core Islamic notion of *tawhid* (the oneness of God) and the complex of related Qur'anic concepts of *'ilm* (knowledge), *'aql* (mind), and *'adl* (justice) *jihad* and (striving or struggle) have all been interpreted anew, with one eye on the sacred texts and the other on the new realities of a global age. In this way, one balances between religion and pragmatism. These Qur'anic concepts serve as markers on the path of resistance to Western intrusions and reform efforts to develop and build exemplary Islamic societies in the face of the daunting obstacles of cruel authoritarianisms. Today, distributed experiences across the Islamic world that in earlier times might have remained isolated, or with only delayed effects, can be absorbed immediately for what they reveal of both opportunities and challenges. Notable in this regard are the practical economic successes of the Malaysians, the democratic theorizing of Tunisian Islamic groups, or the democratic practices of their Turkish and Iranian reformist counterparts. Ordinary people doing extraordinary things on behalf of reform and resistance also find a space of appearance.

What emerges from these complex and unpredictable interactions results neither from a division of labor nor a model of specialization. The relationship of part to whole is organic rather than mechanical. Experiences are absorbed into the organic whole that is the *Wassatteyya* rather than remaining localized in its parts. Thus, the ways to economic success of Malaysia or the victories of practical politics of Turkish Islamic groups or the trials of Iranian reformists become lessons that circulate throughout the *Wassatteyya* network. The pragmatic vision of progress that emerges from these efforts is insistently Islamic. The inspiration comes from the experience of Islamic groups, although including of course those Islamic groups unafraid to borrow from the successful experiences of others. Self-criticism is essential for such a project. It is recognized as such. The midstream vigorously resists the temptation to attribute all ills to outside forces. However, there is also a realistic assessment of the damage done by forces hostile to the vulnerable Islamic world, often with horrific levels of violence and destruction.

Everywhere, the revitalized *Wassatteyya* also confronts the fringe minorities that attempt to capture the Renewal for their own criminal purposes. The deadly aims and the terrible means of criminal Islam are even more at odds with centrist understandings of Islam than they are with the West. The midstream has been far more consistent in its opposition to Islamic extremism than have Western governments. The United States, in particular, has far too often succumbed to illusions that such groups could be used, without cost, for its own purposes. Centrists regard the distortions of Islam by the often-ignorant marginal groups as so dangerous that cooperative projects with the militants, such as those undertaken by American intelligence agencies, are far more difficult to imagine. For much the same reason, the midstream has developed a principled opposition to compliant, official Islam that makes itself the handmaiden of authoritarian rule. In the eyes of the midstream, the damage from extremist forms of Islam, as well as the compromises of domesticated Islam to the inherited tradition, if unchecked, threaten Islam itself. For the *Wassatteyya*, the importance of this battle of "religion against religion," to borrow Ali Shariati's phrase, stands second to none.[10]

The Co-Evolution of Islam and American Empire

This story of the Islamic Renewal and of the challenges faced from within the Islamic world by the midstream engine that drives it cannot be told in isolation. The turbulent years of the 1970s witnessed not only the appearance of the wave of Islamic Renewal but also the rise of the American empire. American power now exercises unprecedented global hegemony, asserted with particular force and willful ignorance in Islamic lands. It does so through an expanding network of bases and client regimes. From the outset, the emergence and evolution of the Islamic midstream have

taken place not only in continuous conflict with the repressive state structures and violent Islamic militants but also in continuous interaction with
the aggressive American empire.

The *Wassatteyya* exists today as a vital, autonomous force, increasingly
capable of resisting U.S. government efforts to manipulate and repress.
This resistance has brought the Islamic midstream into conflict not only
with U.S. policies but also with the regional regimes the United States
maintains. All too often, it is forgotten that the established regimes in
the Arab Islamic world are for the most part the products of the colonial
era or the Westernized outcomes of the struggles for decolonization. As
such, they have made themselves available as the instruments of American power in our own time. Those regimes in turn correctly regard the
independent Islamic midstream, not the violent extremists, as the most
important opposition force they confront. These authoritarian regimes,
whether monarchies or dictatorships that originate from the military,
often receive Western and particularly American support to combat the
midstream Islamic challenge to their repressive monopoly of power. The
periodic announcements of American support for democracy and moderation are simply rhetorical cover, as the historical record makes clear.
The ease with which the American administration facilitated and accommodated the military seizure of power in Egypt in 2013 is only the most
recent case in point.

These various connections and interactions mean that Islam and the
American empire, the heir of earlier such imperial ventures, cannot be
disentangled without severely dimming the prospects of understanding
either. They shaped each other through decades of complex exchanges
and continue to do so today. Both have also drawn strength from the explosive changes in technologies, production, and administration, occurring first in the 1970s in the United States and eventually engulfing the
world. In this precise way, both have defined themselves in important, although rarely acknowledged, ways, by their co-evolution in the new space
and time of globalism. Indeed, the points of connection have been so prolonged and so intense that Islam and empire function in some ways as a
composite whole, responding continuously to each other. However coun-
terintuitive such a notion might seem, for some analytical purposes some
Islamic movements and empire are best considered a single unit of study,
forged through continuous interactions.

Those interactions between Islam and empire have taken various
forms in the past that will all be considered in the analysis offered here.[11]

At the same time, I want to raise the question of the likely form of those interactions for the future as well. It is my hope that this book will be of interest to those in the Islamic world, not least Islamic groups themselves, who have an interest in developing a richer, more nuanced and self-critical sense of the meaning and implications of the Islamic Renewal both as history and contemporary reality. I also have another audience in mind. As an American scholar with strong democratic and social commitments in the best critical traditions of my country, I have written this book as well for my fellow Westerners, genuinely committed to the ideals of justice and democracy. They are often quite bewildered by the almost exclusive focus in the Western media and scholarship on the violent and antidemocratic forces at work in the contemporary Middle East. That focus obscures our own American contributions to the sum total of human misery in the region. One purpose of this book is to show concerned Western democrats, faced with our own democratic struggles at home, that they do have de facto allies on the ground around the Middle East. They are rightful partners in the broader global struggle for democracy and justice, although they simply are not on our radar screen (nor we on theirs). The *Wassattayya*, the chapters that follow show, does represent a positive global force in the struggle for democracy and progress. Although we use different vocabularies to describe and defend our aims, we are committed to the same transnational project on behalf of justice and freedom. We can participate together in the emergence and strengthening of an effective, global public. The democrats in Islam of the *Wassatteyya* are no more perfect in attainments and commitments than we are. However, if there is any basis at all for hope about the triumph of constructive forces over foreign mischief, extremism, and authoritarianism in the Middle East, they are an indispensable part of it. Thus, while the primary focus of this study is assessment of the role of the midstream in the Islamic Renewal, it inevitably and consistently brings into view the co-evolving American empire as well and considers the possibility that the interactions of Islam and the West might yet take more progressive forms.

Arabesques, Networks, and Egypt as Point of Entry

Focus, of course, is not quite the right word for coming to grips with the complex and decentered living web that is the *Wassatteyya*. After all, how can you focus on something that is always in formation and never fully formed, always emerging and evolving without ever achieving final shape, endlessly interacting with its environment and never fully distinguishable from it? Seeing the Islamic midstream in this way as a complex, adaptive system with many of the characteristics of a living organism brings to mind the arabesque, the prototypic Islamic art form.[12] Like the arabesque, the interacting patterns of the *Wassatteyya* remain open-ended. They extend infinitely around the globe, adapting in unpredictable ways to the most varied settings, while remaining recognizably Islamic. There is no one focal point or single privileged point of entry to such a system, although in any given period one node may be more important than another for some specific purpose. All we can do, really, is to grasp hold of a few useful threads that will lead us into the complex arabesque of the *Wassatteyya*, without expecting any completely satisfying sense of finding either the most appropriate beginning or the most conclusive ending for the exploration. A comprehensive, definitive mapping is out of the question. The patterns of meaning and social action shift too rapidly for that. Such total understanding is the dream of idle fools and strategic planners in powerful centers and think tanks whose well-paid job it is to come up with such definitive analyses, however unreal they may be.[13] But we can hope for enough understanding to feel more at home, to find our way around, to recognize potential partners for our projects when they emerge.

The threads pulled here originate in Egypt, although they extend throughout the Arab and Islamic world beyond. This starting point, like any other, builds distortions into the analyses. Perhaps the most damaging is the reinforcement of an Arab-centric view of the Islamic world. Surely by now we all should know that Islam does not belong to the Arabs. It never did, as the Qur'an makes clear. Of the 1.6 billion Muslims worldwide, only a minority of some 350 million are Arabs. Muslims today constitute a majority in some forty extremely diverse countries, and there are Muslim minorities in nearly every country on the planet. Moreover, the largest Muslim population is found in Indonesia rather than the Arab lands. Still, it does make a certain sense to start our journey to the pluralistic Islamic community or *ummah* through its Arab quarters. All Muslims know that their beloved Prophet was an Arab, that the language of the Qur'an is Arabic, and that the Arabs were, as the historian Albert Hourani notes, "the 'matter of Islam' (*maddat al Islam*), the human instrument through which it conquered the world."[14]

The choice of Egypt in particular as beginning point, while arbitrary, is also a reasoned one that affords considerable advantages. Not least, of course, is the Islamic ethos that permeated Midan Tahrir, the epicenter of the quite miraculous Egyptian revolutionary uprising of January 2011.[15] In early July 2013 the Egyptian revolution entered its second phase. Once again, Islam was everywhere a presence. One striking incident makes the point. When the pro-Mursi activists gathered near Cairo University, the military forces that surrounded the intersection where they gathered did all the usual things. They moved established barriers, they moved tanks into place, and they prepared to do battle. Then, once again, they did the extraordinary. Ordinary soldiers, Muslims, spontaneously responded to the call for prayer in the streets in clear sight of the men and women, supporters of the Muslim Brothers, they were sent to contain. Islam itself made itself felt on both sides of those barriers. Later, pro- and anti-Mursi Egyptians prayed in exactly the same way in Rabaa al 'Adawiya and Tahrir squares. The social culture shaped by Islam was the same. The differences were political and, in the end, brutally so.

This pervasive Islamic ethos that has defined the unfinished Egyptian revolution should not be a cause for surprise. Egypt experienced the Islamic Renewal early on and continues to be an exceptionally important node in its evolution. Even more decisively, from an Egyptian school of Islamic intellectuals, this book argues, has come the most impressive and influential formulations of midstream positions and guidance for effective action for the twenty-first century. More specifically, I take the position that a school of Egyptian centrist thinkers has generated the most significant advances in midstream *fiqh* (understanding of Qur'an and *Sunnah*) for the twenty-first century. *Fiqh* has come to mean not simply substantive understandings but also articulations of the rules and guidelines on how those understandings are reached. *Fiqh* for this reason has a very practical function. While Turkish and Iranian thinkers, in particular, have made their own important contributions, the Egyptian *Wassatteyya* has a distinctively transnational character that gives the record of their thought and action the greatest usefulness for our purposes here.

The choice has a personal dimension as well. I have lived and traveled widely for over more than four decades in the historic Islamic world, from Córdoba in Spain to China. Precisely for that reason I am painfully aware of the barriers of language and culture and lived experience that make it hard for a single scholar to make sense of what is happening in great swaths of that vast cultural continent where the most concentrated populations of diverse Muslims live. Egypt is the place I know best. Its rich intellectual and spiritual life, while delightfully elusive, is still more accessible to me than any other. It is the site where, over these many years, I have developed and refined the pragmatic method of understanding others that informs every page of this book. For these substantive reasons Egypt makes sense as point of entry into the networks of the *Wassatteyya*.

More than any others, it is my professional and personal experiences with Egyptian family members, friends, and colleagues that ground the faith I have that, for all the barriers, we can talk to each other through cultural differences. With some luck and considerable patience we can also manage to engage in moral argument and even reach agreement, thanks to those little, always unexpected miracles of breakthrough that enliven human interactions.

Small stories sometimes carry large messages and effect real changes. A conversation I had some years ago with the daughter of a very close Egyptian friend had precisely such an effect. My friend Kamel was one of the very first to introduce me to some of the centrist Islamic figures who will play such a large role in this book. I played with Samar as a toddler and shared with her father his delight in his strong-willed, highly intelligent child. Her only fault, from my point of view, was the astonishing speed with which she spoke. I regularly had to plead with her to slow the "train," a request that always amused her. In her teens, like many of her generation, Samar took the headscarf and I also noticed her sleeves and skirts getting longer. Samar's dad, who died suddenly and tragically just as Samar was entering high school, was a religious man, well read in both classic and contemporary Islamic writings. He and I often discussed Islamic issues. Although an engineer by training and occupation, Kamel loved the classic Islamic texts more than any others, and he avidly followed developments in contemporary Islamic thinking. I first met Kamel in 1968 at the Russian cultural center in Cairo, where my wife and I were studying advanced Russian so we would not lose that daunting language under the pressure of our study of Arabic. Later, as friends, when Kamel and I made our yearly treks to the Cairo book fair, two stops were required before the aimless wandering in which we delighted most. We had to know first what was new in children's books and then in Islamic philosophy. Admittedly, there was something just a little odd about our obsession with children's books. When the tradition began, he didn't have any and neither did I. But Kamel was convinced that, whatever else we did with our lives, being good fathers had to be a high priority. Given our limitations, he would slyly note, we had better get started acquiring the skills and sensibilities we would need. I agreed, worried that I had not had the best experience of just what it means to be a good father. Before his first child was born, Kamel already had a considerable library waiting for him, not to mention the old computer he refused to throw away because Mostafa could play with it.

It was Kamel who introduced me to Shaikh Muhammad al Ghazzali, whom I consider one of the two or three most important Islamic thinkers of the twentieth century, quite possibly the greatest. Kamel didn't know Ghazzali personally, but he loved him. He insisted on several occasions that I stay over with his family so we could hear Ghazzali lead the dawn prayer for the vast crowd in a large public square near his apartment in Cairo. There was nothing forced or artificial about Kamel's religious commitments. He treasured them, while wearing them lightly. He was always amused when, pretending to forget, I would invite him for his favorite lunch in the middle of the Ramadan fast. I never minded opening my computer to hear Qur'anic verses that he had surreptitiously planted on my hard drive for my enlightenment, knowing full well I would never figure out how to remove them. His faith was so much a part of his life that the notion that we somehow couldn't talk, argue, or even joke about it never occurred to either of us. Islam was part of the air that Kamel breathed. It was an integral part of our lifelong friendship.

Still, with all this background, Samar's sudden decision to wear gloves and not shake the hand of any males still startled me. In my mind, I saw the *niqab* (face veil) as the next step. The *niqab* covers the entire face and not just the hair, as the *hegab* (headscarf) does, and I feared her countenance would disappear from my life. Kamel disliked extremisms in all forms. I had no doubts that he would have regarded this sudden turn in his daughter's life as one worthy of thought and serious reflection, although I also understood that it would be the subject of conversation and not a diktat.

Samar was used to my involvement in her life in those early years, so she wasn't really too surprised when I asked her bluntly why she was adopting "Saudi" manners and dress. I knew the comment would displease her, as Egyptians hardly view the Saudis as mentors in matters of faith, fashion, or lifestyle. I also knew that she would reject any attribution to Saudi Arabia for the adoption of what she took to be proper Islamic dress and behavior. She pointed out that modest dress was an Islamic obligation. I asked her how she knew that modesty meant gloves. She said that Islam enjoins modest dress for women, noting that the gloves were perhaps not obligatory but nevertheless pleasing to God. I asked her how she knew what was pleasing to God. She told me about her shaikh, who conveyed this wisdom. How did he know? I inquired. Samar didn't hesitate to say, from the Qur'an.

Kamel had given me my opening. Never resisting the opportunity to remind me that his familiarity with the Bible exceeded mine, Kamel had for years encouraged my reading of the Qur'an. I had frequently discussed particular verses with him, most often in his living room with TV blasting and the children playing between our legs. More often than not, we would turn to Islamic scholars like Yusuf al Qaradawi or Muhammad al Ghazzali for help when understanding of a particular verse or concept eluded us. So, there was nothing unusual in my suggestion to Samar that we first check the actual texts. Samar couldn't remember the precise verse her shaikh had alluded to, but from the description it seemed to me it might be in the *Surah* of Women. We searched but, to Samar's disappointment, she could not find the verse that matched the description the shaikh had given in his loose Qur'anic reference. She resolved to ask him for the precise text. The next time we met, Samar announced that the verse was indeed in the *Surah* of Women, but Samar had discovered that neither the face nor the hands were mentioned explicitly as requiring covering. The verse called instead for modesty in dress of both men and women, indicating that the area of the body to be covered was that private domain from above the knees to the waist. It took a considerable imaginative leap to relocate either the hands or the face to those areas. Samar then learned that the shaikh had relied for his interpretation of the verse on certain *hadiths*, or traditions of the Prophet. *Hadiths* can be verified and evaluated as to their reliability, and it turned out that these *hadiths* cited were weak ones. Samar's sense of certainty in her course began to erode. At that point, I suggested she read an important book by Muhammad al Ghazzali, one of her father's favorites, on women's role in Islam in which he supports the headscarf but not the face veil.[16] Samar was, of course, familiar with Ghazzali as a figure whom her father respected. The book itself was still nestled on one of the shelves surrounding the family entertainment center that Kamel had designed. I am not sure if she ever did read it, but I do know that Samar still wears a stylish version of the headscarf, although the gloves disappeared without comment, and I can still see Kamel in her face.

2

Oases of Resistance and Reform

Each of those gardens brought forth its produce,
And failed not in the least therein:
In the midst of them We caused a river to flow.

QUR'AN 18:33

"ISLAM," SHAIKH MUHAMMAD al Ghazzali pronounced, "has become an orphan and a stranger in its own lands."[1] The terrible years of the twentieth century were particularly disastrous for Islam. Writing in the early seventies, Ghazzali expressed great apprehension for the threatened state of *Dar al Islam*, as the century entered its final quarter. His words echoed a *hadith* of the Prophet Muhammad that recounted that "Islam started as a stranger and will become a stranger again."[2] Ghazzali was not referring to attacks on particular Islamic activists or movements. He was lamenting the undermining of the broken *ummah* as a whole. What disturbed him most was that "hatred of Islam itself" had become commonplace.[3]

The West and the Culture of Violence

The disasters suffered by Islam in the twentieth century were the culmination of processes long in motion. At the end of the eighteenth century and beginning of the nineteenth century, the British, French, and Russian empires had all invaded Islamic lands. Out of the body of the *ummah* the colonial powers carved all manner of artificial entities to facilitate settlement and dominance. The twentieth century opened with the empires of Britain, France, and Russia using overwhelming force to consolidate their occupation of Islamic lands. Imperial powers came to the Islamic world as the carriers of a racist culture of violence. Murderous European civil wars, fueled by the blood and soil nationalism on which the West prided itself, had bred the terrible virus. Imperialism acted as its disseminating agent.

European armies, whether from western or eastern Europe, waged wars of casual extermination in their quest for global domination.[4] It inspired the horrific violence of settler colonialism in Algeria and Palestine. The terror was not restricted to Islamic lands, although Muslims numbered disproportionately among its victims. Horrors, without limits and without remorse, were unleashed on the hapless Islamic world.

A memo by Winston Churchill captures the imperial mood that remained strong into the early twentieth century. Churchill intervened in a high-level debate over what weapons should be used to crush the revolt in the 1920s of the people of Mesopotamia. "I am strongly in favour of using poisoned gas against uncivilised tribes," Churchill intoned. "Gasses can be used which cause great inconvenience and would spread a lively terror," he continued.[5] Routinely Churchill expressed his disdain for the Arabs in the most graphic terms. On another occasion he pronounced that "the Arabs are a backward people who eat nothing but Camel dung."[6] There was nothing exceptional about such dismissive racism. The British *Manual of Military Law* stated that the rules of war applied only to conflict "between civilized nations." An elaboration noted that "they do not apply in wars with uncivilized States and tribes."[7]

Americans are prone to distance their own national story from such European attitudes and their bloody consequences. History is far less forgiving, especially when viewed through an Islamic lens. Islamic historians note that the African slaves that subsidized American prosperity with their labor and their lives were at least 15 percent Muslim. A rarely noted dimension of the slave narratives is the struggle of the Muslims among them to preserve their faith and the Arabic language that conveyed its message. It is the American record in the Philippines, however, that stands out for its barbarism when the focus is on Islam. The brutal American seizure and occupation of the Philippines extended from the Spanish-American War of 1896 through World War I. It has a rarely acknowledged Islamic dimension. American forces of approximately 120,000 brought death and destruction on a genocidal scale. The historian Bernard Fall has argued that the American conquest of the Philippines was "the bloodiest colonial war (in proportion to population) ever fought by a white power in Asia; it cost the lives of 300,000 Filipinos."[8] The American assault was waged with particular viciousness against the Muslim resistance in the south.

The United States succeeded the Spanish as colonial power in the Philippines.[9] The American era opened with a proclamation of "benevolent assimilation" issued by President McKinley on December 21, 1898. The proclamation explained that "it will be the duty of the commander of the forces of occupation to announce and proclaim in the most public manner that we come not as invaders or conquerors, but as friends, to protect the natives in their homes, in their employment, and in their personal and religious rights."¹⁰ In practice, the American rules of engagement for this imperial adventure matched and surpassed in unrestrained violence those of the European colonizers. Resistance was most determined by Filipino Moros, as indigenous Muslims were called. Most Americans are familiar with "The White Man's Burden" by the English author and poet Rudyard Kipling. However, very few are taught that this poem was written to support American imperialism in the Philippines.

President McKinley explained that the Philippines were thrust on an innocent America as a result of its victory over the Spanish. There was no choice but "to educate the Filipinos, and uplift and civilize and Christianize them, and by God's grace do the very best we could by them, as our fellow-men for whom Christ also died."¹¹ Mark Twain sardonically praised the U.S. government's success in the "civilizing mission" of U.S. diplomacy over the Muslim inhabitants of the southern Philippines that ended in mass murder. Christian attitudes found perverse expression among the officers who led the American forces. One Major Edwin Glenn, to cite but one example, proudly reported how he had forty-seven prisoners kneel and "repent of their sins" before ordering them bayoneted and clubbed to death.¹²

Mark Twain, in uncensored versions of his work, wrote bluntly of American imperialism. As with so many genuine American heroes, Twain is encased in a neutering mythology. It must be broken for an encounter with the politics of the father of American literature and my neighbor for many years: The Mark Twain House, where his spirit rests, was just down the street from my first house in Hartford, Connecticut. Hartford has its problems, but it also has the West End with its charming Victorian houses, including Mark Twain's. As an ardent anti-imperialist, Twain spoke for Americans of enlightened conscience in a flood of articles denouncing England, France, Germany, Russia, and the United States for their imperialist depredations. In his "A Greeting from the 19th Century to the 20th Century" for the *New York Herald Tribune* on December 30, 1900, Twain wrote acidly that "I bring you the stately matron named Christendom, returning bedraggled, besmirched and dishonored from pirate-raids in Kiao-Chou, Manchuria, South Africa and the

Philippines, with her soul full of meanness, her pocket full of boodle and her mouth full of pious hypocrisies. Give her the soap and a towel," Twain concluded, "but hide the looking-glass." He followed up in 1901 with his essay "To the Person Sitting in Darkness." Twain explained that not only the United States but each of the strong powers of the day was advancing "with its banner of the Prince of Peace in one hand and its loot-basket and its butcher-knife in the other."[13]

Even against such a dark background of nineteenth- and early twentieth-century crimes, the Western atrocities of the mid-twentieth century still stand out. Not all the wounds in this most violent of centuries were to the "uncivilized." In the twentieth century fratricidal bloodletting engulfed Europe on a scale without precedent in world history. Two European civil wars, labeled misleadingly as world wars, took over fifty million souls. Firebombing of "enemy" European cities numbed all sensitivity about the loss of civilian lives. The use of atomic weapons against Japanese "enemy cities" highlighted the utter lack of humanitarian restraint in the new American center of Western power. Islamic intellectuals witnessed these spectacular wars against all notions of civilized behavior with shock and dismay. They assessed the twentieth century, so completely dominated by the West, as one of the bloodiest in history. They felt great and justified apprehension for the fate of Islam in a world dominated by the West and its culture of violence.

Ending of the Caliphate

For Islam the twentieth century was the era that brought the demise of the caliphate. In 1924 Mustafa Kemal Atatürk (1881–1938) officially ended the caliphate. Weakness and rampant political and financial corruption had long since diminished its role as the repository of the collective aspirations of Muslims. Nevertheless, it had provided a symbolic expression of the bonds that connected them. For the first time in their history, Muslims worldwide found themselves bereft of an overarching Islamic political framework and political figure symbolically representing the unity of the *ummah*. The "father of the Turks" went still further: He launched an unrelenting campaign to strip Turkey of its Islamic character. Turkey was declared to be secular.

Atatürk took secularism to mean the elimination of any role for Islam in public life. Politically, the regime reserved a privileged place for the military as the "guardian" of the nation's secular and republican character as Atatürk had defined it. The elitist arrangement sharply limited prospects for democratic development. This Turkish model, greatly admired and actively supported by the West, paved the way for other countries to follow suit, most notably Iran and to a lesser extent Egypt. Three critical centers at the heart of the Islamic world seemed on their way to abandoning Islam. Western delight at any weakening of the Islamic world was tempered by fears that a strong and assertive nationalism, like Atatürk's, would be equally or perhaps even more problematic. Over the coming decades the West at times did support Islamic movements as a counterweight to strong nationalism. The underlying consistency was abhorrence of any strong and unified alternative to imperialism, whether nationalist or Islamic.

By the mid-1970s, Atatürk-style Westernization had reached unprecedented proportions. Most disheartening for Islamic intellectuals was the systematic weakening of *Shari'ah* (the provisions from Qur'an and *Sunnah* to regulate human behavior) in most Arab and Islamic countries. The damages were not confined to the religious and cultural sphere: Two entire countries, Zanzibar and Palestine, had already been lost for Islam. The success of the Zionist project in establishing the state of Israel meant that the bulk of historic Palestine was severed from the Arab Islamic world and its remnants were left defenseless. In 1964 an uprising led by local African revolutionaries succeeded in overthrowing the Arab-dominated government of Zanzibar. A massacre of hundreds of local Arab and Indian Muslims ensued. Zanzibar as an independent entity with an overwhelming Muslim majority was swallowed up in a union with Tanzania.

Great traumas seared the violent history of Western assault on the *ummah* into the collective memory of Muslims. The wounds were old. The memories and the pain remained fresh, and they included direct assault on Islam. The French conquered and occupied Algeria in 1830. An estimated one million Algerians were killed by the occupiers. The French, having themselves suffered losses of some 30,000, were determined to occupy Algeria permanently. They aimed to systematically destroy its Islamic culture, replacing it with their own. Mosques were converted into churches. Old Arab city centers were torn down and replaced with the French version of an orderly city. The French attacks on Algeria's Islamic identity culminated with the conversion of the historic eleventh-century Great Mosque, believed to be the oldest in Algeria, into the Cathedral of St. Philippe. Qur'anic inscriptions in the interior were encircled with gold letters that read: "Jesus Christ yesterday, today, and forever." A large cross was placed on its high minaret to signal, as the colonial officials announced, that "French domination of Algiers is definitive." In his inaugural sermon, the new Archbishop of St. Philippe announced that the mission of the cathedral was to convert the Arabs from "their barbaric faith."[14]

The assault on Algeria's Islamic character extended to displacement of the country's Muslim people. Prime agricultural land was distributed by the French rulers to an amalgam of European settlers, including Maltese, Italian, and Spanish as well as the French. These European "pied noirs" settlers, as they were called, exerted a political and economic stranglehold on the colony. The tragedy of Algeria was repeated at sites throughout the Islamic world. Most familiar is the colonization of Palestine by European Jewish settlers of mixed national origins. In the West, the colonization of Palestine is rarely understood in this way. In the Islamic world note is taken of the fact that in 1917 the Jewish population of Palestine represented less than 10 percent of the total. On this modest foundation, it is understood by Muslims everywhere that aggressive settler-colonialism, with many similarities to the Algerian experience, erected the Israeli state. By the mid-1970s the Palestinian Arabs were either second-class citizens in a Jewish state, living under oppressive occupation, or refugees.

Nasser's Anti-Western Westernization

The twentieth century opened with renewed imperial assaults that once again targeted Islamic lands. It ended with postcolonial, anti-Islamic regimes on the Turkish model in power throughout the Middle East. The rulers were indigenous, but, from an Islamic perspective, there was little difference: All such postcolonial regimes pursued strategies that took the West as the model of progress. Invariably, movements under Islamic banners emerged as its major opposition. Some of the imitative new regimes allied themselves with the West. Others took anti-Western positions. Nasser of Egypt was the most successful of the "anti-Western Westernizers."[15]

Ghazzali in the early 1970s had called for resistance, although the precise forms it should take were not yet clear to him. "We have decided that we will remain present," he pronounced. "A willful and obstinate *nabqa* (presence)," he continued, "represents the heart of the message we bring." Ghazzali pledged that "Islam will endure, even if those who struggle for it die. We will bequeath the message and the struggle to the next generation."[16] Ghazzali's rhetoric of resolute refusal had solid historical grounding. Islam in the face of violent assaults from the West had consistently refused to play the role of passive victim. Although rarely emphasized in Western accounts, the history of the *ummah* from the eighteenth century to the twentieth century witnessed three great waves of Islamic reform and resistance to foreign intrusions.

Three Waves of Resistance

The successive waves of mass resistance to Western depredations wrote an impressive chapter in the history of Islamic lands. Over the course of the three centuries, from the eighteenth to the twentieth, Islam responded like a living entity to threats to its existence. It had, like any living thing, desperately searched for the means to defend itself against the odds. In doing so, it lodged itself more deeply in the hearts of ordinary Muslims. The story Islamic historians tell of Islam's renewal is always and everywhere a story of the power of the faith in the lives of the masses of ordinary Muslims rather than a tale of charismatic leaders. The mention of key leaders is simply a shorthand. These figures represented a new way of thinking and acting to meet the dangers. By the time they emerged, that way of resistance had already taken shape in the minds of hundreds of thousands of ordinary people. The leadership figures of each wave of resistance had only to speak its name to win mass support. In every era, resistance drew on the Islamic heritage rather than foreign sources.

The first great surge arose in the second half of the eighteenth century and continued through the first half of the nineteenth.[17] Reformers of this period aimed to return Islam to its most essential sources in the Qur'an and *Sunnah*. They sought intellectual and *fiqh* (Islamic legal reasoning) reform. The great movements of reform included Muhammad Ibn Abd al Wahhab (1703–1791) from Najd in the Arabian Peninsula, Muhammad Ibn Nuh (1752–1803) from Medina, Shaikh Muhammad Ali al Sanusi (1778–1859) in Morocco, Muhammad Ibn Ahmed al Mahdi (1843–1885) in the Sudan, Muhammad al Shaukani (1758/9–1834) in Yemen, al Shehab al Alus (1802–1854) in Iraq, and Wali Eddine al Dahlawi (1702–1762) in India. From an Islamic perspective, the large number of reformers and the massive followings they won indicate that a great deal more than personal charisma was at work in these diverse settings. These highly successful mass movements appear as the products of the Islamic environment itself as sustained by everyday Muslims. In some cases the reformers not only focused on a call to return to the sources but also built a political movement on these new intellectual foundations. The Wahhabi in the Arabian Peninsula, the Mahdi in the Sudan, and the Senussi in Morocco all had this dual intellectual and political character. Others remained movements of thought and *fiqh* without a distinctive political character.

The second great surge of mass Islamic resistance arose in the last quarter of the nineteenth century and extended into the early years of the twentieth. Its proponents arose in opposition to deepening imperial intrusions. The West at this time completely dominated the Islamic world. The British had taken Egypt and the Sudan, the French Tunis and Morocco, and the Italians Libya. Mass movements of national resistance arose. They were inextricably tied to Islam. The mass uprisings included those of Abdul Qader al Jazeiri (1808–1883) in Algeria, Abdul Karim al Khatabbi (1882–1963) in Morocco, Ahmed Sharif al Senussi (1873–1933) in Libya, and Muhammad Ahmad al Mahdi (1845–1885) in the Sudan. In Egypt, the arc of Islamic resistance extended from Gamal Eddine al Afghani (1838–1897), Muhammad Abduh (1849–1905), and Rashid Rida (1865–1935) to Mustafa Kamel (1874–1908). Afghani and Abduh left the most durable imprint as theorists of Islamic resistance. The Algerian thinker Malek Bennabi (1905–1973) has aptly described Afghani as the spark for the resistance to the Western assault and Abduh as the figure who stimulated reform to address the underlying vulnerability that had made assault possible. Afghani agitated tirelessly for the unification of the Islamic world to resist the incursions of the violent Western intruders. He sought the unification of Sunnis and Shi'i, notably of Turkey and Iran. Abduh for his part added a more nuanced notion of resistance that included strenuous efforts to reform traditional Islamic institutions and the traditional ways of thinking they embodied. He argued that the Islamic world must be not only united but reformed as well. The challenge facing these reformers was far more complex than those of the first wave, when the focus was essentially on the reform of the heritage. Imperialism, by the time of the second wave, had sunk deep roots into Islamic lands, seriously threatening not only the heritage but also the Islamic identity and way of life of the people themselves. Westerners had established protected foreign enclaves or outright colonies in the heart of the Islamic world. Particularly destructive was the impact of Christian missionaries who arrived in the wake of Western armies. By the end of the second wave, it had already become clear that the Islamic character of both the land and the people was threatened. It was not enough to respond to colonialism itself; it was essential to deal with the cultural destruction that came with it.

The third great surge of Islamic reform arose in the wake of World War I (1914–1918). It lasted through World War II (1939–1945) and the subsequent decades of the 1950s and 1960s. World War I represented the first great European civil war of the modern period. It brought the ascendency of the French and the British. They proceeded to divide the heartlands of the Middle East between them. The British took Palestine and Iraq. The French exerted their control over Syria, Lebanon, and Algeria. Russia in turn took Bukhara, Samarkand, and Tashkent, consolidating control over the Islamic lands of central Asia. The British and the Dutch dominated the islands of southwest Asia that had majority Muslim populations.

By the third wave, the threat to Islam and Islamic identity of relentless Westernization no longer came only from the outside. The colonial presence in Islamic lands created a whole new set of challenges for which the responses of the earlier eras were no longer adequate. The occupying powers set about building entirely new institutions to parallel and ultimately displace inherited Islamic institutions and the ways of thinking and living they made possible. Western political and legal structures were imported wholesale. Educational and health facilities on Western models were built. A debilitating dualism came to characterize the colonial situation. Islamic societies were split in two and suffered an inevitable erosion of social and cultural coherence.

The collapse of the caliphate opened the way for a variety of transnational Islamic societies that sought to address these ills. These included the Muslim Brothers, founded by Hassan al Banna in Egypt in 1928; the Islamic Society, by Abul Ala Maududi in India in 1941; and the Nurcu, inspired by Said Nursi in Turkey in the 1950s. During this third wave, resistance initially drew on both Islamic and nationalist sentiments that appeared indivisible. Gradually, however, strains appeared between those with essentially nationalist motivations and those whose loyalties derived from broader Islamic commitments. While the nationalist trend emphasized political and economic independence, the Islamic trend focused as heavily or more on cultural demands. Islamic intellectuals argued strongly that only civilizational independence could provide a shield for Islam. Both trends evoked popular support. They were often at odds, even though their demands were complementary. This divisive split persists to this day.

Despite this history of resistance, by the decade of the 1970s it looked as though Islam would be decisively defeated. In the Middle East nationalists with secular orientations were everywhere dominant. On the global level the general picture was not all bleak, although new dark shadows were coming into view. The European bloodletting had ceased. The European empires withdrew from their overseas territories, vacating Islamic lands. Europe itself was at peace. Competition among European imperial powers for imperial acquisitions was no longer the major threat to Islamic lands.

However, a new danger just as deadly had already appeared on the horizon, although the nature of the threat it posed was not yet clear. The United States was establishing itself as the dominant world power. The Cold War, a supposed rivalry between equally balanced world powers, had masked America's rise as a global hegemon. Only calculated exaggerations of Soviet power and assertiveness created the illusion of parity. Emphasis on the perfidies and infinite evil of the communists deflected any critical self-examination in the United States, as it renewed its taste for imperial adventures. More importantly, the inflation of the Soviet threat also justified the immense arms buildup that within a remarkably short time would make the United States the sole superpower. America would be the driving force and major beneficiary of globalization, as the soft version of American empire would be called.

Even before the end of World War II, the United States had focused on the vast energy resources of the Gulf region. Not surprisingly, Islamic lands hosted the most important of the string of American bases that with time defined the new face of the American successor empire. From the skies and on the seas, American power shadowed the lives of Muslims. The full violence to which Muslim peoples would be subjected by this ominous presence was as yet beyond comprehension. Still, the final decades of the twentieth century were years of profound and rightful apprehension for Islamic intellectuals. History, or so it seemed, had turned decisively against the *ummah*.

The Fourth Wave and New Reserves for Reform and Resistance

At the very brink of despair, Islam defied all the trends and reasserted itself in multiple yet complementary ways. In the great Shi'i arc that stretched from southern Lebanon through Syria, Iraq, and the Gulf to Iran, centuries-old religious connections defined durable commonalities. Islam would find resources in those venerable Shi'i connections, not only to preserve the faith but also to make Islam a force to inspire mass revolution. In Arab lands a network of loosely connected associations of Muslim Brothers provided a generative matrix out of which came all manner of Islamic groupings. Among the Turks a spiritual revival centered on the works of Turkish Islamic mystics, notably Said Nursi. Remarkably, these diverse resistances flowed together in ways no one could have foreseen. The energy from these creative fusions fueled the Islamic Renewal.

The Shi'i Arc from Lebanon to Iran

The Shi'i arc represented the most improbable of all the reserves for Islam's capacity to resist, in the face of overwhelming Western power. The lands of the Shi'a stretch from Lebanon to Iraq, Iran, and the Gulf. The venerable connections between the Shi'i communities of Mount Amel in Lebanon to such centers of Shi'i learning as Najaf in Iraq and Qom in Iran date back to the mid-sixteenth century. They remain vital today. As a minority community estimated at under 15 percent of the world's Muslims, the Shi'a represent a distinctive Islamic presence. In the popular imagination, Shi'a are defined by emotional rituals of self-flagellation. They shed oceans of tears as part of *Ashura*, the yearly commemoration of the martyrdom of the Prophet's grandson Hussein. Community leadership is understood to reside with learned ayatollahs. These accomplished Shi'i scholars command moral deference and wield material power. Traditionally, their leadership has leaned to political accommodation and quietism as the most appropriate strategies to protect a minority community. Shi'i vulnerability crystallizes in the distinctive concept of *taqiyya* (dissimulation), which justifies the concealment of adherence to Shi'ism when believers are under threat. *Taqiyya* is permissible where the dangers to life or property are clear and when no damage to the faith results from the deception.

This characterization of the vulnerability and passivity of the Shi'a is accurate, but it is also incomplete. Critical contradictions are integral to the Shi'i legacy. Both an inclination to quietism *and* a contrary propensity to dissent have consistently characterized Shi'i communities and given them a volatile character. Moreover, extreme emotionalism and rigorous rationality both find their place. Rivalries and intense debates among the

Shi'i ayatollahs are not at all unusual. Shi'i scholars do privilege gnosis and intuition. They retain a profoundly mystical conception of the infallible power of interpretation of the Shi'i imams. At the same time, Shi'i scholarship draws on a strong rationalist tradition. In the absence of the last imam, scholars are called to deploy reason in the service of *ijtihad* (an effort of interpretation of the sacred texts) to guide the community. Rationalism, intuitive understanding, and extreme emotionalism coexist comfortably in the Shi'i tradition.

The imams of the Shi'a occupy a place midway between the human and the divine. They were not created from clay into which God breathed life as ordinary men and women. Rather, they originated from a divine beam of light that appeared before the world itself was created. Imam Ja'far al Sadiq (702–765) teaches that God reserves certain knowledge for himself, while knowledge of other things is taught to his angels, his messengers, and his imams. The judgments of imams were regarded as protected from error by God and therefore infallible. The majority Twelver Shi'a believe that in the absence of the imam the ayatollahs should take responsibility for the guidance of the community. Deprived of their beloved imam, Shi'i communities turned to the most learned among them for leadership. From the ranks of the learned ayatollahs came the grand ayatollahs. Those grand ayatollahs of outstanding scholarly weight and moral authority might then ascend to the position of *marja'* (the highest rank of authority among Shi'a religious scholars). The *maraji'* (plural) have been at the very core of the Shi'i capacity for community building that has proved so durable and resilient.

The process by which an ayatollah is elevated to the position of *marja'* is fluid and reserves an important role for the followership. A *marja'* emerges through his reputation for learning and high moral principles. The most important sign of the emergence of a *marja'* is the publication of a collection of important rulings that establish his strong scholarly record. What matters even more is the reception of the *marja'* by ordinary Shi'i who look to him for guidance. It is the number of such self-selected adherents that has the greatest weight in establishing a figure as a *marja'*. Followers of a particular *marja'* can come from widely dispersed communities, located in a variety of different states. They typically render to the *marja'* the celebrated *khums* (payment of one fifth of acquired wealth). The *maraji'* often command great wealth and the accoutrements of power that it makes possible. Grand ayatollahs and *maraji'* would arise across the Shi'i arc, and not just in Iran, to mobilize movements of mass resistance that would startle the world. In 1979 an Iranian ayatollah from the second ranks who was neither the most learned nor most influential as a scholar created the alchemic formula that would transmute traditional quietism into the extraordinary revolutionary energy of Iran's Islamic revolution.

The Muslim Brothers in the Sunni Heartland

A very different Islamic assertiveness has had a venerable tradition in Egypt, the confident heart of the Sunni world. Egyptian associations with the mission of protecting and fostering Islam were the earliest and most numerous in the Arab world.[18] From Egypt came the most important movement of politicized Sunni Islam, the Muslim Brotherhood.

The Organizational Genius of Hassan al Banna

The origins of the most important of Sunni Islamic associations were extremely modest. An Egyptian schoolteacher in the provincial city of Ismailia joined with his brother and a handful of followers to found the Muslim Brothers. It is difficult to verify the details. What we do have is the clear projection of the founding myth by Banna himself. In his telling, Banna makes clear the intended link of the new association to the quest for justice. Banna relates that in March 1928 six laborers from the British camp for the Suez Canal Authority came to him to thank him for his teachings. They went on to say that "we know not the practical way to reach the glory ('izza) of Islam and to serve the welfare of Muslims. We are weary of this life of humiliation and restriction. Lo, we see the Arabs and the Muslims have no status (manzila) and no dignity (karama). They are not more than mere hirelings belonging to the foreigners." The laborers explained that "we possess nothing but this blood . . . and these souls . . . and these few coins. . . . We are unable to perceive the road to action as you perceive it, or to know the path to the service of the fatherland (watan), the religion, and the nation (ummah) as you know it. All that we desire now is to present you with all that we possess, to be acquitted by God of the responsibility, and for you to be responsible before Him for us and what we must do."

Banna, who was twenty-two years old at the time, accepted the obligation. Together the small group swore an oath to God to act as junud (soldiers) for the message of Islam. Banna pronounced that "we are Brothers in the service of Islam; hence, we are the Muslim Brothers."[19]

The Islam Banna sought to protect was an inclusive Islam. Banna explained to his followers that "we are a Salafiyya message, a Sunni way, a Sufi truth, a political organization, an athletic group, a cultural-educational union, an economic company, and a social idea."[20] The Islam for which the Brothers spoke was also a worldly Islam, deeply committed to transforming Muslim societies. It was very much motivated by fierce opposition to colonialism and the positive struggle for moral rectitude and social justice. To achieve these social aims, Banna believed that strong and tightly organized leadership would be essential. He wed his notion of community service to an authoritarian conception of leadership.

Traditional conceptions came naturally to Banna. He was born in 1906 into a pious lower-middle-class family in the village of Mahmudiyya to the northwest of Cairo. As a boy, Banna attended village schools. His father was a religious teacher who often led the community prayers in the village. By the age of fourteen, Banna had memorized the Qur'an. While still in his early teens, Banna began attending the mystic circles of the Hasafiyya Sufi Order. He totally immersed himself in the activities of the order and attained the status of an initiate. Banna remained an active member in the Order for some twenty years. For a brief time, he even wore the tasseled turban and white outer garment of the Order. His readings lead him to the work of the medieval scholar Abu Hamid al Ghazzali (1058–1111), who played a key role in bringing Sufism into mainstream Islam. From the great scholar, Banna drew the paradoxical lesson that scholarly pursuits should be limited to just enough learning to secure an occupation and perform one's religious obligations in an informed way. Throughout his life, Banna maintained the position that the bulk of the vast literature of *fiqh*, developed over the centuries by Islamic scholars, was irrelevant to the current conditions of Muslims. He turned instead directly to the Qur'an and urged his followers to do the same.

Banna's involvement during these same years in a variety of religious associations reinforced this strong practical streak. He regularly rose to leadership positions and showed a gift for recruitment. Banna consistently sought to think through an issue and then *act* on conclusions, bringing others along with him. Ideas and principles really came alive for him when they were embodied in social actions. Social and political activism demanded the practical discipline of embodying ideas in concrete projects.

Banna left his village for Dar al Ulum in Cairo, a Western-style university where he trained for a teaching career. Upon graduation, he accepted a post teaching Arabic in the public system in the city of Ismailia. In an essay from his last year of studies, he wrote that "I believe that the best people are those who . . . achieve their happiness by making others happy and counseling them." Banna concluded that Sufism offered one path to that end of "sincerity and work in the service of humanity," while teaching offered a second. He chose the second path, explicitly preferring it because of "its involvement with people."[21] Banna remained a teacher for nineteen years. He taught his young students during the day and their parents at night in voluntary adult education programs. He described his calling as "preaching and guidance." Banna found his students not only in mosques but also in coffee houses and other public gathering places that he regarded as "people's institutes."

During those same years, Banna actively participated in demonstrations against British rule. Ismailia hosted the Suez Canal Authority, and consequently there was a very large British presence in the city. Throughout his life, Banna's deep faith and gentle personal manner coexisted with his passion to free Egypt of a degrading occupation and return Islam to its rightful place as the moral anchor of community. Banna had no formal higher education in the Islamic sciences. The paths to leadership in traditional Islamic organizations were closed to him. He defined a new trajectory through social activism, wedded to a call for Islamic renewal.

Hassan al Banna developed an innovative organizational formula aimed explicitly at reflecting the *shumeleyya* (comprehensiveness) of Islam. The insistence on Islam's all-inclusive character provided an essential response to efforts by the colonizers to marginalize and neutralize Islam. Banna could not accept the Christian notion of relegating religion with its moral and ethical principles to a sacred sphere separate from the rest of human life. Banna believed, and sought to demonstrate through the activities of his movement, that Islam was a complete way of life, fully capable of generating political, economic, social, and faith institutions to respond to the needs of a modern society. Banna's conception was an innovative one. Outside observers have done their best to force the Brotherhood into recognizable Western molds as a covert political party, social movement, or fellowship of faith. Islam as Banna conceived it could not be contained by any of these "buckets." Banna himself said simply and directly to his followership that "my Brothers: you are not a benevolent society, nor a political party, nor a local organization having limited purposes. Rather, you are a new soul in the heart of this nation to give it life by means of the Qur'an."²² The Brothers were to be, quite literally, an Islamic society in embryo.

Banna never synthesized into a critical intellectual system these powerful impulses. His writings have more the character of tracts designed for mobilization, rather than serious intellectual works. He had absorbed his insights directly from the humiliations of the colonial situation. He expressed these insights in organizational forms, rather than in theoretical treatises. His writings and speeches were enlivened by flashes of insight, captured in powerful aphorisms like "eject imperialism from your souls, and it will leave your lands."²³ However, Banna left no systematic contribution to contemporary Islamic thought. When asked why he did not write books, Banna famously explained that he authored men who authored books. Muhammad al Ghazzali characterized Banna as a synthesizing vehicle for reformist influences from Abduh, Afghani, and Rida. From Afghani he took a sense of the dangers coming from the West, from Abduh the notion that the *ummah* should reform itself, and from Rida guidance to deeper understanding of the Qur'an. Ghazzali believed that Hassan al Banna sowed knowledge the way a farmer sows seeds. Ghazzali regarded himself as a lifelong student of Banna. He believed that Banna had a skill that allowed him to explain complex things in simple terms that the Islamic world had not seen since the great Abu Hamed al Ghazali (c. 1058–1111).²⁴

Hassan al Banna possessed the imaginative power to envision organized actions in a wide variety of spheres, all within reach of ordinary Muslims. He then created the new institutional arrangements on all levels to make them possible. The depth of his insights can be read from the very practical activities of the Brothers. They taught proper forms of worship. They explored issues of Islamic morality in group settings. However, the real burst of transformative energy came as social activism among the people. The Brothers established schools and clinics as well as factories where wages and benefits were higher than in state-owned enterprises. They launched a modern Scout movement. They ran literacy clinics and night schools for workers as well as tutorial programs to assist with civil service programs. Here was the real strength of the Brothers. Banna's activism united people around social activities, permeated with Islamic teachings. The Brothers could live an alternative, more meaningful and moral life. They could build their identity on that basis. In contrast, the Marxists, with whom the Brothers competed for the loyalties of the youth, focused on study groups to explore interesting ideas, but the ideas themselves were for the most part disconnected from life around them. Banna understood his community works as essential planks of his strategy to resist colonial encroachments. Politically, the mainstream Brothers stressed moderation and gradualism in the service of a very long-term vision of social transformation. They opposed any headlong rush to power and strongly opposed the use of violent means to achieve the Brotherhood's aims.

Banna's achievements were not without deep and disturbing contradictions. There was an inherent tension between the cohesive and adaptable social networks he built and the rigidly disciplined leadership structures that managed them. Governance of the Brothers was authoritarian and secretive. The absence of a coherent overall theoretical understanding of the mission of the Brothers also created its own dangers. Banna emphasized the call, rather than a drive for political power. However, he was aware that power would in fact be necessary to accomplish some of the goals he set for the movement.[25] Banna never resolved these ambiguities about power. Nor did the Brothers under Banna develop a coherent economic philosophy. In practice, this shortcoming meant that, despite their support for some progressive measures, especially in health and education, they left the structures of economic privilege in place and worked through them.

Perhaps most fateful of all was Banna's ambivalence and contradictory responses on the question of violence. Like all political trends in Egypt at the time, the Brothers did develop an armed wing ostensibly for defensive purposes in a climate of escalating violence. That secret apparatus proved difficult to control. It threatened to turn the Society in a more overtly political direction, laced with violence. Banna's gradual and moderate vision of change through "Qur'anic wisdom and sound counsel" had difficulty holding its own in the face of calls to take political paths to hasten the Islamization of Egypt. Banna famously spoke against the violent actions of militants with a political agenda. He charged that they "are not Brothers, they are not Muslims."[26] However, there were inconsistencies in his statements. At other times, he spoke loosely of *jihad* (struggle for the faith) in both spiritual and physical senses, giving it a militant meaning. At any rate, Banna never incorporated his warnings into an effective institutional mechanism to contain the extremists within the Brotherhood. Their violence, including the assassination of political figures, eventually turned back on the Brotherhood. In February 1949, at of the age of forty-three, Banna himself was assassinated by an Egyptian government agent near his office in Cairo. He reportedly was shot seven times and then denied medical care until he died from his wounds. Banna's murder by the palace left the Society vulnerable to its extremist elements. The political vision that the extremists championed, with the scent of violence surrounding it, haunts the Brotherhood to this day.

The Utopian Political Vision of Sayyid Qutb

In his *Milestones*, Sayyid Qutb gave the extremist alternative its most cogent theoretical expression.[27] Qutb's writings contain very forceful condemnation of the predatory violence of colonial powers in the Islamic world. He also attacks the corruption and brutalities of ruling secular regimes. His arguments on these circumscribed matters are well reasoned and well founded. Few intellectuals of the Islamic Renewal would disagree with either of these basic positions. Qutb went further: He called for the support of revolutionary resistance to the crimes of Western empires and to the tyrannies of Westernizing, postcolonial regimes. These positions, too, have widespread support among centrists. However, for many in the midstream, Qutb crossed a red line in his thinking when he pronounced existing regimes as un-Islamic rather than simply deeply flawed or even criminal.[28] Qutb argued that these systems were only nominally Islamic and open to the charge of *takfir* (declaring Muslims to be unbelievers). This formulation left the implication that killing their leaders was not only permissible but even a duty.

Qutb's stance read as a declaration of war against existing regimes across *Dar al Islam* and of the global order of which they were a part. Qutb argued against accommodation with either the regime or the Western-dominated world system. Here we have the most radical of all his ideas. With the charge of *jahilliyya* (belonging to the pre-Islamic age of ignorance), Qutb forcefully challenged a centuries-old Sunni compromise with ruling power. In the wake of the assassination of the fourth caliph Ali in 661, the Sunni community acquiesced in the capture of the caliphate by the ruler of Damascus. The Umayyad dynasty followed, with its secular orientation and commitment to hereditary rule, both contravening the Prophet's example. Henceforth, the majority Sunni community would accept dynastic rule that had little to do with Islam. It did so on condition that internal order and territorial integrity were maintained, while religious matters were left largely to the *'ulama* (Islamic scholars).

Qutb called for a clean break with that tradition. He considered the Sunni historic compromise with ruling power to be the greatest mistake in the history of *Dar al Islam*. More than any other single factor, it explained, in Qutb's view, how the Islamic world lost its place of world leadership. The compromise had opened the way to *jahilliyya*. Qutb applied this reasoning to the contemporary challenges facing the *ummah*. Acceptance of the Western imperial order and of regimes that accommodated that order was unacceptable to Qutb. To implement his radical challenge to Sunni tradition, Qutb called for the formation of a vanguard that would galvanize true Muslims both by persuasion and "physical power and *jihad*."[29]

Centrist Islamic intellectuals agreed with the dissent from the tyrannies of the Egyptian regime. They did not agree that the road to reform and accommodation was closed. Moreover, they feared that such a position opened the door to an even more violent repression of the Islamic trend. In the view of the mainstream, the "dark ideas" of Qutb's later writings reflected an extremist interpretation of Islam that had more to do with the terrible provocations of the Nasserist state and the criminal depredations of dominant powers than the message of Islam.

Western critics are fond of charging that Islamic moderates have failed to challenge such extremist positions. The charges are without merit, no matter how endlessly repeated. In fact, centrist Islamic intellectuals produced volume after volume of refutations of Qutbist positions.[30] Virtually none of this important work in Arabic is read or discussed in the West. It does receive attention in Egypt and the Arab and Islamic world, however. Islamic centrists have been remarkably successful in countering the influence of Qutb's extremist ideas for the overwhelming majority of Muslims.

It should be noted as well that while Qutb did reach extreme conclusions on the theoretical plane, he himself never participated in actions that relied on the "physical power" that he foresaw as necessary to face such repressive regimes. It is a serious mistake to see him as an engaged advocate of armed struggle. Qutb's vision was utopian on a grand scale. He looked to the vanguard not as a violent underground movement but rather the embryo of an Islamic society that would grow organically as a movement until it formed a truly Islamic community "in some Islamic country." He reasoned that "only such a revivalist movement will eventually attain the status of worldwide leadership, whether the distance is near or far."[31]

The frequent comparisons made between Qutb and Lenin are without merit. Qutb was no Lenin. Sayyid Qutb did not *act* to create and lead a revolutionary party of militant revolutionaries, committed to employ violence without restraint to impose their will. There is more mystical fantasy in

Milestones than the ruthless realism of *What's to Be Done*, Lenin's most influential revolutionary tract. On the political plane, Qutb advocated utopian ideas. Lenin, in contrast, led the first workers' revolution in history. Qutb's political philosophy was closer to anarchism than the militant Marxism and party dictatorship that Lenin advocated and succeeded in installing in revolutionary Russia.

Qutb's ideas were in no sense those of a democrat. But neither his radicalism nor antidemocratic stance makes him an advocate for theocracy, as is often charged. Qutb was indeed unimpressed with the Western-style democracy that he observed firsthand in the United States. He had total disdain for the kind of society it enabled. In his view, Muslims should stand against both "rule by a pious few, or democratic representation." Qutb in full anarchist mode actively opposed *any* system where men are in "servitude to other—other human beings . . . from the clutches of human lordship and man-made laws" that Qutb regarded as "un-Islamic and a violation of *hakemeyya* (God's sovereignty) over all his creations."[32] Qutb opposed theocracy as strongly as he did Western-style democracy.

For his writings and utopian speculations, Sayyid Qutb was imprisoned for ten years, periodically tortured, and eventually hanged. One incident from his decade-long imprisonment left an indelible mark. It can stand for all the brutalities that overwhelmed his spirit. Qutb witnessed the slaughter in 1957 of twenty-one defenseless Brotherhood prisoners, who had balked at reporting for backbreaking manual labor. A regime capable of such crimes, in his view, was not redeemable. In a final show trial in 1966, with none of the most elemental requirements of a genuine court procedure, Qutb and five other Brothers were charged and convicted of plotting to kill the president and other state leaders. The trial came in the wake of an alleged Muslim Brother assassination attempt against Gamal Abdel Nasser. It has never been firmly established that such an attempt was real. It is instructive that the "evidence" used against Qutb in the trial consisted essentially of passages from his radical writings, primarily *Milestones*. If hard evidence of a plot and Qutb's role in it actually existed, it made no appearance at the trial. Qutb vigorously denied the charges of criminal and treasonous actions. At the same time, he adamantly refused to disavow his ideas, knowing what the price would be. A legend has grown up around Qutb "kissing the gallows."[33] Stories are told about the smile that passed over his face as he faced death. Nasser reportedly had offered Qutb a reprieve, provided he renounced his ideas. Qutb refused, just as he had years earlier refused offers of a high-level position

in the new military regime. Qutb's principled martyrdom utterly captivated a great many youths in the Islamic world in the late 1960s.

Sayyid Qutb is now a man routinely described as "the father" of
modern terrorism, usually in a few declarative sentences that brook no
rebuttal. The indictment typically jumps from a sketch of Qutb's undeniably revolutionary ideas, his show trial and hanging, and then to the hei-
nous crimes of later terrorists who distorted Qutb's thinking in the most
ruthless ways. The suggestion takes shape that violence erupted from
Qutb's pen, inspiring murderous actions from al Qaeda to ISIS. Such a
view exonerates the bloody deeds of the regime that murdered him and
of the imperial powers that despoiled *Dar al Islam*. Unlike Frantz Fanon,
Sayyid Qutb did not argue for the cleansing force of violence as a way to
ameliorate the damaging psychological effects of a racist, colonial occupation. But he did respond to it. He explained that "it is not that Islam
loves to draw its sword and chop off people's heads with it. The hard facts
of life compel Islam to have its sword drawn and to be always ready and
careful."[34] Qutb did not choose violence. Violence chose him, and it left
its marks on his body and spirit. To exhume the tortured body of Sayyid
Qutb and drag him into the company of al Qaeda's Osama bin Laden and
Ayman al Zawahiri or, more recently, ISIS's Abu Bakr al Baghdadi and
other such violent criminals makes any reasonable understanding of his
actual role in history extremely difficult. Qutb was never linked to any violent or criminal act. Sayyid Qutb was murdered by the Nasserist state for
his ideas. Each time accounts of Qutb's life and thought implicitly justify
that judicial murder by reference to crimes committed by others years or
even decades later, Sayyid Qutb is murdered once again.

The pervasive caricature of Qutb blocks from view the real human
being. Qutb was a man given to theoretical and rhetorical excess. He was
also a principled man and an intellectual of depth and sensibility. In any
serious attempt to understand the sources of the exceptional strength
and resilience of the Muslim Brothers, the intellectual Sayyid Qutb must
stand second only to the activist Hassan al Banna in stature and enduring
importance. Qutb's influence has been multifaceted. It has flowed abundantly in centrist as well as extremist channels.

My own effort to know Sayyid Qutb in all his complexity was a personal quest embedded in the kind of theoretical conundrum that in-
trigues graduate students. I became aware of Sayyid Qutb first as a man
in a box, with an intellect and a spirit that was transparently available for
scrutiny. Nadav Safran, my Egypt-born mentor in Middle East Studies at

Harvard, introduced him to me in the early 1960s in just this way. Safran believed that the intellectuals of his land of birth could be understood by grasping the worldview that animated their beliefs and action, a worldview presumably carried around in their heads. Qutb was no exception. Once you grasped the worldview of a radical fundamentalist, you knew the man and could assess his historical weight. Qutb, in Safran's explanation, represented a "Weberian ideal type" of a fundamentalist extremist. That box was all that was needed to contain him. A second boxing of Qutb confirmed the analysis. In 1966, while I was still a graduate student, Qutb was hanged in Cairo. The most enduring image of that travesty is an iconic picture of Qutb in a cage during the show trial. The image was still fresh in my mind when I first arrived in Cairo in 1968.

Through the years that followed, and, to my astonishment, I encountered the footsteps of Sayyid Qutb everywhere I traveled in *Dar al Islam*, from Bosnia to Turkey and on to Iran and central Asia. He was a presence in all these places, his writings banned and his name pronounced only in whispers. I wondered how a one-dimensional figure so easily boxed and caged could have escaped to such far-flung places.

The answer turned out to be quite simply that there is weight and there is substance to Sayyid Qutb. Men in boxes don't evolve. Sayyid Qutb did. There were at least three important waystations on Qutb's short life voyage. At each of them he produced substantial work. The Qutb of the first station is an educator and an author, with a liberal nationalist orientation. He first established himself in Cairo's celebrated literary salons as a poet, one of the many prodigies of the towering figure of the writer and poet Abbas al 'Aqqad (1889–1964).

Qutb himself wrote prodigiously throughout his life, a pattern set in this first waystation. He published some 130 poems. He also wrote several novels, including one that drew on his experience as a boy in a poor Egyptian village. However, Qutb had his greatest success in Cairo intellectual circles as a literary critic. It was Sayyid Qutb who first brought the work of Nobel laureate Naguib Mahfouz, then unknown, to the attention of a wide Egyptian and Arab public. Qutb's own prolific writings from these early years merit attention for their limpid style and insightful critical analyses.

Once Qutb moved out of the shadow of al 'Aqqad, he gave clearer emphasis to his own Islamic commitments. In his second waystation Qutb emerged as a moderate Islamic intellectual. He wrote his important *Social Justice in Islam*. Sayyid Qutb, the man from a poor village, the schoolteacher, and the social activist, explained how the Qur'an spoke directly to the yearnings for justice of those oppressed by poverty. Qutb explored the notion of justice in a third voice that was neither capitalist nor socialist. His discussion of the concept of property, central to any system of economic thought, gives a sense of the Islamic quality of his thinking. "The individual," Qutb writes, "is in a way a steward of his property on behalf of society; his tenure of property is more of a duty than an actual right of possession." Making the Islamic dimension still clearer, Qutb continues that "property in the widest sense is a right that can only belong to a society, which in turn receives it as a trust from God who is the only true owner of anything."[35] With *Social Justice*, Qutb established himself as an original Islamic thinker who gave Islam a progressive cast that went beyond the thinking of the liberals of the day. The work had a significant influence on the Free Officers around Gamal Abdul Nasser, the authors of the 1952 coup. These nonideological military officers took a great deal of the left-leaning social program they enacted after their coup from the more progressive wing of the Muslim Brothers. Sayyid Qutb was the mediator. He met with the young officers and for a time served as a mentor on social and political affairs to the men who were to eventually orchestrate his murder.[36]

The third waystation saw Sayyid Qutb establish himself as both a major Qur'anic scholar and a radical Islamic thinker. Despite their support for his coup, Nasser turned against the Muslim Brothers, fearing their independent mass base. Nasserists contest this version of events. They argue that Nasser did respond sympathetically to the Brothers, giving them a position in the cabinet and more. However, the Brothers both insisted on more power and advocated for a diversionary agenda that focused on imposing the veil and closing cinemas. In any case, an attempt was made to woo Qutb from the Brothers with promises of a high government post. By then, Qutb understood the Westernizing thrust of the emerging Free Officer regime. He declined. That decision led to a lifetime of persecution by Egypt's military rulers. During this third period Sayyid Qutb completed his *In the Shade of the Qur'an*.[37] He also wrote *Milestones*. Undoubtedly, angry young Muslims will continue to turn to *Milestones*. In far greater numbers, Muslims of all shades will look to *In the Shade of the Qur'an* for a creative and beautifully written companion for their own explorations of Islam's holy book.

It is only very recently that serious scholarly treatments of Qutb have begun to appear in the West, although Islamic scholars have long appreciated his contributions. The more recent Western work invariably gives

rightful attention to *In the Shade of the Qur'an*. Qutb's intellectual achievement is staggering.[38] The impact is even greater still when one learns that
Qutb began *In the Shade of the Qur'an* in the early 1950s and completed its
thirty volumes during his imprisonment from November 1954 until May
1964. Qutb spent a good deal of his time in cells with up to forty other
prisoners, many of them criminals. It was the practice in Nasser's jails to
blare the speeches of the president some twenty hours a day. Under these
conditions, Qutb completed a monument of will, intellect, and faith. I
know of no other like it in the history of prison literature. Today the work
is read quite simply as one of the most admired Qur'anic commentaries ever written. During the month of Ramadan devout Muslims aim to
reread the Qur'an in its entirety. When I ask acquaintances and friends
which commentaries on the Qur'an they find most helpful, *In the Shade
of the Qur'an* is frequently mentioned. Usually, readers appear quite unaware of the circumstances under which it was written.

By Qutb's reading, the Qur'an through all its verses issues a call to freedom and social justice. As a Qur'anic exegete, he brings out as no other
the subtle literary qualities of the Qur'an—the sounds, the rhythms, the
images, the stories—that continue to make its reading such a moving experience for millions.[39] Qutb also makes clear the imperatives for action
built into Qur'anic ethical teachings. Qutb's influence on Islamic radicals
is undeniable. However, it is only one strand in his story and not the most
important one. Sayyid Qutb, the literary figure and scholar of the Qur'an,
had a deeper impact on the far broader and far more important moderate
center.[40]

Sayyid Qutb lingered at each of the waystations of his life. He, therefore, came to his revolutionary thinking and Islamic activism as a Muslim
Brother late in life and by a route with some very strange loops. The most
fateful twist in his life story came with a two-and-a-half-year trip to America in 1949 on a scholarship to study education. His adventures began
on the liner across the Atlantic when an inebriated foreign woman tried,
unsuccessfully, to seduce him. American analysts and policymakers are
fond of attributing anti-Western attitudes to jealousy and the progress
and prosperity of American society. The notion of America the beautiful,
implicit in such analyses, eluded Sayyid Qutb. What he saw was the dis-
tasteful character of American consumerism, pervasive violence, and the
brutality of American culture, as typified by such sports as football, and
the moral and ethical failings of a people for whom the quest for material
acquisitions overshadowed struggles for moral and ethical refinement.

Qutb registered shock that in America elderly parents were often left by their children to fend for themselves. A man of dark skin, Qutb experienced firsthand the rampant racism of American society. He tells of one incident when he and a group of Arab friends were denied entrance to a "whites-only movie theatre." When one of the group explained that they were Egyptians and not African Americans, the doors opened. Qutb refused to enter. Qutb pronounced the American dream, that so captivated Egyptians, and indeed so much of the rest of the world, a grand deception.

Reading of Qutb's disappointments in America heightens awareness of the profound frustrations that seemed to confront him at every turn. Escaping from village life, he succeeded in establishing himself as a literary figure of some stature in a sophisticated urban milieu. Soon, however, the materialist appetites of the elite in Egypt under the monarchy, their imitation of Western culture, and their tolerance of glaring social inequality eroded his sense of having found a world where he belonged. Qutb's commitments to social justice opened the way for connection to the young officers who would overthrow that order. Yet, again having through his intellectual talents found footing with the emerging new political elite, he suffered crushing disappointment at the Westernizing character of the project they envisioned for Egypt. Given the very great promise of the original connection, the break with the Free Officers represented yet another profoundly disquieting experience.

For some, disappointments in political or public life are offset by the solace of the happiness that relationships in the private sphere bring. There is little indication that Qutb ever enjoyed that kind of comfort. All his life he was plagued by ill health, variously attributed to asthma or even tuberculosis. He always appeared frail of body and dour of personality. There is also a clear record that not all of the frustrations in Qutb's life were political in nature. Sayyid Qutb was very much the fastidious, effete intellectual, but one with no hint of the romantic adventures of any kind that were part of his mentor al 'Aqqad's mystique. For all his acquired urban sophistication, he retained strands of rigid conservatism in his thinking, including a hostile attitude toward Christianity and Judaism and little development of his ideas on the role of women. Qutb's biographers report that his first romantic attachment ended in painful failure, as did a later one. Qutb never married. He explained, unconvincingly, that he had not found a woman of sufficient "moral purity and discretion" and therefore remained single.[41] An uncomfortable relationship to sexuality pervades Qutb's work.

An important source of the appeal of Sayyid Qutb's work is the sense of the many dimensions of the real human being who shows through. His work is not summed up by his most radical tract, *Milestones*. His life voyage as an Islamic intellectual cannot be reduced to its endpoint on the gallows. Sayyid Qutb, with all his talents and flaws, did manage to escape the boxes and cages designed to contain him.

Turkish Mysticism and the Triumph of Said Nursi

The policies of Kemal Atatürk, the founder of modern Turkey, made clear the terrible repression that Islam would suffer at the hands of the secular postcolonial rulers who dominated key Islamic states. It would be an exaggeration to argue that Atatürk's assault on Islam precipitated the Islamic Renewal and the massive mobilizations that swept through *Dar al Islam*. Yet Turkey's military, as the guardians of the Atatürk legacy of extreme secularism, did set a terrifying and galvanizing example. The Turkish military spared no excess in their campaign to eliminate Islam from Turkish public life. Given Turkey's historical role as the base of the Ottoman Empire and the site of the caliphate, the anxiety and anger caused by this active repression of Islam registered with Muslims worldwide. The fervent embrace of this Turkish "model" by Western governments did not go unnoticed. For decades the Turkish military that Atatürk ensconced in power appeared to be firmly in control and without serious Islamic opposition. The trauma of Islam's fate in Turkey haunted the imagination of Islamic intellectuals. Extreme secularism, or so it seemed, was poised to triumph throughout *Dar al Islam*.

Few noticed that for decades the Turkish military guardians of the secular idea waged a battle with a ghost. Their prolonged struggle did not go well. In the end, it was the phantom that triumphed. The opening salvo in that decades-long war came on the night of July 12, 1960. It took place just weeks after the first of the Turkish military coups that punctuated the twentieth century. Tanks entered the town of Urfa in southeast Turkey. The military imposed a curfew. They surrounded the shrine of Abraham in the city center. Troops stormed the shrine, smashed a marble tomb, removed a shrouded body, and drove to an airfield outside of town. The body was placed in a military plane and disappeared.

In March the body of Bediuzzaman Said Nursi (1878–1960) had been laid to rest in that shrine. The site almost immediately attracted thousands of mourners. The military feared Nursi's tomb would become a focal point for anti-Atatürk sentiment and a tangible symbol of Islamic resistance. The effort to contain the impact of Nursi's spirit failed. Even an empty shrine attracted mourners in large numbers. More importantly, Nursi's ideas continued to inspire a spiritual movement that drew Turks by the hundreds of thousands into its informal ranks. The current ruling party in Turkey has its roots in the Islamic soil that Nursi preserved and nurtured. The spirit triumphed over the tanks.

Said Nursi of Turkey, although far less well known outside of *Dar al Islam*, is a figure whose importance to the Islamic Renewal bears comparison to that of Hassan al Banna. Nursi felt profoundly the threat to the *ummah* in the early decades of the twentieth century, declaring that "the pain and suffering of the Muslim *ummah* have always bruised me so deeply. I feel as though the stabs directed at the Muslim world are directed at my heart, first. That is, my heart is often wounded."[42] While Banna acted to fortify Islam's public presence, Nursi focused on preserving Islam's hold on the interior of minds and hearts. Over the course of the long and difficult decades of the 1940s, 1950s, and 1960s, ordinary Turks inspired by Nursi quietly nourished and deepened their private commitment to Islam. It appeared that extremist secularism had gone from victory to victory. The West exulted. These surface impressions were profoundly misleading. Nursi had successfully laid the groundwork for oases of Islamic resistance in the hearts of ordinary people.

The deep spirituality and personal character of Nursi's writing, so different from the prosaic pamphlets of Banna, left an indelible stamp on Turkish Islam. Banna's genius turned interpersonal relationships, anchored in shared commitments to Islam, into organizational strengths to advance common goals. Nursi lived his life in the shadows cast by the massive slaughters of World War I, the abolition of the caliphate, and the onset of extremist secular rule. Nursi nurtured the spirit as the only means to offset these terrible defeats and preserve Islam for a time to come. In Nursi's work, a pervasive sadness coexists with an improbable sense of hope. Nursi shed "tears of blood for Islam," as one of his followers expressed it.[43] Yet he never faltered in his belief that Turkey would play a central role in preserving and advancing the Islamic *ummah*. His writings come alive in this core contradiction of profound grief and irrepressible optimism.

This reading of Said Nursi as an emblem of Turkish spirituality came easily to me. I first encountered his work precisely in this way. For years, Said Nursi was to me a mystic figure with a very personal role that had little to do with Turkey. Nursi helped me shape an attitude to the world and life experience that has never left me. "When I enter a garden, I choose its most beautiful flower or fruit," he writes. "If it is difficult for me to pick it, I take pleasure in looking at it." Then he wisely adds, "if I come across a rotten one, I pretend not to notice it, according to the rule: Take which pleases and leave what does not. This is my style."[44] I found in him a spiritual adviser who spoke to me at times of apprehension, deep disappointment, and grief. Above all, Nursi helped me understand how trauma can echo through a lifetime and what one can do to ameliorate its effects. "O Long-Suffering One!" Nursi writes, "when a misfortune is sent to you, do not divide your patience by confronting both past and present misfortunes." Nursi advises that we "focus on the present one, for the painful past has joined with the remaining spiritual blessings and rewards they gained for you in the Hereafter." Nursi continues: "Do not use up your patience confronting possible future misfortunes, for what the future brings depends on Divine Will. Use your patience for today, even for this hour. Reinforce it by smiling at misfortune and loving it so that it will join your patience and help you rely on your OWNER, the ALL-munificent, All-compassionate, and All-Wise. When you do that, your weakest patience will suffice for the greatest misfortune."[45]

All of Nursi's writing reflects a painful awareness of the human capacity for cruelty and the perennial risk of slipping into barbarism. At the same time, Nursi also understands the strange power of impossible dreams and unfounded hopes. Islamic mystics, like Nursi, understand the human capacity to dream large in the most adverse of circumstances. They know that hope springs from action, however small the steps, modest the gestures, and distant the realizations. They express those thoughts and feelings that you know absolutely cannot be expressed. Such is your understanding, that is, until these mystics succeed in doing precisely that. They are the purveyors of the impossible in the realms of the spirit. It is helpful to have the writings of Said Nursi close at hand when considering the sources of the Islamic Renewal.

The years of Nursi's early adulthood saw the savagery of World War I and the painful final decades of the collapsing Ottoman Empire. The young Nursi regarded the Ottomans as the guardians of Islam. He actively served the Ottoman cause. As a fighter, Nursi commanded the militia forces on the Caucasian front against the invading Russians. Nursi's valor attracted the attention of his superiors and won him a medal. Undeterred by the constant shelling in one battle with the invading

Russians, Nursi declined to fight from the trenches. He inspired his troops to advance by his personal bravery. To this story, Nursi's followers add a revealing detail. They tell us that, while battling the Russians on horseback, Nursi dictated to a scribe his Qur'anic commentary, *Signs of the Miraculous.*[46]

It is Nursi's driving spirituality that is the secret of his astonishing hold on Turks in numbers beyond counting. His spiritual depth has made him a major source of the Renewal. For Nursi the spiritual is very much enmeshed in the world. Despite the richness of his spiritual life, Nursi knew the feel of the ground beneath his feet. Captured by the Russians, he spent two years in Siberia until he managed to escape. He made his way to Istanbul, where he achieved a certain prominence as an advocate of educational reform. The backwardness of Turkish education distressed Nursi. In particular, he decried the neglect of math and the sciences in Turkey's Islamic schools. His reforms centered on the integration of classical Islamic studies with a fully modern education. The capstone of Nursi's planned reforms was to be the founding of a university that would exemplify this integration. Nursi managed to get his proposals before the last of the Ottoman emperors. However, the war intervened and the plans for the university lay dormant.

A turning point in the war came with the British and French attempt to secure a sea route to Russia by forcing passage through the Dardanelles. When that failed, a landing was undertaken to capture Constantinople. Eight months of heavy fighting ensured with heavy losses on both sides. Casualties are estimated at about half a million. The Allies conceded defeat by withdrawing. For the Turkish fighters, this Battle of Gallipoli represented a great national victory. The Allies had already made plans for the dismemberment of the Anatolian heartland. When the Ottoman Empire collapsed, this military success galvanized the Turks for their War of Independence. Eight years later, Mustafa Kemal Atatürk, one of the commanders at Gallipoli, led the successful struggle to found the modern Turkish state.

Nursi rallied. He never wavered in his embrace of Atatürk's founding of modern Turkey and in his commitment to Turkish independence. Atatürk, in turn, recognized Nursi's enormous gifts. He offered him several government positions. By that time, however, Nursi saw the dangers to Islam of the extreme secularism that Atatürk had wedded to his version of Turkish nationalism. Nursi could not accept that aggressive secular agenda and declined. The decision was momentous. The break between the two figures never healed. The rupture it signaled meant a lifetime of harassment, imprisonment, and exile for Nursi.

The republican regime sought to contain Nursi's influence by exiling him to distant Kastamonu. The limitations imposed by exile and house arrest did not work. His physical movement was sharply circumscribed. But Nursi's spirit soared. Nursi internalized his disillusionment with Mustafa Kemal Atatürk and the republican regime dominated by the military. He ended his public role and ceased even reading the newspapers. Nursi concluded that participation in the affairs of the state Atatürk founded would mean complicity in efforts to undermine Islam. Instead, a "new Said" emerged who, Nursi himself explained to his followers, had turned his back on politics. The new Said would devote all his intelligence and energy to spiritual matters.

In conditions of exile, Said Nursi produced his most important work. Deprived of libraries and the company of scholars, he focused on an extended personal reflection on the Qur'an, *Risale-I Nur*. He completed his grand project in the years from 1925 to 1948. His work fell outside of traditional Islamic scholarship. Nursi made no attempt to connect to the religious establishment. He had lost hope that they could be a force to save Islam. In turn, the establishment scholars showed indifference to his work. Attempts are made at times to cast Nursi as a Sufi and to describe his followers as a neo-Sufi *tariqa* (a school or order of Sufism). Such attempts to press Nursi into a traditional mold simply do not work. They greatly devalue the innovative character both of his writings and of the associational forms that emerged from his work as an independent Islamic scholar.

Out of Nursi's followership, there emerged self-organizing networks of an entirely new kind. They took shape without central direction and without any model. Totally new relational connections emerged as a consequence of very practical activities that Nursi inspired. He had neither wealth nor power. Spirit proved sufficient to generate one of the most extensive and successful networks the contemporary Islamic world has ever seen. The new forms had nothing do with the traditional practices that were under siege by the secular state. The Nurcu, as the network of Said Nursi was known, did not engage those old battles. Rather, energies migrated to entirely new fields for action. Nursi handwrote his massive commentary of some six thousand pages. He had no access to any means for printing or distributing his work. Instead, his followers stepped in to hand-copy and circulate the texts. The process of copying the manuscript gave thousands of ordinary Turks the justified sense that they were them-selves a part of Nursi's message. With the Qur'an in one hand and the *Risale-I Nur* in the other, the Nurcu gathered in small reading groups to discuss Said Nursi's message for the age. Spontaneously, these read-ing groups of Nursi's students became the essential connectors of the Nurcu network. First, they numbered in the hundreds, then in the thou-sands, then hundreds of thousands. Nursi's popular title was *Bediüzza-man*, which means "the Wonder of the Age." The extraordinary story of how Nursi's deeply spiritual writings safeguarded Islam in secular Turkey gave substance to the title.

The political Nursi had a deeply spiritual commitment to Islam that drove his public activities. The spiritual Nursi had an astute political sense that enabled him to understand how best to serve Islam in changing cir-cumstances. Nursi avoided the temptation of a drive for power in a set-ting decidedly unfavorable to direct Islamic resistance. Nursi succeeded in leaving an indelible imprint on Turkish Islam, precisely because both the political and the spiritual informed his work at every turn. Nursi's apparent passivity in the face of the aggressive secularism of the Atatürk regime was misleading. By appearing to cede the political kingdom at a time when Islam in Turkey had no prospects at all of confronting Turk-ish secularism in power, he preserved and deepened the wells of Islamic belief and commitment in the lives of ordinary Turks. At the time of his death, estimates of the size of his movement ranged up to one million. The Nurcu spread from Turkey into central Asia and the Balkans.

The shift in Nursi's personal stance from political activism to with-drawal from public life only strengthened the coherence to his legacy. Nursi grounded a firm commitment to freedom of conscience and expres-sion in an unwavering conviction that people required these freedoms to know God. The corrosive effects of materialism and decades of systematic attacks on Islam could only be reversed by the collective efforts of believ-ers who could make use of such freedoms to strengthen their faith. In Nursi's view, such a collective force could only take shape in a pluralistic society and democratic political order. This logic led to an accommodation with moderate secularism that has ever since been characteristic of domi-nant trends in Turkish Islam. For Nursi, secularism was anti-Islamic only in its extreme versions. He believed that a moderate secularism would be neither for or against any religion, provided that religious figures did not rule and basic freedoms, including freedom of conscience, were guaran-teed. To Nursi, moderate secularism would mean that all citizens of any faith, or of no faith at all, would have equal status and the same protected rights.

At the core of Nursi's thinking, through all stages of his life, was the commitment to reverse the damage of Western materialism and undemocratic governance that Atatürk had fostered. Several decades before the appearance of recognizably Islamic parties, Nursi had worked out a theoretical politics, rooted in Islam and in accommodation with moderate secularism. The Islamic political culture he imagined would be committed to both constitutional democracy and development. He believed that such a politics could only be achieved under conditions of the existence of basic freedoms, including the freedom for Turks to reaffirm their Islamic faith. In such an open society it would be possible to counter the negative effects of extreme secularism. Nursi looked to a democratic political system to strengthen pluralistic society. The Turkish political system did open to multiple parties in the 1950s. The legacy of Nursi's sophisticated thinking that merged Islam with democracy gave parties under an Islamic banner a distinctive advantage. Nursi prepared the way for the Islamic trend to seize the democratic banner and to win power democratically in one of the most important states in *Dar al Islam*.

Diverse Cultures of Resistance and the Survival of Islam

It is clear, in retrospect, that Islam was not nearly as exhausted in the early 1970s as surface indicators suggested. Islam was gathering strength just below the surface. What Shaikh Muhammad al Ghazzali and others could not yet see clearly, as they surveyed the desolate landscape of *Dar al Islam*, were the subterranean springs that kept Islam alive as a river of life. Resistance under Islamic banners would arise from dispersed oases fed by Islam's regenerative capacities. The differences among the diverse sites in Iran, Egypt, and Turkey were profound. Remarkably, however, the improbable ties that connected them were stronger. Everywhere, the Qur'an was a presence. Prayers provided constant reminders of the oneness of God and the unities of his community. Invocations of the Prophet reminded Muslims everywhere of his example and the worldly miracles of human effort and commitment it inspired. When Muslims prayed, they understood that all their fellow Muslims, wherever they might be in the world, also prayed in the direction of Mecca. These essential elements of the faith had the power to transcend difference.

Ever-shifting patterns of complex interactions made it possible for the cultures of resistance that arose in these diverse sites to flow together, even if only intermittently and largely in symbolic ways. They are what make it possible to speak of an interconnected, although not unified, Islamic world. There were strange loops in the complex connections that yielded the Islamic Renewal. They explain how it is that the Renewal only seemed to come out of nowhere. Drawing on these hidden sources of strength, Islam would defend itself in the final quarter of the twentieth century. It did so at great cost but with a measure of success that defies the imagination. No one predicted the unexpected triumphs of the Islamic Renewal that would arise from the hidden oases of reform and resistance to sweep through Islamic lands. Even Ghazzali did not recognize as such the heralds of the fourth historic wave of Islamic resistance who emerged from those oases. The mesmerizing figures, who were appearing across *Dar al Islam*, pronounced the name of resistance for the millions of ordinary Muslims who were to drive the Islamic Renewal of our time. Shaikh Muhammad al Ghazzali was himself one of the most important of their number. He did not work alone.

3

Guidance from the Center

Of those We have created are those
Who guide in truth and justice.

QUR'AN 7:181

JOHANN WOLFGANG VON Goethe warned that "the hardest thing to see is what is in front of your eyes."[1] For four decades, *al Tagdid al Islami* (the Islamic Renewal) has fostered reform and renewal in Islamic communities across the globe, while supporting legitimate resistance. Yet its presence has barely registered in Western commentary. When we fail to see things right in front of our eyes, we are generally either looking at something else or simply do not have adequate ways of making sense of what stands before us. Both failings are at work with the Islamic Renewal. Apprehensively scanning the horizon for the threatening "political Islam" of movements, parties, and charismatic personalities, we look right through Islam itself. Yet Islam cannot be reduced to its political dimensions. There is politics. There is politicization of Islam. But there is no political Islam. There is just Islam itself.

The unhelpful focus on "political Islam" is only part of the story. The inability to see centrist Islam, with its distinctive understanding of deep spirituality and Islamic civilizational identity, as the heart of the Renewal represents, an intellectual failure. However, to reduce the problem to misperceptions or even the systemic distortions of an inherited Orientalist discourse underestimates the analytical challenge. Scholarship along these lines has made important contributions. Such work explains a great deal about how the West views the Islamic world that is important and especially relevant to Western policy considerations.[2] However, it tells us far less about Islam. Islam itself is quite simply not the main subject of such studies.

Islam has a comprehensive character that is knowable ultimately only from the Qur'an and the example of the Prophet and never transparently so.

The Qur'an speaks clearly of Muslims as people of the center, an *"ummah,* justly centered and a witness over the nations."[3] To bring Islam into view, the focus must be on the midstream rather than the margins. The challenge is compounded by two factors. The first arises from the complexity of contemporary midstream Islam, now more fully articulated in the logic of what Manuel Castells has usefully called "the network society."[4] The second factor is the exhaustion of critical resources able to assess the innovative character of the network structures of the Islamic midstream. Those networks connect the oases of reform and resistance from which the Islamic Renewal has emerged. The philosopher Mark Taylor has aptly labeled this theoretical deficit a "critical emergency."[5] These two barriers to understanding the contemporary evolution of Islam are rarely considered in tandem. They should be.

The Islamic Renewal as Complex Cultural System

Complex systems, like the networks that constitute the Islamic Renewal as a cultural system, have their prototype in the dispersed mode of production and distribution of the global economy. The new structures are enabled by the technologies of the Information Revolution. Such systems are emergent and self-organizing. They have horizontal structures that interact so intensely with their environments that they are difficult to recognize as distinct from it. Not all such systems are economic. They are cultural as well. Midstream Islam today articulates itself in precisely this way. Such systems are usefully thought of as "difficult wholes." They are "difficult" in the sense that as complex composites of disparate parts they are not easily seen as constituents of a larger whole. The dispersed points of origin and the very different character of the heralds of *al Tagdid al Islami,* and of the mass followings they generated, have consistently made it difficult to grasp the interconnected character of the Renewal as a cultural system of this kind. The extreme cultural diversity of Muslims compounds the issue. You have an interconnected Islamic Renewal with a common Islamic thread, coming in strikingly different cultural colors.

Systems such as the Islamic Renewal that take on these complex forms typically arise from circumstances of disruption when old structures have been hollowed out and come close to collapse. Such was the case with inherited Islamic structures, battered by imperial intrusions and secular attacks. In such challenging circumstances, such systems make collective action possible without fixed, hierarchical means. Their forms are always in process, rather than fully shaped. They are constantly remaking themselves to respond to new conditions and new demands.[6] Their suppleness makes it virtually impossible for such systems to function as a means of containment and repression. They are simply too flexible and yielding for such purposes.

Complex adaptive systems belie the fears that have driven and ultimately paralyzed the most promising recent social and cultural criticism, such as Derrida's deconstruction, Foucault's social constructivism, and Baudrillard's theory of simulation. Each of these innovative perspectives advanced the project of critical theory. They each sought to reveal the totalizing effects of all systems. Each left a direct imprint on Islamic studies. Each also contributed to the current theoretical impasse. They did so essentially for the same reason. These postmodern approaches are all reactions to a dominant and repressive system. The bipolar world system of the Cold War represented precisely such a system and fostered ways of thinking and cultural forms that took such an underlying system for granted. Postmodern thought seemed to capture key aspects of reality precisely because the theories mirrored the bipolar confrontations of the hierarchical world system. Critiques of that hegemonic world, despite their important differences, all shared a consuming opposition to the "system." It made little difference if the system presented itself as American corporate capitalism, Soviet state capitalism, or postcolonial kleptocracies in the Islamic world. Ironically, the interest in freedom behind this visceral antipathy to these repressive formations produced a new dogmatism that endlessly generated the very same condemnation of the totalitarian character of *all* systems.

Yet, at precisely the moment when these despairing approaches were capturing the liveliest minds, the Information Revolution and the global market it enabled generated transformations that gave the lie to the essential premise of these reigning theories of cultural criticism. The collapse of the Soviet Union ended the bipolar configuration of the world order. Old hierarchical structures yielded to new horizontal network structures that roamed across the globe, organizing themselves in entirely new ways. Theorizations of complex horizontal systems emerged as a central intellectual task to make sense of these new formations.

The relevance of this shift to the study of contemporary Islam has registered only slowly in the West. Clusters of theorists outside midstream currents, notably complexity theorists, began to argue bluntly that it is simply wrong to conclude that all systems and structures totalize and repress. In the self-organizing network structures that were transforming human social life could be found precisely those nontotalizing systems judged to be impossible. Applied work in complexity studies suggested that such systems were not merely theoretically conceivable. From the right angle of vision, they could be recognized as already operative in contemporary networks.

The examples of the new forms included cultural networks such as those of the Islamic midstream that guides the Islamic Renewal.[7] Such complex, adaptive systems rest on flexible foundations—that is, they have foundations that move. These systems regularly assume the character of difficult wholes. What was not noticed in the work of complexity theorists was that Islamic civilization from its very earliest history had found its most suitable incarnation in flexible networks of this kind. Without a theoretical grasp of the nature of such systems, not only the Islamic Renewal but Islam itself remained largely unseen.

Islamic intellectuals did not share this dilemma. Our "critical emergency" was not theirs. They had developed a perfectly adequate understanding of the wellsprings and character of the Islamic Renewal as a flexible network. Unfortunately, their scholarship is largely unknown in the West. Their starting point is the work of interpretation of Qur'an and the *Sunnah* of the Prophet Muhammad. Fixed texts are interpreted in flexible ways. Relying on an organic descriptive vocabulary and concepts drawn from the Islamic heritage, important Islamic theorists developed an approach well suited to characterizing midstream Islam as a complex system. They focused on centrist Islam as the outcome of an adaptive interpretive project. That project was at once responsive to the timeless truths of the Qur'an and to the concurrent demands to give meaning to those truths in exceptionally diverse environments and times. They understood that linkages between such dispersed communities of interpretation would be horizontal rather than hierarchical, given the absence of overarching political structures in the Islamic world. Unifying political and economic linkages had proven elusive for *Dar al Islam* (the Islamic world). Yet Islamic intellectuals were confident that the flexible unities of culture and civilization remained and could be strengthened in organic, nonrepressive ways.

Islamic midstream intellectuals are quite aware of the new trends in Western thought. They are broadly familiar, for example, with works that draw on complexity theory to understand globalization.[8] It is not difficult to imagine their reaction to such explanatory frameworks. It is suggested in the scant attention they give them. There is a well-known historical parallel. Khedive Muhammad Ali (1769–1849), the founder of modern Egypt, is reported to have heard promising things about Machiavelli's advice to Italian princes. Illiterate until age forty-five, he nevertheless regularly had books read to him at a pace of ten pages a night until he finished them. He never made it to the end of *The Prince*. Muhammad Ali concluded that the Italian thinker had little to say on power manipulations in the service of rule that he did not already know.[9] It is almost certain that Islamic thinkers would have much the same reaction to a full-blown exposition of the work of complexity theorists. Complexity theory argues for an emphasis on the organic versus the mechanical. It emphasizes the advantages of horizontal and networked structures versus hierarchies and grids. It argues that complex adaptive systems represent those most suited to global conditions. Islamic intellectuals have a long-term familiarity with all of these ideas. They developed them independently out of their Islamic heritage, embraced them fully, and incorporated them into their understanding of Islam in God's world.

A larger conclusion suggests itself. The unexpected success of the Islamic Renewal may well have a great deal to do with the aptness of these inherited ways of thinking and the kinds of structures they generate to the new conditions of the global age. This insight raises new and different questions: What are Islam's prospects in a global age, given its inherited civilizational advantages? What can be learned from the experiments of Islamic intellectuals in drawing on their inherited tradition to project a transformative project identity in the face of the forces of globalization? What does the work of the New Islamic intellectuals tell us about the capacities of the new network structures that complex adaptive Islamic systems are now generating? Developments in the Islamic world, rather than confirming the soundness of past Western pathways, might just open new possibilities for organizing human communities of the future in a new era of accelerated change.

Islamic Renewal in a Global Age

It is no accident that the great successes of the Islamic Renewal began to register in the early 1970s, precisely the time of the dawning of the global age. Scholars of Islamic history, like the geographer Gamal Hamdan (1928–1993) and the contemporary historian Tareq al Bishri,

have little to learn from complexity theory. In fact, their theoretical understandings of Islam have a great deal to teach, if the West were interested in learning. Bishri has produced deep historical studies that rely
consistently on an organic image of Islam that has profoundly influenced my own thinking. Bishri does not consider Islam mechanistically
as an isolate, a separate variable acting on other equally distinct factors and closed onto itself. Rather, Bishri sees Islam as a living organism. He explains the way it interacts with rather than acts on its diverse
environments.[10]

Organic imagery is concretized in a variety of ways by Islamic intellectuals. A particularly insightful elaboration comes from Hamdan.
He compares Islam to a coral reef. Coral is a living creature. Classified
by scientists as an animal, coral assumes a wondrous variety of forms,
some rigid and rocklike, others supple and vegetative. Coral does not
live as an individual. It always establishes itself as a part of a complex
colony of interconnected individuals that cooperate in ingenious ways
to secure food for constituent elements, often vast in number. Coral
also takes on a variety of splendid colors, thanks to the algae it ingests.
That variety mimics the diverse forms of Islamic community. Like such
communities, coral adapts to very different oceanic environments. It
also shapes its marine settings in quite remarkable ways. Coral generally grows by extension. The extensions have a horizontal character
that create living linkages among the interacting colonies as the coral
procreate, increase in density, and populate new territories. Coral also
expands when small buds, known as polyps, break off and establish
themselves as the core of a new colony in a more distant setting. Coral
may also fragment, with each of the pieces establishing itself as an independent colony.

In all such characteristics of coral, Hamdan sees mirrored essential
features of Islam itself as a cultural system. To intellectuals with an Islamic formation, these organic parallels are so striking and so obvious
that they require only the briefest commentary. They regularly use organic images like the coral reef to explain the ways that Islamic communities function. Islam lays strong communal foundations, yet those
foundations move and adjust to very different settings, much as living
coral would. Islam may take shape as a product of highly rational, legalis-
tic thought and institutional processes that have a very solid, at times even
rigid character. Such structures, like the great schools of *fiqh* (Islamic
legal reasoning, based on interpretation of Qur'an and *Sunnah*) and the

grand mosques that house them, endure through the ages much like the great coral barriers. Yet Islam also assumes ethereal and highly spiritual forms, suggested by those corals that take the plantlike forms of fronds, moving seductively in ocean waters. Sufi Islam has these very same characteristics. Throughout the history of the Islamic community (*ummah*), segments of the community have broken off, acquiring distinct characteristics while preserving certain essentials of an Islamic character. Shi'i Islam was the most notable of these diversifications. They include as well an enriching variety of small, break-off communities of both Sunni and Shi'i Muslims that acquire distinctive features that make them no less Islamic entities.

The core achievements of the Islamic Renewal all flow from the character of Islam as a living organism. Underground oases of reform and resistance fed *al Tagdid al Islami*. Dispersed heralds of the Renewal won support in their separate contexts for the Renewal. These pioneering figures differed greatly in character and the challenges they faced. Yet all were nurtured by the river of Islam. Their efforts advanced the Renewal across *Dar al Islam*. They did so without an overarching institutional structure or a unified leadership structure. Their coalescence was neither forced nor backed by power. Yet the collective work of the heralds of the Renewal flowed together in a great fourth surge of renewal and reform. They shared the centrist commitment to rethink Islam and to engage the modern world constructively in its new terms. Following the Qur'an, Islamic intellectuals who sought an understanding of contemporary Islam adequate to provide *tarshid* (guidance) to the *ummah* insistently looked to the center rather than the margins.

The aim here is to characterize the ways in which centrist intellectuals and activists have succeeded in providing guidance for the Islamic Renewal across *Dar al Islam*. The effort to do so will draw on the two alternative vocabularies that the analysis thus far has brought into view. The first is the Islamic vocabulary that originates with the work of centrist Islamic scholars. The second derives from Western efforts to theorize, notably by complexity theorists, the impact on human societies of the Information Revolution that reshaped the international order in the post–Cold War era. The parallels between the two vocabularies are hard to miss. They complement each other in useful ways.

The organic conceptions of the Islamic intellectual tradition deploy a mind–body analogy to capture the nature of leadership and followership in Islamic communities. The mind is understood as a collective one that enables coordination without coercion. The New Islamic thinkers understand their own scholarship as part of the workings of the collective mind of the Renewal. They welcome the tremendous growth in the last quarter of the twentieth century of the Islamic body. However, they understand as well the dangers of rapid expansion. They explain that a robust and growing body, without a mind that has also increased its capacity, lacks balance. At the same time, a mind detached from the energies of a strong collective body may well create elegant and sophisticated visions. However, if the mind remains detached or is overwhelmed by the body, such visions will be unable to provide guidance. This notion of "balance" between mind and body is inherently flexible. What is "balanced" in one set of historical circumstances might not be so in another. There is no set formula. The collective mind is open and avoids definitive formation. It resides in shifting sites. The mind lives comfortably with differences in decisions made for the community. There is no final arbiter. Competing and even contradictory outcomes remain authoritative.

Such fluid, moving, and noncoercive patterns characterize Islam. In *Shari'ah* (the provisions from Qur'an and *Sunnah* to regulate human behavior), for example, are four different schools of interpretation. They agree on many issues. They disagree on others, including very important social and political questions. There is no resolution of the differences in the abstract. The distinct interpretations are all authoritatively Islamic. Individual judges may draw on any of them in reaching verdicts in concrete cases, guided by reason and the evidence of particular circumstances.

The second descriptive vocabulary, notably complexity theory, affords an alternative way to express basically these same ideas. The collective mind is discussed in terms of distributed intelligence and parallel processing. Concepts from computer science help us understand how dispersed thinking and independent calculations by multiple actors can indeed achieve coherent outcomes that have the capacity to generate a shared general orientation. The parallels with contemporary Islamic thought are striking. There is nothing accidental in the fact that a noteworthy characteristic of Islamic schools across *Dar al Islam* is their attention to both English and computer science. Islamic intellectuals and activists have often been leaders in the use of the new forms of communication made possible by information technologies. Early on, they embraced the Information Revolution.

Muhammad Abduh and the Centrist Networks of the *Wassatteyya*

The *Wassatteyya* (the Islamic midstream) brought into view by these vocabularies today consists of a complex network of centrist Islamic scholars and activists. There is no room in the usual mapping of Islam in the West for such networks of "radicals of the center." They are centrists but they are engaged in a transformative project. In a global age Muslims are our neighbors. With even minimal interaction, it soon becomes clear that very few of them are six foot six and committed to violent attacks on "the great Satan" or the beheadings of hapless innocents who fall into their hands. Centrist Muslims, living quite ordinary lives and occasionally doing quite extraordinary things, are all around us, although we do not always see them. The Islamic midstream now claims more than the lion's share of the world's 1.6 billion adherents to the faith. It is growing steadily. These Muslims are not obsessively concerned with the West or jealous of its achievements. They do not hate us. They do not seek our destruction.

The networks of midstream Islam do embrace a common orientation of resistance, peaceful when possible, to Western intrusions into the Islamic world. They reject subservience and oppose violent assaults and occupations. Such centrist groupings as the Egyptian New Islamic trend, and their counterparts across *Dar al Islam*, are open to principled accommodation to superior Western power on the global level. Counter-violence for the midstream is always a weapon of last resort. They do recognize, however, that the provocations of assault and occupation require no less. At the same time, the midstream everywhere pushes relentlessly for reforms of the inherited Islamic tradition. They seek reform to meet the needs of the new age.

For all of these commonalities, the midstream owes a deep debt of gratitude to the work of the nineteenth-century Egyptian reformer Muhammad Abduh (1849–1905). His influence is pervasive. The commitment to reform of the heritage in no way contradicts the impulse, also widely shared, to articulate Islam's timeless values for rapidly changing and exceptionally diverse circumstances.[11] Clusters of midstream intellectuals and activists across *Dar al Islam* arose independently to provide leadership to the Renewal. My travels over several decades across *Dar al Islam* allowed me to witness the unfolding of the Islamic Renewal under the guidance of midstream figures in all of these diverse settings.

For the *Wassatteyya* today, the single most important concept taken from Muhammad Abduh remains the guiding idea that while the strength of a nation has important economic and political dimensions, cultural independence provides the essential foundation for autonomy. It preserves the sense of a distinctive identity that is based on a valued common history and aspirations for a future of one's own making and in line with one's own Islamic values and collective purposes.[12] From Abduh, the intellectuals of the Renewal learned that the Islamic heritage as a civilization in all its richness provides the essential framework for this cultural autonomy. They assess the ways in which civilization identity can be articulated as a broad project to energize efforts of reform and social change. The New Islamic conception of the *maslaha amma* (common good) is directly related to the realization of an Islamic civilizational identity. The common good is thus understood in terms of a fluid conception of an identity to be realized rather than a particular public space, whether of politics or civil society, to be dominated or defended. This consistent privileging of the fluid and elusive over the rigid and fixed confers great advantage.

In making a civilizational identity the highest *maslaha amma* (common good) for Muslims worldwide, the students of Abduh clearly differentiated between an Islamic society with such a cultural foundation and one based on religious authority, narrowly understood, that would inevitably be restricted to Muslims and therefore exclusionary. Abduh insisted that the notion of a religious state, sanctified by divine authority, was the exact antithesis of what an Islamic order would mean.[13] No other single idea was as important as this one in shaping the Islamic *Wassatteyya* and enhancing its appeal as a centrist force. Islam, Abduh explains, is "a world religion and a human system to guide people to do what is right and realize justice and spread peace and announce the common brotherhood of human beings without reference to skin color, gender, or language." He continues that "this is the humane path to build the Earth and protect its goods and resources."[14] The inclusive character of Abduh's vision found a particularly compelling statement during a visit to Europe, where the day-to-day moral behavior of ordinary people impressed him greatly. "I saw Islam without Muslims," he pronounced.[15]

In their own time, however, the nineteenth-century pioneers like Abduh never attracted wide popular support beyond the intellectual classes. In part because of this failing, leadership of the cause of national resistance passed to nationalist forces, and reform came to mean the adoption of Western social models and even Western notions of independence. The legacy of

Abduh was not lost. It was, however, eclipsed by the tangible achievements of the nationalist wave that won national independence and then launched initially promising social and economic development projects.

With time, however, it became clear that the national gains in political and economic terms brought only a circumscribed independence. More importantly, the imitative modernization strategy left a cultural void. From within the Islamic wave, a new kind of leader and a new kind of organization with linkages to a mass following emerged to counter rampant Western influences. New Islamic intellectuals and activists see Hassan al Banna, the founder of the Egyptian Muslim Brothers in 1928, as an Islamic leader who carried forward the centrist project of Abduh and the pioneers. He did so in competition with extremist elements.

The Extremist Challenge

Once the Islamic midstream is brought into view, it becomes clear that the distorted and criminalized Islam of the networks of violent groups is not the Islam most important or most in need of sustained attention and analysis by scholars. This perspective can have a calming effect, in sharp contrast to the hysterical and interested overreaction in the West to the threat that extremists pose. Centrist Islamic intellectuals understand perfectly well the dangers of extremism. They know from the outset that they themselves would be a prime target of violent militants. "If Islam were to come to power by force," explained Selim al Awa, "it would be far worse than the current situation. Those who are in power today are in dialogue with us, which is far better than being slaughtered in the name of Islam."[16] Yet midstream intellectuals also have an understanding of Islam's 1,400-year-old history that told them quite clearly that extremists mattered far less than the center. They project confidence that extremist currents will eventually be reabsorbed into the midstream, although they might do damage from the margins in the interim. That damage, however, never rises to a level that warrants reducing Islam itself to the militants of the margin.

The Power of Islamic Civilizational Identity

Remarkably, alongside the denizens of caves, the Islamic world has produced these New Islamic radicals of the center who renounce aggressive violence and commit to a project of strengthening an assertive Islamic identity project, capable of flourishing in the global age. They look to profound but peaceful social transformation and deep reform of inherited traditions. They support armed resistance, in line with international and humanitarian law. They are building global networks for the exchange of ideas and joint actions in line with Islamic values and higher purposes. These centrists move with particular deftness through the new public spheres of our electronic age. They ignore old borders in the interest of sharing the lessons of successful resistance and constructive "building of the world."

At the very heart of those lessons learned is deep appreciation for the power of Islamic identity. The New Islamic trend explains that in contemporary conditions of severe destabilization, the realization of the common good is tied not so much to particular arenas of civic and political action but rather to the strengthening of an Islamic civilizational identity. The midstream argues that this struggle cannot be reduced to a political struggle for power. Muhammad al Ghazzali warned that a focus on a political route to power, through whatever means, represented an unhelpful diversion of effort from the most compelling tasks at hand. Ghazzali noted, in particular, that groups like the Muslim Brothers that organized around political issues were mistaken in their conviction that the goal should be the establishment of an Islamic state. Ghazzali argued that "such political work should take no more than 1% of the effort of the Islamic trend, while 99% should go to the call for Islam and to efforts of Islamic education and upbringing to heal destroyed societies and broken people." Ghazzali wrote presciently of his "suspicions" of those who call for an Islamic state and of his "fears for the future of Islam in their hands."[17]

The heightened importance of identity is widely appreciated as a phenomenon of the global age everywhere.[18] Critical distinctions are made between the restrictive politics of narrow, exclusive identities and the more expansive political possibilities of more inclusive project identities. This shift poses far more problems for Western theorists than it does for Islamic intellectuals. The idea of multiple identities that commingle as part of a defining project is intrinsic to the Islamic legacy. The Islamic Renewal has provided precisely such an inclusive project identity for millions of Muslims. The narrowing of political identities to the nation-state is a Western conception. It was only recently imposed on Islamic societies. Today, older Islamic identities almost always coexist with the more recent national attachments, at times creating tensions, at other times blending seamlessly. Such processes of synthesizing identities, and generating projects that express them, have long been under way in the Islamic world. These efforts find their most tangible expression in concrete efforts to rebuild societies in a self-directed way, despite extreme pressure from intrusive external forces. The turn to the heritage to provide inspiration for rebuilding can be observed in sites throughout *Dar al Islam*. Everywhere, there is a contest with the Islamic trend between those with inclusive and those with exclusive conceptions of identity. New Islamic intellectuals explicitly embraced the notion of multiple identities and deplored the narrowing down of identity to the Islamic dimension only. They affirmed, for example, the Coptic and African dimensions of Egypt's personality, against the dangerously exclusivist and potentially violent conceptions of the extremists.

Muhammad al Ghazzali and the Renewal Incarnate

The heralds of the Renewal all adopted such strategies and cultivated such project identities. In the analysis that follows, the Egyptian New Islamic school will stand for the larger universe of centrist Islamic scholars and activists engaged in such work across the Islamic world. The decision to focus on the Egyptian New Islamic trend finds justification in the impressive body of scholarship and record of activism their school has produced. Moreover, as Islamic intellectuals they now have a presence that reaches throughout the Arab arena and deeply into the larger Islamic world beyond.

My life in Egypt also gave me an extraordinary opportunity to observe up close one of the greatest of the heralds, Muhammad al Ghazzali. My friend Kamel made sure that I didn't miss it. For several decades Kamel and I were inseparable. Deeply religious, Kamel would guide my reading of the Qur'an. Quite literally, he would also drag me to public morning prayers, if he had learned that Ghazzali was presiding. Kamel adored Ghazzali. Of course, Ghazzali was perpetually out of favor with the Egyptian regime, and that complicated things. As a result of his official disfavor, Ghazzali's public appearances had to be carefully managed. It was imperative that his assistants not announce publicly where he would speak. It was even more important that the event end quickly before there could be a confrontation. The rumor would circulate that Ghazzali would be speaking to commemorate some special Islamic holiday or one or another of the endless occasions that Egyptians love to celebrate. Until the very last moment the square where he would actually appear was not identified. Quite magically, often just hours before the prayer, hundreds of thousands of followers would converge to see and hear their beloved Shaikh.

Kamel always knew where Ghazzali would be, although I am still not quite sure how. Kamel often insisted that I come to his apartment the night before so we could get to the site early. There were many such occasions. One stands out. It was in August 1981. Kamel called me, absolutely sure that Ghazzali was speaking the next day in a square near his neighborhood. I spent the night at his place. Very early the next morning, Kamel announced that we were instead going to Abdin Square in downtown Cairo, actually a good distance from his suburban apartment and not too far from where I now live near Tahrir Square. The event had been moved in the last hours. We took a cab. Kamel wore a long white *galla-beyya* (a traditional Egyptian garment native to the Nile Valley). Once near the Abdin area, we proceeded on foot. We found ourselves a part of a mass of humanity, in purposeful motion. Egyptians by the thousands were moving, still before sunrise, toward the square at a distinctive pace, faster than normal walking but not running. Most dressed like Kamel, but the pace of their walking alone already signaled where they were headed. My estimate of the crowd at the time was about 250,000. To see them coming together to pray, hear Ghazzali's message, and then quietly disperse and blend back into the city made the whole experience unforgettable. Ghazzali had filled a massive public square in Cairo.

To this day, when I walk through that square, I have the very same feeling of just how important was that occasion that I shared with a quarter of a million Egyptians. I had seen the Islamic Renewal and heard one of its most compelling centrist voices. In lectures, writings, and conversations, Yusuf al Qaradawi frequently referred to Ghazzali as a *mugadid*, one of those renewers of Islam who have appeared in every century throughout the fourteen centuries of Islamic history.

From the Qur'an, centrist Islamic scholars understand that God charged all of humanity with the task of building the world. To play their part, Muslims are called to draw guidance from the Qur'an and the example of the Prophet Muhammad. Inevitably, there would be shortfalls in this great interpretive project to serve the *ummah*. Shaikh Muhammad al Ghazzali embraced a sense of the inexact character of the interpretive project, of the limitations of human knowledge that would inevitably plague all efforts to guide the *ummah*, and of the unknowable contingencies that circumstance would bring. There is nothing in his work of the hubris that regularly derailed mainstream Western thinkers. Western theories of economic and political development had fixed the endpoints of human history and struggles for progress. That kind of certitude, Ghazzali explained, belonged to God alone. Faced with the depredations of the West and the failure of practical plans for the defensive unification of the Islamic world, Muhammad al Ghazzali understood, more clearly than most, how critical a coherent intellectual framework was to the task of guiding the Islamic Renewal. He also understood that it would have to be accomplished in flexible, decentered ways, given the fragmentation that the *ummah* had suffered. He realized that great uncertainties would inevitably hover over all such efforts.

Ghazzali broke with the very traditional Muslim Brothers with their hierarchical leadership and conventional thinking that skirted such complexities. He also kept his distance from official Islamic institutions, like al Azhar. Ghazzali was, nevertheless, frequently mistaken as simply a traditional Islamic scholar in Egypt and in other parts of the Arab Islamic world. In the West, he was regularly denounced as a reactionary fundamentalist. He was neither. In fact, Ghazzali lived his life as an incarnation of the new kind of centrist intellectual that Islam would need not just to survive but to flourish in the new conditions of globalization in the post–Cold War world. Having moved out of the traditional structures of al Azhar and the movement institutions of the Brotherhood, Ghazzali sought to ground his intellectual project elsewhere. He turned to the Qur'an. He spent a lifetime in Qur'anic studies and established himself as a leading twentieth-century authority on the Qur'an, producing a score of influential and controversial Qur'anic studies. His reputation as a preeminent Qur'anic scholar was his passport to the entire Islamic world.

Ghazzali brought these impressive resources to the Egyptian New Islamic school, where he was a beloved figure in a circle of world-class Islamic intellectuals. Ghazzali himself consistently expressed extreme modesty in his own assessment of his capacities and achievements. He did not, for example, regard himself as a *faqih* (an Islamic scholar, specially trained and recognized by peers as qualified to contribute to Islamic legal reasoning). Ghazzali did not believe that he had the mind of a *faqih*, but judged that Yusuf al Qaradawi did. Qaradawi disagreed. Qaradawi said simply that he regarded Ghazzali as his teacher. Ghazzali, he explained, did not apply himself as an independent interpreter to secondary issues, as many *faqih* do. Rather, he directed his attention to the great questions of the day. On those issues, noted Qaradawi, he made substantial contributions, and he made them as a *faqih*. Ghazzali always demurred. Even on the question of his knowledge of the Qur'an, Ghazzali insisted that "I have accompanied Qur'an since my childhood. I memorized it by the age of ten, and I continue to read it in the eighth decade of my life." Yet Ghazzali concluded that "it seems to me that what I know of it is little and does not rise above the direct meanings and repeated phrases."[19]

Such an attitude carries an explicit openness to the collaborative work with others for reform that the collective mind of the *Wassatteyya* would enable. Ghazzali strived tirelessly to contribute to a unifying framework, modernist and based on the Qur'an, for the work of the school. He believed that such a framework would allow centrists across the globe to cooperate in informal networks. In this way, Ghazzali's scholarly work contributed to a broad consensus that brought midstream Islamic centrists together through persuasion and the power of example. At the same time, he saw himself as a warrior for truth and never hesitated to take the most controversial positions or to tackle the most sensitive issues.[20] Truth for Ghazzali meant above all honesty about one's own failings and shortcomings.

Ghazzali did not spare his beloved *ummah* from scathing criticisms. He bemoaned the ways in which Islamic intellectuals had failed to nurture and safeguard Islam itself. "Wounded Islam," he wrote, "stumbled half dead, half alive through the tortured and violent decades of the twentieth century."[21] It was not until the last quarter of the century that the Islamic midstream found the right combination of intellectual and organizational resources to shield Islam from the terrible blows that rained down and begin the work of repair. Ghazzali was at the very center of that effort. Only with those resources in place could the ground be prepared for the impressive revival of Islam in our own time.

Islamic centrist intellectuals insistently took an accurate measure of the history of the *ummah* over the course of the eighteenth and nineteenth centuries. They recognized the external assaults it suffered. They also acknowledged the internal weaknesses that created such vulnerability. The Islamic Renewal was born in terrible pain and misery. Centrist Islamic intellectuals displayed a steely capacity to face directly the violence and denigration the Islamic world experienced. All the harbingers of the Renewal felt the blows sustained by Islam in the twentieth century. None expressed the painful impact more powerfully than Muhammad al Ghazzali. He did so in a voice that was profoundly personal yet intensely political, enriched with great Islamic learning yet expressed simply by a man who never forgot his own modest beginnings. Like so many in the Islamic world, Ghazzali felt the humiliation of foreign occupation and rule. He refused to be shamed by them or to use them as an excuse for inaction. He catalogued the terrible crimes of Western imperialism against the Islamic world. Yet the deepest anger welled up in his voice when he reviewed the ways contemporary Muslims had made their lands so vulnerable. He decried in particular the cruel and irresponsible tyrannies that littered the Islamic landscape. He complained bitterly of the deterioration of Islamic scholarship and culture. He ridiculed the useless books and tracts on Islam by the hundreds that demeaned the faith by the triviality and antiquated character of their preoccupations. He saw Islam as a worldly and spiritual force of great potential power. He called his fellow Muslims to think and act to realize that potential. Why waste time bemoaning suffering at the hands of powerful outsiders, he asked, when the responsibility for this terrible vulnerability rested in no small part in the hands of Muslims?

Inspiration for Ghazzali's stern position came from the Qur'anic verse that pronounced "verily never will God change the condition of a people until they change it themselves (with their own souls)."[22] To read Ghazzali's most important work in the period of the late 1960s and early 1970s is to understand just how unfounded are the Western claims, endlessly repeated, that Muslim peoples and Islamic intellectuals are in some mysterious way genetically programmed to blame others for their predicaments. Ghazzali spoke at once to the learned and the masses of ordinary people. He spared neither intellectuals nor the people a harsh recitation of their failures and a spirited insistence that they do better, much better.

Nor did he spare himself. Ghazzali said plainly that a new understanding of Islam was imperative. He charged that contemporary Islamic scholars like himself had failed to do the serious intellectual work required. Ghazzali set about doing it. He worked tirelessly to meet the challenge, producing a flood of articles and some fifty books. Still, Ghazzali recognized that scholarly production on the scale that *al Tagdid al Islami* required could not be the work of one person. He acknowledged that in the midst of the intellectual desert there were surprising exceptions in the writings of clusters of Iranian, Indian, and Turkish intellectuals across *Dar al Islam*. Ghazzali's opening to cooperation and collaboration set the stage for his own lifework as a leading figure of the influential Egyptian New Islamic trend. That productive collaboration extended over four decades and immeasurably increased the depth and impact of his own scholarship.

In the classic mode of *talab al 'ilm* (travel in search of knowledge), Ghazzali set about traveling in search of knowledge. He made major contributions to intellectual life not only in Egypt but also in the Gulf and North Africa. Before talk of networks became fashionable, Ghazzali had already updated the inherited tradition of meaningful connectivity through the writings of scholars. Ghazzali spoke in a voice that echoed the venerable Islamic sciences taught at al Azhar. He did so, however, with the distinctive modernist inflections of a figure for whom the nineteenth-century reformer Muhammad Abduh was a major inspiration. Membership in the Muslim Brothers provided the formative experience of his early work as an Islamic thinker and caller to the faith. Yet the Brotherhood displayed clear limitations of intellectual and organizational means to meet the new challenges of the late twentieth century. Those limitations became all too apparent when the Muslim Brothers came to power for just under a year following the Egyptian revolution of January 2011. The shortcomings of the leadership would not have surprised Ghazzali, although he would have deplored their overthrow by the military.

Out of the Brotherhood, and thanks precisely to its limitations, came a succession of Egyptian Islamic thinkers of world-class stature who found themselves unhelpfully constrained within the organization. Centrist Islam had found a way around the shortcomings of the inherited Islamic institutions like al Azhar that had lost its independence to the political rulers. The docile official Islam of Azhar was brought to heel by Egypt's postrevolutionary military rulers. Centrist Islam moved out of the sphere of the Muslim Brothers as well. The politicized Islam of the Muslim Brothers undoubtedly suffered defeat in the year of Brotherhood rule in Egypt. Islam did not.

Collective Mind: The New Islamic School

The New Islamic intellectuals coalesced as an intellectual school in the late 1970s and early 1980s. They aimed to establish a public intellectual presence to guide the Islamic Renewal without inviting repression. To this end, they constituted themselves loosely as an "intellectual school" of Islamic thinkers rather than a political party or social movement. The core group of diverse Islamic intellectuals, including both lay and religious figures, wrote the manifesto for the group in 1981. They initially circulated their statement informally among approximately 150 intellectuals with a variety of orientations. They did not actually publish the document until a full decade later. From the outset, the school has had the horizontal structure of a flexible network rather than a rigid vertical hierarchy. The boundaries of the network were never sharply demarcated, giving the school a permeable and open character. The group explicitly presented its manifesto as a statement of broad principles, rather than a precise working program. They advocated for a centrist Islam focused on the values of justice, freedom, and equality that had the greatest relevance to political and social issues. Their vision of nonviolent peaceful change advocated democracy and pluralism. The trend avoided tying the manifesto to a specific time and place. They aimed to invite like-minded centrists to recreate the school in their own environments, adapting the flexible format to their special circumstances. With this approach, they sought to foster a capacity for self-organization and reorganization and to foster extension of their model throughout *Dar al Islam*. The statement of inclusive principles, coupled with the flexibility of the forms in which they can be expressed, would give the emerging networks an infinitely adaptable character, while still remaining recognizable as articulations of centrist Islam.

Guiding intelligence for the school emerges through spontaneous intellectual exchange, dialogue, and debate, rather than by direction of a fixed leadership in any formal sense. In these ways, the intellectual school of the New Islamic thinkers contrasts sharply to the rigid organizational structure of the Muslim Brothers. Their approach avoids the common pitfall of leadership figures vulnerable to repression or to the temptations of authoritarian leadership. Both of these shortcomings have plagued the Muslim Brothers throughout their history. The school works through informal and spontaneous cooperative efforts that are very similar to the parallel processing of computer networks. Over several decades the school has evolved in this way as a guiding component of the broader phenomenon of Islamic Renewal, from which it could be distinguished only with considerable difficulty.

The New Islamic scholars consistently set their sights on the long term to better absorb inevitable setbacks under authoritarian conditions. They focused on education and culture, critiquing the shortcomings of national institutions and encouraging the development of alternatives in the interstices of official life. The New Islamic trend proved able to accommodate ruling power, without losing sight of long-term transformational goals. They paid attention to the experiments of the growing number of activists of the Islamic wave in the political arena and in civil society, notably in projects in the economic arena, elections of professional associations, and parliamentary alliances with non-Islamic political parties. They have quite frequently expressed sharp criticism of the shortcomings of these on-the-ground efforts. At the same time, the scope of their own work as a school has been much broader. In their scholarship and activist interventions in public life, they reach beyond politics and civil society, and beyond Egypt's borders, to address the challenges of renewal that arise throughout the world. New Islamic scholars have pioneered new ways to accomplish these ambitious goals.

Islam Online

Historian Tareq al Bishri reasons that the task of reviving the sense of belonging to a shared Islamic world just needs patience and alertness the keys to bring people together in ways that empower them to influence states and the relations among states through infiltration just like water flows from one land to another. Quite unexpectedly, one example of just such a "coming together" took place in Qatar in the mid-1990s, and in a way that reflected the new opportunities of the global age. The original idea came from Maryam al Hajery, a student at Qatar University. A course assignment required that this young woman familiarize herself with the resources of the Internet.[23] As she became aware both of the misinformation among Muslims about their faith and the attacks on Islam by hostile external forces, particularly in the West, she wondered why Islamic thinkers had not established an Internet site to explain Islamic beliefs and correct inaccurate characterizations of Islam. Within months, the new transnational site Islam Online was operating from Qatar.

The presence of Yusuf al Qaradawi in Qatar gave the project both an anchor and a magnet. With Qaradawi at the helm, it proved possible to attract and coordinate resources from across the Islamic world. A staff in Cairo prepared the Arabic-language content, working with a group competent in English in the United States, and supported by a technical crew from Bahrain. The day-to-day collaborations on which the site relies fostered a computer-age sense of belonging to the Islamic world.

Qaradawi's leadership also helped to infuse the effort with the New Islamic commitment to the Islamic *Wassatteyya*. This transnational, moderate Internet project succeeded because, in the idiom of the new age, the world of Islam was already hardwired by culture and history. The new technologies simply brought to the surface these submerged connections that had survived. With Yusuf al Qaradawi playing a leadership role, the new Internet site provided a midstream "software program" with a *Wassatteyya* vision that could be widely shared.

Distributed Intelligence and Networked Islamic Scholarship

The collective scholarly work of the New Islamic trend provided strong but supple intellectual foundations to undergird the Renewal not just in Egypt but throughout the Islamic world. New Islamic thinkers have most effectively advanced their claim to speak for centrist Islam and to guide the Renewal by boldly engaging the most controversial issues of the final decades of the twentieth century. Figures including Yusuf al Qaradawi, Tareq al Bishri, Selim al Awa, Kamal Abul Magd, and Fahmi Huwaidi combined their efforts to develop an innovative body of Islamic thought. Their scholarship inevitably has direct reference to the Egyptian context. However, it always carries implications for the Islamic world beyond. The New Islamic thinkers made themselves an important and durable presence in Egyptian public life with frequent and often very effective interventions in the affairs of the nation. At the same time, their scholarship elaborates centrist Islamic positions on broader questions with relevance throughout *Dar al Islam*, such as Ghazzali on social justice, Abul Magd on globalism, Bishri and Huwaidi on the rights of non-Muslims in an inclusive framework, Awa on the centrality of *ijtihad* (an effort of interpretation of the sacred texts), and Qaradawi and Huwaidi on democracy in Islam.[24] Huwaidi clearly stated the broad conclusion of the New Islamic trend that "no one can imagine the people being without Islam, just as today they cannot imagine a righteous nation without democracy. Without Islam, the spirit of the nation would die and without democracy the work of the nation would be frustrated. Consequently, it is understood that it is absolutely necessary for the two to be together."[25] Centrist positions like these developed under the *tarshid* of the New Islamic thinkers were widely circulated throughout the Islamic world.

In developing this body of independent Islamic scholarship and supporting the activism it underwrote, Egypt's New Islamic thinkers extended their circle to intellectuals across *Dar al Islam*. They did so through a complex network of networks that give a loose, overall coherence to the intellectual and activist work of the transnational *Wassatteyya*. No homogenizing unity is imposed on their efforts. Islam of the center is an active, positive force that aims to guide men and women in their struggles to be better human beings and to build a better world. It inspires the struggles of ordinary men and women for freedom and justice under an Islamic banner. Those struggles burst into international consciousness with the Green Revolution in Iran and the Arab revolutions that swept through Arab lands in 2011. Everywhere, centrist Islamic inspiration braids easily with besieged local nationalisms and struggles for justice. Centrist Islamic intellectuals inspire resistance to tyrannical rule, including dictatorships cloaked in Islamic rhetoric and external forms of religiosity. Such commitments are never merely tactical and strategic. They arise naturally out of the moral universe of Islam, defined by the values and higher purposes of the Qur'an and elaborated by sound *hadiths* (sayings of the Prophet that illuminate his thoughts and actions) as the Islamic midstream has come to understand both. This moral grounding means, in practice, that centrist intellectuals do not hesitate to step forward as bold critics of the excesses of so-called Islamic regimes and movements. They have issued harshly critical assessments of conditions in Saudi Arabia, Iran, Sudan, and Pakistan. Fahmi Huwaidi pronounced, for example, that despite his great sympathy for the Iranian people and appreciation for the accomplishments of the first stages of their revolution against the regime of the Shah, Iran could in no way be considered a model of Islamic rule.[26]

Egypt's New Islamic thinkers coalesced as an intellectual school at a time when similar developments were taking place in various sites in the Islamic world, notably those around Necmettin Erbakan in Turkey, Rashid Ghannouchi in Tunisia, and Alija Izetbegovic in Bosnia, to cite but three examples. The intellectuals and activists in these circles have also been profoundly influenced by the Brotherhood example. They also understood its limitations. They were open to New Islamic thinking.

The new thinking took the idea of a broad and inclusive project identity that was first put forward in the manifesto of the thinkers of the New Islamic school.[27] In the years that followed, their collective scholarship insistently advanced a synthesizing, theoretical thrust that argued for a pluralistic mainstream project. Islamic values and higher purposes would be central. However, they aimed to find points of connection and areas of agreement on the level of values and objectives between the major competing trends. They argued that future cooperation could be built on such a platform. The New Islamic school brought into clear view a civilizational

Islam that projected a consensual vision of democracy and progress that would appeal to centrists across the political spectrum. Quite explicitly, the new thinking embraced the possibility of cooperation of moderates from both Islamic and secular trends for the common good. These creative thinkers never diluted their commitment to the idea that midstream Islam would make a major contribution to this effort. However, they insisted as well on the necessity of a broader coalition of all major social and political trends that were afoot in the land. The new thinking opened especially to the young across much of *Dar al Islam*, whose lives were clouded by despair and the sense that the future held little for them. The ability to reach disaffected Arab youth was of great importance to all trends. The inclusive and sophisticated approach of the New Islamic thinkers helped bring these insights within reach of all groups. Such inclusive thinking aimed to overcome divisions and enable moderates of all kinds to build coalitions and other forms of cooperation for their often courageous and always daunting efforts to act politically in an authoritarian political context. There was nothing automatic about these formulations. The New Islamic thinkers understood that there was no way around the uncertainties and tribulations of political engagement in very diverse and often dangerous national circumstances.[28]

What Egypt's New Islamic thinkers accomplished was the delicate task of building on the contributions of the Muslim Brothers in ways that, at the same time, indicated how their limitations might be bypassed. By the time of his death in 1996 Muhammad al Ghazzali, for example, had established himself as a far more influential Islamic intellectual and moral force than any of the Brotherhood guides who succeeded Hassan al Banna. Although a critic of the Brothers, Ghazzali never confused them with the destructive extremists. Ghazzali saw the extremists and their distorted interpretations of the faith as a threat even more deadly than the repressive security regimes for the damage they did to the souls of their youthful adherents. Beyond official Islam, movement Islam, and extremist Islam, Ghazzali understood that "Islam itself" defined an expansive centrist space of hope and untapped opportunity where the serious work of "building the world" could take place.

While Islam does lend itself to diverse interpretations, it does not lend itself to "hijacking" by extremists. Such an alien and interested formulation says nothing at all about Islam. It speaks rather to the interest of imperial powers in having an "enemy," real or imagined, to rationalize to their domestic publics endless wars of expansion. The implausible idea that a small band of criminals could pose an existential threat to a super-power makes minimal sense only if those criminals have somehow managed to capture and manipulate the faith of millions. Islam is not a thing to be seized and held for ransom. Islam is transcendent. It is out of reach of all such purposes. Nevertheless, despite its patent absurdity, the idea of a hijacked Islam has its uses. Such an imagined Islam helps justify to frightened Western publics' profitable imperial ventures and disciplinary restrictions on democracy at home.

There are lessons to be learned from the historical experience of the *Wassatteyya*, but at no point do the New Islamic thinkers mistake historical insight for rigid models that can be applied in all times and places. The Renewal contains a wide variety of groups, all of which differ from traditional expressions of religious belief in their active concern for the major issues of national life. Qaradawi also notes that these varied groups "differ on many issues."[29] In this precise way, Qaradawi understands the environment of the New Islamic school in terms that a complexity theorist has described as "a seamy web that draws together and holds apart the elements of which it is constituted."[30] Speaking for the New Islamic thinkers generally, Qaradawi explains that their school speaks in the name of "the largest of these currents, which I name that of Islamic *Wassatteyya*." The *Wassatteyya* trend, as Qaradawi sees it, "comprises the broadest base, from which others branched off or separated." Qaradawi expresses the belief of all the New Islamic thinkers that the *Wassatteyya* "is the ablest of the trends and the one we hope will survive and continue to grow because in our opinion, it is the correct current, representing the moderation of the Islamic method, path, and way."[31] In the New Islamic view, it is the *tarshid* of the *Wassatteyya* that would matter most.

Ijtihad *for a Global Age*

Underlying all such practical initiatives is the commitment of the intellectuals of the *Wassatteyya* to a creative and collective *ijtihad* in the interest of the common good. They act consciously and deliberately to recover and rejuvenate the roots in the faith for a bold interpretative project to renew Islam for our time. Islamic civilization reserves this kind of exceptional role for religious scholars.

Quite explicitly, the New Islamic thinkers explain that their interpretive efforts must address the priority challenges of the age rather than confine themselves to arcane matters of the faith. Tareq al Bishri, for example, asserts the necessity in the new globalized conditions of accelerating changes for an *ijtihad* that produces a new *fiqh*, consistent with these turbulent times.[32] The Islamic world, Bishri adds, will be left at continued disadvantage unless the dramatic transformations that the world is experiencing are analyzed and understood within an Islamic framework. The new global realities must be addressed in the light of the core values and higher purposes of Islam. He argues that this essential work of *ijtihad* represents the highest priority of the Islamic world.[33]

The New Islamic thinkers insist that the duty of *ijtihad* cannot be suspended. Here they stand firmly against the traditionalists, who argue that the possibility of *ijtihad* has been closed for centuries to protect the *ummah* and to preserve the heritage unchanged. In defiance of such views, they assert their collective right to exercise this function today. The school in general and Selim al Awa, Muhammad al Ghazzali, and Yusuf al Qaradawi in particular have achieved prominence and some measure of notoriety for their scholarly work on interpretive method, applied to a wide range of pressing societal issues. They emphasize the distinctive positions on *ijtihad* that defined their school just as strongly as the substantive conclusions on issues related to the common good. At the same time, they clearly recognize that no one, including themselves, has any monopoly right over *ijtihad*.[34]

Islamic intellectuals never accepted the Western fantasy that history would end with a universal civilization based on Western forms and values. At the deepest level, they believed that certainty about the course of human history is reserved to God. They refused the notion that the West's past defined the future of the *ummah*. They also rejected out of hand parallel fantasies of a unitary future of exclusionary dominance for Islam, advanced by Islamic extremists. Innovative groups like the New Islamic trend looked instead to a common future in a pluralistic, multipolar world. They understood such a world to be consistent with the Qur'anic vision for humankind. They believed that there was evidence all around us for the unfolding of just such a world that would enhance the sense of common humanity on, for the first time, a truly global scale.

Islamic intellectuals always knew that they would face the profound uncertainties of all manner of contingencies in a pluralistic world. They actively embraced the challenges these uncertainties posed. Islam from the outset shared God's world with the non-Muslim Jews and Christians of Arabia. They were enjoined to respect and acknowledge these non-Muslims as the adherents, like themselves, of the Abrahamic tradition. The diverse world of the early Muslims extended to the Greeks, the Persians, and the Indians. These encounters translated into the grand philosophical tradition of medieval Islamic thought that is quite simply incomprehensible without attention to the Greek tradition with which the Islamic scholars entered into a dialogue from the ninth to the thirteenth century. Islamic scholars had been immunized against any illusions that the fate of human societies could be known with the precision of mathematics and the natural sciences. The great Islamic medieval philosophers, still read and studied today, had laid to rest such "scientific" illusions centuries ago.

The New Islamic thinkers as a school have produced important new theoretical and practical work on all spheres of social life, including pioneering work on such fundamental issues as social justice, human rights, the advancement of women and minorities, economic development, and democracy. Against the odds, in authoritarian landscapes disfigured by a dismal record of torture and other violations of basic human rights that have targeted Islamic activists in particular, these thinkers and public figures of the New Islamic school have also left a public record of speaking and acting on behalf of reason and science, democracy and human rights, and economic development strategies that aim to close the gap between the wealthy and the poor. While their support comes primarily from the lower middle classes, they position themselves to provide assistance to the disadvantaged in the name of Islamic justice. While women and non-Muslims still play only a limited role in their organizations, they project a self-critical vision of the need to fully include both in the new world that is coming into being. More to the point, the policy positions that the New Islamic thinkers take in existing public arenas emphatically aim to translate the promise of inclusion into emerging social realities. These accomplishments were possible in no small part because the New Islamic thinkers never constituted the kind of direct political threat to the regime that would provoke their suppression. Their stature as distinguished public figures to this day provides an important measure of protection as they undertake the tasks of guiding the Islamic wave toward their goal of much broader and more inclusive consensus.

The weight of the New Islamic thinkers of the fourth surge of renewal resides in their ability to articulate broadly inclusive projects that attract the attention and commitments of centrists throughout the Islamic world. They speak for Islam as a way of being in the world without fear. They do so in direct opposition to traditionalists and extremists, who project fearful representations of Islam that use the threat of hell to win the support of the young and to discipline followers of all ages. In the eyes of the New Islamic thinkers, Islam can never be so fearful for its own future that it turns to extremism for self-defense. The Islam they evoke is unafraid, even when faced with the hostile power and might of the most powerful empire on the planet. At the same time, the story of the Islamic *Wassatteyya* is always about more than fear and courageous defense. Islam of the center is a positive, active force that aims to build a better world, inspiring the struggles for freedom and justice. Such struggles arise naturally out of the moral universe of Islam, defined by the core values and purposes of the Qur'an as understood by the midstream. Battles for political freedom and economic and social justice, mounted by midstream forces, draw their strength throughout the Islamic lands from the power of Islamic identity, created and recreated through the networks of the *Wassatteyya*, to meet the needs of particular times and places.

For decades, Islam's centrists have been raising their voices in condemnation of criminal political violence by extremists of all kinds, including those who hold abusive power as well as those who oppose them. They champion a model of gradual social transformation that aims to preserve the best of what has been accomplished worldwide, including in the West, while insisting that humankind can do better. They seek development with a strategy that begins with cultural and educational reform, based on reason and science. They speak out against the resort to un-Islamic violence in their own societies, whether by the regime or its opponents. They have been particularly effective in countering the distorted views that prompt militant assaults on the arts, women, and non-Muslims.

With the same forthrightness, the New Islamic thinkers have condemned the rise in violence around the world. In the face of the mass murders of September 11, 2001, Islamic intellectuals speaking for the *Wassatteyya* issued timely and unequivocal condemnations of the killers. On September 27, 2001, Shaikh Yusuf al Qaradawi, Tareq al Bishri, Muhammad Selim al Awa, and Fahmi Huwaidi issued a condemnation of "the terrorist acts . . . considered by Islamic law . . . to constitute, the crime of *harabah*, waging war against society."[35] The influence of their views on this matter has expanded widely in the transnational Islamic centrist networks. Yet the actions of these New Islamic thinkers for the most part remain unseen and their words fall on deaf ears in the West. Despite its very public character, their record leaves little trace on Western understandings of Islam or developments in the Islamic world. The very existence of such Islamic centrists is openly and repeatedly denied.[36]

This willful Western ignorance of the pursuit of peaceful remaking and repair in Islam's name has a straightforward explanation. The centrists of the Islamic wave have one fatal flaw from the dominant Western perspective. All of the major figures of the *Wassatteyya* advocate a future for the peoples of the Islamic world of their own making. Moreover, their condemnation of the violence of the Islamic extremists does not translate into forgiveness for the violence of the West, particularly the United States and Israel.[37] On a whole range of foreign political and economic issues, the New Islamic thinkers directly criticize currently existing Arab regimes for their failure to protect the right of self-determination of Arab Islamic peoples. They seize whatever opportunities that public spheres provide to urge that, when ruling regimes fail them, the people themselves should act directly through boycotts and other peaceful means to refuse destructive plans made by others for their future.[38] They have not hesitated to criticize all such excesses of Western and particularly Russian, American, and Israeli power. Yet, as their total record indicates, the intellectuals of the *Wassatteyya* are neither pro- nor anti-Western. Rather, they stand emphatically *for* the peoples of the Arab Islamic world. They speak for a *maslaha amma* that is defined in Islamic civilizational terms. They vigorously defend their right to shape their own future in line with the higher purposes of Islam. These sentiments that steel opposition to the West thus have deeper roots and a rationale far more compelling than the prevailing explanations that emphasize irrational hatred and the slanderous notion of some inherent Islamic propensity to rage and violence. Even before 9/11 provided the domestic support for the direct U.S. assault on the Islamic world, beginning in Afghanistan and then Iraq and now extending to Syria, the centrists had recognized in American foreign policies a threat to the Islamic world and its right to an independent future. They consistently opposed an American-sponsored "peace process." They judged reasonably that it was little more than a cover for the continued Israeli "settlement" of the West Bank and the collective imprisonment and punishment of the people of Gaza, in violation of international law and universal concepts of justice and decency. In their public commentaries, they asked all the hard questions: Wasn't the American bombing in 1998 of the only pharmaceutical plant in the Sudan (which provided medicine for more than half the country) on the charge that it was making chemical weapons (later proven false) as much a "war on society" as the destruction of the World Trade Center?[39] Was the world right to grieve less for the children of Iraq who died by the hundreds of thousands as a result of the Western blockade than for the innocents slaughtered in New York? Isn't the ongoing and U.S.-supported colonization of Palestine (i.e., the appropriation of land and water and the displacement and containment of an indigenous people) an act of violence? Should "moderation" mean acquiescence in the relentless Israeli settlement of land in the Occupied Territories and imprisonment of an entire people within so-called security walls on the West Bank and an open-air prison in Gaza? For opposing all forms of illegal and criminal violence, whether by the powerful or the weak, the New Islamic thinkers earn the active and dangerous enmity of the violent criminal groups in the Islamic world. For that same offense, compounded by their support for the self-determination of Arabs and Muslims, they are ignored, or worse, by the West.

The most impressive forces of resistance to this U.S. strategy are not coming from the expected quarters of power politics. Neither Europe, young or old, nor China nor Russia mattered much when it came to restraining George W. Bush from attacking Iraq. Rather, opposition is springing in unexpected ways from the new, worldwide networks of social forces, mobilized in flexible and adaptive ways. The place where these new forms of global political action appear is now emphatically the alternative media, originating in the Internet and enhanced by satellite transmissions. This new electronic public square, despite market and political encroachments, has become the most promising site of political creativity in the new conditions of the post–Cold War world. It is sometimes overlooked that the Information Revolution that made these electronic sites of opposition possible was itself a product of the same creative upheavals of the 1960s that gave rise to the sexual liberation, anticonsumerism, and antiwar movements. Still, it would be a mistake to allow the nostalgia in some quarters for the return of the "movement" to cloud appreciation for the radically new forms and prospects of contemporary resistances. The old forms of social movements, beginning with labor and ending with the classic antiwar movements, are being hollowed out as effectively as the nation-state. The shells and the memories remain; however, it is already clear that vital functions are moving into the new network systems of the electronic age. The great Arab uprisings of 2011 made it perfectly clear that these processes are well under way and probably irreversible in the Arab Islamic world.

An essential charge to a free press is the ability to monitor the inner workings of power at home and record what power does in the name of America abroad, including acts of criminality that violate international and humanitarian law. Figures like Edward Snowden, Chelsea Manning, and Julian Assange have shined lights on criminal actions taken in the name of the American people. Important, too, are the contributions of investigative reporters like James Risen of the *New York Times*, who has reported on the constitutional violations that occurred in the wake of 9/11 and the massive corruption that accompanied the government practice of simply throwing money at terror.[40] Muslims have not failed to notice just how often they are the victims of the crimes that whistleblowers reveal. Americans need to know what the U.S. government is up to; so, too, do Muslims around the world. The revelations of these men have lifted the curtain on the terrible costs of American plans for the remaking of the Islamic world. The calculated destruction of Iraq stands not only as one of the great war crimes of the twenty-first century but as searing witness to the horrific means the American empire is willing to use to pursue them.[41]

The Challenge of Spirituality, Identity, and Resistance in a Global Age

The New Islamic school warns of the dangers that erupt from "the arrogance, tyranny and ignorance" of a flawed humankind that has abandoned the values of "justice, humane betterment and sense of balance."[42] The rebuilding of community and repair of the Earth is everywhere, not just in the Islamic world, the challenge of the age. The writings of the New Islamic thinkers also alert us to the fact that this time of dangerous transition has created the conditions for yet another threat every bit as ominous in its consequences for our species as divisive poverty and environmental degradation. In societies around the globe, they argue, we are now faced with a terrifying intellectual fundamentalism that leads inevitably to violence. Despite variations in its cultural forms and content, this deadly threat is recognizable for its futile longing to return to the formalistic values and rigid structures of an imagined past. They read effects of such thinking in the slaughter by a criminal minority of thousands of defenseless civilians of a rainbow of colors, ethnic origins, and beliefs in the most cosmopolitan of world cities; in the devastating consequences of a rigid and inhuman market fundamentalism imposed by global financial institutions on the wretched of the Earth and the poor in their own societies; and just as clearly in the numbing spectacle of the world's only superpower waging war against an opportunistically defined "terrorism."[43]

On the ground of midstream Islam, the New Islamic thinkers join enlightened intellectuals and activists everywhere to stand squarely against these terrifying simplifications and the failure of moral and intellectual courage they represent. They insist on making distinctions and seeing nuance and contradiction, notably even in their thinking about the threatening policies of the United States. Recognizing that America has made itself the enemy of a scarcely understood Islamic world, Tareq al Bishri nevertheless insists that Islamic intellectuals and activists recognize and embrace those within the United States who struggle against the abuses of unconstrained American power. Even in militarized America, Bishri argues with compelling moral clarity, there are partners in the cause of peace and reconciliation.[44]

The New Islamic thinkers urge "a leap into the time and space" of a world of accelerating change. They insist that the faith, understood through the nuanced prism of an *ijtihad* for a global age, calls on Muslims to learn to live creatively and humanely in the fluid circumstances created by the Information Revolution. The challenge is not new, although the conditions are. They are experimenting boldly to create new forms adapted to the changed conditions that the Information Revolution has brought. It makes no sense to ignore their efforts or predetermine their outcome. The New Islamic record of public activities provides important lessons that can contribute to our more general efforts to "provide an account of the distinctive operational rules and principles of networks."[45] The products of an inherited culture built on the impressive worldwide networks for scholars, merchants, and travelers, these centrist Islamic intellectuals are uniquely well positioned to understand the codes that create cohesive identity out of difference. In doing so, it is likely that they will also help us better understand the mystery of Islam's stunning adaptive capacities through the centuries.

The *Wassatteyya* guides the Islamic Renewal to speak for the pluralism and opening out of identity that is a critical dimension of the Islamic heritage. This openness contrasts sharply to the Western emphasis on nationalism that has historically narrowed and closed off identities. Just as forcefully, it argues against the sectarian and ethnic impulses that pulse through the *ummah* as polluting subterranean currents, pitting Sunni against Shi'a, Arab against Persian, Turk against Kurd. Pluralism, as

Muhammad al Ghazzali emphasized in all his writings, holds a central place in Islamic political thinking. Indeed, Ghazzali wondered whether pluralism should not be considered an Islamic invention.[46] Those who live within the embrace of the *ummah* represent, by God's deliberate design, a mosaic of cultures and ethnicities. They are bound together by a shared, inclusive Islamic sensibility that embraces difference. The Qur'an sees men and women as having the high calling of building a just community where even the poorest and the weakest are entitled to respect and the material means for a dignified existence. The struggle to realize such a human community and the experience of building and living in it are intended to transform and elevate. Islam takes the flawed character of humanity as a given. The *al jihad al kabir* (the great *jihad* or personal struggle to be a better person) of Islam thus calls humanity above all else to strive to rise above human weaknesses and aspire to a better self. The work of building community together aims to provide a practical and uplifting reminder of "those truths everyone already knows."[47] Such truths, all too often dimmed by human limitations of circumstance and vision, attain in their view greatest clarity from the uncoerced experience of living together in the ways that reflect God's intentions for humanity. The experience of struggling in the task of "building the world" provides a practical, worldly intimation of divine purpose.

The New Islamic thinkers reach back along inherited pathways to the Islam of timeless higher purposes and values. At the same time, the school reaches forward into the new economic, social, and cultural realities created by the Information Revolution and the global market. There are strange and extraordinarily productive loops in the historical experience of *Dar al Islam*. The irony, as we have seen, is that the ultramodern configurations that complexity theory identifies have characteristics that mirror those of the classical Islamic world. The vast and sudden expansion of Islam in its first centuries preserved its cultural and religious unity. However, politics and economics could not keep pace. Viewed from the vantage point of *tawhid* or unity, varying degrees of chaos in political and economic terms prevailed across *Dar al Islam*. Out of the chaos came self-organized economic and political structures. In their extreme diversity, they reflected local needs and circumstances. Flexible networks, based on religion and culture, provided just enough connectedness to preserve a sense of the shattered whole.

The Western imperial onslaught of the eighteenth and nineteenth centuries brought fragmentation once again. Islam responded in much the same way. Political and economic schemes to achieve unification under pan-Arab or pan-Islamic banners faltered. Flexible ties of culture and faith held. From protected oases, watered by the river of Islam in Iran and Turkey, erupted creative assertions of renewal and reform. Despite their diversity, the contributions from Egypt, Turkey, and Iran flowed together to strengthen *al Tagdid al Islami*. Contemporary Arab journalist and Islamic intellectual Fahmi Huwaidi brings developments in these important nodes of the midstream networks into view as he navigates the tumultuous byways of the Islamic world today and records in countless articles what he has experienced. The heavy-duty intellectual work of *ijtihad* over four decades has produced an imaginative *fiqh* of text and a compelling *fiqh* of reality that charts the fate of the faith in a globalized world. The work of the Egyptian New Islamic thinkers makes it perfectly clear that Islamic civilization in general does have the resources to achieve civil, humane, and balanced social orders. More pointedly, the unexpected success of the Renewal suggests the ways that the new conditions of a globalized world enhance the prospects of such outcomes. The New Islamic reliance on both inherited pathways and evolving contemporary networks gives renewed substance to what Gamal Hamdan has called Islam's "planetary" reach.

4

Heralds of Renewal

And We cause springs to erupt therein . . .

QUR'AN 36:34

ISLAM'S "River of Life" fed subterranean springs that sustained oases across *Dar al Islam* (the Islamic world).[1] During the repressive decades of the 1950s and 1960s, these nurturing springs created improbable islands of green in Egypt, Turkey, Iran, and countless other sites in Islamic lands. Such sites provided refuge for a wounded Islam and kept the prospect of renewal alive. In the late 1960s and early 1970s, heralds of the Islamic Renewal burst on the scene from each of these oases. The heralds only seemed to come out of nowhere. Oases in Egypt, Turkey, Iran, and more distant Islamic lands had allowed these figures to repair, gather strength, and act for Islam. By their example, they called forth unexpected mass energy in a fourth great historic surge of Islamic resistance and reform in the early 1970s, inspiring millions across *Dar al Islam*. Islam did more than survive: It experienced a dramatic revitalization to become once again a major player in human history.

Muhammad al Ghazzali was one such herald. He himself did not see clearly the signs of the great Renewal to come. A deep despair and fear for Islam run through his early writings. In his *Notes from Prison* Alija Izetbegovic writes, "Is there anything more beautiful than a rainbow? But the man who is inside it, cannot see it."[2] A rainbow in so parched and desolate a landscape was just too improbable. Like Ghazzali, Izetbegovic contributed to the coming of the Renewal with his bold and insightful *Islamic Declaration*, issued from the 500-year-old community of Bosnian Muslims. Izetbegovic called Muslims across *Dar al Islam* to action. He, too, could not foresee the impact of his work. He, too, was in the rainbow.

The messages of figures like Muhammad al Ghazzali and Alija Izetbegovic as well were precisely the signs that ordinary Muslims were looking for. They responded in the millions. Muhammad al Ghazzali sounded his compelling call for revival from Egypt, the land of al Azhar and Muhammad Abduh. Ghazzali and the other Egyptian New Islamic intellectuals were joined in their efforts for renewal by Muhammad Hussein Fadlallah in Lebanon, Necmettin Erbakan in Turkey, Ali Shariati in Iran, and Alija Izetbegovic in Bosnia. These men were not alone. Heralds of Islamic Renewal appeared in all quarters of *Dar al Islam*. They rallied the masses to act for Islam. Few in the West understood the importance of these heralds of Islamic Renewal or even took note of the collective character of their work. Rare are the ordinary Western citizens, or even intellectuals, who will have read any of the prolific works of such figures. Western cultural imperialism seeks not only to project its own culture but also to discourage exposure of its citizens to the world's intellectual currents.

Conventional Western analysts insistently pointed to a secular future. An unchallenged certainty reigned that all religions faced inevitable decline and marginalization. God was dying, if not already dead. Creativity of distinctly Islamic inspiration gave the lie to these false certainties. Each of the figures who contributed to *al Tagdid al Islami* (the Islamic Renewal) did so in highly inventive ways. It proved impossible to force them into existing categories of understanding and classification, although the effort was endlessly made. The heralds of the Islamic Renewal simply did not fit. Western scholars were ill equipped to take their measure. They have yet to grasp the nature of their collective role in shaping the character of *al Tagdid al Islami*.

Muhammad Hussein Fadlallah, the Poetic Voice of the Fourth Wave

Understanding unanticipated events of such extraordinary emotional energy and density of meaning may well exceed the descriptive and analytical capability of the prosaic prose of the social scientist. Poets have a better chance of capturing their import. The fourth Islamic wave found such an interpreter in an Iraqi-born Lebanese grand ayatollah. Muhammad Hussein Fadlallah (1935–2010) was a poet as well as a religious scholar and himself a force for renewal. Fadlallah held the rank of *marja'* (the highest rank among Shi'i scholars). All Shi'a must choose a *marja'*. They seek his guidance on religious matters. His teachings guide their life decisions. They financially support his scholarship and community social work. From the Shi'a arc, Fadlallah defined as no other the call to freedom at the heart of the spirit of the Islamic Renewal.

The Iranian Revolution of 1979 was so dramatic and influential an event that it overshadowed the many other important contributions that came to the Islamic Renewal from Shi'i communities. Lebanese and Iraqi Shi'i scholars, like Fadlallah from Lebanon and Muhammad Baqir Badr (1935–1980) from Iraq, rose alongside the Iranians. They had central but now rarely noted roles in defining *al Tagdid al Islami*. Given the long shadows that the Iranian Revolution and Ayatollah Ruhollah Mostafavi Khomeini (1902–1989), in particular, have cast, it is especially important to bring them into view. For many who know little of the Shi'a and their rich historical legacy, Ayatollah Khomeini, and the repressive theocracy he established in the wake of the Iranian "earthquake," has become the definitive face of Shi'a Islam. Close attention to the lifework of Fadlallah will help cultivate a more accurate sense of the richness of the contributions of the Shi'i tradition to the Renewal. It will also act as an antidote to the common perception that there was something inherent in Shi'ism that explains the authoritarian character that Khomeini gave the Iranian Revolution.

The second voice of the Shi'a, less poetic and more philosophical, sounded a parallel call to resistance, social justice, and Islamic reform. Badr came from a distinguished family of scholars. He was a prolific writer and a deep thinker on contemporary issues. Today he goes unread and rarely even mentioned in the West. It was Saddam Hussein who silenced that voice. He did so with unimaginable brutality. Arrested and tortured by Saddam's henchmen, Badr's torment ended with a nail driven through his skull. Part of the appeal of figures like Fadlallah and Badr is quite simply that they were men of great personal courage and deep conviction. They took unimaginable risks for the causes they advocated. Even without the Iranian Revolution of 1979, the work of figures like Fadlallah and Badr guaranteed that the diverse Shi'i communities of the *ummah* would have a powerful role in shaping the inclusive Islamic Renewal.

It is Fadlallah's voice that most effectively breaks through cultural barriers to reach the widest audience. In "To Be Human" Ayatollah Fadlallah identifies resistance as the heart of the broader Renewal aimed for the assertion of one's humanity:

Freedom comes from the will to freedom within oneself.
    Freedom cannot be issued by a decree,

Nor can it be given by others.

Freedom is exactly like a spring that erupts from the depths of the earth.

It imposes itself.

When a spring erupts,

It doesn't seek the approval of this and it doesn't ask the opinion of that.

And it does not accept refusals

Because *giving* is the secret essence of the spring.

Fadlallah continues:

Only a freedom that erupts from within can give a man his humanity:

The freedom to say "NO"

When "NO" is your thought,

Even if the whole world says "YES!"

The issue is not being self-centered.

The issue is simply being human.[3]

Fadlallah uses the metaphor of erupting springs to suggest how only freedom can bring forth the thinking individual as a free human being. He links the freedom to develop and express one's own thoughts to the attainment of a full humanity. He does not speak of movements or parties. Rather, Fadlallah addresses politics in its broadest sense of the relationship of individuals to the community of Muslims. Politics understood in this way addresses large issues that concern all Muslims. He connects the individual freedom of Muslims to the inclusionary struggle for the transcendence of sectarian divides that fracture the unity of the *ummah*. It demands resistance to all manner of colonial and imperial intrusions into the body of the *ummah*. It calls for the realization of a free Palestine. To experience this freedom and to fulfill the responsibilities it entails, Fadlallah calls ordinary Muslims to recapture their capacity for independent thought and action from the tyrannies of persons and enthrallment with things.

As a Shi'i *marja'*, Fadlallah commanded a massive following that extended well beyond Lebanon to Shi'i communities in Pakistan, Afghanistan, Iran, Iraq, the Gulf, and central Asia. Many Sunnis, too, responded to his call and looked to him for guidance. Both Western and regional media outlets regularly identified Fadlallah as a Shi'i religious leader, but the ayatollah himself never accepted the designation. He quite deliberately sought to address all Muslims. He appealed to an inclusive "true Islam" that "wants us to base our lives on reason and to elevate it by means of knowledge, so as to enrich it and be enriched by it."[4] Fadlallah's many contributions to the renewal of Islamic thought and legal reasoning aimed to strengthen a modern and nonsectarian Islam.

Fadlallah did speak from Lebanon, and that grounding did make a difference. The American-backed Israeli invasions of Lebanon in 1978 and in 1982 gave Fadlallah's work a clear focus, although never an exclusive one. Throughout his long and productive life, he never lost his conviction of the threat to Islam posed by Israel and the United States. Fadlallah took for granted the necessity of resisting the 18-year Israeli occupation of southern Lebanon (1982–2000). He understood that the United States consistently defended Israeli positions in all international forums. Hope rested with resistance mounted from Lebanese soil and by the Lebanese people, notably the Shi'a of occupied southern Lebanon. Fadlallah's unequivocal advocacy of that position was fully in accord with international law and in no way criminal. In parallel fashion, Fadlallah remained all his life a staunch supporter of those Palestinians who struggled with justice on their side to establish a Palestinian state.

Muhammad Hussein Fadlallah was always more than a political figure. He took great pains to elaborate both the moral basis and the logic of resistance. There can be no doubt that his calls for resistance against occupation did inspire the fighters of Hizbullah. His message of social justice and concrete social projects did uplift the repressed and degraded community of Shi'i Lebanese. It is out of that community that Hizbullah as a national resistance movement emerged. In his *Islam and the Logic of Force* Fadlallah called upon Shi'a to reject their traditional passivity in the face of injustice and foreign domination. He called on them to reject centuries of quiescence. He did so from within Shi'i traditions. He urged the freedom fighters to seek inspiration in the behavior of the Prophet's son-in-law Ali and his grandson Hussein. Both heroic figures martyred themselves in struggles against tyranny.[5]

Fadlallah's call for resistance earned the profound animosity of both Israel and the United States. Israeli and Western intelligence agencies held Fadlallah responsible for all attacks against Western targets in Lebanon, including the kidnapping of foreigners and the 1983 bombings of the barracks of the multinational force in Beirut that killed 241 U.S. Marines and 58 French paratroopers. However, neither the Israeli nor the American authorities ever produced any persuasive evidence linking the ayatollah to these attacks, although he clearly believed that Lebanese had the right to oppose military occupiers who intervened in their affairs.

Fadlallah refused outright the Israeli–American narrative on Palestine. He explained that, in his view, Palestine is for the Palestinians who used to live there as the overwhelmingly majority population. Fadlallah, like most Arab intellectuals, rejected the Israeli claim to Palestine because their ancestors had lived there thousands of years ago. He asked if any people would recognize such a claim as the basis for the displacement of the contemporary population who lived on the land for generations. Fadlallah faced squarely the dilemmas of resistance to an overwhelmingly powerful occupying power in both his Lebanese homeland and in Palestine. He reminded Muslims that the Qur'an rejects passivism and legitimizes the resort to force by those violently oppressed and "driven from their homes."[6] As an Islamic scholar, Fadlallah reasoned that since Israel used the terrible violence of its American-supplied advanced weaponry, Islam permitted the defensive use of the classic weapons of the weak by resistance fighters. Since Palestinians had neither a regular army, nor an air force, nor a navy, Fadlallah defended the use by Palestinian fighters of their own bodies as weapons to defend their land, their way of life, and their faith. When Israel deployed F16 aircraft against civilians in 2002, Fadlallah pronounced that "they have had their land stolen, their families killed, their homes destroyed, and the Israelis are using weapons, such as the F16 aircraft, which are meant only for major wars. There is no other way for the Palestinians to push back those mountains, apart from martyrdom operations."[7]

The ayatollah refused to call such operations "suicide bombings." Fadlallah explained that "I was not the one who launched the idea of so-called suicide bombings, but I have certainly argued in favour of them. I do, though, make a distinction between them and attacks that target people in a state of peace—which was why I opposed what happened on September 11." Fadlallah explained that "the situation of the Palestinians is quite different, because they are in a state of war with Israel. They are not aiming to kill civilians but in war civilians do get killed. Don't forget, the Palestinians are living under mountains of pressure." Fadlallah did encourage the pragmatic discussion of how effective such attacks were in advancing the Palestinian cause. He expressed no doubt, however, that they were justifiable in Islamic terms.[8]

Fadlallah would have none of the hollow rhetoric and hypocrisy of the West. Violence, he argued, began with occupation and dispossession, not with the resistance to them. All violent resistance struggles inevitably find innocent civilians caught in the crossfire. However, Fadlallah would not tolerate the suggestion that this deplorable outcome was somehow restricted to the Palestinian resistance fighters. He asked Americans a simple question: "During the Second World War, how many civilians did the West kill? Were the bombs which fell on Hiroshima and Nagasaki dropped on civilians or not?" Fadlallah dismissed out of hand the endless Western attempts to establish a link between Islam and fanaticism. He reasoned that, "of course, there are extremists and fanatics in Islam, just as there are extremists and fanatics in the West. For example, you have people who are fanatical about the race issue. In Muslim countries, there are even fanatics against other Muslims, but that doesn't prove that Islam creates them, any more than that Christianity creates fanatics in your society." With unfailing logic, Fadlallah exposed how double standards and sheer hypocrisy had compromised the West. He appealed to universal standards, applicable to all, and he did so to great effect.[9]

It is quite impossible to take accurate measure of Fadlallah and his contribution to the Renewal from the point of view of his sharp criticisms of Israeli and Western policies only. Such an approach overlooks the ayatollah's frequent attention to shortcomings closer to home. He did so with equal bluntness and the same moral clarity. Above all, the grand ayatollah was a lifelong advocate for the unity of the Islamic *ummah*. He warned presciently of the dangers of sectarianism to the *ummah*. Fadlallah regularly used his Friday sermons to call for the unity of the *ummah*. Over and over again he emphasized: "O Muslims: The Shi'as are not the Sunnis' problem and the Sunnis are not the Shi'as' problem." Sectarian strife, he insisted, was deliberately stirred up by hostile outside powers to weaken the *ummah*.[10] Fadlallah did not hesitate to challenge those among the Shi'a who saw the imamate as the foundation of irreconcilable differences between Sunni and Shi'a. Ali's legacy as a man of great wisdom and a revolutionary in his view transcended the sectarian divide:

When there are outside threats, the leadership and the whole Ummah should freeze their differences and unite in preserving Islam and the Muslims. Therefore, all those who incite sectarian strife are in reality acting against Ali, because his principles, teachings and practice have always called for preventing the arrogant and disbelievers from exploiting our sectarian, religious and national differences in order to destroy Islam.[11]

Fadlallah argued, in short, that the beloved Imam Ali was a champion of the unity of all Muslims.

Fadlallah also did not hesitate to denounce violent Islamic extremists who imagined that their indiscriminately violent means somehow defended Islam. He charged that, on the contrary, they did clear and lasting damage with their fanaticism. Fadlallah issued especially harsh condemnations of the extremist resort to *takfir* (declaring Muslims to be unbelievers). He found it shameful that

> at a time where the Muslim *Ummah* faces severe challenges from the outside, a fanatic *takfiri* group from within continues its war on Muslims inside their mosques, armed with an alienating sectarian mindset and a murderous mentality that violates the sacredness of mosques, and eventually ends up killing groups of believers and worshippers in a brutal and criminal manner that has nothing to do with Islam and its principles.[12]

The grand ayatollah insisted on a sharp distinction between freedom fighters and criminal extremists. Fadlallah was among the first of the Islamic scholars to condemn the horrific 9/11 attacks as a violation of *Shari'ah* (the provisions from Qur'an and *Sunnah* to regulate human behavior). The ayatollah likewise sharply condemned all such operations that deliberately killed civilians, such as the murders that took place in the Moscow subway in 2010.

Fadlallah's stature as a revered *marja' al-taqlid* allowed him to go further in Shi'i self-criticism. He called for an end of Shi'i blood-shedding ceremonies at *Ashura* (the day of mourning for the martyrdom of the Prophet's grandson in Shi'i Islam). More remarkably, he did the unthinkable for a Shi'i religious scholar of his time. Enormous prestige flowed to Iran in the wake of the revolution of 1979 that overthrew the Western-backed shah's regime. Yet the grand ayatollah consistently and quite deliberately made himself a thorn in the side of Iran's theocratic regime. In Lebanon, Fadlallah criticized Hizbullah's dependence on Iran. Western critics, unaware of the dynamics of political life in Lebanon, consistently missed the fact that Fadlallah's enormous following provided one of the few obstacles to the complete dominance by Hizbullah and their Iranian mentors of Lebanese Shi'a.

Efforts to silence the grand ayatollah's defiant and uncompromising voice remained a constant threat throughout his life. They consistently failed, with a regularity that suggested miraculous protection to Fadlallah's followers. In 1985 a massive assassination attempt was engineered against him. A 440-lb. car bomb was placed along the road from his apartment to his mosque. The ayatollah just barely escaped the explosion. The huge bomb destroyed an apartment block, killing more than eighty and wounding several hundred, including large numbers of women and children. The United States denied any responsibility. However, Bob Woodward, the American investigative journalist, connected the Central Intelligence Agency (CIA) to the operation. There were contrary indications that right-wing Lebanese Christian extremists were behind the attempt. In any case, to date no credible investigation to establish the identity of the perpetrators has been undertaken. We do know with certainty that the Israelis made a second serious attempt to kill Fadlallah in 2006 by bombing his house in south Beirut. They did not disguise their intent. Fadlallah's house was demolished, but the ayatollah was not there.[13]

American and Israeli intelligence agencies and Christian extremists were not the only enemies of Lebanon's most distinguished Islamic scholar. Profiles of this complex figure rarely note that he was also attacked and threatened for his modernist and progressive social views. Conservative Islamic scholars and their activist supporters denounced Fadlallah's stance on a wide range of social issues. Foreign occupiers, in Fadlallah's view, were not the only enemies of human freedom. Fadlallah regularly described men and women as equals and consistently argued for women's rights. Freedom for him was not the preserve of males alone. In 2007 the grand ayatollah issued a *fatwa* (religious opinion by an Islamic scholar) condemning domestic violence against women. The ruling defended the right of a woman to defend herself in such situations. In subsequent *fatwas* Fadlallah banned female circumcision and "honor killings." The ayatollah openly discussed issues of female sexuality, including masturbation and the right of a woman to an abortion when her health was at risk.

Following the pathway to social justice charted by Hassan al Banna, Fadlallah registered exemplary charitable and welfare achievements that many judge as far more advanced than Banna's. He founded a public library, a women's cultural center, and medical clinics, as well as an extensive network of eighteen schools, nine orphanages, and a large number of religious and cultural centers in the Shi'i suburbs of Beirut and in southern Lebanon. All of his work was suffused with a personal kindness and gentleness that was itself an inspiration for spiritual regeneration.

Inevitably, Israel and Western governments placed Hizbullah on their arbitrarily compiled lists of terrorist organizations. Routinely, Fadlallah was described in Western scholarship and journalism as the spiritual advisor of Hizbullah, irresponsibly exposing the ayatollah to attacks in the "War on Terror." Such arbitrary pronouncements aside, there is no credible evidence that Fadlallah was directly affiliated with Hizbullah in any institutional capacity. Hizbullah looked to Ayatollah Khomeini and his successor Ayatollah Khamenei in Tehran. Fadlallah had, in fact, distanced himself ideologically from Hizbullah when the group accepted Ayatollah Khamenei, the successor to Khomeini, as their *marja'*.

Undeterred by these inconvenient facts, the corporate international media endlessly repeated the myth of Fadlallah's role as spiritual advisor to Hizbullah. The independent journalist Robert Fisk, personally acquainted with Fadlallah and in a class by himself for his direct knowledge of Lebanon, knew otherwise. He said so, simply and convincingly. In a defiant tribute to the ayatollah at the time of his death, Fisk pronounced that "Fadlallah was a very serious and very important man whose constant sermons on the need for spiritual regeneration and kindness did more good than most in a country constantly flooded in a rhetoric bath." Fisk reported that "hundreds of thousands attended his funeral in Beirut . . . I am not surprised."[14]

The Iranian Earthquake

Attention to the important work for the Renewal by Shi'i scholars in other sites does not diminish in any way the importance of the Iranian Revolution of 1979. Out of the suffering of the Iranian people, one of the greatest mass movements in human history erupted. The Iranian Revolution of 1979 sent tremors felt around the world. It galvanized Muslims everywhere, and not just those of the Shi'a arc. These voices of millions could not be silenced at Iran's revolutionary moment. Like other such momentous developments, the nature of the revolution's long-term effects was far from clear. What was clear was that the Iranian people had launched the first genuine mass revolution of our time, not inspired by Western ideologies.

As Iran's cities exploded, the glowering image of the black-turbaned grand ayatollah inevitably became the face of the Iranian Revolution. Khomeini's character and background tell a great deal about the nature of the Iranian Revolution and the regime that emerged from it, but they obscure even more. When Khomeini stepped from his plane to return triumphantly from exile to an Iran in revolution, a young reporter asked the ayatollah what he felt at just that moment. "Nothing" was Khomeini's chilling reply. Within a year, that young man had been executed, along with thousands of others, as the cruel and dictatorial features of the new regime took shape.[15] There are many examples of brutal authoritarian and theocratic rulers in the history of the Islamic world. However, they were interpreted as contraventions of Islam. Khomeini, in contrast, had crafted an elaborate theological justification for his theocratic rule. Such a justification in Islamic terms was unknown to Islam in all its centuries. Although sharply contested on Islamic ground, he succeeded in imposing it by force. The new regime concentrated power in the hands of one man, and that man felt nothing. Rivers of blood flowed. The screams of those tortured and killed under the watchful gaze of the "Imam," as his followers called him, were as frequent and as wrenching as those from the time of the shah.

The temptation is overwhelming to see this authoritarian outcome, engineered by Khomeini, as inevitable, but it should be avoided. Whatever came later, it is undeniable that Iran did experience a revolution. It was genuine. The revolution removed the American-imposed shah. It fundamentally transformed state structures. It called for their rebuilding on new foundations of Islamic inspiration. These momentous events inspired ordinary Muslims across *Dar al Islam*. The Iranian people did register a signal victory in the human struggle for freedom. They did so in Islam's name. It was *al Nas*, the people, who poured into the streets to make the revolution. Hundreds and hundreds of thousands did so, carrying the banner of Islam. In the end, their cries for freedom and social justice went unrealized, as the new regime degenerated into a theocratic autocracy. Yet that degeneration should not obscure the importance of the event itself. The liberating promise of the revolution did not take Iranians further than the elimination of the shah. Yet that accomplishment was in itself a gain for freedom. A close look at events in Iran makes the further point that there is no iron code that Shi'i Islam inevitably generates theocratic despotism. There were contingencies, both internal and external, that ultimately shaped developments in Iran. There were power struggles within the ranks of Shi'i scholars. The outcomes were not preordained. They were resolved, for the time being, in ways adverse to the more liberating outcome for which the Iranian people had launched their revolution. The pathways not taken remain to shadow the current authoritarian structures.

From the very outset, the unfolding of the revolution harbored contradictions. They defined alternatives to Khomeini's brand of authoritarianism that centered on his commitment to *wilayet al faqih* (rule of the *faqih*; the system of government in which a leading Shi'i religious leader exercises absolute authority). It is now almost forgotten that even among Iran's senior religious scholars there were staunch opponents to the rule of "the *faqih*." Grand Ayatollah Sayyid Mohammad Kazem Shariatmadari took the lead. In Qom, the center of Islamic learning in Iran, Shariatmadari was generally considered to be the highest-ranked and most influential of the grand ayatollahs. Earlier, Shariatmadari had intervened to rescue Khomeini. Khomeini's outspoken political criticism had brought him to the attention of the shah's security apparatus. Shariatmadari supported Khomeini's elevation to the rank of grand ayatollah, thus placing him out of reach of the shah's security forces. Shariatmadari's support carried great weight with the palace. He belonged to the quiescent school of Shi'a scholars and had provided important support for the shah's rule.

As Iran moved toward revolution, Ayatollah Ruhollah Khomeini made his bid for leadership. He advanced his radically revisionist conception of *wilayet al faqih* that would concentrate absolute power in the hands of the *faqih*. Ayatollah Shariatmadari forcefully opposed Khomeini's innovation. He saw it as a dangerous and unprecedented break with tradition that opened the way to theocracy. Shariatmadari was no democrat, as his unwavering support for the shah had made clear. Yet the grand ayatollah concluded that a far greater danger than even the shah's rule lay in dictatorial rule with theological underpinnings. Khomeini responded fiercely to Shariatmadari's criticisms, recognizing just how high the stakes were. The grand ayatollah's supporters were killed in street clashes, and his family was harassed. "Death to the detractors of *wilayet al faqih*" became a street chant of Khomeini's minions. Shariatmadari himself was arrested. Shockingly, the elderly ayatollah, a man of immense learning and great dignity, was physically abused. He was forced to recant publicly his opposition. He did so but in a way that left no doubt that the confession had been extracted by brute force. Many read that signal as the final act of defiance of a brave man. Not long after his public confession, Shariatmadari fell seriously ill. He was diagnosed with cancer. The grand ayatollah, the leading religious figure of Qom and the man who had rescued Khomeini, was denied the medical treatment his condition required. In a final vindictive act of disrespect, Shariatmadari was buried near the toilets on the grounds of the hospital where he had languished untreated.

Given the vocal opposition of very senior figures like Shariatmadari, it is unlikely that Khomeini would have prevailed without the support of other senior scholars to offset the opposition of figures like Shariatmadari. The support for Khomeini of Ayatollah Hussein Ali Montazeri (1922–2009), in particular, proved critical. Montazeri had impeccable credentials for resistance to the shah, having been jailed and tortured more than once. At the same time, his scholarly work would earn him the rank of grand ayatollah and the status of a *marja'*. Although he was from a modest background and was a simple man in habits and speech, Montazeri was regarded as among the most learned of his contemporaries, with significant works on mysticism, ethics, and legal reasoning. Khomeini recognized how indispensable his distinguished former teacher was to his rise. He designated Montazeri as his successor.

Khomeini proceeded to consolidate his hold on power with Montazeri at his side. In time, the scale of the postrevolutionary bloodletting exceeded all expectations. It proceeded more and more recklessly. Estimates of those killed in the revolutionary struggle itself number some 2,000. During Khomeini's postrevolutionary consolidation of power, it is likely that close to three times that number perished. For Montazeri, a turning point came with Khomeini's decision to execute approximately 3,000 political prisoners who had opposed his rule. Already jailed and therefore no immediate threat to the regime, Khomeini nevertheless ordered their slaughter. Montazeri dared to speak out publicly against this outrage. Friends and associates asked later why he had not just kept silent; with Khomeini's passing, he would assume the leadership and could have righted the wrongs into which the revolution had fallen. Montazeri expressed himself plainly: "I could not sleep knowing that people were being killed." Khomeini would not tolerate the open break. In his letter removing Montazeri from his official position and the succession, Khomeini's earlier regard for the man he called "the fruit of my life" lingered.[16] Described as a brilliant exponent of legal reasoning, the ayatollah was ordered to retire to Qom and resume his teaching and research.

Montazeri ended his years engaged fully in his scholarly work while at the same time acting as the spiritual mentor of all those who opposed the tyranny of Iran's theocrats. Montazeri produced path-breaking works that extended the legal tradition from protection of the rights of the faithful to protecting the rights of all Iranian citizens, notably including the Baha'is in Iran.[17] Periodically, he issued ringing criticisms of the Iranian religious establishment, not sparing Ayatollah Ali Khamenei, Khomeini's successor as Supreme Leader. His former protégé, Montazeri pronounced bluntly, was unqualified for the position. Moreover, he lacked the standing of a senior religious scholar, entitled to issue *fatwas*.[18] Iran's most prominent human rights advocate, the Nobel Peace Prize laureate Shirin Ebadi, issued a statement of gratitude to him at the time of the ayatollah's death in 2009: "I call you Father because I learned from you how to defend the oppressed without using violence against the oppressor. I learned from you that being silent is helping the oppressor. Father, I learned much from you, although I never (got the chance to) show my appreciation for being your child and student. Father, forgive us."[19]

Many other leading Shi'i scholars, despite serious reservations about Khomeini's claim, choose silence over overt opposition. That position was very much in line with the traditional stance of Shi'i religious scholars. But not all took this path. Among Shi'a grand ayatollahs, Shariatmadari and Montazeri were not alone in registering courageous opposition to the doctrine of *wilayet al faqih*. The Lebanese grand ayatollah Muhammad Hussein Fadlallah lent his powerful voice to augment that of Shariatmadari and Montazeri. Fadlallah had enthusiastically welcomed the Iranian Revolution. Initially, he expressed support for Khomeini's leadership as well. However, as the authoritarian and arbitrary character of Khomeini's rule became clear, Fadlallah mounted a sharply critical attack. He did so on Islamic grounds, pointedly challenging Khomeini's notion of *wilayet al faqih* as an unacceptable innovation of Shi'i doctrine.

Fadlallah refused outright Khomeini's claim that he, like the Shi'a imams, should be regarded as offering an interpretation of Shi'a doctrine that was beyond challenge. Fadlallah's dissent was clear and forceful. It carried the imprimatur of one of the most respected and beloved of the Shi'a *maraji'*. His critique of the Iranians had broader implications. Fadlallah found the Iranian Islamic scholars loyal to Khomeini arrogant and over-reaching. He said so bluntly. In his view Iran under Khomeini, whatever the initial successes of the revolution, should not be allowed to set itself up as the epicenter of Shi'i Islam. Fadlallah believed that the Iranian *marja'iyya* (collective of *maraji'*) dominated the upper echelon of Shi'i thought to its detriment. He rejected outright the fact that "the Iranian theologians believe that Iran is the only Shi'ite Islamic authority, because they consider Iran as the headquarters of Shi'ite influence. The Iranians believe that all decisions regarding Shi'ite Islam must come from Iran."[20] Fadlallah positioned himself quite purposefully as an Arab Shi'i *marja'*, whose standing in the Shi'i hierarchy equaled or surpassed that of the Iranian clerics. He forcefully made it clear that he did not consider the Iranian religious establishment beyond criticism. Fadlallah rejected outright the Iranian claim that Khomeini and his successor, Ayatollah Ali Khamenei, had a monopoly on truth. "Like all other believers," Fadlallah pronounced categorically, "leaders are fallible and open to criticism."[21]

The opposition of these dissenting ayatollahs was not the only challenge Khomeini faced. The story of the left and liberal opponents of the Iranian theocracy is better known and can therefore be treated in brief. They represented the unrealized progressive possibilities of freedom, democracy, and universal human rights that were all part of the Iranian constitutional tradition. Khomeini, as a senior Shi'a scholar and the symbol of resistance to the regime of the shah, did stir millions in Iran. Nevertheless, he was acutely aware that the possibility of revolution did not belong to him and his followers alone. Khomeini's rise was shadowed by the challenge from the Iranian left and the legions of young people who responded to its appeal. Khomeini's successful crushing of the secular opposition has pushed them out of view. Their significance is now forgotten. Yet none of the cold realists who were players in prerevolutionary Iran had the slightest inclination to underplay the role of the left, not the shah and his brutal SAVAK, not the CIA and its army of paid informers and Iranian co-conspirators, and not Khomeini and his most trusted advisors. They all, rightly, took the challenge from the liberals and the left seriously.

Iran had a strong liberal and constitutional tradition. The country experienced a constitutional revolution in 1906 and that tradition remains very much alive in the Iranian political imagination. The Iranians had a long history of struggle for democracy. They had registered some notable successes, despite the power of those arrayed against a democratic Iran. That prospect shined brightly again in the 1950s under an extraordinary Iranian nationalist, Prime Minister Mosaddegh, who successfully nationalized Iranian oil. In the face of such assertiveness with overwhelming popular support, the United States played its classic, antidemocratic role.

A CIA-engineered coup against the constitutional government installed the shah's regime. Iranians were subjected to decades of his brutally repressive rule. Liberals and leftists were targeted with particular viciousness that aimed for their elimination from public life.

Khomeini was aware that the left and the liberals constituted a serious force. The grand ayatollah was too astute a political figure to ignore them. He took note of those forces and individuals who exerted influence on those hostile segments of the population. Ali Shariati was the most influential of such figures. Shariati appealed to the Iranian left and liberals alike, using an innovative Islamic political discourse with modernist and progressive shadings. We know that Khomeini read Shariati's work, although the grand ayatollah kept his assessment to himself. He must have grasped how different was the revolution Shariati imagined. Yet he also understood how useful Shariati's charismatic appeal, cast in an Islamic idiom, could be to his movement. Shariati died in London in 1977 before the outbreak of revolution. Most believe he was assassinated by the shah's secret police, but, however he died, this charismatic Iranian intellectual had already left his mark. His influence in Iran has endured and now runs through subterranean channels. It remains important for ongoing efforts to conceive of an Islamic alternative to the repressive theocracy Khomeini established.

When *al Nas* (the common people) first erupted onto the streets of Tehran and other major Iranian cities in October 1978 until October 1979, when the shah left the country, Khomeini's was not the only name they chanted. Shariati's name was also on their lips. Today, however, this charismatic figure known to millions of Iranians, especially the youth, is almost always left out of the most influential accounts of the Iranian Revolution. In parallel fashion, Shariati is almost never engaged critically in any of the major works on the broader Islamic Renewal, whether by Western or Muslim authors. At best, there are passing references, sometimes laudatory but more frequently hostile. The misguided message in either case is that Shariati had only marginal influence on the revolution and has had no continuing relevance.

While Khomeini emerged from the conflicted heart of Shi'i Islam, Ali Shariati came from its permeable margins. That difference was not the only one between Shariati and the grand ayatollah who felt nothing. Shariati was a man who felt deeply the suffering of the least of the Iranians, a man whose empathy for the dispossessed gave him an appeal that rivaled that of Khomeini. Shariati himself explained in words that could be taken as a self-description that "the enlightened soul is a person who is self-conscious of his 'human condition' in his time and historical and social setting, and whose awareness inevitably and necessarily gives him a sense of social responsibility."[22] Shariati was not primarily a religious scholar. Nor was he an ideologue of fundamentalist Islam, nor a philosopher in the mold of Sartre or Fanon. He eluded all these categories. For Iranian youth, in particular, Shariati was much more. He was a Shi'i storyteller who, in the guise of a university lecturer, gave them access to the emotional energy and spiritual power of the most progressive strands of their distinctive Islamic heritage. In his writings and lectures Shariati regularly invoked Abu Dharr al Ghifari, Islam's "first socialist" and a companion of the Prophet. In his influential "Where Shall We Begin" Shariati explains that "in the tradition of Abudhar [sic], who is my mentor, whose thought, whose understanding of Islam and Shi'ism, and whose ideals, wants, and rage I emulate . . . I begin my talk with the name of the God of the oppressed (mustad'afan)."[23]

All too often we neglect the power of emotions and feelings when assessing the factors that explain the Islamic Renewal. The reduction of matters to intellectual formulations, political impulses, and movement manipulations misses a great deal. Remarks made by Shariati about a visit to Egypt illustrate just how much. At the pyramids, Shariati marveled at the enormity of the stones used as walls and ceiling for the base of the pyramids. He was entranced by his guide's description of the way in which the countless blocks of stone for the construction were brought to Cairo from Aswan 980 miles away. At a short distance from the site, Shariati noticed scattered mounds of stones. He learned that of the 35,000 slaves who carried stones, uncounted hundreds were crushed to death under the weight of their loads. The site he had noticed was a collective grave. The slaves were buried in a ditch near the pyramids, the guide reported, so their souls could be employed as slaves just as their bodies were.

Shariati asked the guide to leave him alone at the site. He went to the graves and sat down. He reports feeling very close to the people buried in that mass grave, recalling that "it was as if we were of the same race . . . I had nothing but warm feelings and sympathy toward these oppressed souls." Shariati reports that, when leaving the site, he "looked back to the Pyramids and realized that despite their magnificence, they were so strange to and distant from me! In other words, I felt so much hatred towards the great monuments of civilization which throughout history were raised upon the bones of my predecessors!" Broadening his lens, Shariati concludes that "my predecessors also built the great walls of China. Those who could not carry the loads were crushed under the heavy stones and put into the walls with the stones. This was how all the great monuments of civilization were constructed—at the expense of the flesh and blood of my predecessors!"[24]

Shariati elaborated the theoretical and political implications of these intensely personal reflections in his sociological writings. His scholarly work opened new pathways. He aimed for nothing less than to craft a revolutionary Islam. All of his intellectual work reflected that goal. Shariati aimed to turn inherited Shi'i commitments in the direction of radical change. The task was a daunting one. Shariati registered far greater success than one could reasonably expect, given the long history of the Shi'a as a quiescent minority community. The messianic Shi'i doctrine promising the reign of justice with the return of the hidden imam had for centuries rationalized inaction in the face of suffering. Shariati's boldest move was the sundering of the conventional link between waiting for the return of the hidden imam and his reign of justice with patient tolerance of injustice and tyranny. Shariati instead tied the future reign of justice to present revolutionary struggles. He advocated mass action in the now and in the name of the triumph of justice to come. Shariati pointed to the experience of redemption in action that comes with struggles for justice rather than as a consequence of them. Acting for the revolution could advance today that ultimate victory of age-old Shi'i dreams.

Shariati was trained in sociology at the Sorbonne. In his scholarly work, Shariati reasons that an Islamic sociology would be based on the distinctive Qur'anic understanding of the major force that drives historical change. He comments on the two major Western approaches to explain the drivers of large-scale social change. On the one hand, there are those that point to uniquely gifted individuals like Buddha, Jesus, or the Prophet Muhammad. Others look to elites of exceptional skills or gifts, such as clergy or intellectuals. Shariati argued that neither approach has a place in Islam. The Qur'an, he explains, does not recognize the Prophet Muhammad as the active cause of development. He is rather the bearer of the Message that shows the people the school and path of the truth. Shariati points out that the Qur'an most often addresses its message to *al Nas*. The Prophet himself is sent to *al Nas*. *Al Nas*, as Shariati sees it, are the motivating force of both spiritual and worldly progress. As a trained sociologist, Shariati concludes that Islam is the first school of social thought that recognizes the masses

as the driving factor in shaping history and society. That essential role does
not belong to the elect, as Nietzsche thought; nor the aristocracy and nobil-
ity, as Plato claimed; nor great personalities, as Carlyle and Emerson believed; nor those of pure blood, as Alexis Carrel imagined; nor the priests
or intellectuals; nor the workers alone, as Marx envisioned. For Shariati it is
ordinary people, the masses, *al Nas*, who drive history forward. In *Religion
against Religion* Shariati points out that the Qur'an opens with God and
ends with *al Nas*. He goes further. Speaking in a sociological rather than
theological sense, Shariati boldly declares that one can substitute *al Nas* for
God in the whole of the Qur'an without altering its meaning.[25]

Revolutions, unlike coups, succeed through mass action. Shariati
was no democrat. He embraced *al Nas* but paid little attention to the mechanics of how the popular will would be expressed. These unaddressed
considerations, however important, did not diminish Shariati's ability to
bring segments of the left and the liberals into a mass movement under
an Islamic banner. Ali Shariati never wore the turban. He never spoke for
the religious establishment. The man who did most to bring the people,
especially the urban and educated youth, to Iran's revolutionary moment
was not an ayatollah, not an Islamic scholar of standing. Inconsistencies
and scholarly inadequacies are everywhere apparent in the body of Shariati's writings. They mattered little. What we have are for the most part
lecture notes, rather than sustained and polished works. They reflect the
status of his thought at the time of delivery, rather than his considered,
scholarly views. The coherence of Shariati's work flows from the extraordinary boldness of his project itself and the eloquence of its articulation.
Iranians revere their poets, as I do. The way thoughts are expressed matters greatly. Shariati used his rhetorical skills to craft nothing less than a
revolutionary Islam. Ultimately, what made it possible for Shariati to play
this role had less to do with his familiarity with the left-leaning thought
of Jean-Paul Sartre, his study of the Third World leftism of Frantz Fanon,
or his graduate training in Western sociology under such luminaries as
Jacques Berque. More important than all of these undoubted influences
was the sheer magic of Shariati as a storyteller who took his materials
from his heritage.

Abdulkarim Soroush, a leading Iranian philosopher and public intellectual, has best described Shariati's inimitable contribution:

Shariati's master stroke was to bring to life the tale of Ashura
and Imam Hussain, Zainab's captivity and the captivity of Imam

Hussain's kith and kin, and the events of Karbala as a whole. He was, in all fairness, an expert—with a magical touch—when it came to cultivating this story and bringing Shi'a's blood to the boil; no one has been able to surpass him in this.[26]

Boldness made Shariati a brilliant and irresistible force for revolution, no matter the inconsistencies in his thought, the disinterest in democracy, and the selective treatment of the history of the Shi'a. Revolutions require blood brought to a boil. Shariati had that magic touch.

Necmettin Erbakan and the Spirit of Islam in Turkey

Turkey is now a destination. For decades, in the wake of the dissolution of the Ottoman Empire, the new Turkish state was generally viewed as a bridge between East and West. The secular elite fashioned by Kemal Atatürk embraced this bridge metaphor with misplaced pride. They made it part of their emerging Turkish national identity. In this formulation, the East and the West were real places. Turkey, by implication, was not. It was simply a passageway from one real place to another. Turkey itself had an insecure and fragmented identity. Turkish identity was presumed to be fractured between the identities of those others who walked over it. Samuel Huntington famously pronounced Turkey a "torn country," with an elite that yearned to be Western and masses who knew they belonged to the Islamic world.[27] The description stuck. A Western political scientist innocent of any deep understanding of Turkey or the Islamic world to which it belonged should be forgiven for not noticing that the Turkish elite was not nearly as monolithic as his observation suggested. An Islamic alternative, grounded in the Ottoman experience, shadowed the secular Turkish republic. It drew its greatest strength from mass support, as Huntington understood. Yet from that mass base emerged an impressive counter-elite with an Islamic orientation that had deep roots in the Ottoman age and a rich tradition of Turkish mysticism. It survived despite Atatürk's assault on all things Islamic. That Islamic counter-elite not only grew in strength but also developed its own distinctive understanding of Turkish national identity and the capacity to repair the tears.

Said Nursi had done the essential intellectual heavy lifting that yielded an Islamic strategy to make post-Ottoman Turkey whole. Nursi and the Nurcu movement prepared Turkey as no other to make a distinctive contribution to the success of the Islamic Renewal and to ensure

Turkey's key role in it. "The Wonder of the Age" cast nationalism in Islamic terms. Nursi and the Nurcu movement that he founded made substantial progress in developing a body of Islamic political thought. They also carried out a program of pragmatic social activism of Islamic inspiration that reinforced connections to the masses of Turks, especially those in the countryside. It was Nursi and his followers who forged the critical link among Islam, democracy, and nationalism in Turkey. He moderated all three elements of this potent synthesis. He blended the three to give Turkey its distinctive contemporary character. Such would be the banner of the Islamic counter-elite. For decades the Islamic nationalism of Nursi's inspiration had remained a subterranean current. It was not until 1950 that the Turkish polity opened to multiparty competition. Only then could political ideas and practices with a clear Islamic character emerge from the shadows. When that time came, the Islamic current demonstrated its impressive strength.

The seemingly absolute ascendency of an extreme secular authoritarianism, fervently backed by the West, had delayed but not derailed the effects of Said Nursi's work. It took several decades to realize his vision. The man who did most to make that possible was Necmettin Erbakan (1926–2011). He rarely receives the recognition his contributions merit. The full scope of his achievements is almost never registered, not even in Turkey. Turkish analysts note that "there are no extensive studies today that deal with the contribution of Erbakan to our political life."[28] At best, Erbakan is regarded as having laid the foundations for "political Islam" in Turkey. At worst, he is denounced as a reactionary fundamentalist.

Nursi envisioned. Erbakan did a great deal to realize the vision. The very notion of political Islam was alien to Nursi and his legions of followers. For them, Islam was a comprehensive system. Nursi was far from a backward-looking fundamentalist. Nursi's complex vision blended a comprehensive and centrist Islam with nationalism and democracy. Erbakan took the crucial steps that made the realization of that larger vision possible by planting the first seeds of a politics that would give it practical expression. Turkey today is a unique place where Islam, democracy, and a robust economic and political nationalism all flourish. That outcome owes much more than is generally acknowledged to Necmettin Erbakan.

Erbakan's story is usually told as the confrontation of an extremist religious ideologue with the Turkish military that is cast as the vigilant guardian of secularism. The high point of his political career is the post of prime minister, which he held for a period of just under a year. The denouement is always the "soft" military coup that unceremoniously pushed him off center stage in February 1997. The tale ends with a marginalized Erbakan lapsing into a paranoid politics of frustrated impotence and shrill rhetoric.

This conventional history is little more than a caricature of the man and his historic role in Turkish political life. It obscures all of the really significant dimensions of a career that made Erbakan not only a major figure in the shaping of modern Turkish nationalism but also a genuine herald of the Islamic Renewal. The portrait of the irrational ideologue begins to blur when we know that Erbakan was a highly educated and accomplished engineer. He studied mechanical engineering in Istanbul Technical University, one of Turkey's most respected universities. He received his Ph.D. in Germany from RWTH Aachen University, renowned for its world-class mechanical engineering program. Returning to Turkey, Erbakan proved himself as an engineer with several important inventions. He went on to success in business. It was his role as a university professor of mechanical engineering, however, that seemed to suit him best. Erbakan's manner was above all professorial, down to his emphatic pointing gestures to drive home a point. Throughout his active political life, Erbakan was known affectionately to his followers as Hodja, "the teacher." Yet even the professorial image only went so far. Erbakan contradicted it on the lighter side with a sartorial taste that found its signature statement in Versace ties. He also undermined the reassuring image of the thoughtful professor with a propensity for hyperbolic attacks on perceived enemies. At various times, the list included Zionists, communists, leftists, secularists, and even former protégés like the current prime minister, Recep Tayyip Erdogan. Erdogan incurred his mentor's wrath when he bolted from his camp to found the Justice and Development Party (AK) that today dominates Turkish politics.

These details of the highly successful and deeply contradictory life of a real human being do spoil the simple lines caricature requires. However, they also point in revealing ways to the balance of impressive talents and serious flaws of a larger-than-life political figure. Erbakan was a major political figure in Turkish public life for decades. On that score alone, he deserves attention. When the field of vision is broadened beyond Turkey to take in all of *Dar al Islam*, the point has even greater force. Erbakan staked an explicit claim very early as a champion of the worldwide *ummah* rather than simply as a defender of Islam in Turkey. In 1969 he published a manifesto, *Milli Gorus* or the *National View*. Turks read the title correctly as the *Islamic View*. They understood that all direct references to Islam were banned at the time the document was first published. Erbakan's manifesto blended Islamic Ottoman influences with Turkish nationalist commitments. He addressed to transnational Islam a call for the solidarity of all Muslim peoples) in order to face what he saw as the unrelenting hostility of Israel and the West. *Milli Gorus*, in short, was a defensive call to Islamic Renewal, addressed to Muslims worldwide.

Based on this program, Erbakan in 1970 founded the first of a series of five Islamic parties. They all had the same general Islamic orientation that challenged the reigning secularism. He faced all manner of obstructions. His party suffered a series of closures, only to have the resolute and remarkably irrepressible Erbakan reconstitute his Islamic party under yet another different name. The Turkish military seized power through coups in 1960, 1971, 1980, and 1997. Erbakan was a preferred and frequent target. He was imprisoned once, banned from political life for an extended period, and exiled for several years to Switzerland. Given these daunting obstacles, his political successes as an Islamic political figure are even more impressive. They were not confined to Turkey but had a transnational reach. He was the founding father in 1969 of Millî Görüş, the leading Turkish diaspora organization in Europe. Reasonable estimates in 2005 placed membership across Europe at close to 90,000, with some 50,000 in Germany alone.

In the Turkish political arena, Erbakan rose to the pinnacle of power, although he was unable to consolidate that position. In the 1970s, Turkey's most prominent Islamic political figure served twice as deputy prime minister. Finally, for almost a year in 1996–1997, Erbakan served as Turkish prime minister. As prime minister, Erbakan immediately sought to reorient Turkish policies. He advanced a bold vision for the new direction. In the domestic arena, he challenged extreme secularists and sought accommodation with moderates. In foreign affairs, he outlined an alternative to dependence on the West. The actual steps taken were modest and practical but they pointed to a bold, new direction.

There was nothing conspiratorial or extremist about Erbakan's Islamic sympathies and the ways he sought to translate them into policies. He was forthright and honest with the Turkish public in the way he presented himself and his party. His policy initiatives lay fully within the range of reasonable actions for a new prime minister with a distinctive electoral mandate. At home, he advanced a program of modest social reforms, designed to reclaim a reasonable space for Islam in public life.

Typical of his program of small steps was lifting the ban on Islamic dress for women in governmental offices, universities, and other public spaces as well as adjusting working hours to accommodate Islamic worship practices.

The prime minister's foreign policy measures were more dramatic, and especially disconcerting to both Israel and the United States. Erbakan's first foreign trip in office was to the Islamic Republic of Iran rather than either Europe or the United States. Erbakan signaled clearly that he intended to use his office to reposition Turkey in the global arena. Erbakan's pain at the suffering of the Islamic world at the hands of the West was heartfelt. It prompted a search for ways of connecting in more meaningful ways to Islamic countries. To that end, he took the lead in founding the Developing Eight (D-8), an international organization of eight Muslim-majority countries focused on socioeconomic development. The members were Bangladesh, Egypt, Indonesia, Iran, Malaysia, Nigeria, Pakistan, and Turkey. The organization's program implicitly criticized the American-dominated world order. It embraced peace rather than conflict, dialogue rather than confrontation, cooperation rather than exploitation, justice rather than double standards, equality rather than discrimination, and democracy rather than oppression. In a parallel track, Erbakan set in motion a series of measures designed to improve relations with Arab countries. When Erbakan was pushed out of office by the military, the mainstream American press reported that the case against him centered on his moving Turkey away from its pro-Western orientation, as though such a reorientation was a crime sufficient to warrant a military coup.

Through his political party experiments, Erbakan succeeded in creating a space for Islam in Turkish public life. The opportunities he created allowed promising young people with Islamic commitments to gain practical political experience. Erbakan's political campaigns were consistently marked by successful grassroots networking across class, gender, and ethnic lines. The fact that important electoral victories were registered gave added weight to this critical political training of a whole generation of politically experienced, Islamic activists. Erbakan created a model of effective grassroots organization. He showed how to combine a revolt against the establishment's injustice, cruelty, and cultural alienation with historical and emotional connection to the people's heritage and sentiments. It is this ability to connect with the masses in culturally meaningful ways that gives Islamic movements an edge over other political trends, notably the Marxists.

Erbakan's practice of a pragmatic politics, suffused with the ethos of centrist Islam, had set strong roots. The Islam for which Erbakan spoke had a modern character that diminished the appeal of Turkish extremists. It is now often forgotten that there were alternative extremist Islamic strategies and militants to implement them during his years of active political work. Erbakan's presence pushed them to the margins, although this signal achievement is rarely noted. Extremists never gained a foothold in the politicized Turkish Islam that Erbakan dominated. On social and religious practice issues, Erbakan was demonstrably a conservative. This stance had its advantages. For years Erbakan provided a centrist political home for socially conservative Turks, thus further diminishing the appeal of the militants.

Erbakan's brief for a centrist, if conservative, Islam in public life had as its corollary a commitment to democratic politics. He understood that the overwhelming majority of Turks had deep attachments to Islam. Democracy would provide the rightful vehicle for the ascendency of Turkish Islam. There is no evidence at all that Erbakan ever seriously considered any other pathway to power for the Islamic trend other than the ballot box. His success in electoral politics validated the soundness of his judgment. Erbakan made perhaps his most important political contribution in accepting the outcomes of a democratic political process, even one at times highly circumscribed and frequently short-circuited by the military.

Erbakan's achievements are to this day overshadowed by charges that he was an erratic and even irrational fundamentalist. Without doubt, Erbakan as prime minister broke all the rules for those days. He was and behaved as the representative of an alternative political orientation. He expressed an identity for Turkey other than that of a bridge to the West. He moved in new ways. He generated new ideas. Americans, Israelis, and secular Turks all felt, quite rightly, that they had no friend in Erbakan. Quite clearly, Erbakan opposed Western policies in the Middle East. Just as clearly and certainly more forcefully, Erbakan was anti-Zionist and pro-Palestinian, although with few consequences on the ground. At the same time, he did not hesitate to challenge the uncontested reign of secularism in Turkey. The label of moderation consistently eluded Erbakan, despite his democratic commitments and importance in containing Islamic extremists. To earn the moderate label a leader must be 100 percent pro-Western and deferential to Israeli power and influence. Erbakan failed both tests. His accomplishments for the Islamic Renewal all flow from those "shortcomings."

Like Ghazzali and like all of the heralds of the Renewal, Erbakan understood contemporary conditions through an unforgiving historical lens. To understand Erbakan, it is essential to grasp first that his core motivations went beyond narrow Turkish interests. His worldview was shaped by a sense of the profound injustice of a predatory Western imperialism that assaulted *Dar al Islam*. Moreover, he regarded as illegitimate the postcolonial regimes that were the stepchildren of imperialism. They most often arose from the military and imposed their rule through coups. For Erbakan, developments in Turkey under a pro-Western, secular, and military-dominated regime were part of a much larger pattern of destructive Western dominance and distorted political development.

Erbakan viewed Israel from this same perspective. Zionism in his view was a virulent settler colonialism ideology, spawned in the West and very much like the colonizing ideology of the French in Algeria. In parallel with leftist and secular trends, Erbakan saw the Israeli occupation and colonization of the remnants of historic Palestine as an extension of the West's colonizing past. The extreme harshness of the Israeli occupation and the systematic repression of Palestinians outraged Erbakan. His language was at times intemperate and un-Islamic, notably when he lapsed into condemnatory language that blamed Jews in general for the actions of the Israeli state in violation of international law. However, you do not need the template of Western anti-Semitism to understand his distaste for the triumphant Zionist state of Israel. The French deserved exactly the same condemnations for their horrific record in Algeria. Erbakan stood with the Palestinians. He suffered with them the pain and loss of displacement and humiliation at the hands of arrogant European immigrants who occupied their country and appropriated their land and natural resources. Erbakan correctly judged that, rhetoric aside, the United States had embraced the project of a greater Israel and lent the expansionist Israeli state extraordinary levels of aid of all kinds.

Erbakan had made it possible to formulate an Islamic political program and organize an Islamic party within a parliamentary democracy. The military eventually moved against Erbakan. The event that pushed them into action appears to be the support of his party for protests against Israeli human rights violations and overt support for Arab national liberation movements: Hamas in the occupied Palestinian territories and Hizbullah in Lebanon. The military leadership prepared an elaborate indictment and forced the prime minister to sign a bill of particulars that included restricting Islam once more in public life, such as a ban on headscarves in universities, the shuttering of Qur'anic schools, and the closing of Sufi orders. Erbakan acquiesced. He refused to resort to violence in response to the military intervention. The prime minister resigned, accepting a five-year ban on all political activity. Erbakan's acquiescence in disabling military interventions in politics is at times characterized in deprecating terms, even by sympathetic observers. One well-informed observer of the Turkish scene comments that when faced with a military ultimatum in 1997 Erbakan "sheepishly left office . . . and accepted a withdrawal from political activity for a period of five years in what amounted to a bloodless coup prompted by his alleged Islamic agenda."[29] This characterization misses an important point. Like Nursi, Erbakan worked for the long term. He sought to accommodate the superior power of the secular forces, while at the same time building a popular base that would eventually make a successful and lawful democratic victory possible. In retrospect, there is more statesmanship than sheepishness in that judgment. The action is a testament to Erbakan's moderation among the Islamic groups. He clearly saved Turkey from unproductive, violent clashes between Islamic and secular forces. Erbakan absorbed the blows, without the resort to violence. However, he also refused to disappear from the political arena and encouraged Islamic political activists to stay the course and take advantage of whatever political possibilities remained open. In so doing, Erbakan secured the banner of democracy for the Islamic trend.

Ultimately, it was an offshoot of Erbakan's party that devised the formula that Said Nursi and Necmettin Erbakan had anticipated. There were no shortfalls in Erbakan's principled resoluteness. However, there were serious limits to the practical course he adopted. Erbakan's Welfare Party was disbanded by a ruling of the constitutional court in 1998. True to form, Erbakan managed its reemergence as the Virtue Party that entered general elections in 1999, but, it too, was banned in 2001. Party activists came to believe they were trapped in a cul-de-sac. Leadership elements from the Virtue Party bolted. Led by Recep Tayyip Erdogan, these young and savvy activists broke with Erbakan to form the Justice and Development Party with a distinctive new approach. The Justice and Development Party presented itself as a secular party, although one with Islamic roots. Erdogan argued for a more inclusive political formula. He sought to combine a respect for religious belief with commitments to democracy, capitalism, and the continuance of Western alliances. More traditional elements continued with the old politics under Erbakan's leadership. They were pushed to the margins and drifted into irrelevance.

Erdogan had found the pragmatic formula, essentially a refined and amended version of the one that Erbakan had pioneered, that eventually brought him to power and has kept him there for over a decade. He was able to consolidate that power in a way that Erbakan had never achieved. Once that power was secure, Erdogan could move legally against the military conspirators. He did so with great effect. Leading members of the military opposition were tried for conspiracy, found guilty, and received lengthy sentences in August 2013. The hold of the military over Turkish political life was broken. It is clear that the formula that produced this dramatic success for the Islamic trend was not one that Erbakan could have invented or embraced. However, it is just as clear that no formula at all could have taken shape without Erbakan's indispensable preparatory work.

Alija Izetbegovic and the Islamic Renewal in Europe

Alija Izetbegovic heralded *al Tagdid al Islami* as a midstream Islamic intellectual and reluctant nationalist. Throughout his career, a strong and consistent commitment to a political project of pluralism and democracy within an Islamic framework informed his intellectual and political work. Yet, despite his very visible public presence and extensive writings, a reasonable appraisal of Izetbegovic emerges only with great difficulty. Portraits abound of Izetbegovic as a radical Bosnian nationalist. They alternate with even more misleading characterizations as an Islamic extremist. He was neither. A very public and easily verifiable record of impressive consistency as a centrist Islamic intellectual and activist defines the main outlines of Izetbegovic's political career and of all his important writings.

For the world, the most enduring image of Alija Izetbegovic will undoubtedly be that of the besieged leader, governing Bosnia-Herzegovina from his sandbagged offices in Sarajevo. Izetbegovic, as the first president of Bosnia-Herzegovina, led his people in the Bosnian War of 1992–1995. After Bosnia and Herzegovina declared independence, the Bosnian Serbs laid siege to the capital with a force of 13,000, stationed in the hills overlooking the city. For almost four years, the world watched as Serbian forces pounded the city with heavy artillery from the surrounding hills. The building housing the presidential office was continuously targeted. Some fifty people were killed in and around that one building alone. An international arms embargo prevented the Bosnian government from acquiring heavy weaponry to match the more advanced Serbian arsenal. Residents of multiethnic Sarajevo included Muslims, Croats, and Serbs. All those who remained in the city opposed Serbian aspirations for a greater Serbia. They paid a terrible price for their resistance. The prolonged siege denied them adequate food, utilities, and communication, Throughout Bosnia, Serb nationalist forces conducted a campaign of brutal ethnic cleansing to "purify" the land of non-Serbs. Entire towns and villages were destroyed and their inhabitants, predominantly Muslim, expelled, imprisoned in detention camps, raped, tortured, or killed. Muslim women were systematically raped as an act of war. Lives lost in the Bosnian war exceeded a quarter-million, with over 11,000 killed in the siege of Sarajevo alone. The single most shocking incident was the cold-blooded massacre of an estimated 8,000 unarmed Muslim boys and men at Srebrenica in 1995.

Izetbegovic refused to surrender. He remained at his desk in beleaguered Sarajevo for three and a half years, the duration of the siege. A sober and unshakable Izetbegovic rallied the forces of resistance while giving blunt and truthful assessments of Bosnia's dire situation. While the West stood aside, Bosnians drowned in a river of blood that ran through their capital and across their countryside. As president of a people facing genocide, Izetbegovic did what he could to find the means to stave off destruction. He turned for assistance to the Muslim world, receiving support from Saudi Arabia and Turkey. A grateful people recognized that Izetbegovic's inspiring leadership and their own incalculable sacrifices made possible Bosnia's survival as a pluralistic, Muslim-majority state.

Alongside his nationalist commitments and achievements, Izetbegovic registered an even greater historical importance as one of the major Islamic intellectuals and activists of the twentieth century. He was an early and insightful champion of the Islamic Renewal. Yet most see only the impressive political role of national leadership. Alija Izetbegovic began his political rise as an anticommunist in Marshal Tito's Yugoslavia. He was imprisoned twice by the government. With the weakening of the Yugoslav state, Izetbegovic, along with scores of other political prisoners, was released, after serving just over five years on his second imprisonment. He immediately organized a political party to participate in the emerging constitutional order. His Party of Democratic Action (SDA) proved to be the most effective in Bosnia. It became known in Bosnia, as well as internationally, as the representative of Bosnian Muslims. As party leader, Izetbegovic was elected head of the Bosnian joint presidency in 1990. The Bosnia-Herzegovina that Izetbegovic headed differed from the other Yugoslav successor states in that no single cultural community dominated. Bosnia came into statehood with a volatile mix of Muslims (44 percent), Eastern Orthodox Serbs (31 percent), and Catholic Croats (17 percent). Power-driven elites in the neighboring republics exploited the latent communal hostilities within Bosnia. Serbia and Croatia schemed openly to divide Bosnia-Herzegovina between them. They looked to their respective co-religionists in Bosnia to support these plans to dismember the country. Their aim, as Izetbegovic described it, was no less than "to wipe our country off the map." In March 1994, Bosnian Muslims and Croats managed to form a joint federation that reduced the combatants to two, a Muslim–Croat alliance versus the Serbs. The war that ensued took some 250,000 lives. The fighting did not subside until NATO, after a long delay, stepped in to bomb Serbian positions in Bosnia in August and September 1995. Izetbegovic signed the Dayton Peace Accord in November 1995, although he did not believe Bosnian Muslims had received full justice by its terms.

In 1996, Izetbegovic was reelected to the three-member collective presidency. He remained in office despite the great difficulties of dealing with a war-torn country. Well-documented fraud and corruption plagued the president's efforts to build a democratic Bosnia. Izetbegovic did not deny the existence of corruption. Yet, for all the limitations of what Bosnia accomplished during the short period of Izetbegovic's postwar leadership, the country reasserted the commitment to a tolerant pluralism that was the hallmark of the Bosnian capital city of Sarajevo. Far from a fundamentalist Islamic state, Bosnia preserved its open and progressive character. Women were prominent in all occupations. No attempts were made to implement a strict interpretation of *Shari'ah*. Non-Muslim Bosnians worshipped freely in Muslim-majority areas. Churches in Sarajevo were protected, in contrast to the mosques in Serbian-held territories, which were systematically destroyed by Serb and Croat armed forces. Dayton did not end the travail of the Bosnians; the accords terminated the overt violence but not the conflict between the three antagonistic communities. The ultranationalist former president Radovan Karadzic remained in de facto control of the Serbian enclave. Under his leadership, the Bosnian Serbs largely ignored the terms of the accords. Large numbers of refugees were not able to return to their homes in Serbian-controlled areas. Serious reconstruction and development efforts were delayed. A greatly discouraged Izetbegovic resigned the presidency in 2000. He announced that he could not live with the unworkable arrangements imposed on Bosnia by the international community.

It is understandable that the high-profile political career in an area that attracted global attention has overwhelmed all else. Yet, from the first, Alija Izetbegovic himself had placed his commitments to a Bosnian state in a larger Islamic framework. By his own measure, it was the revival of Islam and the renewal of the *ummah* that defined his most important lifework. The battle to protect vulnerable Bosnians was always part of this larger transnational struggle for an Islamic renaissance. At heart, Izetbegovic's life struggle was a spiritual one. Izetbegovic had great success as a political figure, yet the trappings of power and privilege left him unmoved. The Egyptian journalist and Islamic intellectual Fahmi Huwaidi reports on his visit to Izetbegovic. He was struck that Bosnia's president continued to live in his very ordinary Sarajevo apartment, without any special guards or ceremonial markings for a president's residence.[30]

A crisis of faith, rather than a political event, precipitated this lifetime journey. Izetbegovic was born near Sarajevo and educated in the city's elite gymnasium that boasted a traditional European education, with a curriculum that included classical Greek. At an early age, Izetbegovic established a degree of personal autonomy from his parents, making his own life choices, including in matters of faith. As a teenager in communist Yugoslavia, Izetbegovic was bombarded with official atheist propaganda. Religion was cast as a villain in the human struggle for freedom and dignity. At age fifteen, he reports, "I began to waiver in my faith." It was easy, he acknowledges, to fall for the line that "placed God on the side of injustice." However, after a year or two of anxious vacillation, Izetbegovic's faith in Islam returned, although in a different fashion. The Islam that he reclaimed was "no longer merely the religion I had inherited: it was a newly adopted faith. I never lost it again."[31] From that time on, Alija was a Muslim by conviction and conscious choice. He remained a committed and practicing Muslim all his life. Izetbegovic always refused to join the Yugoslav communist party, despite great pressure to do so. He was equally repelled by fascism as ideology. From his early manhood, Izetbegovic chose Islam as a third way. That decision proved to be a fateful one. It set the course of his life. The very bookish young man read prodigiously. In his late teens and early twenties, Izetbegovic built on his excellent secondary education, devouring major Western works of philosophy, social thought, and history. Izetbegovic acquired familiarity with the best of the European intellectual tradition, from the Vienna Circle to Marxism. Such diverse key figures as Kant, Bergson, and Spengler left a visible imprint on his intellectual and moral development.

Izetbegovic read this Western literature against the backdrop of his heightened commitment to Islam. He saw clearly the weaknesses of the Islamic world. Yet the shortcomings of Muslims did not diminish his sense of the contribution that Islam had made to human progress and its continued promise for humanity. Izetbegovic judged that, under the leadership of the West, the world had gone terribly wrong. The disasters of the twentieth century, he concluded, had intellectual roots in the short-comings of Western thought and moral roots in the limitations of Christianity. Izetbegovic was neither anti-Western nor anti-Christian; he was pro-Islam. At the same time, Izetbegovic was deeply dismayed by what he saw as the degradation of Muslims. "Islam," wrote Izetbegovic in a much-quoted passage, "is the best. But we Muslims are not the best."[32] These were the key ideas that lay behind Izetbegovic's momentous *Islamic Declaration*, written and circulated in 1970.

It was the *Islamic Declaration* that placed Izetbegovic in the company of Ghazzali, Erbakan, and Shariati as a herald of the Renewal. The *Declaration* also positioned Izetbegovic squarely in the sights of the security authorities. Izetbegovic was accused and tried as an Islamic fundamentalist. The charges opened with his role while no more than sixteen years old in founding the Muslim Youth organization. They closed with extensive references to the *Islamic Declaration* that the prosecutors used as evidence of his subversive fundamentalism. Izetbegovic defended the work and refused to disavow any of his ideas and commitments.

Izetbegovic's manifesto is very much a committed Muslim's *cri de coeur*. It sounds the alarm for an Islam vulnerable and under assault. The *Islamic Declaration*, despite all the misrepresentation to which it has been subject, makes a strong case for a spiritual revival on the basis of centrist Islam. The work cautions against the excesses to which nationalism is prone. It is no less wary of the extremisms to which religion can succumb. Izetbegovic calls on Muslims in the shattered and dangerous world of the Balkans to find the strength and resources to rebuild their lives on the foundation of an inclusive Islamic identity, as part of the worldwide *ummah*.[33] The case for Izetbegovic as a radical nationalist requires overlooking the fact that Bosnia is not mentioned even once in the entire document. The characterization of Izetbegovic as an Islamic extremist is typically made by a tendentious reading, supported by the selective use of quotations taken out of context. Both sets of distortions effortlessly disappear when the complete text is read.

The *Islamic Declaration* seeks to "Islamize Muslims." Izetbegovic's is a work of severe Muslim self-criticism. The harshness of judgments is all self-directed. The portrait of contemporary Muslims and their failings is unsparing. The moral state of the Muslim world, Izetbegovic writes, is one "of depravity, the rule of corruption and superstition, indolence and hypocrisy, the reign of un-Islamic customs and habits, a callous materialism and a disturbing absence of enthusiasm and hope."[34] Equally harsh is the judgment that the postcolonial secular regimes throughout the area are incompatible with Islam and are destined to pass from the scene. Turkey, as shaped by Atatürk, is taken as the most egregious example. Such imposed un-Islamic systems that imitate the worst of Western structures contradict the values and beliefs of Muslim peoples. In forceful terms, Izetbegovic judges that "there can be neither peace nor coexistence between the Islamic faith and non-Islamic social and political institutions."[35] This sentence is endlessly quoted to make the point that Izetbegovic opposes accommodation between Muslims and non-Muslims or between Islamic states and non-Islamic states. In fact, the reference is purely internal: It refers to non-Islamic regimes imposed on Muslims in the postcolonial era. Izetbegovic argues that such alien postcolonial regimes imposed on countries throughout the *ummah* should not be tolerated. Centrist Islamic intellectuals across *Dar al Islam* share that judgment.

Although often mistaken as essentially a radical nationalist, Izetbegovic is quite clear that the preferred way forward is the path of Islam rather than nationalism. Moreover, his Islamic vision and mission is a broad one that is not confined to the Balkans. It is a common misreading to see Izetbegovic's lifework as centered on forging a sense of identity for Bosnia's Muslim community. Many Bosnian Muslims were nonpracticing, while others identified themselves as either Serbs or Croats. Izetbegovic clearly did encourage, not least by his own example, stronger commitment to the practice of the faith. However, from the outset Izetbegovic's own Bosnian nationalism and Islamic commitments developed within the much larger framework of the *ummah* as a moral community for Muslims everywhere. Izetbegovic, like other heralds of the Renewal, insisted that the Islamic notion of community was inherently pluralistic. Islamic civilization was not the product of Muslims alone. Islam was never alone in God's world. An Islamic identity was not an exclusionary one.

In Izetbegovic's own mind there was never any confusion as to where his priorities resided. He regularly explained his reservations about all varieties of nationalism and his unbounded commitment to the worldwide Islamic community. Islam generated large dreams. Izetbegovic shuns local nationalisms and looks to the strengthening of the universal *ummah* that extends as a spiritual community from Morocco to Indonesia.[36] Izetbegovic does know the history of political disunity that has characterized the Islamic world. It is perfectly clear that he did not aim, in any practical way, for the political unity of the *ummah*. Rather, he explains how the spiritual trumps the political to preserve a higher form of unity. Historically, Izetbegovic records, such has been the case since the Middle Ages. The political divisions that shattered the early Islamic empires "did not lead to the breaking of cultural links, and that was characteristic for the entire Islamic Middle Ages."[37] From these facts of history, Izetbegovic concludes that Islamic culture was unified in the spiritual values of Islam. There are no political boundaries that impede the value connections. Spiritually, Muslims are a single, supranational community, despite all the variations in their political conditions.

Like Ghazzali, Erbakan, and Shariati, Izetbegovic understood that global Islam's most important reserves of unifying cultural and spiritual ties had taken root in the hearts of millions of ordinary people rather than in state structures. These figures are great inasmuch as they represented the unarticulated sentiments and aspirations of Muslims around the world, as much as Nasser was an expression of the longings of Arabs throughout history for social justice, independence, and progress. The *Islamic Declaration* explains:

> the real support which a Muslim people gives to the regime in power is in direct proportion to the Islamic character of that power. The further the regime is from Islam, the less support it will receive. Un-Islamic regimes remain almost totally deprived of this support and therefore have to seek it, willy-nilly, from foreigners. The dependence into which they sink is a direct consequence of their non-Islamic orientation.[38]

Izetbegovic elaborated his assessment of nationalism by contrasting it to pan-Islamism. He noted that "pan-Islamism always came from the very heart of the Muslim peoples; nationalism was always imported stuff."[39] Addressing his fellow Muslims in the very personal and reflective *Notes from Prison*, Izetbegovic advises his fellow Muslims everywhere to "start thinking of yourself as a Muslim, in order to rescue yourself from the narrow confines of the tribe or nation. Become protagonists of the Islamic Renewal and Islamic culture."[40]

President Gamal Abdul Nasser of Egypt once asked Marshal Tito what he thought of Alija Izetbegovic. Tito collaborated with Nasser and Nehru of India to lead the nonaligned movement. Arab analysts report that Tito told Nasser that he considered Izetbegovic far more dangerous than the Muslim Brothers, whom Nasser regarded as his major opponents. At that time the Brothers did not advocate the formation of an Islamic political party. In contrast, Tito explained that Izetbegovic believed that those who advocate an Islamic revival should organize politically to seek power. Moreover, Izetbegovic believed that the preferred route to power would be the ballot box in democratic elections. Such democratic political views naturally alarmed authoritarians like Tito and Nasser. Izetbegovic clearly spelled out their logic in the *Declaration*. The essential premise of Izetbegovic's thinking is the necessity for both a religious and political revolution. The *Declaration* explicitly states that "the religious renewal has a clear priority." The starting point for the religious transformation would necessarily be Islam itself. For all the battering that the faith had suffered, Islam, he wrote, is "alive . . . not a desert." Yet Izetbegovic also cautioned that Islam is one thing and the historical record of Muslims another. Great damage had been done to Muslim peoples. The renaissance would necessarily follow "from the principles and nature of Islam and not from the dismal facts characteristic of the Muslim world today."[41] As a first step to the ultimate renaissance, Izetbegovic called for a moral revolution to close that gap between the higher principles of Islam and the disappointing behavior of contemporary Muslims. In the wake of that religious reform, the political revolution would follow. The heart of the political revolution would be the democratic exercise of power by the post-reform Muslim majority.

The journey would be a long one to prepare Muslim peoples for these responsibilities. Izetbegovic portrayed that struggle for moral rebirth in classic Qur'anic terms. At heart, the struggle would be the great *jihad*, the internal moral struggle to be a better human being. This Qur'anic understanding places a sense of responsibility front and center on the individual Muslim. Izetbegovic argued forcefully that while criticism of others can be merited, the real sign of maturity is self-criticism. In a particularly insightful passage, he elaborated on this notion:

When I think about the situation of Muslims throughout the world, my first question always reads: Do we have the destiny that we deserve, and are others always to blame for our situation and defeats? And if we are to blame—and I believe so—what did we miss doing, but should have done, or, what did we do, yet should not have? For me, these are two unavoidable questions regarding our unenviable situation.[42]

Izetbegovic took particular care to warn against succumbing to the destructive temptation to demonize the dominant Western powers and attribute all failures to Western machinations. In a stunning passage in a later work he elaborated on these terms:

> The West is neither corrupted nor degenerate. It is strong, well-educated, and organized. Their schools are better than ours. Their cities are cleaner than ours. The level of respect for human rights in the West is higher, and the care for the poor and less capable is better organized. Westerners are usually responsible and accurate in their words. Instead of hating the West, let us proclaim cooperation instead of confrontation.[43]

That plainly expressed admiration for certain characteristics of Western societies stands out against the dominant anti-Western conspiracy theories that proliferate in the Arab and Islamic worlds. However, Izetbegovic did not extend his admiration to imitation of a Western model of transformation or to the terrible Western culture of violence that haunted Western pathways. The Turkish example of Westernization from above was a powerful negative one for Izetbegovic. His anticommunism did not translate into admiration for all things Western. Turkey was too close at hand to allow such unwise indulgence. Izetbegovic argued that "Turkey, as an Islamic country, had ruled the world"[44] but had dropped to the level of "a third-rate country" when it emulated Western nationalism. The universal values of Islam, rather than Western-style nationalism, would make Muslim nations strong.[45]

Like Ayatollah Fadlallah, Izetbegovic understood that the struggle for freedom was at the heart of the Islamic renaissance. In the battles for freedom, Izetbegovic leaned decisively toward reliance on nonviolence. In the *Islamic Declaration* Izetbegovic condemned the casual resort to violence or a coup and forced change from above.[46] At the same time, he understood that no one gives you your freedom. To a large degree, the means used to achieve freedom will depend on the moral and material capacity of the insurgents, although not completely. An abstract commitment to violence or nonviolence will not, in Izetbegovic's view, determine the character of a movement for freedom. He understood that the nature of the adversaries faced, and the situation within which the struggle takes place, would also shape the struggle in important ways. In Izetbegovic's view, choice does not always figure into the ways the battle for freedom takes shape. But when it does, Izetbegovic argued that peaceful means should be chosen.

In addition to his influential manifesto, Izetbegovic produced a body of writings far more substantial than one could reasonably expect from an activist and national political leader. *Islam between East and West* provides the most developed presentation of his ideas and is generally regarded as the most sophisticated of his writings on Islam. While the *Islamic Declaration* established Izetbegovic as an important activist and advocate of the Islamic Renewal, it was *Islam between East and West* that made his most substantial intellectual contribution. No less a figure than Muhammad al Ghazzali has provided an authoritative evaluation of his status as a major centrist Islamic thinker.

In an appreciative, posthumous review published in 1997, Muhammad al Ghazzali judges the book a "momentous contribution to contemporary Islamic thought."[47] Ghazzali notes that Izetbegovic presents in his work not only a critique of Western thought but also an insightful elaboration of preferred alternative modes of thinking. Ghazzali explains that he does so by drawing in sophisticated ways on the original sources of the Islamic tradition.[48] Ghazzali illustrates this quality with reference to the discussion of human rights. Apologetic literature simply asserts that Islam already contains whatever is positive from the West. In contrast, Izetbegovic provides an erudite explanation of the quite different sources of human rights in Islam. Izetbegovic explains that for Muslims human rights are rooted in the Qur'anic principle of *istikhlaf* (the divine call to humanity to act as God's regent on Earth). Islam grants a unique and matchless position to man in the order of existence. In contrast, Western materialism explains away man as merely a certain stage in the natural evolution of nature. The Qur'anic conception presupposes an essentially free agent with a choice. Izetbegovic goes further: He makes the argument that Islam embodies the very principle according to which man was created—that is, the unity of the material and the spiritual. For that reason, Ghazzali elaborates, Izetbegovic is making the critical point that "there is an inherent harmony between man and Islam" that he juxtaposes to the necessary tension between religion and human nature in otherworldly Christianity.[49] In Islam, humanity is entrusted by God to live life in accordance with God's laws, calling for righteous deeds and action against evil in practice. Human beings have a role that is at once worldly and spiritual. In just the same way, Izetbegovic argues that Islam provides a unity of religion and social order, without any conflict between the two. This unity, which is foreign both to Christianity and materialism, he concludes, is "the basic and the 'most Islamic' characteristic of Islam."[50] Ghazzali commends Izetbegovic's ability to offer very broad and insightful generalizations, such as his view that all intellectual approaches fall into one of three categories of thinking: materialist, religious, or Islamic. He positions Islam as a distinct and unique tradition that is neither wholly worldly nor entirely otherworldly. Islam he explains, correctly in Ghazzali's view, "is neither exclusively concerned with the material amelioration of human life here, nor does it dictate its followers to wholly dedicate themselves to the other-worldly concerns. It is a combination of both."[51] Ghazzali credits Izetbegovic with a lucid explanation of the elusive concept that Islam simultaneously affirms this world and all it holds for man as well as the promise of "the Home of the Hereafter."[52]

Islam between East and West provides a very effective antidote for the denunciations of Izetbegovic as an anti-Western fundamentalist. The work contains an extensive and highly laudatory evaluation of key phases in the development of Western culture, notably of the art and literature of the Renaissance. Izetbegovic's major focus on Western philosophy contains a very positive assessment of what he considers an Anglo-Saxon school of social theory that comes in for high praise. He contrasts the principled and flexible practicality of American thought with the abstract and speculative European philosophical tradition. The Anglo-Saxon tradition, he notes, sought a middle way between science and religion. Particularly noteworthy is Izetbegovic's striking conclusion that there are critical parallels between Islam and American pragmatism. He concludes that the similarities are so extensive that they justify considering philosophical pragmatism "the Islam of the West."[53] Principled, determined, and practical: These are all fair adjectives for the commitments of the great American pragmatists like John Dewey. Izetbegovic identified these same characteristics with the centrist Islamic tradition. They also aptly describe the career of Alija Izetbegovic himself.

Ghazzali, who is generally regarded as one of the major Islamic thinkers of the twentieth century, concludes his essay with an extraordinary assessment of Izetbegovic's place in the Islamic tradition. He writes that

"Alija Izetbegovic belongs to that galaxy of savants and intellectual mas-
ters of the Muslim scholarly tradition that include such luminaries as al
Ghazali, al Razi, Ibn Taymiyya, Ibn al ʿArabi, Ibn Rushd, Shah Wali Allah,
Ashraf ʿAli Thanvi and Muhammad Iqbal." Ghazzali adds, however, that
"Muslim scholars of the present times have yet to give Alija Izetbegovic
the place and recognition that are his due."[54]

Alija Izetbegovic died on October 19, 2003. His funeral in Sarajevo
was extraordinary in many ways. There were world leaders in attendance
who celebrated the large role Izetbegovic had played. From *Dar al Islam*
came the prime minister of Turkey, Recep Tayyip Erdogan, who remarked
simply that "Alija Izetbegovic enjoys great respect and has a special place
in the hearts of Turkish people."[55] However, the day belonged to the thousands and thousands of ordinary Bosnians who poured into Sarajevo.

Variations

To see these heralds of the Islamic Renewal together is to marvel at the
rainbow of their colors, representing distinctive interpretations of Islam
suitable to very different settings. They were Sunni and Shiʾa, Kurd, Turk,
Arab, Bosnian, and Iranian. They were lay intellectuals with intense commitments to Islam. They were mystics who reveled in Islam's spiritual dimensions. They were callers to Islam close to the people. They were learned
scholars of Islamic legal reasoning who wrote for the ages. These figures
exemplify the "variations" celebrated in the Qurʾan as part of God's plan.[56]

The heralds of the Renewal were innovators. For all their differences,
they shared the three fundamental commitments of resistance against
foreign dominance, insistence on the cohesiveness of the *ummah*, and
transcendence of sectarian divides. In pursuit of these core objectives that
reflected the higher purposes of Islam, these historic Islamic intellectuals
and activists created new forms of association that would enable Muslims
to be Muslims in a world dominated by the West and threatened by its
culture of violence. They strived to secure the future of the *ummah*. In all
their instructive variety, they acted in parallel but uncoordinated ways to
protect Islam. They were the signs, for the most part ignored in the West,
for the coming of the fourth great historic surge of Islamic Renewal and
reform. That fourth wave continues to work its way around the globe today.

The world was quite unprepared for these heralds of the Renewal. The
conventional wisdom in the West did not question the continuing rise of
secularism and the decline of all religious orientations. Islam was of only

marginal interest and importance. It was seen as part of those phantoms of the past that would rise periodically and cast meaningless shadows on the forward march of a science-based progress and development that sharply circumscribed the scope for religion. That march would eventually leave all such phantoms behind. In the East, including the lands of *Dar al Islam*, powerful anti-Islamic and insistently secular forces seemed poised to have done with Islam. The dismal state of Muslim countries, especially according to the terms defined by the West such as the rate of economic growth or the percentage of women in the workforce, blinded the West to the latent power of Islam in the hearts and minds of its believers.

Human creativity of distinctly Islamic inspiration gave the lie to all these certainties. Each of the figures who contributed to the Renewal did so in strikingly inventive ways that defied conventional analyses. The new associational forms eluded standard categories. The Islamic Renewal to which they all contributed would take the world by surprise. Muhammad al Ghazzali was in the vanguard of a distinguished group of intellectuals who founded a "school of intellectual thought" that bore little resemblance to the Muslim Brotherhood organization from which most of its major figures emerged. It was emphatically *not* a social movement. Necmettin Erbakan created an Islamic political party of a totally new kind. It was committed at once to a conservative Islam and to technology-driven development and democracy. Erbakan's was *not* a party of Islamic extremists. Neither Marxist nor Fanonist, Shariati reintroduced to the modern world Abu Dharr, the Prophet's companion, whom he declared to be Islam's first revolutionary socialist. Shariati found in university lectures the perfect vehicle to convey his creative rethinking of Islam. The throngs of students and others who came to hear the charismatic speaker knew, just as he did, that these were not ordinary lectures of a university professor. Shariati retold all the great stories of the ancient Shi'i communities. He aimed to generate the mass energy to drive a revolutionary Islam and *not* a Shi'a revival. Alija Izetbegovic, plagued his entire life by unfounded charges of Islamic extremism, demonstrated just how pragmatic and pluralistic a Bosnian Islamic consciousness could be. He was *not* an extreme nationalist, nor was he an Islamic fundamentalist. It proved impossible to force any of these figures into the available categories. Each one created entirely new forms to energize and inspire the mass of ordinary people, new ways suffused with the spiritual power of Islam. Their astonishing creativity made the heralds of the Renewal virtually invisible, *except* to the millions of Muslims who responded to their message.

5
_____

Medieval Pathways and Ibn Battuta

Moving through the land seeking of God's bounty.

QUR'AN 73:20

THE QUR'AN EXPLICITLY speaks to *al Nas*, all humanity. In Islam, all human beings are chosen. "One single community" is the description of humankind in the Qur'an.¹ The universal message of Islam recognizes no human or geographic boundaries. There is no ethnicity, tribe, or other human grouping exalted above others. To guide personal and communal life and to resolve conflicts, God sent "messengers with glad tidings and warnings along with the Book in truth." The messengers all brought insights into the human connections that the Qur'an exalts. By God's grace, those messengers sent to *al Nas* (the common people) showed the way to "the truth." None is excluded from the invitation to follow "the straight path," although the Qur'an recognizes that not all will choose it. The affirmation of God's intent that humanity should display diversity comes with the admonition that there should be no compulsion in questions of religious faith. The embrace of pluralism could not be more explicit. The Qur'an pronounces simply and directly that "they have their faith and you have yours."²

Those who do respond to Islam's message regard the Prophet Muhammad as the last of the line of these messengers from God to humanity. The Seal of the Prophets, as he is named in the Qur'an, opened the Islamic path to all of humanity.³ By his example in building the first community of Muslims, he also clarified the ways in which Muslims would be a distinctive element in the human community. Throughout the ages, the Qur'anic revelation and the efforts of believers to interpret its meaning have given spiritual and cultural coherence to those worldwide who embrace Islam's call. In every age, the strength of the worldwide connection finds simple human measures. Through some fourteen centuries and to the present day, for example, it has been possible for a

Muslim to travel through the ancient pathways of *Dar al Islam* (the world of Islam) and revel in the human variety without ever feeling a stranger. Ibn Battuta in the fourteenth century left such a record. In his work one experiences the worldwide reach of Islam in his day. The Information Revolution has undoubtedly made some aspects of such a venture more accessible. However, electronic connections cannot give us the internal understandings of what those connections mean as only the traveler on the ground can. Today, the prominent Egyptian journalist Fahmi Huwaidi is providing such a contemporary account. Such personal and direct witnesses speak to the coherence of the *ummah* (Islamic community) through the ages. At the same time, they affirm that crossing from *Dar al Islam* to the world beyond has never for Muslims meant leaving the company of human beings who are also God's creations. Muslims are called to recognize that God's world is a plural world. They are called to strengthen the coherence of the *ummah* in a larger world of human difference.

The Prophet, himself a traveler, represents in body, mind, and spirit the distinctive features of the community of Muslims. The Prophet was a husband, a father, and a fighter for justice. For Muslims he is the exemplary human being in all three guises. Islamic scholars entertain a simple and compelling explanation for Islam's ability to win adherents on all the world's continents. Islam, they judge, looks to enhancing and uplifting the human character. However, it never goes against it. Islam of the Qur'an is uniquely compatible with human nature. In all their complexities and contradictions human beings are God's creations. For Islamic scholars, it is no cause for surprise that God's word reflects an understanding of the essential characteristics of humanity. Islamic communities, wherever they take root, explicitly order themselves in ways to meet the needs of the human body, mind, and spirit. There are no contradictions between demands of the faith and the intrinsic nature of men and women. In Islam, there are no unrealistic demands for celibacy or turning of the other cheek when attacked and dispossessed. Qur'anic verses explicitly allow Muslims, even during Ramadan when fasting is enjoined, to have sex after breaking the fast, while numerous verses also affirm the moral right of self-defense.

Islam raises human beings above all other creations for their capacity to worship God with awareness of all that such worship means. They are called to make Him part of all aspects of their lives from the most private to the most social. The instincts and needs of the body are to be respected. God is a presence in even the most intimate of human connections. Communities of Muslims are saturated with Islam in all personal matters, just as they are in social, economic, and political dimensions of human community. God has set high expectations for the work of the human mind. Men and women from different cultures and geographies are invited to use their thought and imagination to look beyond surface differences to see the imprint of God on all his creations. They are called to use their splendid capacity for reason to understand the human heart, the social world, and the larger natural world and universe beyond. God filled the social world and the world of nature with his "signs." They point to mysteries to be explored and wonders to challenge the mind. No individual can accomplish such tasks alone. For this mission, human beings must build communities that allow them to work together on the daunting common projects that God has assigned them. To sustain themselves in struggles to build better selves in a better world, Muslims embed reminders of God's presence in the time and space dimensions of their communal lives. As all who live in the Islamic world know, the words of the Qur'an are spoken into their ears throughout the day. Verses appear before their eyes in an endless stream.

The Qur'an calls on scholars to travel the world to seek wisdom (*talab al 'ilm*) to guide this human task of completing God's work on Earth. It is part of the lore of wisdom that surrounds the person of the Prophet that we should "search for knowledge even as far as China."[4] Such work requires strong and healthy bodies that are not denied essential needs. It demands minds that are creative and innovative but always aware of the limits as well as the glories of reason. Creative human spirits must soar and exalt in capabilities, while never losing sight of the truth that it is God, and not man, who is to be worshipped. The boldest and most ingenious of human achievements are viewed in this same way. Spiritual guides, scientist of all kinds, political leaders, and generators of wealth and prosperity are all to be appreciated, but they are not to be deified. New discoveries in science and technology and the wondrous devices they generate are manmade; they are to be celebrated and used but never venerated. Such is the Qur'anic message to men and women in all times and places: God alone is to be worshipped.

Dar al Islam is structured neither as a political unit nor a singular civilization. It is rather an interconnected community of believers in the revelation. All are strugglers to interpret its meaning. Islamic communities are always communities of interpretation. The common translation of the

Arabic phrase *Dar al Islam* as the "Islamic world" misleads to the degree that it suggests a delimited geographic entity. An older phrase, "abode of Islam," comes closer but is simply too archaic in English. It can also be understood to connote a fixed rather than variable place. For that reason, the phrase *Dar al Islam* is best left untranslated. It refers simply to those very different places in God's world where Islam is to be found and where communities of Muslims have established themselves.

From the time of the Prophet, Islamic communities have been diverse communities in a plural world. Islam embraces human variety and the complexities of human nature as expressions of God's deliberate creation. The Qur'an tells us that God chose to make humanity a heterogeneous community. God also conveys his intention that Muslims are to share the world he created with non-Muslims. The Qur'an is clear: "If the Lord had so willed, He could surely have made all mankind the same; they will not cease to differ."[5]

The Prophet with his companions built the first community of Muslims in this world of intended difference. They have inspired and guided the efforts of those who have followed across the globe. Struggles for Islamic community engage the full range of human experience, from the most intimate to the most global. Each effort to build community and to make rich personal and social lives possible inevitably bears the distinctive marks of particular circumstances. At the same time, each search for community also reflects the shared characteristics that flow from the higher purposes and values of the Qur'an and that are exemplified by that first community of Muslims.

Non-Muslims have always had a rightful place in the communities Muslims establish, as well as in the larger world outside their boundaries. Islamic scholars highlight the invaluable contributions non-Muslims have made through the centuries to the development of *Dar al Islam*.[6] They are judged to have done so not least by their very presence that represents the blessings of human variety. During the times of the great Islamic empires, with their myriad of ethnicities, religions, and languages, Qur'anic values shaped shared ways of thinking and feeling that transcended all such differences. Connections of mind, body, and spirit have made it possible for the worldwide Islamic community of revelation and interpretation to sustain itself through the ages as a networked system of believers. The human failings of particular Muslims, no matter how frequent or egregious, cannot abrogate this demanding Qur'anic vision of a plural human community of Muslims.

Binding the Ummah

Across the centuries, durable yet flexible ties have woven together the lives of those who live within the embrace of the *ummah*. At times these threads have been strong and vibrant, as they were when Ibn Battuta made his journeys in the fourteenth century. At other times they have weakened and faded. The early and middle decades of the twentieth century, before the fourth surge of Islamic Renewal, represented such a time. Although the character and salience of the ties that bind have varied, there has been one constant: the presence of the holy Qur'an. God's final message to humanity, articulated in a language of incomparable beauty, enjoys an uncorrupted presence wherever Arabic is understood. The *ulema* (Islamic scholars) have sought to understand the Message, as well as the larger world within which it works its effects. Their quest has always been for knowledge of the text and its changing worldly context. Scholars have sought to deepen understanding of the values and higher purposes of the Qur'an. No less important have been the efforts of the best among them to know as much as could be known of the natural and social world where those values and purposes find expression. Through the centuries, *talab al 'ilm* has led scholars to crisscross Islamic lands. By their interactions with merchants, saints, and simple travelers along the pathways of *Dar al Islam*, they have acted as the human threads that bind the community. Islamic scholars continue to do so today. The life force making the Islamic community real and resilient has always been these threaded patterns of human interaction that Islam inspires.

Ibn Battuta represented this life force and the extraordinary human connections it is capable of generating in a compelling way. As a *rahal* (traveler), Ibn Battuta visited more of the fourteenth-century *ummah* than any other man of his time. Ibn Battuta's travels began in 1325 in a completely conventional way. He set out from his home in Tangiers in present-day Morocco to make the pilgrimage to Mecca. From Mecca and Medina, he made his way to Yemen, Mogadishu, Africa, and Oman. He then voyaged across Anatolia and on to Persia, Afghanistan, and India, where he worked for several years. Travels down the Indian coast took him to the Maldive Islands for a year and a half, and then on to Ceylon, Bengal, Sumatra, Java, and finally China. Ibn Battuta eventually returned home to Morocco across the Middle East but not directly, visiting Timbuktu in west Africa and Granada in al Andalus on the way. In all, Ibn Battuta logged an estimated 75,000 miles over the course of some twenty-four years. His *Travels*, as no other single work, brings the fourteenth-century *ummah* clearly into view.[7]

Ibn Battuta's record highlighted the character of the human interactions that defined the *ummah*. The caliphate, often more symbolic than real, expressed the ambitious aspiration for the political unity of the far-flung and loosely connected communities of the *ummah*. That political unity has never been realized. The modern era brought the dissolution of the caliphate. It has also seen the undermining of the traditional learning centers that educated the *ulema*. Both blows signaled a weakening of the *ummah*. They should have been calamities, but they were not: Instead, these setbacks made possible creative rethinking about the nature of the contemporary *ummah* and of the human networks that sustain it.

Muslims around the world responded in innovative ways to the setbacks suffered. Their responses fuel the contemporary Islamic Renewal. The Renewal illustrates for our time the way diverse and informal human networks, rather than formal structures, sustain the *ummah*. Muslims today have invented entirely new forms of organization, mobilization, and enactment, such as the original Egyptian "society" of Muslim Brothers of Hassan al Banna, the "intellectual school" of Egypt's New Islamic scholars, or the "study circles" of the Turkish followers of Said Nursi. These associations are loosely organized around commitments, leadership, and organizational poles at a far less formal level than either the earlier caliphate structure or contemporary social movements or parties. Only some of such poles of emergent cohesion are political. Moreover, those that do have a political character are by no means the most important. The selective attention to things political comes at a high cost to understanding *al Tagdid al Islami*.[8] Today the networks of the *ummah* do include Islamic political groups, movements, and parties, but they are in no way limited to them. Far more varied collaborative activities give substance to the Islamic Renewal. They center as well on religious, professional, cultural, economic, and social justice commitments. Their efficacy depends not simply on ideas or structures held in common. Great passions, complex feelings, and shared sensibilities have an importance that is just as important. The psychological dimension, inaccessible to external observation, may well be the most cohesive of all. The *ummah* has an interior life.

The Information Revolution and the *Ummah*

The new technologies of the Information Revolution have been enthusiastically embraced by Islamic groupings of all kinds. They mesh naturally with the borderless character of the *ummah*. They have been useful in

enhancing the flexible ties on multiple levels that such decentered organizational patterns require. Centrist Islamic intellectuals, guided by the
New Islamic scholars, have counseled reassuringly and accurately that the
new information and communication channels complement rather than
subvert older unifying forms. They recognize that the new technologies
can provide accelerated connections and more expansive linkages. They
explain that technology, too, is part of God's world and always has been.

It is neither an innovation nor a surprise that the networks of the
ummah in a global age constitute themselves in ways that make use of the
new possibilities the Information Revolution has brought. These contemporary changes in the nature of the Islamic networks that bind the *ummah*
are important to note. However, it is unhelpful to exaggerate the ways
they transform the character of the worldwide Islamic community.[9] *Dar
al Islam* is not flat. It does not present itself as a blank surface on which
modern technologies of communication and power can inscribe new beginnings, incommensurate with what has come before. The *ummah* has
historical, cultural, and spiritual depth. It has an astounding continuity,
to which the work of Islamic scholars, merchants, and simple travelers,
like Ibn Battuta, through the centuries testifies.

Islam is always about infusing a spiritual dimension into the practices that bind across the full spectrum of human possibilities. Collective
struggles to interpret the Qur'an and the relationship of its message to
contemporary realities forge powerful bonds that are physical, intellectual, and spiritual. Islamic communities have always been realized in
struggles of interpretation: What does the revelation mean in our time
and place? What does Islam mean for my day-to-day interactions, and how
can I live day in and day out? Meanings and emotions held in common
and experienced collectively permeate Islamic communities. The practice
of Islam brings God fully into the individual lives of believers and into
the most intimate spaces of their personal lives. At the same time Islam
responds to human social needs by fostering a sense of *sillat* (connectedness) to others in communities that strive to organize themselves in what
they understand to be the ways God intended for humanity. In Arabic
the root of *sillat* is the same as the word for prayer. Divine intentions for
humanity extend into all areas of human life, from the public spaces of
politics and economics to the private spheres of friendship, family, and
sexuality.

In the most general terms, the universal drive for human connections
of all kinds displays a relentless capacity to articulate itself anew for each

generation and for every age. Such renewals are invariably experienced as more distinctive than they really are and not just by Muslims. Young people everywhere claim sex as their own secret discovery. Who among us, in our youth, could entertain the thought for long that our parents or, more unthinkable still, our grandparents, actually have sex? These irreverent thoughts came to mind when working my way through the overgrown literature on globalization and its impact on human affairs. An unwarranted breathlessness characterizes even the best and most thoughtful work about the new information technologies and electronic linkages they make possible. The argument is made that these innovations have precipitated an unprecedented break in human history. Now, suddenly, everything has changed. A new epoch is upon us. This assessment is extended to *Dar al Islam.* Muslims, a leading Western scholar of Islam has announced, must now come to terms with a "globalized Islam," as though that challenge were a new one. In keeping with this view, Muslims are called to "the search for a new *ummah*."[10]

Islam and Sexuality

The truth is that our parents, like our grandparents, did have sex. So, too, did earlier generations, including the Muslims among them. Indeed, few of the world's cultures have as rich and sophisticated a literature exploring human sexuality, and the complex behaviors and emotions that surround it, as medieval Islamic thought. After all, the *ummah* is sustained by the resilient threads of human connectivity in all its forms, including the most physical. There is no domain of human experience that lies beyond Islam. As with all else, the Qur'an helps most in understanding why. One of the most beautiful Qur'anic verses makes God's purpose clear:

> O mankind! We created you from a single (pair) of male and female, and made you into nations and tribes, that ye may know each other (not that ye may despise each other). Verily, the most honored of you in the sight of God is (he who is) most righteous of you. And God has full knowledge and is well acquainted (with all things).[11]

God is the only singular in Islam. The Prophet Muhammad is seen in the company of the long line of prophets. He is surrounded by his companions, wives, and children. One cannot be a Muslim alone. God's command to humankind to "know each other" extends to human connections of all kinds, including the sexual.

Human sexuality has an honored place in the moral universe of Islam. It is regarded as no less important than air, water, and food. Sexual behaviors are understood to make a critical contribution to human physical and psychological well-being that goes beyond procreation. Authoritative Islamic texts provide abundant resources for appreciation of the spiritual dimensions of human sexuality and the pleasures it brings, without stigma or a sense of shame. Discussion of the appropriate boundaries of those pleasures has continued through the ages, many of which are detailed in the Qur'an. The discussions are complex, but two firm conclusions inevitably emerge. First, boundaries in some form for sexual expression consistently provide important guidance, although different communities of Muslims have calibrated them differently. Second, the strange notion of celibacy has no place in Islam.

Qur'anic insights into both the physical characteristics of the human body and the higher purposes of the human spirit are both integral to the classical heritage. So, too, is an understanding of the connections between the two. Human beings, the great medieval thinkers understood, are endowed with the startling power to connect the purely physical with the higher realms of the spirit. Medieval scholars explored these connections in matters cosmic and personal. The power of the human mind, Abu Hamed al Ghazali (1058–1111) explains, extends to an improbable capacity to move the body without activating the muscles or touching. The two realms of mind and body are linked in powerful ways that only seem to be mysterious because we are not mindful of the small miracles of everyday existence. Ghazali made the point in a wonderfully playful way. In dialogue with the philosophers, Ghazali discusses a class of miracles that even the most skeptical of philosophers accept. Ghazali summarizes that when the mind conjures up an image, the body may respond to it. A vision of tasty food may cause the mouth to salivate, although no actual food or even the smell of food is present. Similarly, and even more decisively, is the situation where "a man imagines sexual intercourse and the faculty responds by making his penis erect."[12] Both men and women understand and appreciate that very human miracle, especially in those dreaded times when things do not go as they are supposed to.

A great deal of the nuance and sophistication of medieval discussions of sexuality has been lost. The Egyptian Nobel laureate Naguib Mahfouz was subject to a steady stream of criticism over the course of his career for the sexual themes woven into his novels. Representations of vigorous heterosexuality, homosexuality, and sexual transgressions of various kinds are threaded through his major novels. Mahfouz treats sexuality as a normal part of the human personal and social experience. Belal Fadl, the contemporary Egyptian writer and social commentator, makes the point that when viewed in the context of the classical heritage, Mahfouz's treatment of sexuality is, in fact, greatly understated. Fadl invokes, in particular, the work of the distinguished scholar Jalal al Din al Suyuti (c. 1445–1505).[13] He comments wryly that contemporary conventions, foreign to the classical heritage, make it unwise to even mention the title of his most important work on human sexuality![14] Al Suyuti was no minor or marginal figure. A prolific Sufi scholar, he was the author of hundreds of published works. He produced major studies in *fiqh* (legal reasoning, based on interpretation of Qur'an and *Sunnah*) and *Shari'ah* (the provisions from Qur'an and *Sunnah* to regulate human behavior). He also wrote in candid ways on sexuality. His work is suffused with an intense and learned interest in what can only be called the arts of sexual expression. There is explicit discussion of the most adroit movements in sexual performance. There is also very sensitive attention to the emotional and spiritual dimensions of the sexual experience.

Sexuality has a sacred character in Islam. Al Suyuti is not the outlier he may appear to be, although his treatment is more explicit and detailed than most. The Prophet Muhammad charted the way. Quite unlike Jesus, the Prophet appears as a figure who balanced spiritual and worldly things. While Muhammad's role as a fighter is often emphasized, it should not overwhelm his equally compelling image as a husband and father. The Prophet is reported to have loved perfume, food, and women best. He judged the sexual union of husband and wife an act of worship for which each would earn *sadaqa* (a divine reward). Sexual intercourse, the Prophet reportedly advised, must be approached in ways consistent with its spiritual character. There are *hadiths* that attribute to Prophet Muhammad some very explicit advice on how men should approach their wives. While the *hadiths* themselves come with weak authority, they are consistent with the Qur'anic embrace of human sexuality and the fully human character of the Prophet himself. In one such *hadith* the Prophet warns men that "none of you should fall upon his wife like an animal; but let there first be a messenger between you." The men ask the Prophet, "And what is that messenger?" He replies, "Kisses and words." The Prophet finds two things unacceptable in male behavior: first, "a man goes to his wife before talking to her and gaining her intimacy," and second that he "satisfies his need from her before she has satisfied her need from him." Elaborating on the Prophet's counsel, Abu Hamed al Ghazali reportedly pronounces that "sex should begin with gentle words and kissing." In a commentary on Ghazali, Imam Murtada al Zabidi (1145–1205) adds that "this should include not only the cheeks and lips: and then he should caress the breasts and nipples, and every part of her body."[15] These sayings are best understood as part of the vast lore around the person of the Prophet that aims to impart *hikma* (wisdom) in matters of human sexuality. They have circulated for centuries in *Dar al Islam*.

These learned Islamic scholars respect the Islamic call for modesty. They also recognize those propitious moments when men and women can safely put modesty aside. We have all heard the demanding modern-day counsel to aim for simultaneous orgasms with our partners. But I still smile when I think of the passage from Imam Jalal al Din al Suyuti when he offers a novel justification for this most gracious way to play the game of physical love. With mutual orgasm, he comments, women can safely set aside their own preferred modesty. A woman knows that her male partner will be fully preoccupied with his own organism and will not notice any lapse in her modesty![16]

Sexual union in Islam, at its most basic level, represents an act of sharing and kindness to one's partner. At higher levels the religious implications of intercourse are more profound, particularly in the eyes of Islam's mystics. For those who strive for closeness to the divine, sexual union opens a pathway. Sufis, particularly those in the school of Ibn al Arabi (1076–1148), believe that in sexual union, each partner, if sensitive enough, has the opportunity to "see God." The Sufis explain that males imitate certain aspects of the divine, females others. The sexual union brings those two aspects, each essential for creation, together. Sexual union, Ibn al Arabi explains, represents "God's greatest self-disclosure."[17]

As he moves through the ancient pathways of fourteenth-century *Dar al Islam*, Ibn Battuta, the greatest of the Arab travelers, displays an inviting openness to all that is laid before him. His engagement with the world, he makes quite clear, has a robust sexual dimension. Ibn Battuta delights in the details and in the naming. Knowing al Suyuti and the numerous other medieval scholars who embraced human sexuality, in sophisticated and uninhibited ways, makes it easier to give the revealing sexual aspects of the work of the great *rahal* the attention they deserve, as he moves through the networks of the medieval Islamic world.

A dismal prudery, alien to the heritage of medieval Islamic thought, has established itself in *Dar al Islam*, although there is far more resistance to it than outsiders imagine. This enforced reticence has restricted the kind of enlightened explorations of the importance of sexuality in human life that characterized medieval Islamic thought. Still, despite such regressions, it is my experience that a great deal of medieval Islamic sexual culture survives into contemporary life. It does so, however, for the most part as a subterranean stream that goes forward without the physical naming and higher spiritual speculations in which medieval scholars delighted.

The Networks of Dar al Islam

The *Travels* of Ibn Battuta provides a reminder that *Dar al Islam* has always been networked. The enthusiasm for network analysis in contemporary Western social thought risks obscuring that historical reality. The networks that connected the widely dispersed communities of the *ummah* in the fourteenth century often took forms quite as intricate as the new electronic webs within which we now live. Undoubtedly, they were never as extensive in their reach or as instantaneous in their capacity to generate new connections. Change, including dramatic change, has always been an important part of the story of the *ummah*. The pace of that change now pulsing through global electronic networks has accelerated greatly. Both for their ancient lineage in the Islamic world and the accelerated speed with which we can now move through them, networks rightly command our attention in the study of *al Tagdid al Islami* (the Islamic Renewal).

Still, a word of caution is in order. The disappointing truth now, as in earlier periods, is that focus on the *architecture* of networks tells us surprisingly little about the human beings who create or animate them. Network analysis inevitably promises far more than it can deliver. It is easy enough, for example, to plot the movements of the mystics, scholars, and merchants who traversed the pathways of the *ummah* in earlier centuries. Yet, without the vivid personal accounts of reactions and feelings left by travelers like Ibn Battuta, just how meaningful would those mappings be? Without the kindness and generosity of those who opened their doors to the wanderers, how much would they have learned of lives lived in Islamic communities founded on other shores? More than network structures bind Islamic communities; they are also linked by the shared experiences, values, and feelings of the people who move through them.

Islam considers communal life itself sacred. Political, economic, social, and sexual affairs are not a distraction from the faith; rather, they are important components of a lived spirituality. The experience of building community and the conduct of its affairs in accord with Islam provide intimations of the sacred. All who live in such a community find reflections of the divine through the day-to-day experience of pleasure, kindness, justice, and generosity, rather than through faith and prayer alone. Mosques do demarcate a sacred space in Islam. It is not, however, a space apart: All the Earth for Muslims is a mosque. Nor do mosques bring spirituality to the community. Rather, they express the spirituality that a community of Muslims makes possible. For this reason, their particular architecture does not matter greatly. Across *Dar al Islam* mosques in all manner of styles can be found. Aside from mosques, which do require a certain level of material investment and often official approval, any small group of Muslims can create a *zawiya* (small informal mosque) on any street in any neighborhood. Spirituality does not reside in external forms. Whatever the forms, there is always an excess of meaning that exceeds the externalities of architectural structures. It is the unseen interiors that define the experience of Islam for believers.

Networks from the Inside: Ibn Battuta and the Pragmatic Alternative

Expectations of access to the interior of networks must be kept realistic and modest. The access will inevitably be incomplete. It will come, if it comes at all, through knowledgeable insiders like Ibn Battuta and Fahmi Huwaidi. We need these fellow travelers at our side as we move through the Islamic networks we seek to understand. We must rely on these traveling companions to provide interpretations along the way of what we are seeing and hearing. Travel literature represents one of the great Arab cultural attainments. It provides a venerable template for pragmatic work of this kind.

Islam suffuses the pathways along which Ibn Battuta travels and the varied human interactions he enjoys along the way. My own infatuation with the great *rahal* is not, I have come to understand, quite as unusual for Westerners as I once imagined. Anthropologists in recent decades have come to recognize Ibn Battuta's *Travels* as a foundational work for anthropology as a field.[18] In quite unexpected ways, as we shall see in Chapter 6, the work of this fourteenth-century traveler provides a useful point of entry to contemporary anthropological literature.

The Learned Networks of Medieval Islam

The most helpful fellow travelers are invariably figures on the move who experience as much of the networks of their community as possible. One needs to get to know them and appreciate all the slants and biases that color their point of view. The dazzling scholarship of the medieval world of Islam adds a multitude of just such critical and highly individualized human voices to external mappings of ancient networks. Ibn Battuta does not travel alone. Muslim scholars, mystics, and merchants in great numbers moved through the networks of medieval Islam. Many left records of their passage. Some have given us their personal and deeply felt accounts of thoughts and feelings, doubts and certainties, as they lived their lives passing through these inherited pathways. These cultural treasures of the medieval era give life to the networks of that time of Islamic ascendancy. They have provided instruction for the sensibilities of generations of Muslims in all areas of life, from probity in commerce to an appreciation for meaningful sexual experience. They give substance to notions of belonging to the worldwide community of Muslims. For the purposes at hand, these records of complex and rewarding human interactions, widely shared throughout the *ummah*, provide helpful inoculation against any notion that a networked global Islam is either a mirage or a product of the new information technologies.

Some of these primary accounts from the classical age rise to the level of great and enduring works of scholarship. All of the major medieval Islam thinkers, including Ibn Sina, Ibn Rushd, Hamed al Ghazali, and Ibn Khaldun, include in their writings references to their own very extensive personal and professional travels. They comment as well on the movement of books and ideas across the great expanses of the medieval *ummah*. In doing so they give us an internal view of how the networks actually functioned in human terms. Through their writings we see how the networks are experienced by real people to whom one can relate on a variety of levels across the centuries. The gifted analyst Ibn Khaldun, for example, offered his services to rulers first in Tunis and then in Cairo, where he worked for more than twenty years. We can register these facts in the life of the great scholar. However, we can also grieve with Ibn Khaldun when he tells us that he lost his entire family at sea just off the coast of Alexandria when the boat bringing them to Egypt from the Maghreb sank.

Great debates animated intellectual, religious, and cultural life as controversial ideas, concepts, and ways of thinking traveled through the classic networks. Ibn Rushd famously argued for scientific rationalism and confidence that the universe was governed by laws of cause and effect. Abu Hamed al Ghazali opposed him vigorously with a mystical "occasionalism" that saw the necessary hand of God in each effect. Their debate echoes through the ages, as a clash of real personalities as well as ideas. Great questions of the day circulated through the networks of the learned. They continue to resonate with educated Muslims today: How should we engage the great Greek thinkers like Aristotle and Plato, the sources for so much that eventually defined the West, from the perspective of the Islamic revelation? How should we integrate foundational notions of prophecy with the legacy of Greek rationalism? How should we interpret the revelation in ways suitable to the diverse circumstances of the *ummah*? What should we do about provocative and unconventional ideas and the subversive circles of intellectuals and activists who advocated them? How should we insulate and protect the unlettered masses from the potentially subversive thinking of the learned?

More than the exploration of an exhausting stream of philosophical and theological question was involved in the exchanges that animated *Dar al Islam*, however: Practical matters were also in play. Islamic intellectuals shared the findings of astronomy that had direct and immediate consequences for the everyday practice of the faith. Exactly when would the fasting for Ramadan begin? Medical learning saved lives. A sophisticated interest in scientific experimentation, rather than just theorization, made its way through the networks. The results have been momentous for human history. The experimental method is an Islamic invention. Islamic scholars built on the speculative work of the Greeks, going beyond it to pave the way for the experimental laboratories of modern scientific and technological research.

The flow of goods and services from one end of the *ummah* to the other gave the networks a very down-to-earth function. The classical scholars themselves displayed a wide range of interests that went far beyond theology to philosophy, mathematics, and medicine. Political insights and bureaucratic skills were also among the most important intellectual goods traded and shared. So, too, were notions of the beautiful and the place of the arts in Islamic communities. The great *rahala* (travelers) traded their firsthand knowledge of conditions and customs in the various lands through which they moved for influence and wealth at the courts of the powerful.

The Grand Theory of Ibn Khaldun

I first encountered the work of this galaxy of impressive Islamic intellectuals and the diverse world of ideas and cultures they inhabited in graduate school, where we read from the classics. Among the very small cohort of graduate students at Harvard interested in the Islamic world in the mid-1960s, Ibn Khaldun attracted the most attention, notably for the generalizing thrust of his thinking. Ibn Khaldun believed that humanity had a natural need to identify with a group and its leadership. The strength of such group feeling was the essential determinate of the rise and fall of dynasties. In his well-known view, a small group with *'asabiyya* (high energy and group cohesiveness) would arise periodically to replace declining, dynastic structures. They would win mass support and sweep away the old order, only to suffer the same fate themselves when the inevitable decline of their own *'asabiyya* set in. Ibn Khaldun put his dazzling intelligence at the service of a string of rulers, including those in Tunis and then in Cairo.

Such findings seemed neither strange nor irrelevant when I first encountered them. The mid-1960s in America was a time for comparable sweeping theories that aimed for the status of science for politics and economics at major U.S. academic centers. It was also a time for preparation for the practical tasks of imperial rulership, although the matter was never put so bluntly. American scholars, nevertheless, did go about readying themselves and their students for the new American world responsibilities, the euphemism used in those days for empire. This period was one of great confidence in models of political and economic development, applicable in all times and places. Although cast in universal terms, these development studies were in fact distillations of the Western, and particularly the American, experience. The distinctive histories and cultures of underdeveloped or developing countries inevitably came into view as obstinate social and cultural materials to be transformed. Area studies programs were launched during these same years to serve Cold War ends. They emphasized language and culture. Such area programs did attract smaller cadres of students who were encouraged to study abroad. Everyone understood that the programs were considered second tier in terms of academic standing. Moreover, students in them were explicitly warned of the dangers of "going native," even though there were those who did develop attachments to the peoples and cultures they studied. For most, however, it did not take long to figure out that the skills acquired would be important primarily for assessing what went wrong with societies that had failed to develop along the lines of the most powerful Western states. It was considered important to have just enough command of the language and just enough familiarity with the culture for the contemptuous project of understanding the "moral basis of backward societies," as one highly influential study put the matter.[19] In this climate of hubris, lessons learned from a marginal, poor Italian village would illuminate the vast geography of empire where the United States had inherited responsibilities from the great European empires. The thought that American scholars and their graduate students might learn anything at all from the histories and contemporary experiences of such failed peoples, particularly the Muslims among them, almost never surfaced. What was needed was general theory that would justify the benevolent transformations of the modernization that America's dominant world position would facilitate. A smattering of "local knowledge" was judged helpful in a very secondary way to tailor the general remedies to specific circumstances. Given his own entanglements with the ruling powers of his day, Ibn Khaldun could reasonably be seen as an Islamic scholar on whose shoulders one could stand.

Moving through the Fourteenth-Century Ummah *with Ibn Battuta*

My own inclinations ran in a contrary direction. Islamic studies, with emphasis on language, literature, culture, and history, provided an important refuge from my power-drenched studies in political and economic development. In those early years of my first encounter with the classic Islamic thinkers, I was not inclined to give my spare time and affections to yet another abstract theorizer, even one with the dazzling intelligence of Ibn Khaldun. In the end, like his modern counterparts, he seemed to have his primary interest in abstract notions of power and its imperial uses.[20]

It was the far less abstract and far more human Ibn Battuta whom I found most engaging. My reasons for the attraction, then as now, go against the tenor of the time. For me, Ibn Battuta was a kindred spirit. He generally seemed to be getting the most out of his present circumstances, rather than seeing the present simply as a way station to some imagined and more attractive future. At the same time, Ibn Battuta embraced his immediate situation with just the right hint of dissatisfaction, always looking around corners, endlessly curious about unexplored pathways, given to dawdling, ready at all times to take a new and unplanned direction, always wonderfully unfocused. Ibn Battuta's mind wandered. So did he. I was all too eager to follow him.

Wealth, influence, and social standing mattered to Ibn Battuta, too much so for my taste. I always wished he paid more attention to ordinary people and was less impressed by riches and social status. However, the acquisition of wealth and power did not define Ibn Battuta's life in practice. In fact, he put a great deal more effort and energy into living in interesting and pleasurable ways. He found the special challenges of doing so with people quite different from himself very much to his liking. He never seemed to mind the fact that all his personal adventures took place in foreign circumstances he could never hope to understood fully. Ibn Battuta reveled in the unknowns of his everyday life. He taught me to do the same. In terms of sheer intellectual firepower, Ibn Battuta was no match for Ibn Khaldun. His attraction rested on his overwhelming drive to see as much of the world as possible and to make pragmatic sense of what he saw and experienced. The great cities of the medieval *ummah* come alive in Ibn Battuta's writings. I can never visit any of them now without feeling his presence and experiencing with him a sense of the grandeur of the architecture, notably the schools and the mosques, and of the pervasive spiritual impact of Islam that soaks into every crack and crevice of those precious stones. Those cities, like a string of pearls, serve as lustrous markers for an inevitable itinerary. The improbable sense of connectedness across such a vast territory creates an irresistible compulsion to see them all. Each of the ancient Islamic cities is precious in its own way, but none beckons more irresistibly than Cairo.

Lingering in Cairo

Cairo is for Ibn Battuta, as it is for me, the inescapable gateway to the Islamic world. The description of Cairo in the *Travels* is quite extraordinary for its sheer poetry.[21] The description resonates through the ages. Cairo remains Cairo. In the *Travels*, we see the venerable mosques and the extraordinary number of schools. We feel the crush of the population and the impossible animation of the streets. We learn of the riches that the land of Egypt yields. More importantly, Ibn Battuta captures the intangible ways in which Egyptians have given their capital a distinctive character that defines the city to this day. It is that definition, in turn, that provides the most durable meaning to the notion of an Egyptian identity, despite the fact that no other Egyptian city, especially not Alexandria, shares its character. In Arabic "Cairo" to Egyptians from other parts of the country is known as *Misr*, which is the Arabic word for Egypt as well as the capital. In the vernacular, the city and the country are one.

Cairo, Ibn Battuta tells us, is a city that makes the stranger feel that he is not a stranger at all. The people of the city embrace all. In Cairo, there is a place for the weak and a place for the strong. Cairo offers exactly what you are looking for, from the wise to the ignorant, from the upright to shady characters of all kinds, from the serious to the superficial, from the limited to those of immense intelligence, and from those who do good to those who do far less than good. In Cairo, every life event inspires a party, organized or impromptu. The youth of the city are its greatest treasure. Cairo as the heart of Egypt, Ibn Battuta reports, wins the heart of all the nations of *Dar al Islam* and beyond.[22] Egypt looms large in Ibn Battuta's account even after he has left the Nile Valley. Then, as now, one encounters educated Egyptians everywhere throughout the lands where Arabs live. They contribute their talents to the lives of brothers and sisters in all parts of the *ummah*. When locals learned that Ibn Battuta was coming from the land of the Arabs, their first questions were invariably about Egypt.

Ibn Battuta's descriptions provide no great single finding, no key to unlock the mysteries of human affairs. He had nothing to offer that could rival Ibn Khaldun's notion of *'asabiyya*, for example. I found that a great relief. His complexly detailed work illuminated the lives of diverse others. He raised questions about specific problems in particular sites. He seemed mercifully to have no interest at all in providing sweeping answers for all times and places to highly speculative questions about the fate of human societies.

The sheer expanse of the world of Islam he traversed leaves a lasting impression. Ibn Battuta's travels through Islamic lands helped define my own itinerary for a lifetime of voyages, as yet incomplete. Just last year, I followed Ibn Battuta to Ras al Barr at the tip of the delta in Egypt, where the Nile empties into the Mediterranean.[23] I first read his description from the *Travels* of that magical site. I did find that amazing sliver of land where you can see the fresh water of the river on one side and the salt water of the sea on the other, just as he promised. I have no doubt from his description that Ibn Battuta had stood on my very same spot.[24]

However, the urge to simply map Ibn Battuta's extraordinary lifelong travels through these lands should be resisted. Maps are always misleading. They are particularly inappropriate representations of Ibn Battuta's travels. They impress for the wrong reasons. Maps suggest purpose. Yet the great *rahal* often has only the dimmest idea where he is headed. He is never lost just because he is never quite sure where he is going. To travel with him demands a readiness to reverse course, circle back, or head in an entirely new direction, all without evident purpose. The extent of his travels, and the destinations eventually reached, matter far less than the adventures along the uncharted ways.

Writing this book provided my excuse to return to Ibn Battuta's *Travels* in its entirety. My early encounters with Ibn Battuta were limited to excerpts from his massive work. I read them first in advanced Arabic-language classes and then in history and politics courses on the medieval Islamic world. Unlike those sad occasions when positive first impressions are betrayed by later intimacy, knowing Ibn Battuta more fully has only confirmed my appreciation for his work and for what it suggests for my own. The full text of *Travels* runs some 700 pages.[25] The author emerges clearly with all his imperfections, contradictions, and complexities. The contrast to the more conventional and quite boring Marco Polo could not be starker. Marco Polo gives us a didactic geography, and we learn little about the sensibilities of the man. In contrast, Ibn Battuta was a man of robust body and mind, and his expansive personality is imprinted on every page. Ibn Battuta responded to the pleasures of the mind and traveled to the ends of the Earth to meet the great scholars of his time, although he himself was no scholar. He pursued Sufi mystics and sought to learn from them the secrets that came to them from their soul searching, although the great *rahal* was no mystic. Ibn Battuta experienced as well and without contradiction the pleasures of the body. He described quite matter-of-factly the attractions of the intoxicants of wine, power, and wealth, although sex in an array of forms appears quite clearly to have been his drug of choice.

Ibn Battuta never failed to comment on the beauty of mosques and *madrasas* (Islamic schools) that adorned the cities of the *ummah*. Yet the focus on the monuments to faith and learning did not exhaust his sense of the beautiful. Beautiful people, especially girls and women but men and boys as well, captured his attention and stirred his passions. He took obvious pleasure in describing in rich detail the sources of their attractiveness and the effect it had on others. Given the breadth and depth of the attractions he experienced, it did not surprise me to learn that Ibn Battuta made himself something of an expert on various aphrodisiacs as well as on sexual practices and positions. At one point, Ibn Battuta reports that a beautiful young *gariya* (female indentured servant) brings an impressive price of one dinar, while a particularly handsome young male servant commands two.[26] He went to great lengths to make these bonded servants a part of his life wherever his voyages led him. Ibn Battuta thought nothing of delaying a voyage to search for a favorite *ghulam* (male bonded servant) who had mysteriously disappeared. Nor does he display any unease about the obvious intensity of the attachment.[27]

Ibn Battuta genuinely wanted to know how others on other shores went about their own experience of living. He wanted to learn about their search for knowledge, their quest for spiritual serenity, and their experiments with the shared pleasures of the mind and body. It was Ibn Battuta's reaction to the tremendous human variety of the far-flung world he encountered that appealed most to me. It was his ability to move with a modicum of success through these varied human spaces that left the most enduring impression.

Responsive Openness and the Wonders of the *Ummah*

Ibn Battuta brings to his travels an attitude of mind and heart best characterized as responsive openness. An unwarranted confidence allowed Ibn Battuta to act as though his understanding of the world was right in its essentials. No matter how exotic to his eyes the setting, this intrepid traveler clung to the expectation that, for all their surface differences, his varied interlocutors saw the world in terms close enough to his own roughly accurate understandings to make mutual comprehension and joint actions possible. Ibn Battuta simply took it for granted that those he met did have a fundamental grasp of their own situation. He also believed that they had the capacity to explain with stories or illustrate with actions the meaning of their beliefs and behaviors to a stranger, willing to listen carefully and linger long enough to really see and hear. In short, his adventures were always those of a man with a resilient capacity to learn from his encounters with others who captured his attention. He struggled to see them as clearly as possible, to hear their voices, and to grasp the essentials of what they had to say. Through Ibn Battuta's stories, we come to know the ways in which he understands the cultural specifics in which he inevitably becomes entangled. We gain insight as well into the larger lessons about the durability of a shared Islamic culture as an independent yet flexible determinate of identities.

At Home in Distant Places

Arriving in a new place in some distant land, Ibn Battuta regales his readers with the often quite startling customs and beliefs he encounters, including novel practices and ideas about Islam. With the catalogue of cultural distinctions and anomalies fully elaborated, he invariably ends his preliminary assessment of the strange new land and its people with the phrase "and they are Muslims."[28] Comforted by that thought, Ibn Battuta gets down to the practical business of setting up a personal and professional life as a *qadi* (judge who decides cases in accord with *Shari'ah*). He does so without undue emphasis on the novelty of his circumstances and the special difficulties it presents. His priorities are timeless. The *qadi* must find employment or make himself available for the patronage of some high personage. With a means of support secured, he then sets about setting up his household. To feel at home and at peace, emotional and sexual needs must be satisfied. All manner of customs in strange lands pique his curiosity, although none more than the sexual practices of the local populations.

Sex, in theory and practice, seems at times to be an all-consuming preoccupation. Ibn Battuta cheerfully assumes his readers have parallel drives. He unabashedly shares his discoveries. Afghanistan, the *rahal* reports, is a country of exceptionally beautiful and sensual women. He comments on their exquisite features, particularly their well-shaped noses and luxuriant eyebrows. The sensuality of Afghan women, the *qadi* notes, expresses itself in knowledge of a range of sexual positions that the experienced *rahal* reports never having encountered anywhere else.[29] In Turkey Ibn Battuta is fascinated by the hold that Queen Taitughli has on her husband, the sultan. She is the sultan's favorite wife and dominates his court. Several courtiers supply Ibn Battuta with what he finds to be a compelling explanation for the power she wields. The sultan sleeps more frequently in her chambers than with all the rest of his wives. From two well-placed courtiers, Ibn Battuta learns that the sultan himself reports that sleeping with his favored wife is like always sleeping with a virgin, despite the children she has borne. Ibn Battuta pursues the matter and learns from friends at court that there are reportedly women with a similar anatomy in China. That critical intelligence is filed away. Ibn Battuta later writes of his travels to several Chinese cities. With disappointment, he reports that he registered no success in finding Chinese women with those special anatomical gifts.[30]

Ibn Battuta's robust interest in sex does not preclude serious attention to the search for knowledge and spiritual enlightenment. Both scholars and saints consistently play their roles in the life he creates in each new site. Moreover, Ibn Battuta's voyages give him the opportunity to see women as more than beautiful adornments and sources of sexual pleasure. He shows no hesitation in reporting these discoveries as well. In the lands of the Turks, Ibn Battuta comments on the extraordinary levels of respect and power that women enjoy. They have, he reports with some disbelief, "a higher place in society than the men."[31] Such revelations could not have come easily to a Maliki scholar from north Africa, where the roles of women at court, especially in political matters, were far more indirect and almost never public. At times Ibn Battuta is clearly taken aback, as when he once observed a well-dressed, unveiled Turkish woman entering the bazaar in the company of her husband. He comments that her male companion might well have been mistaken for her servant.[32] The impressionable *qadi* cannot fail to notice the great wealth enjoyed by the wives of the sultan and the extravagant ways they displayed it. Ibn Battuta also notes just how much respect the sultan himself shows to his most senior wife. When she enters the golden tent, he reports that "the Sultan advances to the entrance of the pavilion to meet her, salutes her, takes her by the hand, and only after she has mounted to the couch and taken her seat does he himself sit down. All this is done in full view of those present, and without any use of veils."[33]

As Ibn Battuta moves through the diverse spaces of *Dar al Islam*, he inevitably encounters beliefs and behaviors of which he disapproves. He is a reformer by nature. His accounts of these struggles, at times in public arenas but more often in the most intimate spaces of his private life, are among the most revealing and engaging in his *Travels*. The specific, grounded details speak to larger and more abstract issues of the role of cultural and religious identity in everyday life.

Ibn Battuta found a great deal to admire in the lives of the Muslims of the Maldive Islands, where he remained for the unusually long period of a year and a half. He comments appreciatively on the fealty of the Muslim inhabitants of the island to their formal religious obligations. He openly admires their honesty in social interactions and probity in their everyday commercial interactions. His descriptions leave no doubt of the sincerity of his admiration. This backdrop of appreciation only serves to highlight Ibn Battuta's private dismay that the married men *and* women of the Maldives regularly establish intimate relationships with "friends" of the opposite sex, whom they entertain privately in their homes when their spouses are away. Ibn Battuta reports his astonishment at visiting the most respected *qadi* in an important city to find him entertaining a beautiful young woman "friend," without the slightest hint of impropriety. To the contrary, the local *qadi* mentions that he had recently made the pilgrimage to Mecca with his young friend. The woman is openly amused by Ibn Battuta's discomfort that she has been invited to join them. Her distinguished "friend," for his part, seems quite mystified by Ibn Battuta's response to the circumstance.

Ibn Battuta learns that such behavior is quite unexceptional. On another occasion, he visits a second distinguished personage at home. In the background, a woman and man are conversing intimately on a daybed. When Ibn Battuta inquires as to the identity of the woman, his host explains that she is his wife. Who is the man, inquires Ibn Battuta. Her "friend," he learns. Ibn Battuta's host is a man who has lived in Arab lands where customs are so different. The *qadi*, therefore, inquires why his host is not disconcerted by such behavior. The man replies calmly that the women of his country are quite different from those in Arab lands. In the islands, he explains, such interactions are perfectly acceptable. Later, the scholar sends Ibn Battuta several invitations to visit again. They are quietly ignored. But what is most revealing is the way Ibn Battuta tells the story. He clearly disapproves. However, he also notes just how well established these cultural practices are. At no point does it occur to him that these Muslims could be induced to change their ways to bring them more in line with the views of a *qadi* from north Africa.

Ibn Battuta is quite delighted on the Maldive Islands with the cleanliness and order of the most important city. He is also struck by the personal dignity and beauty of its inhabitants. However, he has a very hard time adjusting to the local habits of dress. The women of the islands, he reports, do not cover their breasts. Ibn Battuta makes a great effort to persuade the local notables and Islamic scholars that such behavior does not comport with the modesty that good Muslim women should observe. The male notables are quite unconvinced by his arguments, and the women of the islands find them even less persuasive. The best that Ibn Battuta can accomplish is insistence that all women who enter his courtroom cover their breasts or be denied entry. In their other activities, the women remained free to dress as they saw fit. For the *qadi* it is a small victory. Yet Ibn Battuta seems content that it represents the maximum change he can effect. Ibn Battuta always accepted with equanimity the idea that he could never understand other Muslims' lives or their stories in quite the same way as they did.

In his own more intimate personal spaces, Ibn Battuta is just as unsuccessful in imposing his notion of preferred behavior when it conflicts with established custom. The women who are so important in his life repeatedly resist his efforts to change their behavior. For the most part, they do so successfully. He accepts their victories. In one instance, he reports that neither his wives nor his female bonded servants are persuaded by his arguments that they should cover more of their bodies. We can almost hear in his accounts echoes of the voices of the women themselves. They chide him for insisting on their wearing clothing that will make them a mockery before family and friends. They object forcefully that the clothes would conceal their beauty. Ibn Battuta's argument for the costliness and elegance of the fabrics he provides carries no weight with women. They tell him that all the draping only diminishes the natural beauty that God has bestowed on them![34]

We also learn that by local custom women do not eat in the presence of their husbands. Ibn Battuta is baffled by the custom and exerts all manner of pressure on his wives to set it aside. He appreciates the attentive care that his wives give him. However, he wishes to enjoy their company as wives and not simply as cooks and caregivers. With some of the women, he has a measure of success. They do agree to take their meals in his company. With others, all his efforts have no effect at all. Once again, he simply learns to live with the way these individual women chose to interpret the latitude of the local custom.[35]

Not all the assessments of Ibn Battuta's encounters are his own. *Travels* also provides instructive glimpses of the ways in which the behavior and beliefs of the *qadi* are themselves evaluated by others, and the evaluations are not always favorable. As a strict Maliki *qadi*, Ibn Battuta seeks to impose the penalty of amputation of the hand that his literalist reading of *Shari'ah* mandates for a crime of theft. Not all Muslims, he learned in a dramatic way, agreed. The stunned *qadi* reports that when he pronounced his verdict, several witnesses in his courtroom fainted. Clearly, the strict enforcement of *al hudud* (punishments provided for in *Shari'ah*) was unacceptable to local sensibilities.[36] Ibn Battuta's story reminds us that apparently fixed aspects of Islam are subject to varying understandings and applications. All of these incidents, and countless others like them, establish not only that cultural differences are real within *Dar al Islam* but also that they are durable and actively resistant to change. Understanding cultural difference may be essential for a process of reform or change, but it is no guarantee that reforms will succeed.

Crossing Boundaries: India and China

The *Travels* does take us on several occasions to the furthest borders of *Dar al Islam* and beyond. Ibn Battuta approaches his adventures outside the lands of Islam with exactly the same attitude of responsive openness to the people he encounters. He appears just as confident that his basic understandings of the world will hold true, even when he crosses civilizational boundaries. There is nothing in Ibn Battuta's account to suggest that leaving the world of Islam means that one has left civilization, per se, or the company of men and women who are fully human. Moreover, he expects that the non-Muslims whom he encounters will have a reasonable understanding of how their society and culture work. Ibn Battuta remains confident that they will be perfectly capable of explaining their customs and beliefs to a stranger who comes to live among them. There will be work and there will be wives and lovers in these non-Muslim lands. In short, to leave *Dar al Islam* is not to leave the company of human beings who live in comprehensible and broadly acceptable ways. Although the reach for understanding may be longer and some of the surprises greater, Ibn Battuta's accounts make it clear that nothing fundamentally new is required of him to make his way among non-Muslims.

The *Travels* contains memorable descriptions of non-Islamic lands, including particularly vivid ones from India and China that stand out for their complexity and sophistication. For such contextualized descriptions, anthropologists like the phrase "thick description," borrowed from the philosopher Gilbert Ryle and popularized by Clifford Geertz. The label works here only in the suggestion of the importance of context. Characters and their actions can be understood only in the moral and physical environment within which they live. However, Ibn Battuta's contextual descriptions are fluid rather than thick. They are not built of layers that can be peeled away. They are rather shifting constellations of elements, all surfaces, on which human experiences take place. Meaning emerges from one constellation of these elements, only to be destabilized by a

competing arrangement that reveals a quite different yet equally compelling understanding of what is going on. That rearrangement, in turn,
may suffer the same fate. Truth, for Ibn Battuta, resides on the surfaces
on which we live. It is always plural. At play on those surfaces are shifting
constellations of meanings. They are available to experience but always
elude definitive description, "thick" or otherwise.

In India, Ibn Battuta takes us to the site of a Hindu *suttee* (widow
self-immolation ceremony). He guides us to the event through multiple
points of entry. We arrive on horseback with a group of other travelers,
not all of whom fully understand what is about to happen. This first approach initially has the feel of attending a village folk festival. We blend
into an assembled crowd with a sense of anticipation. Gradually, particular characters begin to emerge out of the crowd. A group from the family
of the deceased husband expresses very public grief for the loss of a son.
Their mourning lends a sense of the solemnity to what is about to tran-
spire. They have come to ensure that their rights and family honor are
respected.

As Ibn Battuta takes us closer to the immolation site, the men responsible for building and maintaining the fire come into clearer view. Established rituals guide the way they tend the fire. At one point the men throw
sesame seeds into the flames in what seems to be a symbolic gesture of
feeding. In fact, the purpose is as practical as it is symbolic: The oil in the
seeds excites the flames and augments the heat of the blaze. At this point,
the fearsome fire itself becomes the central character in the scene.

That dominance of the fire is eclipsed only with the arrival of the
widow. She is dressed in her finest, as though for a wedding ceremony.
Her family is arrayed around her. They evince pride that the honor of
their family, too, will be vindicated. The crowd is silenced and awed by the
widow's presence. Moving closer to the site, she calmly removes her jew-
elry and passes it to the women who accompany her. As she approaches
the site, the men tending the fire hold up a screen to shield her gaze from
the fearsome flames. Their gesture is meant to be protective. The widow,
with quiet disdain, pushes the shield aside. She calmly acknowledges the
full force of the fire. Her self-assured glance at the keepers of the fire
announces that she has accepted her fate. She moves toward the flames,
ready for what is to come. Ibn Battuta, however, has reached his breaking
point. He can bear no more. But for the intervention of his friends, he
would have fallen from his horse to the ground. The description breaks
off abruptly.[37]

Ibn Battuta accepts the reality of cultural difference. He is never indifferent as to its meaning and consequences. He nevertheless believes that the beliefs and actions of those from another culture can be brought into view. He accepts with equanimity the notion that knowledge of others will always be incomplete. He also understands that knowing does not mean approval or acceptance; it just means that one has a sense of what other human beings are up to. Knowledge of that kind generates confidence that one can successfully navigate difference, and sharpen one's own sense of self in the process.

The descriptions of Ibn Battuta's experiences in China are equally instructive. He learned from his travels that the borders between civilizations are very real. Still, he shows us that Islam finds them permeable. In China, he discovers large communities of Muslims. *Dar al Islam*, he teaches, is multicivilizational. The demographic sea of the Han Chinese presents to him human beings whose cultural world, like that of the Indian subcontinent, is radically different from his own. It emerges in his descriptions as no less human for that. In the end, China is a place with which Ibn Battuta chooses to minimize his interactions. He withdraws more than is his custom into protected personal spaces to flee from "unacceptable" sights and sounds.[38] Still, his curiosity about this quite different culture drives a characteristic quest for at least minimal understanding. While he finds certain aspects of Chinese culture intolerable, he finds other dimensions of thought and behavior not only acceptable but admirable. He manages to find in Chinese culture values he shares. Ibn Battuta praises the impressive cleanliness of the Chinese, a virtue important as an ideal to Muslims everywhere. He is also greatly impressed by the public orderliness of Chinese cities and the relative absence of crime. In the arts, too, Ibn Battuta finds things to celebrate. He judges Chinese porcelain and ceramics to be among the finest he has ever seen.

My admiration for Ibn Battuta's work is not blind. I am quite aware of the limitations of this particular exemplar of the great Arab and Islamic travel literature. I know that the sober Ibn Khaldun, for one, thought him a liar, although the harsh judgment invoked telling criticism. In the *Muqaddimah* Ibn Khaldun reports

One day I met the Sultan's famous vizier, Faris ibn Wadrar. I talked to him about this matter and intimated to him that I did not believe the man's stories, because people in the dynasty were in general inclined to consider him a liar. Whereupon the vizier Faris said to me: "Be careful not to reject such information about the condition of dynasties, because you have not seen such things yourself."

Ibn Battuta had other defenders as well. Muhammad ibn Marzu, a famous scholar in the city of Fez where Ibn Battuta composed his work, cleared the *rahal* of the charges of lying and declared that "I know of no other person who has journeyed through so many lands as (he did) on his travels, and he was withal generous and well-doing."[39]

At times, Ibn Battuta did make grand and sweeping statements, unsubstantiated by the facts at hand. You just have to learn to scale down the hyperbole and keep things real. Clearly, the pearl divers Ibn Battuta observed in the Arabian Gulf could not actually hold their breath for two hours or more, although Ibn Battuta's observations of their diving techniques are quite accurate.[40] And I suspect that Cairo did not really have the astonishing number of mosques that he claimed to have seen, although I suspect the skyline was dominated by a forest of minarets. I do not doubt that the city then, as now despite contemporary ravages, was quite magnificent. Undoubtedly, the rulers for whom Ibn Battuta worked, particularly in some of the more remote sites he visited, appreciated his services and were reluctant to see the *qadi* from the Arab lands of the Prophet Muhammad move on. However, it seems unlikely that the tears of dismay of one such minister actually splashed on his shoes, as Ibn Battuta reports.[41] Despite the evidence for his outsized libido, I am particularly skeptical of Ibn Battuta's claims that he managed to uphold his conjugal duties to the eight women, four wives and four *gawari*, who depended on him during his time in the Maldives. I have no doubt Ibn Battuta worked out a clever system of rotation. Nor do I question that he consumed the maximum of a certain fish that he firmly believed to be an aphrodisiac. Ibn Battuta himself certainly acknowledges no inadequacies: Male performance illusions reverberate through the ages.[42]

Learning from the Great Rahal

Ibn Battuta after all these centuries repays the effort to think and to travel with him. He has lessons, still important today, on how to live with human difference. Like many Americans, Christopher Columbus was quite naturally one of my boyhood heroes. How devastating to get to know him better as an adult! Columbus, history soberly records, was a marauding adventurer in the worst of the Western tradition of the quest for gold,

God, and glory. His record of theft, enslavement, and murder is quite appalling. What an embarrassment it is to have identified with him. How disconcerting to have the myths of the innocent voyages of discovery of the *Niña*, the *Pinta*, and the *Santa Maria* imprinted forever in your mind. The contrast to Ibn Battuta as an iconic figure is stark and revealing. Ibn Battuta did little harm as he roamed the world in a quest for knowledge, and for more worldly pleasures as well. His adventures were not all of the mind or the soul, and I have always found him all the more engaging for just that reason.

What makes Ibn Battuta so important for anthropology is that the knowledge he sought was practical and grounded knowledge of how other human beings live their own distinctive lives. Moreover, Ibn Battuta sought to understand the men and women he encountered well enough to live among them in peace. He invariably joined with them in pursuit of a measure of happiness and pleasure that could be shared. What makes Ibn Battuta's classic so durable and so instructive is that he does not simply describe the various networks that link the diverse parts of the *ummah* of his day. He lives through them and shares that life experience with his readers in the most intimate and vivid ways. Then he moves on.

The lessons from Ibn Battuta's work are in the details, and often the most intimate details of how social and personal spaces are shared. We learn, for example, precisely how cultures differ on the most basic questions of how basic human needs are fulfilled in diverse cultural contexts. Moreover, we learn with Ibn Battuta that variations within cultures also have great and often overlooked significance. Such differences are durable and highly resistant to change. They have considerable weight in influencing human behavior. They have a profound effect on feelings and sensibilities. They are not easily changed or altered in fundamental ways. Yet, for all the resilience of cultural differences, Ibn Battuta teaches that they do not preclude conversation and cooperation, although they may require some ingenuity and even boldness. In a diverse but connected social world, like the *ummah*, accommodation to important and deep differences must be made. Or, to put the matter in a more positive way, the acceptance of pluralism is a necessity. Islamic civilization has no enthusiasm whatsoever for the idea of a melting pot for human beings. Ibn Battuta, over six centuries ago, observed and recorded the mechanisms by which constructive accommodation could come about in matters large and small. These same mechanisms are still operative in *Dar al Islam*, as the voyages through *Dar al Islam* today by the Egyptian journalist Fahmi Huwaidi make clear. Human differences challenge mutual understanding. However, they do not end the possibilities of productive interactions of all kinds. The Qur'an, as we have seen, makes it clear that an exalted humanity must be both plural and productive. Muslims, indeed all human beings everywhere and in all times, are charged to cooperate in building the world in ways that celebrate human diversity as one of God's gifts. The practical lessons of Ibn Battuta's work all point in that direction. They are as relevant today as when he wrote his *Travels* in 1355.

6

Contemporary Networks and Fahmi Huwaidi

Do they not travel through the land, so that their hearts (and minds)
may thus learn wisdom and their ears may thus learn to hear?

QUR'AN 22:46

I ANTICIPATED A lifetime of travels, following the itinerary laid out by
Ibn Battuta. I reveled in the opportunities to experience, in his wake, Islam's inventive adaptations to local conditions across the globe.¹ I traveled along historic routes from Andalusia in Spain, across north Africa,
the Middle East, and central Asia, and on to China. Impressed by the
contrasts, I searched as well for the commonalities that made all these
far-flung and very different places *Islamic* lands. By observation and conversation, I sought to discover the ways ordinary Muslims across *Dar al
Islam* expressed their faith, as they went about the business of living. I
looked forward to adventures of all kinds in the large communities of
Muslims in Africa, India, and southeast Asia that I had not yet visited.
The ancient pathways that pass through those lands insistently beckoned.

Just when I had the timing of the final stages of my itinerary sketched
out, the unexpected happened. In the mid-1970s new issues began to
dominate my thinking and shape my interests. I continued my voyages,
but gradually my focus shifted. The great historic puzzle of sameness
and difference that lingers over the history of *Dar al Islam* gave way to
new questions. After several years of living in Arab countries, notably
Egypt, I concluded by the early 1980s that a great deal of the unifying history and heritage of classical and medieval Islam has survived
into the modern world. Contemporary Islam, for all the talk in those
years of its eclipse, remained a powerful force. The conviction gradually
took hold that millions of Muslims were succeeding in their daily struggles to live in accordance with their faith. Islam was renewing itself

and growing in strength. It was the efforts of ordinary people, I came to believe, rather than the grand battles of politics and foreign policy that ensured the spiritual coherence and worldly future of *Dar al Islam*. From this perspective, *al Tagdid al Islami* (the Islamic Renewal) of the late 1960s and early 1970s presented itself as a heightened awareness of everyday struggles already under way. Ordinary people aimed to bring Islam more centrally into their daily lives. They sought to strengthen the sense of connection to the worldwide *ummah* that Islam created. At sites across *Dar al Islam*, I took note of the impressive successes they registered, as Islam moved into the public square. Social and political movements under Islamic banners proliferated. Women, including my female students at the American University in Cairo, took the veil, often against the advice of their parents. Regular reading of the Qur'an became more and more a social norm.

Only a handful of Western scholars agreed with this broad conclusion that Islam was experiencing a rebirth, although that realization left me unmoved. For the majority of Western analysts the human future would be a secular one. Islam would be relegated to a historical museum. The Qur'an would have its place as an antiquarian artifact in a glass case.[2] The violent onslaught of nineteenth- and twentieth-century colonialism and imperialism had undeniably done great damage to the connective tissue of *Dar al Islam*. The great European empires dismembered the Islamic world with particular savagery. Yet, in my view, the Renewal and the popular response it evoked promised an improbable transcendence of those terrible ruptures. That promise raised intriguing questions for the most part ignored in Western scholarship: How did ordinary Muslims, responding to the Islamic Renewal, hope to reassert and strengthen their sense of connection to the *ummah*? What actions, all a form of resistance, were they taking to restore the vitality of the faith? How did the intellectuals of the *Wassatteyya* (Islamic midstream) propose to guide the efforts of Muslims to resist external Western intrusions and act to revitalize the heritage?

From my travels and experiences of living in Islamic lands, I was convinced that these questions were real and important ones, although almost no one in the scholarly community took them seriously. I wanted to get a more intimate sense of the great contemporary affirmation of Islam that was occurring across *Dar al Islam* from those who were making it happen. Ibn Battuta had made his point about the coherence of the *ummah*, but his influence in my consciousness began to wane. An absence occurred.

Enter Fahmi Huwaidi

Before long, I realized that a new presence had appeared. Without any conscious decision on my part, a more suitable companion for my new *talab al 'ilm* (travels in search of knowledge) appeared. The Egyptian journalist Fahmi Huwaidi moved figuratively into my life. He arrived without formal introduction. He didn't need one. I had begun following leading Egyptian political journalists in the 1960s, notably the Nasserist Ahmed Bahaeddine and the leftist Mohamed Sid Ahmed. Bahaeddine's combination of political intelligence and commonsense decency exerted a powerful appeal, while Sid Ahmed's nuanced leftism exerted its own attraction. Both were highly influential public figures. Both mentored younger journalists. Huwaidi emerged as a protégé of the secular Bahaeddine. From the outset he had a very distinctive voice. Even Huwaidi's earliest work had an Islamic coloration. His masterful Arabic and deep knowledge of the heritage set him apart as a journalist. His Islamic formation and often provocative views stirred endless controversies with prevailing secular and nationalist trends. Huwaidi commanded more and more of my attention. There was just something more *engaging* about Huwaidi. At the time the leftists and liberals among my colleagues were displeased, given his overt Islamic commitments, with my new companion for travels through the contemporary networks of *Dar al Islam*. They still are.

The Iranians and their extraordinary mass revolution cemented the new relationship with Huwaidi. In 1979 Huwaidi was working as a journalist in Kuwait. He arrived in Tehran on the first civilian plane into the airport after the revolution. I was initially convinced that Huwaidi was really a *rahal* (traveler), disguised as a journalist. However, Huwaidi's frequent travels were not an end in themselves. He makes his living as a widely syndicated columnist. Yet, before anything else, Huwaidi was emerging as a leading Islamic public intellectual. The *real* Fahmi Huwaidi at any given moment is always some shifting combination of the three identities of *rahal*, journalist, and Islamic public intellectual. Over time it is the Islamic intellectual who has come to dominate.

In *Iran from Within* Huwaidi provides his account of the Iranian Revolution of 1979.[3] The book is a modern-day classic, although it remains untranslated into English or any other Western language. Huwaidi traveled five times to Iran in the period between his first visit in 1979 and the publication of his book in the mid-1980s. His work in the Gulf before that among the large Shi'i communities there provided critical background even before his first visit to Iran. Huwaidi hit the ground in Iran running, aware of issues and personages, religious and ideological debates as well as political differences. *Iran from Within* provides an accumulative, layered picture of the revolution. It emerged only slowly, captured in shifting and fluid patterns as Huwaidi's own understanding deepened. As the picture of the Iranian Revolution and Islam's role in it sharpened, so, too, did my sense of Huwaidi as a serious Islamic thinker who had a deep understanding of both the faith and worldly history, including rare depth in his understanding of Shi'i Islam.

Huwaidi frames all his commentary on Iran with a broad vision of the importance of the revolution to the larger Islamic Renewal. For an American, Huwaidi provided an indispensable antidote to the hysterical reaction in the United States to the loss of the brutal, corrupt, but endearingly compliant regime of the shah. Huwaidi's perspective, in contrast, allowed one to grasp the historical importance of what the Iranian people had accomplished. For all that came later of sorrows and profound disappointment, Huwaidi makes clear the basis for his judgment that the success of the Iranian Revolution in removing the despotic regime of the shah ensured Ayatollah Khomeini's place in the history of the *ummah*.

Huwaidi wrote for fellow Muslims who advocated for the Renewal. I positioned myself imaginatively to overhear the conversations. From those travels and Huwaidi's commentaries, I learned of the places and people important to visit. I was made aware of the way the Iranian Revolution related to the other great unifying issues that mattered most to the future of the *ummah*. At Huwaidi's side, I could feel in particular the searing impact on the body of the *ummah* of the relentless Israeli colonization of Palestinian lands. I sensed with him the ominous threat it posed to Islamic Jerusalem. Huwaidi's published commentary yielded a practical record as well of the small actions of resistance that rippled through the *ummah* and gave unexpected life to the Renewal. Moving with Huwaidi, I was positioned to gauge precisely those subterranean developments, notably the heightened role of the faith in the everyday life of ordinary people, that Western scholarship missed.

I made it a point to know as much about Huwaidi himself as possible in order better to take the measure of his observations. Fahmi Huwaidi began his career in journalism very early. His father, an employee in the Ministry of Justice, had participated in the Muslim Brotherhood from its earliest years, under the leadership of Hassan al Banna. Although Huwaidi himself never joined the Brotherhood, he grew up in its presence.

While still a secondary school student, Huwaidi drew caricatures for the Islamic journal *al Da'wa* in the mid-1950s. He was detained by the authorities twice. At the time of his arrest in 1956, he was among the youngest political prisoners in the country. On his release, Huwaidi studied at the Faculty of Law at Cairo University, graduating in 1961. Before graduation, he joined the Research Department at *al Ahram* newspaper and worked there until 1976. During that period, Huwaidi supervised the religious page of the paper. In the early 1960s, President Sadat banned him from writing. Huwaidi moved to *al Arabi* magazine in Kuwait, where he served as managing editor. He never stopped writing and traveled frequently across the Middle East. In 1982, Huwaidi moved on to London to work as deputy chief editor of *Arabia*, the first English-language magazine addressed to the entire Islamic world. In 1984, he returned to *al Ahram*, where he remained until 2006, when the oppressive censorship under the Mubarak regime in its last years prompted his decision to leave. Huwaidi began to write regularly for *al Sharuq* newspaper and has remained a fixture there to this day.

Huwaidi from the outset wrote from a consistent centrist Islamic perspective. That viewpoint is midstream yet, paradoxically, is largely unstudied by Western observers. Most Western specialists focus their attention on the violent Islamic extremists. The countless articles that Huwaidi has produced over the decades represent a treasure trove of direct observation and experience moving through the centrist networks of the *ummah*. It has yet to be tapped for scholarly analysis in any systematic way.

Fahmi Huwaidi's close and often impassioned identification with the *Wassatteyya* (the Islamic midstream) may raise objections that he is too biased to provide reliable witness. After decades of reading Huwaidi, I find the description of his overall orientation accurate. I also find little merit in the charge. Huwaidi puts his centrist Islamic commitments forward directly.[4] Their effects are quite obvious. He makes no attempt to conceal them. They are no more pronounced than the conservative principles of my first graduate school advisor and mentor, Samuel Huntington, or the strong Zionist commitments of my second mentor, Nadav Safran. Neither of these Harvard scholars did much to mask their political commitments. Since their views were in line with dominant points of view, no one seemed to mind, and neither did I (although for my own reasons). Whether an academic, a public intellectual, or a journalist, we know where such forthright figures are coming from. It is really quite easy to take such explicit value commitments into account when evaluating their work.

Painting Fahmi Huwaidi with a black brush is a thriving cottage industry in secular Arab intellectual circles. From Huwaidi's vast body of published work, quotations taken out of context or the presentation of occasional excesses as representative can make the case that he is an Islamic extremist. For Arab and Islamic intellectuals with strong secular commitments, Huwaidi's insistent Islamic orientation can itself be a source of consternation. For those who support Israel's expansionist goals and America's imperial ambitions in the Islamic world, the task is even easier. Huwaidi staunchly and unapologetically opposes both. But so do I. Those positions, shared by anticolonialists and anti-imperialists around the world, hardly make one an extremist. Nor, for that matter, do they make one anti-Israeli or anti-American. Huwaidi, despite his personal elegance and the gentle formality of his personal interactions, can be abrasive in print. The seasoned journalist does have his rough edges. For *all* of these reasons, I considered myself fortunate that Fahmi Huwaidi had slipped into Ibn Battuta's shoes. Classic Islamic travel literature is drenched with an insatiable curiosity and a will to know more about Muslim brothers and sisters living close at hand or in distant lands within and beyond *Dar al Islam*. So, too, are Huwaidi's articles and books. Rarely do I come away from reading them without imagining I have learned something important. Of course, Huwaidi himself bears no responsibility for what strangers imagine they have learned about the Islamic networks through which he has moved for decades.

The Networks of the Islamic Midstream from Hardwiring to Software

Ibn Battuta first exposed for me the historic hardwiring of the Islamic world. Fahmi Huwaidi in turn has facilitated exploration of its most impressive contemporary software, designed and updated periodically by the Islamic midstream. As a columnist at *al Ahram*, Huwaidi was in constant motion. For many decades the paper was the largest and most influential of the official Egyptian newspapers and one of the most important Arabic-language publications in the world. Based for most of his career in Cairo, Huwaidi roamed all over the Islamic world. He generated a rich and instructive record of contemporary happenings. His accounts were as vivid as those of Ibn Battuta of places visited and personalities encountered. With time, however, Huwaidi's scholarly work eclipsed the journalism. The status of Islamic thinker was something the great *rahal* never achieved. In Cairo, Huwaidi surrounded himself with some of the most creative Islamic intellectuals anywhere in the *ummah*. He engaged with them on the great issues facing *Dar al Islam* with thought-provoking and original work. An impressive library of books by Huwaidi resulted. They reflect his sustained efforts, very often collaborative, to formulate a broad and inclusive centrist Islamic vision responsive to the needs of the late modern world.

My new companion for travels through the networks of centrist Islam could not have differed more from the great *rahal* who first inspired my voyages across *Dar al Islam*. Reserved about his personal affairs, Huwaidi's passions have consistently been Islam and the well-being of the worldwide Islamic community.[5] Huwaidi is a model of personal propriety. He evinces none of the character of the worldly rogue of my first companion. The man I have sought to know is the public intellectual whose weight is most directly felt in Egypt and other Arab societies but appreciated throughout the Islamic world. Huwaidi's public presence has been crafted over some five decades. The reactions and sentiments it arouses are always themselves instructive, particularly when Huwaidi plunges into heated debates about Islam's proper role in the struggles of Muslims to build better societies.

Huwaidi's work, like Ibn Battuta's before him, reveals a great deal more than the intellectual, political, or economic interests that animate the networks of *Dar al Islam*. The existence of *Dar al Islam* is sustained as much by shared social practices, memories, and emotions. Unities of subjective experience and feeling cannot easily be observed. They must be experienced. There is no alternative to experiencing the pervasive presence of Islam and the improbable coherence of the contemporary Islamic world from the inside. No single figure has had more privileged access to those interiors than Fahmi Huwaidi.

My travels throughout *Dar al Islam* since the early 1970s following Huwaidi have coincided with the emergence and development of the momentous Islamic Renewal. Many, both within and outside the Islamic world, have been alarmed by the increased role for Islam in public life that this shift has brought. However, it is my clear impression that the overwhelming majority of ordinary people have welcomed the enhancement almost everywhere of Islam's presence. The embrace, it should be noted, often does come with sharp criticism of particular Islamic parties and movements. It is a common mistake of outsiders to underestimate the capacity of ordinary believers to make such distinctions between their faith, on the one hand, and the claims to speak for it of particular Islamic groups, on the other.

My earlier prolonged experience with Ibn Battuta had suggested how best to make sense of the wealth of experiences gained moving through the *ummah*. With time, I had come to recognize Ibn Battuta as a forerunner of contemporary anthropologists. It seemed natural, therefore, not only to embrace Huwaidi as Ibn Battuta's successor but also to immerse myself in the anthropological literature that Ibn Battuta had helped pioneer. My aim was practical in my forays into the extensive anthropological literature on the Islamic world. I wanted to know what insights anthropologists provide into the sensibilities and skills of interpretation that I would need as I moved imaginatively with Huwaidi through the contemporary networks of midstream Islam. I wanted to know how much progress the anthropologists had made toward a useful anthropology of Islam that might assist my own work on the Islamic Renewal.

The Quest for an Anthropology of Islam

The guiding premise of my work on the Renewal has from the outset been that efforts to understand the experience of Islam in the time of the Renewal could not proceed by an exclusive focus on accessible exteriors. Other scholars have reached similar conclusions. Olivier Roy, in his influential *Globalized Islam: The Search for a New Ummah*, suggests a useful place to start the quest for internal understanding. Roy tells us that real knowledge of global Islam and the groups that actually people worldwide Islamic networks will require what he calls a "religious anthropology."[6] Knowledge of Islamic networks, he explains, cannot avoid the human encounter. We must acquire a sense of specific histories, geographic settings, and cultural contexts. Yet their human meaning can only be read from the inside out. There must be interaction with the human subjects of our quest. Knowledge of the interior life of the *ummah* is a critical part of the promise of an anthropology of Islam.

Roy himself posits this ideal only to back quickly away from it. With refreshing candor, he states plainly that the breadth of his subject matter and his own limitations as a scholar dictate that he opt for a network rather than anthropological approach.[7] Roy follows his praise of the rich fieldwork of anthropology with the admission that he does not have the range of skills and sensibilities necessary to generate the kind of contextual understanding that alone can bring the worldwide nodes of Islamic networks to life. Indeed, who among us does when the subject is the global community of Muslims? Instead, in *Globalized Islam* Roy gives us a focus on the networks themselves rather than the meaning they have for those who move through them.

Now, as Roy successfully demonstrates, we can quite competently trace much of what takes place in the new Islamic forms of electronic connectivity. Documents and communications are posted. Pathways between sites can be plotted. The frequency of connections can be tallied. The overall structure of the network can be sketched. In all these ways and more, mountains of data can be amassed. Yet just how useful for internal understanding are all the data that network analysis generates? Unless we have insight into the actual meaning to particular groups and individuals of those electronic postings and the grids that enable them, how much of value have we really learned? The externally viewed mechanics of human interactions are rather basic and generally of only very marginal interest. There is no way around talking with insiders. Inevitably, that means learning their language and traveling to meet them, although travel in itself is never enough. It is important to allow conversations to happen on their own turf or simply to be invited into the room to hear those already under way.

Travel, of course, need not be only physical. An artfully crafted story can carry us off to distant shores. The beautiful, whether in nature or the arts, has the power to transport. As a child in an inner-city neighborhood, I discovered that beauty in everyday life brings this gift of transcendence as well. I experienced it in the unlikely gardens of Italian immigrants who were our inner-city neighbors on Brown Place. They somehow produced grapevines and flowers on urban patches of abused soil in a neglected neighborhood of Jersey City. Arriving at Harvard for graduate studies, I was nevertheless caught unawares by just how far the beautiful can take us. I was quite unexpectedly captivated by Qur'anic Arabic, which leaves no one unmoved by its unexpected aesthetic power. Fahmi Huwaidi writes frequently of the importance of Arabic to Muslims. He revels in the beauty of classical Arabic. His own prose is a model of a stunning command of modern standard literary Arabic. References to the great figures of the classical era are threaded through his work in a language worthy of the references.

For me, it was the study of classical Arabic in graduate school that granted admission to the company of the intellectual giants who shaped the medieval Islamic heritage. The Orientalist scholars with whom I studied and whose works I read revealed very early on their limitations as guides to the contemporary world of Islam. Nevertheless, they did know classical Arabic and had experienced its beauty and power. Their love of the classical heritage and the great scholars of those times was as strong and genuine as their disdain for contemporary Arabs and Muslims. They immersed themselves especially in the contributions of the giants who forged the corpus of medieval Islamic philosophical writings.[8] They insisted their students do the same. Most influential for me were al Farabi (870–950), Ibn Sina (980–1037), Ibn Rushd (1126–1198), and al Ghazali (1058–1111). I have found Ghazali, in particular, endlessly engaging, as does Fahmi Huwaidi. A mystical experience transformed Ghazali's personal life. His attack on the philosophers and embrace of Sufism had a momentous impact on Islamic thought and spirituality through the ages. However, after all these years since our first encounter in the 1960s, I have still not forgiven him for refusing to characterize in any detail for his readers through the centuries just what his encounter with mysticism meant to him. The mystical experience, he reports, always entails "a kind of proximity to God," which various mystics represent in different ways. Ghazali himself refuses any such effort. He takes refuge in a line from the poet Abdullah Ibn al Mu'tazz (861–908) that says simply, "I do not remember what happened, so assume the best, and do not ask for a report!"[9] Ghazali dazzles by his speculative brilliance. He also exasperates by his silences, secrets, understatements, and inclinations to a mysticism that cannot be shared.

Ghazali's silences were splendid in themselves. They were also the perfect foil for Ibn Battuta. I was mesmerized by Ibn Battuta's loquacity, endless revelations, and proclivity to hyperbole. However, with so much action and chatter, it was the unspoken that moved me most. One of the great mysteries of Islam hovers over the work of Ibn Battuta. How was it possible to live in so many profoundly different ways and in such diverse circumstances and still remain a Muslim?

Ibn Battuta himself never engaged this issue directly. However, his great work does suggest a way to tackle this question and others like it. By his own example, he argues for gaining entry into the social world of those you seek to understand and for spending as much time as possible simply moving with them. That talent is very much in evidence in the work of Fahmi Huwaidi. The seemingly ordinary human interactions of daily life, both Ibn Battuta and Fahmi Huwaidi understand, are never really mundane. The ordinary takes on much larger meaning as part of the quest for the gratifications of love, friendship, spirituality, and know-ledge alongside the frequent struggles for sex, power, and wealth that characterize human communities. Most importantly, simply living with people creates spontaneous opportunities to connect with them in ways that exceed anything one could plan for.

Anthropologists are rightly annoyed when their work is viewed as an offshoot of travel literature. However, at the risk of causing such irritation, I must acknowledge that it was indeed Ibn Battuta who set me on the path that led eventually to the sophisticated work of contemporary anthropolo-gists. The encounter with anthropology, however, came only after I had made my own voyages from one end of the Islamic cultural continent to another, from Spain to China, in the thrall of the *Travels*. Ibn Battuta justified the meandering and quite purposeless character of my early voy-ages that I treasure to this day. He was at that point in my life the best of companions. The tireless Ibn Battuta emerges from the *Travels* as equal parts real historical figure and crafted illusion. I never minded: After all, every friendship, not just those of childhood, is inevitably at least one part imaginary.

Decades of living abroad in a wide variety of places has reassured me that diverse human beings can talk to each other and experience all manner of other pleasures together. The heavy lifting required of the stranger is not really so distinctive. It is not all that different in kind from the parallel work of those born in a village or city neighborhood as they try to understand each other well enough to live together peacefully and productively. That everyday achievement represents yet another of those miracles in small places that I have come to love. Of all the social scien-tists, it is the anthropologists who recognize and celebrate these miracles. They radiate an enthusiasm for knowing others. With fieldwork as the centerpiece of their approach, they are inevitably travelers. Moreover, an-thropologists have made notable progress in explaining how travels can become fieldwork that yields knowledge. They point to the ways in which casual experiences can become participant observation, or at least some reasonable approximation to it.

Some reserve, however, is in order when the aim is anthropological knowledge of the networks that define the *ummah* today. If the barriers were simply the limitations of any one scholar for so large a task, as Olivier

Roy suggests, one could assemble a team with the area skills and language competencies required. Unfortunately, there are more serious problems with the putatively ideal solution of "religious anthropology." Reading in anthropology made it clear to me that what we need is an anthropology of religion, rather than a religious anthropology. One need not be a religious believer to observe the role that faith plays for individuals and the groups to which they belong. The language of believers differs from the language of observers who seek to know them. In that unavoidable gap resides a host of challenges. There is quite simply no ready-made anthropological solution to our difficulties. Instead, the rich anthropological literature offers an instructive record of a *quest* for an anthropology of Islam. It is the thoughtful search and reflections on difficulties encountered, rather than any at-hand method, that are most instructive. That search will necessarily focus on particular interpretations of Islam that are shaped by the particular times and places where they occur. Believers may or may not recognize this reality, although anthropologists take it for granted.

As I moved along pathways brought into view by Fahmi Huwaidi, I turned to the work of the anthropologists to help make sense of what I was experiencing. Clifford Geertz, Paul Rabinow, and Michael Gilsenan are the three anthropologists who were most helpful in clarifying my own sense of how to work toward an anthropology of Islam. Like so many others, I found my introduction to anthropology in the elegant writings of Clifford Geertz. His slender and seductive volume, *Islam Observed*, opened the floodgates. For that I am grateful, despite my critical view of his work from the very first reading.[10] There was something magical about the promise of traveling from one end of the *ummah* to the other, from Morocco to Indonesia, and coming back to say something meaningful about Islam. There were obvious shades of both Ibn Battuta and Fahmi Huwaidi in the promise. I was also genuinely delighted to discover that at least one variety of social scientist could write pleasurable prose.

Geertz defined the starting point but not the destination. What disappoints in Geertz's most influential volume for Islamic studies is the silencing of the Moroccans and Indonesians with whom he presumably interacted. We learn very little about the nature of those interactions. How well did he know the local dialects, one wonders. It is Geertz himself who emerges as the central character in this most influential book, and indeed in all of his writings. His contribution consists of speculative interpretive essays that impress as a form of literature. They are not ethnographies at all. In fairness, it should be noted that Geertz's sweeping generalizations

ultimately do derive from what he has intuited, what he has grasped
from his field studies. Yet Geertz's greatest influence has come through
the essays. In these writings, Geertz the anthropologist emerges as the
master interpreter of a symbolic code. He stands apart, out of reach of
the subjects of his work. Behind the backs of those observed, the symbolic code to which he somehow has privileged access shapes beliefs and
behaviors. Behind their backs as well, Geertz explains the workings of
the code. Here Geertz reminded me of the Orientalists. Like them, he
seemed to believe he had captured some essence of Islam that obviated
the need to deal with Muslims. There was no need to engage the ways
their understandings, beliefs, and emotions gave the faith a distinctive
worldly reality. The Orientalists read actual texts, while Geertz read what
he constructed as social and cultural texts. With either approach, a disembodied Islam of the text could indeed be brought into view. But what do
we learn about the Islam of flesh-and-blood human beings?

I learned much more from Paul Rabinow, although not all the lessons
were positive. I read *Reflections on Fieldwork in Morocco* soon after it was
published in the late 1970s.[11] My undergraduate college roommate was a
Moroccan exchange student. With his help, in my senior year of college I
made plans to run off to Morocco with a woman I had met while studying
in France my junior year abroad. I therefore had a very focused interest
in fieldwork in Morocco. That personal plot unraveled; I went to graduate
school instead. Morocco, though, had won a secure place in my imagination, representing to this day the road not taken.

Over the years, I have traveled often to Morocco and worked there on
several occasions as a higher education consultant. As a kind of ritual, I
periodically reread *Fieldwork*. The book is a casual treasure. Fieldwork and
participant observation have come to define anthropology, and Rabinow
makes both real in unvarnished and instructive ways. I was taken by his
acknowledgment of an awkward sexual experience with a prostitute in
the village. Now, as graduate students, we knew that interactions in the
field covered the full range of human possibilities, spiritual and worldly.
Although rarely discussed in print even today, sexual encounters were not
then, nor are they now, unusual or, for that matter, always diversionary.

Knowledge, Rabinow explained, has a negotiated, created character. So
does the experience of sex, at least the more sophisticated varieties that
regrettably eluded the young Rabinow in the village. Learning in all these
areas always entails a process of negotiation, with both partners playing
an active role. Knowledge, as Rabinow insisted, was not something to be

collected like driftwood on a beach.[12] There can be no paid or passive partners in the quest for knowledge.

Rabinow's book helped me sort out my own experiences in the field. In particular, he put the travails of fieldwork in perspective. The battles invariably start with the debilitating intestinal wars. Those bouts, and the humility they impose, may well explain why those distinguished Orientalists whose work I first encountered at Harvard preferred classical texts to the field. Rabinow, in contrast, did make his way to a small and poor village in Morocco. He commented perceptively on the multiple challenges encountered with more frankness than usual.

There were, however, important limits to what could be learned from *Reflections*, especially given my own interest, like Fahmi Huwaidi's, in Islam. The book brought instructive disappointment. From the outset Islam was a problem for Rabinow. It cast a debilitating shadow over his life in the village. Rabinow gained entry to village life through a connection to a dominant family. He was assured access to informants and the general cooperation he would need to complete his fieldwork. However, what he could not overcome, from the first until his very last day in the village, were deep suspicions on the part of the villagers as to his intentions toward Islam. Rabinow explained to the villagers that his stay in their village was part of his graduate student training. His university had sent him to write a systematic history of the village, he told the villagers. The work would, he hoped, result in a book that would lead to a professorship, God willing. The notion of a history or even a systematic study of village society posed no problems, but the idea of a student identity did. *Taleb*, student in Arabic, had religious connotations for the villagers that they could not quite shake. The term also means to ask for or demand, with all the open-ended implications that definition carries. The villagers knew the young stranger was a Christian, thus triggering, as Rabinow reports, "the widespread fear that I was a missionary."[13]

Rabinow describes his continuous efforts throughout his village stay to disabuse villagers of this conviction. Yet, to the very last day, the conviction persisted that his true intent was to win converts from the faithful despite the fact, as he puts it, that "it should have been clear that I had not interfered with, denigrated, or tried to alter anyone's religious beliefs." Rabinow's frustration is palpable. What is even more revealing is his explanation of why his efforts failed. "The constant expression of pure and noble intentions," Rabinow explained, "is a rhetorical art which Moroccans have raised to the level of cultural performance, and they never take such profession of purity at face value." In frustration he concludes, "I did my best to assuage these fears during my stay. I stressed time and time again that my interests were historical and social, but I doubt that I was very convincing."[14] Rabinow believes that the truth of his explanations was blocked by a tradition that saw his protestations as simply a cultural performance of practiced dissimulation. This explanation preserves his innocence, in this regard at least. In Rabinow's account the culturally conditioned anxieties of the villagers, immune to argument, seem irrational and more than a little paranoid. They are *their* problem, not his.

There is a simpler explanation. The malaise of the villagers was perfectly reasonable. Some wariness at the presence of a wealthy young Westerner in such an unlikely setting is clearly warranted. No matter how little their formal education, Moroccan villagers had an idea of what powerful Europeans had done in Algeria and Palestine. It was not unreasonable to see the young American as an advance scout for a coming horde that would seize resources and undermine the Islamic character of their village. No European in such a setting should presume that his innocence will be taken for granted. Furthermore, Rabinow's response shows him to be quite unreflective about the Western fears and hostile attitudes toward Islam that he inevitably brought into the field with him. His own frustrations with Islam seem an important part of the problem. Travelers need to make sure they know exactly what is in their luggage. Rabinow's unhappy encounter with Islam drove him from Morocco. What Rabinow teaches has most to do with the ins and outs of fieldwork rather than any insight into the faith. In the end, he repositioned himself very far from Islam and that disquieting village in North Africa. His later research focused on postmodern theory and such subjects as molecular biology and genomics in which the subject of research doesn't question why it is being studied.[15]

In *Recognizing Islam* Michael Gilsenan explains how he shed such unreal innocence and latent cultural hostility.[16] It opens with one of the most memorable vignettes in the anthropological literature of the Middle East. Gilsenan tells the story of his introduction to the world of Islam as a nineteen-year-old overseas teacher in what is now Yemen. The narrative is recounted in an enchanting, dreamlike key. The young volunteer was living with a friend in Seyyun, an historic town ruled by British-appointed sultans. A family of *sherifs* (descendants of the Prophet Muhammad) dominated the area. Gilsenan reports meeting two young men of that family during a morning walk. They invited him to visit their home. He noticed immediately how their dress and manner, with a green band around their turbans, flowing cream-colored robes, and trimmed beards signified the "holiness and precedence of their position."[17] The experience was intensified when the small party encountered one of Gilsenan's own students. The teenager immediately stopped to kiss the hands of the young *sherifs*, signaling his respect and appreciation for their position. "The world was a perfectly formed magic garden," Gilsenan writes. "I was entranced. All my images of Islam and Arab society were brought unquestionably together."[18]

Soon Gilsenan and the young *sherifs* arrived at their impressive home that reflected the prosperity the family enjoyed from business interests in Indonesia. The door was closed firmly behind them. The windows were quickly shuttered. Lights were turned on, along with Western pop music. Whiskey came out of the cupboard. There was no talk of the faith but only of "stifling boredom, the ignorance of local people, the cost of alcohol, and how wonderful life had been in Indonesia." Several days later the dissolution of the "magic garden" was completed when Gilsenan, this time alone, encountered his own student once again. "We kiss their hands today," the teenager confided, "but just wait till tomorrow."[19]

The student was of the first generation of a peasant family to be educated. He was a Nasserist. His Arab nationalist and socialist commitments called for resistance to imperialism and to the conservative and reactionary social forces allied to it. He would talk to me, Gilsenan reported, "but I, too, was part of the apparatus of colonial administration, *a fact that he realized much more clearly than I did.*"[20] For the student, the young men whose hands he kissed were obstacles to independence and social justice. They had nothing to do with true Islam. Islam had no need of *sherifs*, or deference to wealthy merchants in green turbans, or forced reverence for a sham religious hierarchy. The real Islam was free of such intermediaries. As embodied in the Qur'an and the traditions, Islam stood for equalitarianism and justice. The young man believed that true Islam was a natural ally in the battle against local tyranny, corruption, and alien power.[21]

Things are not what they seem. Yet surely it does not take a trip to southern Arabia to recognize this universal truth. If there is a community on the planet, Muslim or non-Muslim, where meanings are clearly and truthfully labeled, where codes of conduct and patterns of behavior are transparent, I have yet to encounter it in decades of restless wanderings. Nor, his writings make clear, has the Egyptian journalist Fahmi Huwaidi. Gilsenan, as a seasoned traveler by the time he wrote his most important book, obviously knew this. Why, then, introduce his book with a vignette of shattered innocence from his youth?

In my view, this introductory vignette is quite artfully positioned as a playful foil for all the discoveries to come. Telling this story of deception usefully invokes the most damaging at-hand stereotypes about the Arabs and Islam. *It is all manipulation. Muslims, and not just the Arabs, do not say what they mean and they do not mean what they say. The faith is merely a screen for deception.* The implications of such views, when generalized, are pernicious: Muslims cannot, in the end, be talked to or reasoned with; they can only be remade, by force if necessary. Gilsenan will have none of this nonsense, although he has felt its force and understands its importance.

Gilsenan uses the story of his own youthful vulnerability to accepted Western notions of Islam to bring these widely held views front and center. His engaging narrative allows him to do so without wearying preaching. *Recognizing Islam* then goes on to provide guidance on how best to elude the grip of these stereotypes. Gilsenan shows us how to engage in fieldwork in Islamic lands that does not reduce itself to a blinkered search for those Muslims and those actions that confirm preconceived notions. I consider his book the most important one we have in Islamic studies on the nature of fieldwork. Gilsenan lays out no grand theory, nor does he claim to have discovered the magic key to all encounters in the field. Rather, Gilsenan illustrates concretely how to conduct fieldwork in ways that avoid the common pitfalls. At the same time, he explains what our knowledge gains will look like. He explains just how modest they are likely to be. Gilsenan reports that "those sentences so laboriously written down in the red-backed reporter's notebooks at one or two in the morning gave me such a sense of having achieved something concrete, having at last found out something." But then he questions: "but weren't they mostly remarkable for the days it took to realize their *slippery and obscure nature*?"[22]

Knowledge of Islam cannot even be aspired to without real human interactions that, for simplicity's sake, can be called "conversations." Islam cannot hold conversations. Only Muslims, always particular Muslims, can do that, and they cannot do so in the name of all Muslims. That reminder is the most important lesson of Gilsenan's work. In all his work the journalist Fahmi Huwaidi reinforces the point. Only particular Muslims can tell us, at times directly but most often indirectly, about the ways in which Islam has become a meaningful part of *their* lives. We can interact with them and take note of their behavior for clues as to what those meanings are. We can talk to them about issues of faith and the ways Islam enters into their lives.

These elements of encounters in the field mark all Huwaidi's experiences as he moves through the contemporary networks of the *ummah*. Huwaidi's work reinforces the point that reconstructions based on such "slippery and obscure" indicators, always twice removed from particular direct experiences of the faith, will mark the only available path to an anthropology of Islam. Along the way, there will be little ground for overconfidence about our footing. Feeling unsteady, however, will encourage the shedding of the heavy baggage of our own preconceptions.

Things are *never* what they seem. Preconceptions are most likely wildly off the mark. It is best to walk slowly into the field. I mean that literally. Western economists and political scientists, not to mention the now-ubiquitous security analysts, stride into unknown territory in far too purposeful a way. They think they know what they are looking for. Unfortunately, they invariably find or invent it. Such findings rarely have much to do with the world into which they have intruded. They are all about their baggage and the litter they inevitably leave in their wake.

Interviews can be arranged. Conversations, in contrast, are always events. Events are not easily scheduled or harnessed. They demand patience and flexibility. Real conversations frequently cause some discomfort. They invariably leave one feeling vulnerable for the unintended revelations about self and the unexpected and sometimes disturbing discoveries about others. Calculated attempts at staging such conversations for the most part end in defeat. Yet real conversations do happen in the field. On very rare occasions they can reveal something about particular human understandings of Islam in the settings into which we have intruded.

Gilsenan writes perceptively of such moments as part of his studies of the Sufi networks that crisscross the Islamic world. Gilsenan on several occasions experienced Islam's presence in the lives of the Egyptian Sufis among whom he did intensive fieldwork. For most Americans neon seems tawdry, associated with strip malls and strip joints. Yet, in many places in the Arab world, including Cairo where I live, green neon lights are frequently used to mark mosques. It is not unusual to have Qur'anic verses in neon both inside and out. The usual effect for a Westerner is distracting, even disconcerting. Gilsenan found it so in his regular attendance at a Sufi *zhikr* (ritual of remembrance of God) that is marked by collective chanting and swaying body movements. Gilsenan explains how with time and without conscious effort the associations that he brought to the scene faded. Eventually, something more abstract and more spiritual replaced them. The verses written in neon became quite simply *green*. It was not that green was recognized as the color of the Prophet, of the revered mystic figure al Khudr, or of life itself. Gilsenan had always known that history of the symbolism of the color green in Islam. Something more basic and less cerebral was at work. Gilsenan explains:

> Then, one day, perhaps eight or nine months after my first hesitant observations of the zikr [*sic*], I turned unthinkingly away from the swaying bodies and the rhythms of the remembrance of God and saw, not neon, but simply greenness. Greenness, and letters that did not "stand for" anything but simply were powerful icons in and of themselves. No gaps existed between color, shape, light, and form. From that unreflecting and unexpected moment I ceased to see neon at all.

He continues that "it is the direct, self-creating, and recreating experience of greenness that 'just is' for Muslims in a particularly ordinary way, both intimately the same as and distinct from our own, that is so vital."[23]

Gilsenan refused to over-intellectualize the experience, but he did try to explain it. The spiritual is *not* otherworldly in Islam. It makes its appearance in this world. The entire Earth for Muslims is a mosque, a suitable place to pray and feel God's presence. The spiritual coexists and commingles with the full range of human experience. As Gilsenan teaches us, we can with patience learn to see Islam as a spiritual force in neon. These moments can only be apprehended in a spiritual register. Yet they reveal that Islam's presence does enter into even quite ordinary activities like Sufi rituals. Gilsenan helps us understand how networks such as those of the Sufi order do bind the *ummah* and give it a distinctive character.

The Promise of Network Analysis

For the most part, however, those who have turned to network analysis thus far have had agendas quite different and largely irrelevant to the quest for an anthropology of Islam. They serve other purposes. They include security analysts, on the one hand, and Islamic studies scholars, on the other. The security analysts, like those of the Rand Corporation, focus on the ways that flattened and horizontal networks of militants represent a threat to established authorities. The Rand structural network studies purposefully avoid engagement with the actual Muslim fighters who populate militant networks. Such distance guarantees that no empathy for the fighters, so often struggling against impossible odds, will seep in. Such analyses, with their deliberate distance from the believers who move through the networks they study, can contribute nothing at all to an anthropology of Islam.[24] They aim for control rather than understanding.

A different kind of distance marks academic network studies. The best aim for a grand rethinking of Islamic studies to "explore the dynamic past but also to imagine an elusive future, both of them marked by Muslim networks."[25] Networks operate as a core metaphor for the connectivities that unify the Islamic world. Such rethinking of Islamic studies along network lines teaches a great deal about how Western efforts to understand Islam have often gone wrong. It usefully addresses longstanding imbalances and distortions, such as the falsifying polarity of Islam and the West and other such deeply engrained Western stereotypes of Islam. Such work has enriched Islamic studies but in the end makes its major and most substantial contribution in what it tells us about *Western* thinking about Islam.

The Pragmatic Alternative: Grounded Network Analysis

This study is driven by practical interests closer to the ground of the everyday life of Muslims. The anthropological focus here entails the modest project of knowing enough about specific people to communicate with them and make reasonable estimations of how they live their lives. For access to that inner life of the communities and groups in which they are interested, anthropologists in the field rely on informants from the community of people among whom they wish to learn to live. The strategy here parallels that effort. Anthropologists frequently identify themselves as "interested strangers." In that guise they turn for guidance and insight to articulate and aware informants, although I agree with the anthropologist Andrew Gardner that the term "sounds too formal and oddly traitorous to stand for these relationships."[26] These critical sources belong to the social world of interest. They also have the awareness and skill to communicate what they experience. Ibn Battuta represented such a figure for *Dar al Islam* in the fourteenth century. The Egyptian journalist Fahmi Huwaidi plays a parallel role for the contemporary *ummah*.

Pragmatic network analysis takes the underlying coherence of the *ummah* as a given. To be sure, Huwaidi is fully aware of the damage that has been done to the wholeness of *Dar al Islam*. Yet he remains convinced that the ties that bind, including the all-important spiritual ties, can be restored. What is required is the revival of the sense of belonging to the *ummah*. As the historian Tareq al Bishri argues, the task of reviving the sense of belonging to a shared Islamic world "just needs patience and alertness to the keys to bring people together in ways that empower them to influence states and the relations among states through infiltration just like water flows from one land to another."[27] Such an imaginative comparison is impossible without its spiritual dimension. The West has convinced itself that the modern era has brought the end of grand narratives and the death of God. Islamic intellectuals like Huwaidi and the historian Tareq al Bsihri disagree. The most influential midstream Islamic intellectuals of our time, both Sunni and Shi'a, have heralded the project of the Islamic Renewal that is nothing if not a grand narrative. In *Dar al Islam*, they announce quite rightly, God is not dead.

Such is the starting point of Huwaidi's work as witness and advocate for *al Tagdid al Islami*. Today, to know the *ummah*, why rely on the hired hands of the world's intelligence services, the ideological polemics of the denizens of overheated think tanks, or the intermittent work of university professors who venture periodically to the field from their campuses in the West, when we have a lifetime of reporting on centrist Islamic networks by one of the most important journalists and Islamic thinkers of our time? Doors open for Fahmi Huwaidi. Tareq al Bishri concluded his analysis of what revival of the *ummah* would demand with the clear recommendation that "the first step toward strengthening that possibility is to revive the awareness of the shared community through a continuous and systematic follow-up of the events and incidents that shape the Islamic world."[28] It would be hard to imagine a more apt summing up of Huwaidi's career and the critical role he has played as a journalist and a centrist Islamic intellectual.

Learning from Huwaidi: Midstream Islamic Networks from Within

With Fahmi Huwaidi as my guide, the pace of my travels in *Dar al Islam* immediately quickened. The task was not so much to study Islamic networks but rather to move through them. Following Ibn Battuta left one open to aimless wanderings and unexpected adventures of all sorts. They were quite frequently more worldly than spiritual but always saturated by the insatiable curiosity that marks the anthropological imagination. There was always time to linger. Diversions of all kinds were to be savored. Huwaidi, in contrast, gives clear purpose to travels. Itineraries are laid out, schedules fixed, and objectives clear. All voyages and the writings they inform became part of an untiring quest for understanding midstream Islam in the modern world. They did so from the point of view of an engaged Islamic intellectual whose work aimed to reveal ways to advance the well-being of Muslim peoples everywhere.

Over the years, as I have traveled imaginatively with Huwaidi, I have managed to add exploratory side trips to slow his pace. I am always pleased when Huwaidi invites a friend to accompany him. It is in the nature of friendship to slow things down. Of such companions the late Egyptian journalist Ahmed Bahgat was my favorite. You cannot have a Sufi soul like Bahgat did and not linger pointlessly, until, that is, the point announces itself quite on its own.

As a fellow columnist at *al Ahram*, Bahgat also traveled widely, although he often did so without leaving home. He is less of a *Wassatteyya* intellectual figure than Huwaidi, although he sympathizes consistently with centrist methods and aims. However, it is also clear that he believes, rightly I think, that a conversation with the greatest of the Sufi poets, such as Galal Eddine Rumi (1207–1273) or Hafiz (1320–1388/9), offers as much to the advancement of the *Wassatteyya* as an interview with Turkish Prime Minister Recep Tayyip Erdogan, Malaysian Prime Minister Mahathir bin Mohamad, or Iranian President Mohammad Khatami. This creative interplay between Huwaidi and Bahgat nicely illustrates the way that both mind and heart are important to understanding the intellectual and emotional strengths of the Renewal.

Fahmi Huwaidi's perceptive self-awareness means that he understands himself to be traveling through *the already interacting parts* of the centrist network. At no point does he set out to theorize centrist Islamic networks in the abstract. Rather, through his travels and his writings he simply makes their existence palpable. He also suggests ways they might be strengthened. In this sense, Huwaidi sees himself as a constituent element in a process already under way. He aims pragmatically to make possible intelligent activity in relation to that process. Huwaidi shows no interest in explaining the way actors in the network, considered in isolation, came to constitute the whole. As a set of interacting parts, the networks of the *Wassatteyya* precede the individual figures like Huwaidi who move through them. The point, by analogy, is that there aren't any flames before the fire is already burning. Nor are there New Islamic centrists like Huwaidi before the *Wassatteyya* has made their presence possible. Before the trend is under way, there simply are not any isolated figures of the *Wassatteyya* with the interests, commitments, and patterns of practical activity that they display when participating in the whole. At no point does it make sense to take the elements we reify from the process and see them as the causal conditions for the process that they constitute. Social scientists, it should be noted, regularly ask precisely such unhelpful questions about how individuals come to form a society or a social movement. Just as Ibn Battuta did not create the ancient pathways of *Dar al Islam*, so, too, Huwaidi understood that he did not generate the contemporary networks of the *Wassatteyya*. He simply moves through them and thereby creates opportunities for outsiders to catch glimpses of their character as insiders experience it.

Huwaidi is more than an observer and analyst. He plunges into the events that shape the Islamic world. He pays particular attention to the creative movements and groups that work to advance the aims of the *Wassatteyya*. Huwaidi brings to his readers vivid and energizing reports about the real-world reforms and experiments in which Islamic centrists are engaged. He suggests the ways these social experiments might inspire parallel work elsewhere. Huwaidi takes sides in ongoing controversies. His widely recognized standing as an Islamic intellectual lends weight to the evaluations he offers. He is, in the words of social practice theory, an "authorized scorekeeper."[29] What is significant about him being an "authorized" rather than a "respected" scorekeeper, for example, is that the people whose work he is assessing take his evaluations seriously. As a recognized Islamic thinker, Huwaidi is entitled to offer his judgments. Islamic activists and theorists generally feel obligated to respond to his evaluations and entitled to make use of his reports.

The purposefulness on Huwaidi's part makes rigorous demands on any effort to provide an overview of his work. The aim here is to identify, among the countless articles and numerous books, those exemplary moments when the quest for wisdom does bear fruit and when the effort to hear does amplify important but long-silenced voices. Huwaidi makes demands on both mind and heart. From the extensive corpus of his work, useful analytical summations of broad patterns do emerge, as well as

informative distillations of what Huwaidi takes to be their larger meaning. Huwaidi's evocations of places and persons are another matter. Only
the heart can respond to their emotional impact. Huwaidi understands
the ways emotions and feelings make their own distinctive contribution
to the Islamic Renewal. From the raw materials of his observations, he
crafts evocative opportunities for readers to feel their force.

The Islamic Strategic Triangle of Egypt, Iran, and Turkey

Huwaidi establishes that the collective history of the *ummah* does show
broad and revealing patterns. Above all, he insistently points to the enduring imprint of what he calls the Islamic strategic triangle of Egypt,
Iran, and Turkey. Huwaidi's work indicates the ways that the histories of
Arabs, Iranians, and Turks are historically bound together. He points out
how the contemporary experiences of these Muslim peoples provide significant reference points for the struggles of Muslims everywhere to live
their own understanding of the faith.[30] Most importantly, Huwaidi argues
that the prospect of the consolidation of those underlying connections
holds great promise for the future of the *ummah*, however distant such
prospects might be at a given moment.

Huwaidi's reporting shows particularly well-worn pathways between
Egypt, Turkey, and Iran. Today each of these Egyptian, Iranian, and Turkish poles has a population of roughly eighty million or more. Together
they represent impressive human and natural resources. Huwaidi directs our attention to the signal advantages of geography that the triangle
enjoys. Arabs, Turks, and Iranians, he notes, represent a coherent block
that extends over territory that includes the most strategic maritime passages in the world. The area boasts the world's largest oil reserves in addition to huge stores of natural gas. Oil and gas pipelines for the whole of
the industrial world pass through this region. Finally, Huwaidi does not
fail to remind us that Islam creates a powerful natural connection among
the majority populations in the region.[31]

Naturally, Huwaidi is most interested in exploring this Islamic dimension. In his commentaries Huwaidi reveals how the histories of Egypt,
Iran, and Turkey remain braided together in loose but important inherited patterns. Those patterns, he argues, remain relevant and important
to *Dar al Islam* today. In the body of his work Huwaidi provides an exhaus-
tive study of the contrasting yet complementary experiences of Islam in
Egypt, Iran, and Turkey. Huwaidi, as a leading member of the Egyptian

New Islamic school, has played a key role in elaborating the centrist New Islamic vision of the future of Islam. He has given almost equal time and energy to efforts to understand Islam in revolutionary Iran. At the same time, he has carefully chronicled the quite remarkable rise to dominance in public life of a distinctive Turkish Islam, rooted ultimately in Sufism.

The Egyptian, Turkish, and Iranian lived experiences of Islam have all three been critical to the global coherence and historical continuity of the contemporary community of Muslims. None of the three points of the triangle appears in Huwaidi's depictions as fixed endpoints. All three are themselves nodes in multiple networks that open to further connections and invite yet more travel and interactions of all kinds. Egypt and Turkey are Sunni, while Iran is Shi'i. Built into the notion of an Islamic strategic triangle is an inclusive commitment to recognize and struggle to transcend the Sunni–Shi'i divide that has for centuries threatened to weaken the *ummah*. Huwaidi carefully registers the distinctions entailed in these designations. Yet, in the end, he tilts decisively to the conclusion that "they are all Muslims," although he is quite aware that not all Muslims have come to this realization.

Centrist reformism in Egypt, revolutionary dynamism in Iran, and quiet and resilient mysticism in Turkey define three strikingly different modalities of the Islamic Renewal. They indicate the way in which Huwaidi gives a distinctively Islamic focus to the notion of a strategic triangle that goes beyond politics, economics, and geographic advantage. All three angles of the triangle represent elaborations responsive to different environments of Islamic *'aqida* (doctrine). Huwaidi explains how these contrasting yet complementary experiences of Egypt, Iran, and Turkey reinforce the underlying coherence of *Dar al Islam*.

Huwaidi, in his situated commentaries from all three angles of the triangle, provides privileged access to experiences as they are processed and understood by millions of Muslims. In hundreds of articles, very often written on site, Huwaidi records developments in Egypt, Iran, and Turkey with an eye to the ways they advance or impede the prospects for the unity of the *ummah*, centered on the strategic triangle. The records from these key sites, weighed and considered by centrist intellectuals throughout the *ummah*, contribute to the common repertoire of the Islamic Renewal. They identify broad patterns that define the Renewal. They provide resources on which movements throughout *Dar al Islam* can draw in ways that respond to their own distinctive circumstances. Huwaidi points to that repertoire as a source for inspiration rather than for definitive prescriptions or models.

Other Travels, Other Broad Patterns

The strategic triangle is not the only pattern to emerge from Huwaidi's travels. It is simply the most important as measured by the analysis and commentary it evokes in the writings of major figures who identify themselves with *al Tagdid al Islami*. Huwaidi does bring into view an array of other such broad patterns. He uses his platform in *al Ahram* and stature as a major Islamic thinker to renew ties with parts of the *ummah* that have been broken, most often by political barriers that isolate Muslim communities. He works as well to overcome the neglect of other areas that merit greater attention from the traditional centers of the Islamic world in Egypt, Turkey, and Iran. At the same time, as an intellectual of standing Huwaidi works to highlight important research findings and the fruits of practical experiments on matters of importance to the *ummah* as a whole, such as democracy or development.

Huwaidi ventures repeatedly into newly accessible Islamic lands of great potential importance to the *ummah*. The exemplar here is his frequent reporting from the Muslim communities of central Asia that have emerged as independent states in the wake of the collapse of the Soviet Union. The purpose is to reestablish historical connections with Muslim peoples absorbed into the Russian and Soviet empires and cut off for decades from contact with the Islamic world. These renewed linkages with the great centers of Islamic learning in central Asia and the sites of some of the most impressive architectural treasures of the classical period are an important enhancement of *al Tagdid al Islami*. Huwaidi's reports have a particular importance to Turkey and Iran since both countries have strong cultural ties to central Asian lands and peoples. However, all of the *ummah* is called to respond to Huwaidi's updated treatment of the reopening of these historical centers of Islamic civilization.

At times Huwaidi travels to areas of the *ummah* with which connections have frayed. The aim is revitalization. Such travels take Huwaidi to neglected parts of the *ummah*, most notably in Africa, with its estimated 250 million Muslims. African Islamic intellectuals welcome the attention to their experience of Islam and the opportunities that Huwaidi often brings with him to enhance educational and cultural ties.

Huwaidi's voyages through *Dar al Islam* often have purely intellectual and academic purposes. He regularly takes his readers to conferences and research centers throughout the *ummah*. From these sites he reports on innovative efforts to reinvigorate Islamic learning and strengthen institutional ties among Islamic research and cultural centers. Huwaidi through his reports encourages debate and discussion on critical theoretical issues and their grounding in particular Islamic experiences. He pays notable attention to ongoing Turkish and Tunisian debates on the relationship of Islam and democracy. He makes sure that the economic advances of Malaysia and Turkey in the development of successful economies in Islamic political and cultural settings receive the attention they deserve.

For many Westerners, the government of Recep Tayyip Erdogan in Turkey, with its clear Islamic roots, seemed to come out of nowhere. Such is not the case for readers of Huwaidi's columns. Over many years he has followed the intricacies and the ebbs and flows of attempts to establish a Turkish political party with an Islamic orientation that can flourish in a secular setting. In parallel fashion Huwaidi has brought insightful attention to the rise of the Malaysian "tiger." Huwaidi documents the role played in that economic success story by Mahathir bin Mohamad who was Malaysia's prime minister from 1981 to 2003. Huwaidi focuses not simply on the impressive measures of economic growth or the intemperate bursts of anti-Israeli rhetoric that distort Western understanding of this pivotal figure. Huwaidi emphasizes the ways in which Mahathir brought a tolerant Islam to the rescue of a country plagued by ethnic and religious divisions. He brings into view a political figure who was also a serious Islamic thinker who made important contributions to contemporary Islamic thought. Huwaidi has repeatedly cautioned that, while the Turkish and Malaysian experiences convey instructive lessons on such critical issues as economic growth and democratic development, there was no Turkish or Malaysian model that could be implemented in any mechanical way elsewhere. Yet Huwaidi does aim to go beyond journalistic reporting to distill important and practical generalizations that advance the aim of understanding the essential political and economic dynamics of the Islamic Renewal.

Distillations: The Modalities of Islam's Response to the Western Threat

An important focus of Huwaidi's extensive work on the strategic triangle of Egypt, Iran, and Turkey has been the relationship between the impact of the West and a heightened presence of Islam itself as well as the emergence of Islamic movements of all kinds. Huwaidi has shared this preoccupation with other New Islamic thinkers, notably the historian Tareq al Bishri. From their collective work over many years, the New Islamic intellectuals offer a simple and compelling generalization on how different modes of resistance are generated. They reason that the deeper the Westernizing trend and the more violent the means used to advance it, the more radical the Islamic response is likely to be.[32] A quietist response to Western and Westernizing pressures takes shape in sites where a secular government with strong nationalist credentials attains a strong measure of legitimacy, especially with urban liberal elites, the higher reaches of the government bureaucracy, and the military. Outside imperial powers are kept at bay and the public appreciates the regime's nationalist successes. When such a secular government, like that of Atatürk in Turkey, consolidates its power, it invariably aims directly and with all means at its disposal to eliminate Islam from all aspects of public life. Islam is seen as the most likely opposition force to the blend of nationalism and secularism that defines the regime. In the face of such a powerful repressive onslaught with considerable popular support, the most effective response is indirect. Islam in its spiritual and quietist dimensions seeps like water into the soil of the nation. It avoids direct confrontation with a hyperempowered secularism. At the same time, it feeds the roots of the cultural legacy and creates the conditions for later resurgence. Turkish Islam, shaped by such figures as the Sufi Said Nursi, survived militant secularist attacks. It did so as a subterranean spring, out of repression's reach until a more propitious moment arrived to resurface in the public sphere.

A centrist middle way of reform and resistance, like that of Egypt, with reliance primarily on nonviolent reform, becomes possible when Western influence is indirect. In such cases the postcolonial national government coopts enough of both national and Islamic symbols to mask to some degree the authoritarian character of its rule. Typically, such a government allows some limited role to civil society. A circumscribed public life takes shape. The regime offers circumscribed tolerance to diverse political forces. An opposition press is tolerated. Movements with an Islamic orientation play a role and the public becomes accustomed to their presence. Such movements, like the Muslim Brotherhood in Egypt, become the seedbed of activist Islamic political forces, primarily centrist with only occasional radical offshoots. The predominant centrists attempt to cultivate broader support that goes beyond the Islamic trend, although without any great success.

The radical revolutionary Islamic response like that in Iran takes shape in a context where Western incursions have been most violent and have penetrated most deeply. Under such circumstances, the dependent, overtly pro-Western regime the Western powers installed is most repressive and most compromised in its claims to represent the nation. Yet it is also deeply entrenched and protected by a complex of security forces and the promise of external support. For these reasons, displacement of the shah required an "earthquake."

Evocations: The Ummah *Has a Soul*

Huwaidi complements these well-founded analytical summaries with more personal evocations of specific persons and places that give emotional depth to his reports. Huwaidi's descriptions in both registers of the mind and the heart allow readers not only to see general patterns but also to feel their emotional impact. Inevitably for an Arab and Islamic intellectual, the great Western crime against Palestine and the Palestinians dominates. The images and sounds of a threatened and humiliated Islamic Jerusalem permeate Huwaidi's work. His writings express the pain of the terrible losses suffered by the Palestinian people. "We are all Palestinians" is how Huwaidi repeatedly expresses his commitment at those times when the suffering is greatest. These cries of anguish and anger over the torment of Palestine ring through all of Huwaidi's work. By no means, however, do the fears for Jerusalem and the Palestinian people stand alone as reflections of the soul of the *ummah*. There are other such evocations of deeply felt sentiments as well. They all center on the unity and inclusive character of the *ummah*. They inevitably begin within the strategic triangle. However, they draw as well on the experience beyond the triangle, from Bosnia in the heart of Europe in the West to China in the East.

Bringing the Islamic Strategic Triangle to Life

An emotional connection to Turkey and to Turkish Islam looms large. Huwaidi's periodic visits to Turkey often meant that Ahmed Bahgat would travel with him. The decision was always a wise one. The Turkish experience is Eastern and it is Western. It is Islamic and it is secular. Huwaidi conveys this complexity analytically. However, it is Ahmed Bahgat, with his Sufi sensibility, who most effectively captures the essence of Turkey's Islamic identity. Bahgat especially loved the poet Galal Eddine Rumi, who fled Persia when the Mongols invaded and eventually settled in Anatolia. Bahgat understood Rumi's relevance to the mysticism at the heart of

Islam in Turkey. Bahgat often introduced that great Sufi thinker into his reporting. From Rumi Bahgat gives us the story of a servant who suffered from double vision. His crossed eyes produced two images, side by side, of any object before him. One day his master called to him from another room to bring a bottle to him. The servant asked which one. The master replied that he only wanted one and that the other could be discarded. The servant broke and threw away what he took to be the second bottle, only to find that both had shattered.[33]

Bahgat believed that understanding Turkey required double vision: Anything less is simply destructive of the complexity of the Turkish experience. Huwaidi's analysis makes it clear that the Turkish people have not renounced Atatürk, nor have they accepted the notion of an Islamic revolution in Turkey. In our own time, to see Turkey whole is to embrace both the secular nationalism of Atatürk and the Sufi Islam of Said Nursi. To deny either is to shatter the wholeness of the Turkish experience, as the story from Rumi suggests. Secularism is far from discredited in Turkey. Atatürk retains his founding father status. All Turks know that in the end Atatürk did protect the Anatolian heartland and kept Turkey out of the clutches of colonial rule at a time when there were armies of four European powers on Turkish territory. This history in no way contradicts the strong attachment to Islam of the Turkish people. Deeply felt Turkish Islam, with pronounced mystical overtones, coexists with intense Turkish nationalism.

To Huwaidi's analytical gift for political analysis, Bahgat juxtaposes a Sufi sensibility. Bahgat writes with astonishing brevity, drawing mostly on his own personal reactions to persons and events. In his reporting, Huwaidi dissects, in overwhelming detail, the meaning of the electoral victory of Islamic centrists in Turkey for all of *Dar al Islam*. At the base of his political commentary is the assumption of the depth of commitment to Islam of ordinary Turks, particularly those from the countryside. Ahmed Bahgat strikes the same chord, but he does so in his own distinctive way. Bahgat tells the story of a visit to Medina in Saudi Arabia, where he was able to pray at the Mosque of the Prophet. Bahgat prefaces his meditation on the experience with the comment on the human inclination to give priority to family ties. Bahgat disagrees: He believes that there are Muslims today who love their fathers very much but love Omar Ibn al Khattab more; who dearly love their mothers but love the Mother of Believers, Khadija, even more; who love their sons very much but love the Prophet Muhammad more. Bahgat explains that to make such connections of the mind and spirit, and not simply biology, we need strong emotions. We need, he writes, a person "whose heart flies with the stars." Bahgat continues that "Man, originally, is a part of the earth and the earth is part of the solar group which is part of the universe. Thus, Man lives in a universe with galaxies, suns, moons, mountains, seas and deserts and without intellectual connection the universe will be a lonely place, and moons and mountains will lose their meaning. Connections of mind and spirit actually give meaning to everything . . ." He explains that "when we find a friend, a lover, or a stranger who thinks like us, then we feel that earth's rotation around the sun has a meaning of love."[34]

To illustrate his point, Bahgat describes an experience with a Turkish Muslim in the Prophet's Mosque in Medina. Bahgat was reading the Qur'an in the mosque. When he finished, a man approached him and said things in Turkish that he could not understand. Bahgat tried to tell him that he did understand Turkish. The man signaled by gestures "it is not important whether you know the language or not. The important thing is that we are more than brothers. Our God is one, our Prophet is one, and our Holy Book is one. That is enough for creating a cultural and spiritual connection."[35]

Huwaidi makes it clear that connections of this kind extend to Iran. He evokes the Iranian angle of the triangle with a surprisingly imaginative reconstruction that brings to life the deep Islamic roots of the revolution. He does so in a novel way. Throughout his career, Huwaidi has paid special attention to the Iranian Revolution and the Islamic scholars who dominate the new order. Yet, of all the affecting portraits in *Iran from Within* and his later accounts of revolutionary Iran, it is not the depictions of personalities that dominate. Rather, the most affecting evocation of the soul of Iranian Islam and of the revolution it inspired is Huwaidi's kaleidoscopic and nuanced portrayal of the holy city of Qom, the heart of the new Islamic order.

Like other journalists, Huwaidi headed first to Teheran in 1979 to take the measure of the momentous events that were transforming Iran. He soon suspected that Qom, the seat of Shi'i Islamic learning, had far greater importance in the new Islamic order. Huwaidi's sense of Qom's new importance was confirmed by an incident involving a group of Muslim scholars who traveled to Iran to gauge the course of Iran's war with Iraq. The group was welcomed very well and a meeting was arranged with six major ayatollahs. After the meeting, the scholars asked whether they could meet with the president or the prime minister. Huwaidi noticed two ayatollahs smile and overheard one ask in a bemused tone, "Why do our brothers want to waste their time with those clerks?"[36]

Huwaidi visited Qom three times to plumb the depths of the city that was the vital nerve center of the revolution. "On first impression," he writes, "Qom takes you centuries back when the Islamic world was full of centers of knowledge in Bukhara and Samarkand in the heart of Asia to Kairouan in Northern Africa." Like Najaf and Karbala in Iraq, Qom is considered holy by Shi'a Islam. The city is the site of the shrine of Fatema Mæ'sume, sister of Imam Reza (789–816). Qom is a destination for pilgrims. Huwaidi comments on the endless bookstores on the narrow streets of the old city and the "huge numbers of scholars who are walking down the streets in their distinct religious outfits." While the religious dimension makes the most lasting impression, Huwaidi explores as well Qom as a modern agricultural, industrial, and trading center. In the end, he understood that Qom was, as he put it, "a city without a bottom." Every time you think you have reached the bottom, Huwaidi explains, "new depth appears and when you explore it a new dimension emerges and so on."[37]

Huwaidi aims quite purposefully for access to deeper levels. He is convinced that "Qom is the lock and key to Iran after the revolution."[38] To get beyond surface impressions, Huwaidi concludes that one must "walk the streets and sit in meetings with scholars and their students and followers in order to unravel the mysteries and learn the secrets."[39] Meetings with major figures in the new order were more easily arranged. In Qom Huwaidi found that the Islamic scholars were more relaxed and more open with visitors than in Teheran. Still, Huwaidi, the experienced journalist, naturally sought ways to verify the things he learned. To that task he brought an insider's strategy. "Scholars may not let you know what you want to hear," cautioned an Iranian friend who knew how Qom worked. However, he also pointed out that those scholars "have students, and students of students and you will hear from them everything. You can trust to a great extent that what they say does reflect what is going on in the mind of the scholars."[40]

The abstract characterizations of Qom and the opportunities it offered took on a liveliness when Huwaidi proceeded to meet with major scholars who reflected the character of the city. He describes two such meetings in detail. These descriptions bring readers directly into the presence of Iran's new political class. More importantly, they effectively conjure up the qualities that made the experience of Qom so central to any attempt to understand the revolution.

Huwaidi was invited to the home of Grand Ayatollah Lutfallah Safi Golpaygani in Brogrody Street in the old city, where a number of other important scholars live. Except for the guard standing at the door, there was nothing to draw special attention to his house. The street, Huwaidi reports, was extremely narrow. The house looked as though it had remained unchanged since the founding of Qom. Huwaidi removes his shoes at the door and passes through the many followers and students who have filled the house. He then finds himself in front of a white curtain. Someone drew the curtain aside. There was the grand ayatollah seated on the floor, with two of his assistants to his right. Huwaidi describes the ayatollah as thin and wearing thick glasses that had extremely dark frames. In front of him there were piles of papers and a stamp with his name. He was dictating answers to questions sent by his followers. The assistants would write out his answer and read it back to him, and he would then stamp the replies. After some time, the ayatollah slowly looked up toward Huwaidi and welcomed him "with a good Arabic accent." He then spoke about the necessity for the unity of Muslims and the need to bring Sunnis and Shi'a together. He counseled me, Huwaidi concludes, with "a voice coming from the past that was very difficult for me to follow."[41]

An equally important interview took place in 1983 with Ayatollah Montazeri, the figure second only to Khomeini in the emerging political order. This meeting was the second, as Huwaidi had met him briefly in 1980 in the company of other journalists. Montazeri at this time was shielded from all journalists by official order. He agreed to meet Huwaidi a second time in his capacity as an Islamic scholar rather than a reporter, conditioned on agreement that the actual interview not be published. As with Ayatollah Golpaygani, what emerges from this encounter is less the portrait of a personality than a still clearer sense of Qom and all it connoted for the new order. In this depiction one feels in the city the continuous presence of a venerable tradition of a religion as a way of life that had just inspired a modern mass revolution.

Huwaidi describes his impression that "I had to travel back 1,000 years to meet him—ten centuries to the early years of Islam." The modest house was crowded with people, sitting everywhere, the men on one side, the women on the other. Some were reading a book, others sleeping, still others playing with children. Montazeri cut a distinctive figure, modest yet imposing, with his long white beard, large dark-rimmed glasses, traditional headdress, and white flowing robe of the shaikhs. Huwaidi adds that his white socks were ripped, although neither the ayatollah nor anyone else attached any importance to the tears. Huwaidi stayed for two hours and again regarded his time in that house in Qom like a voyage to the first days of Islam. In the extreme modesty of his person and his home, Montazeri himself evoked for Huwaidi one of Islam's first converts, Abu Dharr, a companion of the Prophet, a friend of the poor, and a figure revered by Ali Shariati. Huwaidi's message is this evocation of a timeless time and an unbounded place that is Qom.[42]

Beyond the Strategic Triangle from Bosnia to China

Learned Iranian scholars thrust into political roles were not the only Muslims to inspire Huwaidi's artful depictions. Yet another Islamic intellectual and political figure captured his imagination and inspired a penetrating evocation. In Alija Izetbegovic the iron will of the Bosnian people found an improbable vehicle. The sober, reflective voice of a philosopher, not greatly moved by material things and deeply committed to Islam, led Bosnian Muslims to nationhood through unimaginable ordeals that called forth sympathies and material support across *Dar al Islam*. In the midst of all that drama and bloodshed, what consistently impressed Huwaidi was the man's calming presence. Trials, imprisonment, and siege did not overwhelm his intellectual and spiritual explorations. Behind the heroic public figure, Huwaidi encountered a man who lived more simply and thought more deeply than one could possibly expect from a national political figure.

What impressed Huwaidi most of all was Izetbegovic's stunning personal simplicity. Huwaidi traveled to Bosnia from Arab lands where rulers inhabit ostentatious palaces, invariably decorated with stolen national art treasures placed in horrific, gilded settings. Huwaidi could not quite believe his experience in locating the president's apartment in Sarajevo. The neighborhood was ordinary. The president had not left his family apartment. There were no guards. Ordinary citizens simply pointed out where their president lived with no sense of just how astonishing the simplicity of it all was.[43] Huwaidi understood just how remarkable such simplicity was, and he enabled his readers to feel the lessons the portrait conveyed.

Huwaidi's travels to China created opportunities to *hear* from China's Muslim minority. Listening to those voices of China's forgotten Muslims provides one of the most moving and insightful of all the experiences that Huwaidi's work makes possible. Huwaidi reminds us that while China's Muslims have had little presence in the consciousness of the *ummah*, Islam itself has venerable roots in China. The opening of China to Islam dates back at least a thousand years. Estimates on the number of Muslims in all of China are unreliable, although Huwaidi, writing in the 1980s, ventured a minimal figure of some 20 million. Estimates now are several times that much, although still unofficial. The largest grouping of Muslims is the Uyghur ethnic group, concentrated in the Western province of Xinjiang and now estimated to number approximately 25 million. In some of the larger cities of China proper, there are also established communities, ethnically indistinguishable from their Han Chinese neighbors. Huwaidi identifies them as Muslim Chinese or Hui.

It is in China that Huwaidi's identity as a *rahal* comes through most clearly. For one thing, his book *Islam in China* shows the strongest and most direct influence of Ibn Battuta. Like his predecessor, Huwaidi uses all the senses to take the measure of the cities he visits. "I listen, I smell, I see and I use all three to understand the reality of the Muslims," he writes.[44] Huwaidi goes out of his way to make the great *rahal* a very palpable presence in his text, invoking his name directly at least a dozen times. Huwaidi takes obvious pleasure in walking in the footsteps of a kindred spirit across the centuries.

While Ibn Battuta drew back from scenes he found disturbing, Huwaidi plunges into different lives lived in oppressive shadows. While Ibn Battuta is rightly regarded as one of the predecessors of modern-day anthropologists, Huwaidi just as clearly brings to contemporary journalism and travel literature even more of the characteristic methods of the anthropologists. From his indigenous sources he learns of the great lengths that China's Muslims in the major cities of Beijing, Canton, and Shanghai go to in order to blend into their surroundings.

Everywhere, China's Muslims conveyed to Huwaidi an acute awareness of their vulnerability. At the time of the communist revolution, Muslims sided overwhelmingly with Mao. They viewed his movement from a social justice prism, given the promise of a tilt to the poor and a progressive nationalism that resisted foreign interference. Still, when China later experienced major upheavals, notably the Cultural Revolution, the Muslim communities across China were targeted, along with other religious minorities, and often with great violence. Muslims had few resources for self-protection.

As Huwaidi moved through Chinese cities, he was very warmly welcomed as an Islamic scholar from a major Arab country and a center of Islamic learning. All manner of doors opened for him. Confidences were shared. Huwaidi took painful note that knowledge of Arabic had all but disappeared. China's Islamic intellectuals had suffered greatly in the times of upheavals. Huwaidi encountered one scholar who had studied in Cairo at al Azhar and translated the work of the Egyptian scholar Ahmed Amin on Islam and Islamic historical personalities. In private conversations, he recounted to Huwaidi how his home had been invaded by hooligans during the Cultural Revolution. They destroyed the personal library that he had built up over a lifetime. We hear the pain of a scholar in his voice. Huwaidi noted that with a great deal of tradition lost or adulterated, people clung with great passion to Islam's dietary restrictions. The refusal to eat pork became a badge of commitment to a tradition whose forms had over the centuries slipped through their fingers, although it remained strong in their hearts.

Unlike Ibn Battuta, Huwaidi did not lapse into depressed withdrawal with what he experienced in China. Huwaidi traveled not just to major cities in China proper but also to the Western province of Xinjiang, the land of the Uyghurs. He described himself as "the first Arab or Muslim journalist who entered the province." Huwaidi reported that in the early 1980s "you were quite clearly in a Muslim society, indistinguishable from other Islamic countries."[45] Huwaidi had an acute historical understanding of just how challenging Chinese conditions were for Islam. The long and repressive rule of the Manchu dynasty took a terrible toll over some three hundred years. The fall of the *ancien regime* and the eventual triumph of Mao brought initial promise, although followed by the terrible years of the Cultural Revolution and the violent repression that came with it. Huwaidi arrived in China at a time when relative political calm prevailed and the Chinese economy had begun its really impressive rise. Huwaidi focused on the resilience of the Chinese Muslims. He was able to celebrate those elements of the tradition that they had preserved in the face of such daunting obstacles. At the same time, he registered a clear sense of guilt that China's Muslims, in all their years of travail, had received so little assistance from the Islamic world.[46] Worse, Muslims elsewhere were for the most part unaware of Islam's forgotten millions in China.

Huwaidi heard that neglect and its consequences in the voice of an imam in a large and crowded urban mosque during Friday prayers. He noted all sorts of irregularities in the way the prayers were conducted.[47]

The voice of the imam haunted him: He spoke in a strange blend of Arabic, Persian, and Chinese, and Huwaidi could understand next to nothing. More disconcerting was his certitude that the assembled believers understand no more. Huwaidi concluded that the "Chinese have a deep faith but little knowledge about the faith itself."[48] He feared that unless there is an opening to China's millions of Muslims, there will only be "something called Islam that bears little resemblance to the Message."[49]

Huwaidi did uncover and report some more hopeful revelations in China. He took note of the large numbers of young people who made their way to the mosques. Chinese law banned children from houses of worship until they were eighteen, but once that age was reached, Chinese Muslim teenagers appeared with their parents and grandparents in large numbers. Genuine piety filled the air. From his deeper conversations with intellectuals, he learned that they were aware *al Tagdid al Islami* was sweeping through the Islamic world. They expressed the desire to be part of the Islamic Renewal, even though they had precious little in the way of resources to act on that commitment. Huwaidi reported on their efforts to acquire and translate books about the revival of Islam and to study Sufism as well as the Sunni and Shi'i teachings. The passion to know and practice Islam was there, and Huwaidi heard it in the stumbling voice of that imam.

So Hearts and Minds Can Learn Wisdom and Ears May Learn to Hear

With Ibn Battuta, the urge is almost irresistible to map his voyages. Yet any such summary sketch of his travels is profoundly misleading. A mapping suggests an underlying purpose of which the great *rahal* was completely innocent. Worse, such a summary obscures the major advantages that came from his meandering ways. It was precisely these qualities that allowed him to help build the foundations for modern anthropology.

With Fahmi Huwaidi, there is a parallel inclination to enumerate the Islamic causes and controversies that he engages. Huwaidi's detailed dispatches from the frontlines lend themselves to the generation of an informative record of insider information on happenings in *Dar al Islam*. Such a catalogue approach misses a great deal of what is most important about Huwaidi. Huwaidi seeks depth of understanding rather than simply coverage of the momentous events that are bringing new life to the *ummah*. He seeks to discern who and what is making a real difference. Huwaidi does not just aim to be a witness of important events, but throws himself into the ongoing efforts to determine their larger meaning to the *ummah*. In short, Huwaidi aims, through sustained attention, timely reporting, and diligent research, to provide the necessary materials so that, as the Qur'an says, "hearts and minds may learn" from the experience of brothers and sisters in Islam across the world. Huwaidi understands just as clearly that his role entails the amplification of the voices of marginalized and forgotten Muslims so that, again in the words of the Qur'an, "ears may learn to hear."[50]

7

God's "Signs" and Democracy in Islam

We sent aforetime our messengers with Clear Signs
And sent down with them the Book
and the Balance (of Right and Wrong),
That men may stand forth in justice.

QUR'AN 57:25

MUSLIMS HEAR THE voice of God in cries for justice throughout human history. In several hundred verses, the Qur'an affirms that God has fixed justice as the lodestar to guide human affairs. The Qur'anic injunction to "build the world" carries the imperative to establish just communities that find their place in a diverse world.

Today, the intellectuals of midstream Islam argue that the surest path to a just social order passes through democracy. Across the globe, the values of justice, equality, and freedom are understood to provide the foundations for democracy. New Islamic intellectuals affirm these values. They explain that in Islam all three values find their place as God's "signs" to guide the building of the world.[1] It is a reflection of God's mercy that indicators appear in the natural and human world to guide human efforts to "build the world." In the view of these centrist Islamic thinkers, the realization of justice in our time depends on the political and social freedoms that democratic governance fosters. They aim to clarify the Qur'anic position on the Islamic core values supportive of democracy, while countering distorted traditional and extremist views actively hostile to democratic aspirations.

The difficulty of the task is clear. In no other arena is the *tarshid* (guidance) of New Islamic scholars and thinkers more controversial and more imperative. Much work remains to be done to create social institutions that respond to God's signs. Islamic traditionalists and extremists focus

their attacks on democracy by arguments that Islam does not call for democracy on the idea of scant attention given to freedom in human affairs in the Qur'an. The New Islamic scholars focus their own efforts on
elaborating and strengthening awareness of the link between justice, the
preeminent Qur'anic value, and both equality and freedom.

The demanding character of this work should not come as a surprise.
Such struggles are not Islam's alone. Anyone reading the Talmud, the
Bible, or the Qur'an and expecting to find in place fully elaborated foundations for a democratic polity will be sorely disappointed. None of the
sacred texts of the three great monotheisms puts forward elaborations of
the values that today define humanity's highest moral and political ideals,
notably including democracy. All three traditions are also suffused with
patriarchal values, some of which by contemporary standards would be
characterized as misogynist. None has much to say directly about human
rights. What is required is interpretation of the sacred texts in ways that
bring their messages into the modern world. Everywhere, the successes
that have come from struggles for democracy and the freedom it brings
have taken centuries and oceans of blood and tears to realize.

Unfinished Struggles for Justice, Equality, and Freedom

These struggles are unfinished. When speaking of the shortcomings of
other traditions and historical experiences, it is important to remind ourselves that these struggles are still far from won even in politically advanced states, notably including the United States and Israel. The United
States may choose to see itself as "the light unto nations" and "a city on
a hill." Israel may regularly pronounce itself "the sole democracy in the
Middle East." Neither claim carries much conviction beyond the sphere
of state propaganda. The terrible erosion of public freedoms in the United
States in the Bush/Obama years in the shadow of the "War on Terror" and
the consolidation of the surveillance state make it clear that freedom's
gains in America are far from secure. At the same time, inequality in the
distribution of wealth in the United States has reached grotesque dimensions. The excesses of American capitalism have generated powerful plu-
tocratic forces that are actively undermining democracy.

Israel faces its own demons. Not all the warnings come from outside the
borders of the self-proclaimed "Jewish state." A growing number of Israeli
scholars and public intellectuals warn that unless policies toward Palestinian citizens of Israel and toward Palestinians living for decades under

onerous occupation are changed, Israel will forfeit forever the democratic possibility in favor of an exclusionary ethnic nationalism, wrapped in the external trappings of religion. Israel today is actively consolidating its character as just such an ethnocracy—that is, a state that is democratic for Jews and far less for all others.[2] Justice, equality, and freedom are unfinished business in both the United States and Israel.

What one does find in the sacred texts of the three Abrahamic faiths are the seeds of these core values on which democracy depends. They are God's "signs" for humanity that point to the possibility of just societies. The seeds of just social orders can be found in all the great monotheisms. They are not evenly distributed among them, nor do they automatically come to fruition in any of them. The seeds must everywhere be protected and nurtured. The journey to a just society has a different starting point and distinctive trajectory in each tradition. The record of actual accomplishments is uneven in all three. Each tradition faces distinctive advantages and obstacles. Yet the revelations in each hold out the promise of freedom guaranteed by democracy.

Islam and the Question of Freedom

Islam provides particularly rich articulations of the values of equality and justice. The pathways to their realization are clearly marked. Both equality and justice in the Qur'an are given very concrete and varied metrics by which to assess their actualization in Islamic social forms. Freedom, in contrast, receives a far less robust elaboration. As a value, freedom is treated in only a handful of *surahs*. These *surahs* point to ways barriers to freedom can and should be lifted. The freeing of a slave, for example, is recognized in two *surahs* as a moral good that can make amends for even serious failings.[3] Divorce that allows a woman to gain her freedom is judged as fully permissible in God's eyes.[4] These invocations of freedom pertain to social questions. In each instance, freedom is given a positive valuation but always indirectly by highlighting negative social practices that infringe on it.

The treatment of freedom in spiritual matters, in contrast, is direct and expansive in Islam. The Islamic injunction to worship God alone calls believers to free themselves from excessive devotion to the secular gods of material wealth, social prestige, or power. For Muslims, there is only one God to worship. No political figure, no matter how wealthy, prominent, or powerful, can rightfully usurp that place. In Islamic cultural contexts, resistance to tyranny always has a religious dimension, whether explicitly articulated or not. Ideas of fated outcomes do appear in the Qur'an. However, New Islamic intellectuals point out that the predominant message is the clear expectation that freedom of moral choice between good and evil is reserved to men and women, as they live their lives and build their communities. While differences between men and women that favor men are specified in certain matters of legal testimony, family affairs, and inheritance, the genders are recognized as equal spiritually in God's eyes. Women have the same moral worth as men. Women are called to be partners with men in worshipping God and shouldering the burdens of "building the world." They face the same final accountability for their actions in this world that will determine their just fate in the world beyond.

Muslims have made the question of freedom of religious belief most controversial. Many *hadiths*, including some judged reliable, decisively deny freedom of religion by specifying that apostates be killed. The *hadith* most frequently cited says simply that death is the penalty for changing religion. Throughout Islamic history, the death penalty for apostates has arguably been the consensus legal opinion. Islamic intellectuals of the midstream stand against such *hadith*-based conclusions to argue that the Qur'an calls Muslims to write a very different future.[5] They point out forthrightly that there is absolutely no Qur'anic provision of a death sentence for those who leave Islam.[6] Nor, they argue, is there any reliable record of the Prophet Muhammad himself having executed such a decision in the first community of Muslims. The Qur'an speaks in a pellucid prose to deliver this message: "Let there be no compulsion in religion."[7] Belief, another verse explains with perfect clarity, entails free choice: "The Truth is from your Lord; let him who will, believe, and let him who will, reject (it)."[8]

The choice of disbelief, the Qur'an does make clear, is a grievous error for which a severe price will be paid. *However, the punishment will come from God and not man.* It will be enacted in the hereafter rather than on Earth. God speaks directly to the Prophet Muhammad to bring his worldly role as political head of the *ummah* into conformity with this divine intention: "Therefore do thus give admonition, for thou art one to admonish." The Prophet's role is to teach and guide and not to direct and punish: "Thou art not one to manage (men's) affairs."[9] New Islamic scholars insist that this crystalline message of the Qur'an takes precedence over the dismal historical record.

Because Islam has a political and a religious role, advocates of death for apostates often make their case by conflating apostasy with treason. The New Islamic trend insists on a sharp distinction between matters of religious belief and threats to the security of the community. The personal right to change one's personal religious beliefs does not extend to a collective right of sedition. Treason, they judge, does rightfully carry the most severe of penalties, including capital punishment in cases where the threat to the community is most severe and clearly documented. A change in personal religious beliefs does not.

The sparse treatment of the idea of freedom in Islam is part of a larger and intentionally imposed challenge. In general, Islam does not specify particular political or economic forms to achieve a just social order. The task of creating political and economic systems in accord with the values of justice, equality, and freedom is left to each generation of Muslims by divine intent. The political and economic realms consistently have posed the most serious challenges for Muslims. Islamic civilization expressed its genius in the realms of law, culture, spirituality, human relations, and the arts. In contrast, the record of the political history of the *ummah*, in particular, is fraught with disappointment with the behavior of Muslims, though not with Islam itself.

The nurturing of freedom has been severely hampered throughout much of Islamic history. God's "signs" have been neglected or ignored completely. A luxuriant overgrowth of tyranny in both theory and practice has overwhelmed freedom's promise. In a memorable judgment the Egyptian New Islamic thinker Fahmi Huwaidi pronounced the political history of the Islamic world "a series of disasters in which only the names and places changed."[10] Islamic political history is marked by the dominance of tyrannical and unjust regimes. Numerous *hadiths* attributed to the Prophet Muhammad, many of dubious authenticity, provide a theological rationalization for this rampant authoritarianism. They explicitly warn against the dangers of freedom.[11] However, other sayings attributed to the Prophet counsel that the obligation to obey the ruler only applies to what is in keeping with God's law and advances human well-being.

Yusuf al Qaradawi attributes the wretched political history of Muslims to "the early abandonment of *shura* (consultation)." The seeds of genuine Islamic rule planted by the Prophet Muhammad did give a voice to those governed, although originally that circle of inclusion was narrow. However, with the principle established, the expansion of the circle of consultation beyond the most important personages existed as a clear and attractive possibility. Instead, Qaradawi explained that the "the virus of dictatorship from the Roman and Persian Empires" infected *Dar al Islam*. Muslims, he argued, "copied the worst features of these imperial systems."[12]

The dreary consequences that followed make a political port of entry to the Islamic world an inevitable disappointment. My own first intellectual encounters with Islam and the Islamic world took precisely this discouraging path. With Cairo-born political scientist Nadav Safran of Harvard as my guide to the Islamic world, I first glimpsed the Islamic world through the prism of the wreckage that defines Islamic political history. In those same years of graduate work, I studied the serious limitations of the Islamic heritage in political thought. No student of that historical and theoretical record can fail to notice the meager attention given to constitutional guarantees for such critical matters as freedom of speech, religious beliefs, and assembly. In his own work, Safran advanced the conclusion that these deficiencies flowed from Islam itself. In his view, the failure in Islam to separate the political from the religious sphere created an inherent propensity to theocratic rule. This tendency proved resistant to correction because the resources of political reason could not be brought to bear. In Islam, Safran saw an unbridgeable opposition between reason and revelation that precluded the elaboration of such reasoned protections.[13] Like many in the Orientalist tradition, Safran concluded that the gate to *ijtihad* (interpretation) had been closed in medieval times.

These classic Orientalist views on Islam were not persuasive to me as a graduate student, nor are they now. Yet, ironically, my work with Safran prepared me as no other for my subsequent encounter with midstream New Islamic intellectuals. Born in Egypt to a secular Jewish family, Safran had close ties not only to Israel but, like other prominent scholars at Harvard during the 1960s, also to the CIA and the larger American imperial project that was just taking shape.[14] Initially, I understood his inclination to paint things Islamic in dark tones as shaded by these affiliations. As a man who had developed Zionist commitments in his teens and had fought for Israel in 1948, it seemed perfectly clear as well why he might focus on the internal weaknesses of the Islamic world rather than external assaults *Dar al Islam* suffered as the cause for its weaknesses. Yet, in the end, it is the arguments and not biography that matter most. For all these shadows lingering over his work, I remained persuaded by the factual accuracy of the broad outlines of Safran's delineation of the political legacy and contemporary political shortcomings of the Islamic world, despite my clear dissent from his assessment of their causes.

What was initially most striking in the work of the New Islamic intellectuals whom I began reading in the 1970s, while still a graduate student working under Safran, was their wholehearted acceptance of the broad outlines of his substantive characterization of the political failings of the Islamic world. At the same time, I was intrigued by their vehement rejection of the notion that Islam itself was at the root of the problem. In particular, the New Islamic intellectuals flatly reject the idea that the gate of *ijtihad* was and remained closed. They assert that such a notion of closure is itself an *ijtihad*. They forthrightly reject it. Reform and renewal of Islam are not only possible but imperative, they argue. *Ijtihad* is indispensable for that effort. At the same time, they explain that while the separation of church and state made sense in a Christian cultural context, it could hardly be imposed on Islam that had nothing comparable to an established church to provide infallible interpretations of the faith. They argue that revelation embraced reason in Islam, as indispensable for the process of interpretation. They affirmed the necessity for new interpretations for changing times and places.

The Islamic Renewal and the Opening to Democracy

Democrats in Islam look to the larger project of *al Tagdid al Islami* (Islamic Renewal) for hope of realizing a pathway to democracy in Islam. They note that, around the globe, Islam grows stronger in numbers from year to year. With some 1.6 billion adherents worldwide, Islam has emerged as the fastest growing of the major faiths. Yet midstream intellectuals argue that the spectacular growth of the Islamic body is far from sufficient. The New Islamic thinkers acknowledge the painful truth that the staggering increase in the size of the Islamic body has not automatically translated into a parallel development of mind and spirit. They recognize the deleterious effects of historic colonialism and the contemporary ravages of poverty, illiteracy, and tyranny across so much of the Islamic world.

Midstream Islamic intellectuals point to a disconcerting intellectual dimension to this backwardness of the *ummah*. Destructive distortions of Islam's message flourish when the body grows and the mind fails to keep pace. Of all the misleading misreadings of the faith, none, in their view, is more damaging than the endlessly repeated mantra within the *ummah* itself that Islam calls for *hakemeyya,* understood to mean the rule of God and not men. This shibboleth serves those elements seeking to use Islam as a screen for their own drive to power. In the end, the rule of God will be their rule. This opportunistic banner, often raised by politicized Islam, is then cited by critics as proof of the impossibility of democracy in Islam. The controversies stirred by extremist views of *hakemeyya* are embedded in much broader issues of how *Shari'ah* and its role in the *ummah* are to be understood. On this plane, too, the New Islamic trend has confronted a plethora of distorted and destructive views in traditionalist and extremist circles.

The New Islamic intellectuals will have none of the simplistic and unfounded conception of *hakemeyya* as the literal rule of God. In their manifesto, written in the early 1980s and first published in 1991, Egypt's New Islamic school directly challenges this slogan of politicized Islam. "It is unacceptable," they write, "to deprive Muslims of their political rights and responsibilities with the assertion that in an Islamic society 'rule is for God and not human beings.'" They explain that in the Qur'an the phrase actually means that "the *values and principles* of Islam are God-given." They interpret this to signal that "God's rule comes at the beginning and the end."[15] By this reading, *hakemeyya* means that the Qur'an defines the purposes for which power should be used "at the beginning" to inspire the effort to build a political system, and "at the end" to assess whether the efforts of a particular community have in fact achieved the just system for which Islam calls. By their lights, the whole process of building the political system, choosing leaders, and devising policies to meet people's needs is all left to human actors. The democratic idea of popular sovereignty is perfectly compatible with such an interpretation.

According to the New Islamic school, the essential interpretive error of distortions resides in the conflation of two issues that in the Qur'an are kept separate. The source of legislation is the first, while the basis for obedience to the ruler is the second. In Islam, they explain, legislation originates in revelation. *Shari'ah* has a divine character in those provisions that come directly from the Qur'an. They do not treat the nuts and bolts of politics but rather the values and purposes that should guide political action. Both ruler and ruled are subject to these elements of *Shari'ah*. In contrast, the legitimacy of the ruler and of the political system itself in an Islamic society depend "on the consent of the people, meaning that Islamic government is a civil and not a religious government."[16] The rightful recognition of the divine character of *Shari'ah* as derived from the

Qur'an should not be extended to the very different issues of the claims to rule by a particular political regime and leadership.

The *ummah* is rife with such flawed understandings of *Shari'ah*. The intellectuals of the New Islamic trend have little patience with those Islamic activists who reduce the responsibility to build just communities to simplistic calls for the implementation of *Shari'ah*. They dissent sharply from claims that Islam has such automatic solutions that can simply be applied mechanically, with force if required. They argue that "Islam is the solution," but it is up to human beings to determine the precise forms and character that solution will take in their own particular environments. Fahmi Huwaidi makes the point that activists are wrong to consider that the Islamic solution is ready and at hand. Rather, he explains that "this solution is 'possible,' *if we work hard at it*. This solution is not 'deficient' as has been rumored by some, nor is it 'impossible' as others would like us to believe."[17]

The New Islamic scholars embrace the view, shared by all Islamic currents, that without *Shari'ah*, there can be no Islamic community. However, they dissent in critical ways from the extremists on what constitutes *Shari'ah* and how it should be implemented. The New Islamic scholars wade into the ocean of competing interpretations over *Shari'ah* and put forward their own enlightened vision. They understand their battle with the extremists as one that juxtaposes two strikingly different substantive understandings of the nature of Islamic community and, more particularly, of the *Shari'ah* that regulates it. The community toward which the exegesis of the *Wassatteyya* strives is open, inclusive, and responsive to the world. The New Islamic conception of *Shari'ah* is consonant with such a community. In sharp contrast, the community of the extremists is closed, exclusive, and hostile to the world. The extremist understanding of *Shari'ah* mirrors those distortions and would inevitably produce theocracies.

With a very pragmatic intent, the New Islamic school argues that *Shari'ah* is already partially implemented wherever there is an Islamic community. The task for them is always the manageable one of using the mind to complete its elaboration and adaptation to specific circumstances. Kamal Abul Magd explains that the preferred course is to begin with these partial implementations of *Shari'ah* rather than dismantling them. "God gave us the mind," he wrote, "to cope with this continuous change and to respond to developments. It is only the mind that can protect *Shari'ah* and achieve its purposes."[18] The New Islamic assessment of such political issues as *hakemeyya* and the implementation of *Shari'ah* takes for granted that Islam reserves all such issues to human discretion. Consequently, the human failings of Muslims rather than any inherent limitations of Islam explain the very long record of tyranny and the recent centuries of economic backwardness in so much of the Islamic world.

The Just Society on Islamic Ground

What does it take to build a just economic and political system on Islamic ground? The transnational *Wassatteyya* has put this question at the forefront of the concerns of all those who would contribute to *al Tagdid al Islami*. Conventional Western thinking already knows the answer: Such an Islamic project for economics and politics is futile. The most concise statement of the accepted wisdom comes from my mentor, Harvard's Samuel Huntington, in *The Clash of Civilizations*. Huntington quotes the Sudanese Islamic scholar Hassan al Turabi to make the unexceptional point that all religions provide "people with a sense of identity and a direction in life." Huntington then adds his own gloss that "whatever universalist goals they may have, religions give people identity by positing a basic distinction between believers and nonbelievers, between a superior in-group and different and inferior out-group."[19] In a later passage, he outlines where this chain of reasoning will take us in the case of Islam. Huntington predicts that in the end the global Islamic Resurgence "will have shown that 'Islam is the solution' to the problems of morality, identity, meaning, and faith, but not to the problems of social injustice, political repression, economic backwardness, and military weakness."[20] These failures, he explains, will fuel envy and rage against the West.

Huntington helped shape conventional thinking by pointedly arguing that the problem for the West with the Islamic world is not Islamic extremism only. He argued that "the underlying problem for the West is not Islamic fundamentalism. It is Islam, a different civilization whose people are convinced of the superiority of their culture and obsessed with the inferiority of their power."[21] In Huntington's view, the prospects for building a political democracy or an advanced market economy on Islamic ground are dim indeed.

The idea that a rich culture and a strong identity have little to do with a strong economic and political order, implicit in Huntington's analysis, can be entertained seriously only when talking about other people's cultures, especially those of which we know little. For how long would we entertain such a notion for Western capitalism and liberal democracy? Exploration of precisely these linkages of culture and identity with the economy dominates Western economic history. It is quite impossible to explain the vitality of Western capitalism and the political dominance it enabled without attention to its "spirit," grounded in Protestantism, as Max Weber famously argued.

The point must be that there are deficiencies in Islamic culture that preclude development. Certain traditionalist schools do erect barriers to development in modern conditions. They believe that the storehouse of traditional *fiqh* contains all that is needed to build a modern Islamic economy and polity. Islamic intellectuals of such schools speak quite legitimately about the importance of isolated elements of the heritage. They point to the rich and suggestive notions of *waqf* (Islamic endowment), *riba* (usury), and *zakat* (religious obligation to support those in need), in particular. However, they then quite misleadingly make the untenable argument that these inherited conceptions and structures contain within them all that a modern economy and polity built on Islamic ground requires.

In parallel fashion, extremist movements claim that they, rather than the traditionalists, are the holders of the keys to a flourishing social order. They reject the traditionalist reliance on inherited *fiqh*. Instead, they argue that the inspired and unquestioned *ijtihad* of their particular *amir* (leader of a politicized and often militant Islamic group) provides just the right combination of inherited elements and new insights to build a prosperous Islamic economy and social order, once they hold political power securely in their hands. Both traditionalists and extremists do entertain unfounded ideas that there is a ready-to-go Islamic model of governance and the economy that has only to be implemented. Such mistaken notions make the real work of building such systems much more difficult.

The New Islamic thinkers have no such illusions. Yet they do believe that Islam has direct relevance to politics and economics. Islam, they insist, is not alone in positing a relationship between the spiritual and the worldly realms of human experience. What does distinguish Islam is the direct and unambiguous character of the connection. In the West shaped by its Christian heritage, the spiritual is understood to play its role in indirect ways. Adam Smith's "invisible hand" has left an indelible mark on Western economic and political theory. Charles Darwin borrowed the conception and reframed it as natural selection and the "survival of the fittest" to explain evolution. Darwin's reframing opened the way for a loop back from biology to social life. Parallels were drawn not only to the economic competition of the market but also to the unregulated contests of power struggles. The invisible hand was thus seen to work its effects in biology, economics, and politics. In the economic realm, the amoral struggle of self-interested competitors is understood to realize a common good without reliance on altruistic intentions on the part of "economic man." In the political realm, the indurate struggles of "political man" are seen to yield order and stability through the alchemy of the balance of power, making no demands at all of empathy or compassion. These formulations provide a purportedly secular foundation for an individualistic and ruthlessly competitive economics and politics. They are presumed to transcend their cultural moorings. They claim universal application as secular social science.

In fact, like so much else in Western culture, these apparently secular conceptualizations of how the biological, economic, and political spheres function rest on theological foundations. The magic of the invisible hand in economics and politics can be none other than the workings of divine providence, most evident in Darwinian natural selection. *The invisible hand is the divine hand.* It distills a collective good from amoral individual struggles for survival. Those struggles provide a model for the workings of markets driven by egotistical self-interest. It secures as well a system of order and stability out of the brutalities of unregulated power struggles. These wonders of biology, economics, and politics work their effects behind the backs of human actors and without any explicit recognition of the divine role. Ironically, when unacknowledged in this way, theology is all the more powerful.[22]

A very different understanding of the relationship of the worldly and the spiritual characterizes Islam. Islamic thought rests on explicit recognition of the existence of a supernatural being. Muslims believe that God's essence cannot be known. However, the divine influence can be experienced in the natural and social worlds. In Islamic thought, higher principles and values that advance the common good do not emerge from the actions of egotistical and competitive human actors that must somehow be squared with the common good. Instead, God calls men and women to their better selves. They are as emphatically enjoined to build just communities.

The Qur'anic notion of man as God's *khalifa* or regent on Earth gives force to these imperatives. The mission itself is known as *istikhlaf* (the divine call to humanity to act as God's regent on Earth). It takes the place of the invisible hand. *Istikhlaf* provides an explicit moral frame for the conduct of the economic and political affairs of the world. In Islamic thought, the theological conceptions that define the essence of man and underlie economics and politics are forthrightly stated. The moral framing of worldly affairs is, at once, unambiguously theological and eminently practical. Moral principles, notably justice but equality and freedom as well, are stated with absolute clarity in order to inspire humanity to creative thinking and real-world positive action to instantiate abstract principles in social forms. The moral framing underpins collective life and makes the community, rather than isolated individuals, the key actor in humankind's worldly activities.

At the heart of these differences are contrasting conceptions of the nature of human beings. In Islam men and women are understood to be set off from all others of God's creatures by their highly developed capacity for rational thought and moral reasoning. Men and women are to be creative builders of the world, *mustakhlifun* in the language of the Qur'an. The Qur'an says of humankind that "We have certainly honored the children of Adam . . . and conferred on them special favors, above a great part of Our Creation."[23] Through impressive rational, imaginative, and moral faculties human beings have the potential to acquire the storehouse of spiritual insight and practical knowledge that *istikhlaf* requires. God calls humanity to use this knowledge to plan and initiate the works essential to build a world in "due balance." The Qur'an summons men and women to work for social justice. They are expected to show kindness and compassion.[24] For a humanity so engaged in the high calling of *istikhlaf*, God lays out the riches of the Earth like a vast carpet, held in place by "the firm and immovable mountains." Those copious resources are set forth to facilitate the responsibilities of a blessed humanity. Humans are called to worship God by performing good works of stewardship to benefit their communities, and to act with others across the globe for the general human welfare and protection of the Earth.[25]

Muslims have not always risen to this high calling. *"Could it be that not all of Adam's offspring were so blessed?"* Such was the bitter question put to Arab Muslims by one of the great Egyptian figures of *al Tagdid al Islami*. Perhaps those who were to benefit from this knowledge and capability were peoples other than our own, bitterly suggested Shaikh Muhammad al Ghazzali. If his fellow Muslim Arabs were forced to rely only on those things they themselves invented and produced, Ghazzali remarked, they would stand naked. He continued:

I look to the sea and see no ship that we manufactured. I look to the air and find no plane that we designed. The Arab is a consumer and not a producer. The pen is Italian, the cloth is English, and the shoe from yet a third country. The Arab does not think of exploring and extracting the wealth of the earth until the foreigner comes and does it for him. The Arab then takes his meager share of the profit and spends it on wasteful luxuries. That is not Islam![26]

While critical of the failings of fellow Muslims, New Islamic thinkers like Ghazzali resist the siren call of the West. They judge the Western conception of an egotistical and self-interested human nature to be not only wrong but repellent. They question whether the implicit sanctioning of humanity's worst selfishness might not explain the terrible violence that the West's imperial armies and continuing drive for global dominance have visited on the world.

The Qur'an makes it clear that although God has created men and women as *mustakhlifun*, they must struggle to rise to that calling. Islamic communities must actively and purposefully strive for balance and justice. The *Sunnah* (all the deeds and words of the Prophet) provides instructive illustrations of the ways the Prophet Muhammad sought to meet these challenges for the first Islamic community. Activists of politicized Islam mistake this exemplary work of the Prophet Muhammad for a model to be imitated and applied everywhere. It is not, the New Islamic intellectuals argue strenuously. Rather, the Prophet's example serves a higher function: It is intended to inspire the spiritual insight, practical hard work, and imaginative thinking that the obligations of *istikhlaf* will require.

In all that pertains to the Message he received from God, the Prophet Muhammad is judged *ma'asum* (infallible).[27] On the other hand, in those matters that deal with his leadership of the community, Islam's beloved Prophet is recognized as fully human. The Qur'an itself gives a striking example of the Prophet's very human failings. Preoccupied with a conversation with pagan leaders of the Quraysh tribe, the Prophet showed a lack of sensitivity in "frowning and turning away" when a blind man asked his advice. The story comes complete with a humbling admonition given directly to the Prophet: "Of him wast thou unmindful. By no means (should it be so)! For it is indeed a message of instruction."[28] In another incident recorded in the *hadiths*, the Prophet himself is quoted as recognizing without hesitation his limitations. On an important issue of fertilizing palm

trees, the Prophet had offered his opinion. The practical results of following his advice were unfortunate. Faced with this outcome, the Prophet
acknowledged that he simply did not have the knowledge required to provide sound advice on such agricultural matters. Without hesitation, the
Prophet explained that "you know your life's practical affairs better."[29]
The Prophet Muhammad's record of community building represents a
treasured exemplar. However, it does not provide a flawless blueprint to
be followed mechanically down through the ages. The *Wassatteyya* judges
that such an imitative project would stifle precisely the qualities of intelligence and imagination needed to build viable communities in new circumstances and different times.

In place of imitation, the intellectuals of the *Wassatteyya* have a complex and nuanced view of what economic and political development on
Islamic ground requires. They give the very idea of Islamic ground a rich
meaning. They explain that Islam has set deep cultural roots in the soil of
Islamic lands. The West has historically viewed the lands of non-Western
peoples as empty and inviting colonization, or cluttered with the debris
of failed civilizations and requiring cleansing to make way for "progress."
The deep cultural roots of Islam have been more successful than most
in resisting both colonization and cultural cleansing. At the heart of all
Islamic communities, one always encounters an obdurate spirit of resistance to external domination.

In Islam, midstream Islamic intellectuals explain, there is no such
thing as a blank slate for human efforts. Those who would defend and build
on Islamic ground know that God is already there. To stand on Islamic
ground means to accept God's presence as an all-knowing and all-powerful
being that must be obeyed and worshipped. Centrist Islamic scholars understand religion as something that comes from God to provide guidance
as human beings interact with reality.[30] In Islam the essential elements of
the creed are braided together with unchanging values and higher purposes that have practical relevance to the task of building Islamic communities. These values and purposes, articulated in the Qur'an, originate
from God to guide an imperfect humanity to right beliefs and just actions
in social life. Religious thought thus differs from philosophical thought
in that its first premises originate from God rather than human reason.
However, it is similar in that, like any system of thought, its elements are
all related and all are developed from its first premises. Its practical significance can be traced empirically in the ways it has shaped human beings
and their behavior in the world. Islam is understood to come to humanity

from the general to give meaning to the particular, from the absolute to guide the relative, from the fixed to govern the changeable, and from the permanent to rule the temporary. Important worldly struggles in particular and variable circumstances, like those for a just political order, take fixed and unchanging Qur'anic values as their starting point.

Democracy and the New Islamic Trend

Centrist trends worldwide have put democracy on their agendas, although the horrific violence in recent years in places like Afghanistan, Iraq, and Syria has inevitably drawn attention away from their work. For midstream intellectuals, struggles for democracy loom large. Important gains on the democratic path have been consolidated in recent years in Turkey under the leadership of a party with Islamic roots. More recently, Tunisia has experienced a successful revolution and a promising transition that have captured the attention of the world. The Tunisian midstream Islamic trend, under the leadership of Rashid Ghannouchi, has been prominent in both successes.

Drawing on and enriching these practical experiences, New Islamic intellectuals, notably in Egypt but in other sites as well, have made significant contributions to contemporary Islamic thought on the question of democracy in Islam. The *Wassatteyya* addresses the issue of democracy with three distinctive questions: Does the *ummah* require democracy in order to flourish in the late modern world? What are the intellectual and practical resources on which Islamic movements of the center can draw to build a democratic political life? What are the prospects for success of Islamic centrists in their ongoing struggles for democracy in sites around the Islamic world, and how might those efforts be enhanced?

Egypt's New Islamic thinkers have given the most theoretically sophisticated attention to these questions as a key component in their rethinking of Islam. Their theorizations rely only partly on the Egyptian experience of both advances and more recent reversals. They draw as well on knowledge of democratic struggles elsewhere in *Dar al Islam*, as that knowledge circulates through the Cairo node of the transnational centrist network. The theory and practice of the Tunisians, Turks, and Moroccans as well have had a large impact on the emerging body of centrist thought on Islam and democracy. The prospects of struggles on the ground for greater freedom and prosperity have the greatest immediate importance.

However, the long-term efforts to develop Islamic thought on democracy also merit far more attention than they have received.

The popular uprisings across the Arab Islamic world in the spring of 2011 expressed democratic aspirations. They did so in a chorus of varied voices that everywhere included those that arose from the Islamic Renewal. Sorrows and profound disappointments came later to Egypt. Still, a new generation that includes Islamic activists and thinkers experienced that intoxicating breath of freedom. Freedom won by mass action now seems possible. Whatever else the recent upheavals may achieve, they have undoubtedly also generated new interest in the efforts of Islamic thinkers to theorize democracy on Islamic ground.

The approach of centrist Islamic scholars to democracy departs in significant ways from conventional treatments. The whole issue of the compatibility of Islam and democracy, which has dominated Western discussion and the work of secular thinkers in the Islamic world, is pushed into the background. Islam as understood by the midstream is fully compatible with a wide variety of political systems, including democratic ones. Islam clashes with democracy, they argue, only when the democratic concept is defined in ways that insist that a democratic political order is one that has removed religion from the public arena and replaced it with an atheistic humanism or nationalism. Such arrangements and the theoretical formulations that justify them are unacceptable to Islamic thinkers. Nor do they exhaust the available understandings of the democratic idea. In Islam, anything of value to human life must have a spiritual as well as a worldly character.

Islamic centrists are not the only thinkers convinced of these truths; the great American pragmatists, for example, held similar views. Democracy in both traditions cannot be solely of this world. Freedom for both has a spiritual dimension.

For Islamic thinkers, the issue for serious consideration, particularly in the decades since the 1970s, has been whether a democratic system or some other should be a priority for the Islamic world. Influential Islamic thinkers of the center have all argued unequivocally that democracy is imperative. The compatibility of Islam and democracy is assumed. They have held such views for decades. Democrats in Islam have contributed to this effort from all over the Islamic world. Islamic thinkers and activists from the Islamic strategic triangle of Egypt, Turkey, and Iran have all contributed to exploration of ideas of how to best advance political and economic freedom in Islamic communities.

Regrettably, Iranians who supported democratic values have been overwhelmed for now by the theocrats with their radical notion of theocratic rule, *wilayet al faqih*, and by the brutal repression of the dictatorial regime that followed from them. Still, it would be a serious mistake to underestimate the legacy of freedom struggles that are part of Iranian history and include the great mass revolution of 1979. Even today, the dominance of repressive ayatollahs should not blind us to recognition of the participatory dimensions of recent Iranian political experience. For all of the restrictions and distortions, the voice of the Iranian people can on occasion be heard in the outcomes of Iranian elections.

Important contributions to the theory and practice of democracy have also come from farther afield. They have greatly enriched the collective conversation. The Tunisian thinker and activist Rashid Ghannouchi, returned from exile to prominence by the Tunisian revolutionary uprising of 2011, has a long track record as an advocate of Islamic democracy. His works are cited and circulated by New Islamic intellectuals in Cairo and from Cairo to all of *Dar al Islam*. Ghannouchi, in turn, discusses the profound impact of Egyptian Islamic intellectuals and activists on his work, from the time of Muhammad Abduh to al Banna and the New Islamic trend.[31] The practical experiences and reflections on their larger implications by articulate leaders of Islamic countries, like Alija Izetbegovic of Bosnia, Mahathir Mohamad of Malaysia, and Recep Tayyip Erdogan of Turkey, also provide an abundance of real-world experiences to deepen the discussions.

The intellectuals of Egypt's New Islamic trend have provided the most compelling synthesis of these complex and free-ranging conversations on democracy. It is important to note that the Muslim Brotherhood did not provide the site for this intellectual development. In the long history of the Brothers, the only world-class intellectual produced was Sayyid Qutb, and even Qutb joined the Brothers later in life, already formed as a public intellectual. Moreover, as we have seen, the radicalism of Qutb's thought, in the wake of the torment he endured in long years in prison, moved him out of the midstream. An important impetus of New Islamic rethinking of democratic theory has been quite explicitly aimed at countering Qutb's elitist and extremist ideas. Several important figures of the New Islamic trend did themselves come out of the Brothers, notably Muhammad al Ghazzali and Yusuf al Qaradawi.[32] While they maintained ties with the Brothers, they did their serious intellectual work outside its confines. Some of their most important writings defend the democratic idea against Qutbian elitist ideologies that continued to exert appeal in certain circles of the Brotherhood.[33]

These figures left the Brothers precisely because the ideological and organizational structures of the society inhibited the kind of independent critical work that studies of the relationship of Islam and freedom required. The loose ties of the New Islamic school provided a collective environment much more conducive to the opening to the outside world and independent thinking and critical exchange that the elaboration of Islamic democracy required. Both Ghazzali and Qaradawi gave considerable attention to questions of critical reason and culture in their more theoretical writings. For the most part, this record has been ignored in the West.

Reason, Culture, and Islamic Roots for Democracy

New Islamic thinking takes as its premise the idea that Islam does provide abundant resources of reason and culture to radically rethink the legacy. Reason in the Qur'an looms large and is invoked in complex ways. Islam provides a distinctive cultural context that imbues the use of reason with a spiritual dimension. God challenges human beings to engage all of the faculties at their disposal to make an assessment of the universe they experience. God warns that the "signs" he has sent down should not be treated lightly or ignored; they demand attention and deep thought.[34] The word *ayah* is the word used for a Qur'anic verse. It is also the word used for a sign, an indicator. It refers to the markings God has made on his world. The New Islamic school argues strenuously that the Qur'an insistently and repeatedly calls humanity to think, contemplate, and reflect. Reflection in the Qur'an calls Muslims to admire the wonders of creation and to appreciate a universe created by one God. However, the demands of thinking go farther. The call to think opens the way to all the empirical sciences that explore God's world. It invites the members of each generation both to explore the natural world around them and to assess the relevance of the knowledge of earlier generations to their own changed circumstances. The New Islamic scholars insist on the richness of the Qur'anic conception of reason. Culture for them is thus not a thing to be mummified as a relic of an earlier age. It is rather an active resource for dealing with the unique and daunting challenges of God's ever-changing world. The New Islamic scholars affirm that wherever their reason takes them, human beings will find that God is already there.

Conceptualizing Reason

In the vast body of their scholarly work, the New Islamic intellectuals insist that Islam has more than adequate reserves of reason and culture on which democrats in Islam may draw. Reason in the thinking and action of the New Islamic thinkers assumes three related forms.[35] *Instrumental reason* that connects means and ends in practical life and cause and effect in science is very much a part of their thinking about the world and humanity's place in it. In particular, they insist that Muslims quite self-consciously consider themselves the heirs of a civilization that absorbed the scientific achievements of the Greeks, the Indians, and the Chinese with whom they came in contact. God's world, as the great medieval Arab travelers like Ibn Battuta taught, is a world of multiple civilizations with varied attainments. Islamic civilization did more than preserve and transmit the human treasure of speculative scientific inquiry of the Greeks. Medieval Islamic scholars contributed impressively to further scientific advances in medicine, mathematics, and astronomy and, most importantly of all, in understanding the methods and aims of experimental science.

New Islamic intellectuals have sought to activate rather than memorialize this impressive legacy of Islamic civilization. In the inaugural lecture in 1998 at a center named for the great New Islamic thinker Muhammad al Ghazzali, who had died two years earlier, Yusuf al Qaradawi chose as his theme the absolute centrality of practical and scientific reason to Islam. Qaradawi reminded his listeners that the very first revelation called on Muslims to use their minds:

> Read!—In the name of thy Lord and Cherisher who created man
> . . . Read! And thy Lord is most bountiful—He who taught (the use
> of) the pen—Taught man that which he knew not.[36]

Qaradawi interpreted this verse to mean that God wanted to begin the era of rationality in education and science and that he was calling Muslims to play a role as leaders in its realization. Qaradawi related how Ghazzali was deeply saddened that the Islamic community, the leading light for science and learning for a thousand years, had become backward and ignorant. What most angered Ghazzali was the blame placed on Islam for this backwardness. How could such an argument be sustained, he wondered, when Islam had proven itself to be the vehicle that brought science and enlightenment to the world?

While recognizing the centrality of the instrumental reason of social practice and scientific inquiry, the *Wassatteyya* also emphasized that Islamic civilization explored and deepened ways in which reason could not only relate cause to effects and means to ends, but also offer evaluative judgments about the hierarchy of such ends and the usefulness of such effects for the forms of collective life they sought to build. *Evaluative reason*, they argued, has played a part as important as instrumental reason in the Islamic world. Islamic thinkers have understood that not all ends are of equal value and not all means are compatible with the achievement of certain prized community goals, as Islam defines them. Means, they quite explicitly argue, must also be compatible with the ends used for their achievement. If they are not, the larger goals and purposes of collective life will be distorted and undermined. No one has conveyed that insight with more force than Qaradawi. He pronounces unequivocally that ends do not justify means, but rather means must always be compatible with the ends they serve.[37]

Finally, *moral reason* in Islam holds out the possibility of generating ethical frameworks that encompass the instrumentality and evaluation that are inevitably entailed in all purposeful social activities. Fahmi Huwaidi brought reason in this sense into very public and controversial view when he launched an attack on the excessive religiosity of what he called the *darawish*. Moral reason in Islam is an intrinsic part of inquiry and social activity. In a candid and widely discussed column, Huwaidi noted that in the village of his origins, people repeatedly raised monies for the '*umra* (the recommended but not prescribed pilgrimage to Mecca at times other than the *hajj*) when the village was in dire need of developmental projects to improve the health and well-being of its inhabitants. Huwaidi did not question the probity of the '*umra* as a supererogatory but positive act of faith. What he did was place it in the larger framework of the Qur'anic injunction to "build the world." He concluded bluntly that those resources would be better spent on social projects for collective betterment. The *darawish*, he explained, reduced their obligations as Muslims to narrow rituals and traditional religious practices in the hopes of securing God's favor. "In doing so," wrote Huwaidi, "they are striving for their own salvation as individuals and ignoring the society around them. This attitude of mind and heart causes a kind of unintended selfishness in their religiousness."[38] Huwaidi decried this distortion of the priorities for practical activities that Islam establishes in the service of a larger moral whole. Reason in this third sense thus goes beyond instrumental and evaluative reason to organize the most valued goals and useful effects into a coherent unity. In Islam such thinking is marked by humility. The effort to see and understand the whole must be made, but with a sense that, in the phrasing of the Qur'an, only God can fully remove the "veil" to grasp the whole picture or complete "record" in all its complexity.[39]

Understanding Culture in Islam

These three understandings of reason that characterize the thinking of the *Wassatteyya* emerge out of the cultural context shaped by Islam. The concept of culture embedded in the intellectual and social products of the *Wassatteyya* is multifaceted. It includes the notion of culture as those habits of mind and heart that are the common possession of the varied human communities of the Islamic world. Culture also has for them the additional sense of those outcomes of human effort that command attention and respect for the beauty with which they imbue the human environment, as opposed to the purely natural world. Thus, there is no inclination among the New Islamic intellectuals to denigrate the role of the arts and, indeed, of all forms of creativity, which are recognized as valued outcomes of the highest forms of human effort. With great courage, the New Islamic school has defended art and artists against what they regard as ignorant extremist distortions of Islam that banish music, dance, and artistic expression, at times resorting to violence to accomplish that goal.[40] They stand just as firmly for creative thinking that refuses rote memorization and the divorce of learning from living. Culture for the *Wassatteyya* is open and inclusive. It is a wellspring of intellectual inquiry and progressive social activity.

Centrist Islam, Pragmatism, and the Democratic Ideal

The open-ended character of midstream understandings of reason and culture has produced some unexpected twists. Midstream intellectuals do not see their Islamic culture as in any way sealed off from the world. They explore a variety of connections and interactions with other civilizations and celebrate the enrichment they provide. One such connection, noted earlier, represents the unexpected loop that intersects with the distinctive

American tradition of philosophical pragmatism. The walk from an American philosophical and social reformist tradition to the contemporary thought of midstream Islam on democracy is less improbable than it might at first appear, although it is rarely commented on. The struggle for justice, equality, and freedom in community is a central preoccupation of both traditions. The pragmatists, especially John Dewey, conceptualized democracy as a call to a distinctive way of life. His lifework centered on educational reform, where he had his most enduring influence. The communal rather than individualistic emphasis in Dewey's work has a particularly strong resonance for the Islamic world. Dewey wrote:

> A democracy is more than a form of government; it is *primarily a mode of associated living, of conjoint communicated experience.* The extension in space of the number of individuals who participate in an interest so that each has to refer his own action to that of others, and to consider the action of others to give point and direction to his own, is equivalent to the breaking down of those barriers of class, race, and national territory which kept men from perceiving the full import of their activity.[41]

Dewey offered a compelling vision of democracy as a way to live together free from arbitrary power in self-determined, participatory communities. Like the New Islamic theorists, he understood that social reform was at once an intellectual and a social project. Knowing in both traditions is always about doing. Truth resides in the practical outcomes of thought and action rather than a grasp of abstract essentials that in both traditions is thought to be beyond human capacity.

There is an irony to the introduction of an American philosophical school into a discussion of democracy in the Islamic world at a time when the United States has globally displayed such an intense hostility to democratic developments in those spheres of the world, like the Arab lands, where American power is dominant. The irony may be lost on Western readers, especially Americans, who take seriously American rhetorical commitments to democracy, no matter how obvious their violation in practice.[42] Islamic intellectuals and activists wear no such blinders, in common with politically aware Arab citizens across the political spectrum who regularly witness American interventions to preclude, block, or undermine democratic developments. Yet, with a turn to pragmatism, even this irony is more apparent than real, for one of the most important and nuanced messages of the pragmatists was the forceful argument that American ideological crusades for freedom abroad and celebrations of freedoms at home more often than not functioned as mere screens for interested interventionism abroad and elite privilege at home. There are striking continuities in American foreign policy. The War on Terror provided an indispensable rationale for the support for odious but compliant dictators, like Hosni Mubarak. Today the same rhetoric is exploited by the counter-revolution to undermine the democratic opening in Egypt. At the same time the War on Terror facilitates the assault on longstanding American freedoms at home. In Dewey's time the official battles against communism at home and abroad functioned in precisely the same way. The pragmatists would find nothing really new in the use of struggles abroad to circumscribe freedom at home.

Pragmatism invokes democracy not as a fixed and rigid political formula or mode. Rather, democracy is understood as a call to practices that enhance such value-laden prospects. Unfortunately, in both the West and the Islamic world the everyday usage of the adjective "pragmatic" has come to mean an approach to life that is purely opportunistic, guided simply by unprincipled exploitation of available opportunities without serious attention to values. *Wusuli*, the conventional Arabic translation of pragmatic, conveys precisely this distorted meaning. Dewey would be horrified by such a deformed understanding of pragmatism.

What is invoked in this chapter, and in such centrist works as Alija Izetbegovic's *Islam between East and West*, is principled pragmatism as philosophy. Izetbegovic reasoned that its democratic commitments and spiritual roots made American pragmatism especially relevant to the work of Islamic centrists, who seek to honor God's signs that humanity *should act* to advance justice, equality, and freedom. Pragmatism like centrist Islam insisted on the spiritual dimension of politics and the political dimension of faith. In the work of the major American pragmatists, one finds a consistent, intermingling of politics and faith rather than the polarization that characterizes much else in Western, and especially European, thought. Izetbegovic argues persuasively that Roger Bacon, centuries earlier and under the influence of the great Arab medieval scholars, had accepted this same premise of the commingling science and faith that has remained in creative tension in Anglo-Saxon although not in continental European philosophy.[43]

Truth Standards of Pragmatism and Representationalism

A pragmatic rather than a representational standard of truth will be used to take the measure of the New Islamic explications of Islam in God's world.[44] The approach here aims for the deliberate cultivation of empathy in the hope that such empathy will have practical consequences in possible joint projects that will require mutual understanding and shared values that rise from very different cultural contexts. Such an attitude of mind represents a break with the standard approaches to Islam and Islamic thinkers and activists by Western scholars. The dominant representational view identifies the world with true descriptions of it. This implicit identification supports a positivist sense that all true descriptions weave seamlessly into a single, authoritative narrative. A pragmatic stance, in contrast, views verbal descriptions as situated interventions in the world that aim to influence behavior. A description is true to the extent that those who adopt it can navigate the situation to which it pertains. Descriptions that cannot be taken for granted in action must be revised. The world is not contained in or mirrored by true, scientific theories. Rather, it is the world that makes true theories true, just as the ocean makes seaworthy ships seaworthy.

On the pragmatic account, the original sin of the representational midstream in Western thought is the idea that the final goal is some ultimate, final account of the subject matter, a description that reveals the core of things, duplicates their essence, and strips them to their bare bones. The problem with this understanding of truth is that words cannot literally duplicate anything except other words. In their work, those who entertain a representational understanding of truth set their sights on the one true account, the single description to be maintained to the exclusion of all others. The very belief that such an account is possible is an obstacle to meaningful conversation and possible joint action. It leads to an inclination to psychological and social disorders, notably a superiority complex regarding one's own cultural or ethnic group. Islamic midstream intellectuals regard the certainty for which such accounts aim as God's alone.

In contrast, a pragmatic account is necessarily available for feedback on the ground from partners in the joint inquiry and common project. The mark of accuracy comes wholly from the ease with which the account can be taken for granted in the contexts for which it is intended. The signature of the paradigm of representation is the phallic impetus to penetrate through the world we live in to the "reality" behind it.

What does that penetration in fact yield other than words? What emerges is always some string of phrases like "essence," "underlying factors," "fundamental reality," or "core meaning" that validates researchers and reassures the readers they seek to persuade. At the same time, these phrases actively undercut those described by pointing out that this true account lies beyond their grasp. A parallel contrast was very much in evidence in Chapter 6 between the work of the anthropologists Clifford Geertz and Michael Gilsenan. Geertz postulates a social reading of an underlying symbolic code of which those observed are unaware. Gilsenan, in contrast, makes it quite clear that the only real competence in navigating the mystical experience lies with those, including an anthropologist in the field, who actually experience it in their thinking and practices.

The Deweyan alternative aims for engagement with subjects whose grasp of what is required for conversation and cooperation is no more or less limited than our own. It involves its own generalizations and inevitable reductions, guided, however, by the pragmatic project of constructive interaction in the real world. It thus does the inevitable work of selection and reduction that thinking requires. However, it does so without the spectral baggage of the quest for pure and ghostly forms and priestly overlording of those who presume themselves to have escaped from the cave.[45]

A Critique of Representationalism

The pragmatists want to move us from representational to pragmatic standards of truth in our accounts of Islam. Pragmatists have a future-oriented focus that looks ahead to the new forms of human interaction that inquiry enables. The dominant trend in Western Islamic studies is representational. Two important Western studies of Islam and Islamic movements illustrate this contrast and make more concrete the ways in which representationalism limits the enhanced interactive outcomes for which pragmatism aims.

Bruce B. Lawrence's *Shattering the Myth: Islam beyond Violence* launches a powerful substantive critique of conventional Western studies that insist on a linkage between Islam and violence. Lawrence's work must be appreciated for the effort to "shatter" that link. However, in methodology the work remains typical of Western studies that search for an ultimate cause or set of causes that explain the surface behavior of Islamic thinkers and activists. Such investigations usually end, as does Lawrence's, with the explanatory focus on the accurate representations of the causal abstractions situated at a depth that is out of reach of Islamic subjects but available to the researcher.

In *Shattering the Myth* Lawrence provides an instructive example of how dismissive of the direct experience of others such an account can be, despite the best intentions of the researcher. Lawrence introduces his work with wise reminders that attention must be paid to local factors and to the creativity of human agents. After this promising opening, Lawrence proceeds to characterize rivalism, reform, and fundamentalism as paradigmatic Islamic responses to what he calls "the ascendant world order." The three phases are shaped by their quasi-automatic reactions to global political economy forces originating in the West and best grasped in Western terms.[46] All that is left of the opening nod to Islamic agency resides in the small margin of gradation that shades particular instances of these fixed patterns of response. The patterns take on a life of their own. Self-understandings of the Islamic actors pale.

Lawrence explains his thinking by quoting Robert Segal on "the difference between *starting* with the actor's point of view and *ending* with it."[47] Lawrence is here guarding against relativism. Muslim subjects are quoted but their statements, in Lawrence's work, are taken as a step removed from real determinants encapsulated in the pure forms that his paradigms represent. In the end, the inseparability of religion and politics simply means for Lawrence that causal political economy factors are veiled with Islamic symbols and rhetoric. Lawrence's work projects the conclusion that it has pierced these veils to gain unmediated access to a reality the veils screen from view, presumably inaccessible to the actors themselves. Lawrence, in the end, succumbs to the illusion that reality is articulated fully in the authoritative discourse of Western political economy.

Pragmatism avoids this reductionist pitfall. It does so by identifying reality with the world we actually live in and experience, rather than with our descriptions of it. The pragmatist rejects the correspondence theory of truth—that is, the notion that true sentences and the world are in any sense isomorphic. On the pragmatic account, we face events forward, while speaking to each other sideways.[48] Such a future-oriented, pragmatic approach can acknowledge cultural variability, such as that represented by the variety of forms that modern-day Islam assumes. However, pragmatism abandons the conceit that these differences are objective discoveries. Rather, it puts the variation in us, as observers and actors in the world.

For Lawrence, the only choice is between an explanation cast in terms of pure but ghostly abstractions or a complicit relativism that takes far too seriously the self-understanding of Islamic actors. He opts for the accurate representation of the abstractions. Lawrence undoubtedly believes he has discovered the real underlying factors that shape the paradigmatic Islamic responses to the political economy forces that he gives causal force. In truth, the abstract patterns of response are not discovered by him in his subject matter at all. Rather, they are grouped and distinguished through his analysis, as a map adds borders and place names to terrain. No one "discovered" the borders of Egypt. The problem is that Lawrence's account would reverse the relation of the factors to what is observed. The factors he identifies are discursive entities, abstracted from a plurality of particular events. Putting them "beneath" what has been observed is a way of encoding the idea that these factors have some sort of causal power. The test of causal power comes, however, from the attempt to use these factors in causal explanation, not from some elusive sense of "depth" that gets to essentials. Instead of "essential factors" a pragmatic approach would speak of descriptions sufficiently generic to cover the broad range of particulars about which some meaningful generalization is sought.

A second and different version of representational scholarship lodges truth in an authoritative narrative rather than deep causation. Stephen Humphrey's *Between Memory and Desire* exemplifies this variant. Scholars working along these lines provide accounts of the words and behaviors of their subjects, apprehended as truth from a privileged external vantage point that makes them an objective representation of a reality only dimly grasped, if at all, by the subjects of study. The representational criterion of truth in such works manifests itself in a variety of strategies that all boil down to "letting the facts speak for themselves." Those facts can be objectively reported and ordered in a definitive way. To do so, however, one must have the right access code, something apparently denied to the real-world subjects of the study.

The shared conceit of such essentialist accounts resides in the conviction that there is such a thing as a disinterested standpoint for description of a reality that is simply "out there." Such a privileged standpoint would mean that there is some neutral, ultimate truth, some singular description the identification of which is the goal of inquiry. In contrast, in the pragmatic view descriptions inevitably involve selectivity. Essentialists deny the selectivity in their inquiries. In the end, such works are revealing for what the agenda that guides their selectivity tells us about Western thinking. Such works are routinely praised for precisely this quality. As Max Rodenbeck writes in his appreciative *New York Times* review, Humphreys's book "ends up revealing as much about our own society as those it describes."[49] I would put the same point in stronger terms: The book is of interest primarily for what it tells us about one style of American thinking about the Islamic world.

Such works as those of Lawrence and Humphreys are instructive and valuable for purposes of Western self-understanding. Humphreys, like Lawrence, does helpfully expose the most pernicious American myths and misrepresentations in his engaging book, such as the myth of the Middle East madman that is routinely evoked to explain the behavior of leaders in the Islamic world. In contrast, pragmatic accounts are of interest primarily for what they tell us about those others who have captured our attention. The subjects of such studies are beings who live rich and complex lives in their own culture with a decent awareness of the contextual influences they face. The aim is to create characterizations that would allow actors in the story to recognize themselves and to stimulate in the reader fellow-feeling sufficient to allow a grasp of the situation these actors face. When an effort is made to describe their environment from their own point of view, we at least have the possibility of experiencing imaginatively the challenges, the hopes, and the fears that actually animate their struggles. Such accounts can serve the aim of making possible cooperation for shared goals, like the attainment of democratic ends. The most influential of the "neo-pragmatists," the late Richard Rorty, made precisely this point with his discussion of the value of detailed "sentimental stories" that can create sympathy with others sufficient to stimulate practical, ethical, and political action. Following Hume, he argues that such accounts have greater practical moral force than abstract rational arguments.

Stories of this kind invoke emotions that do encourage identification and sympathy. For Rorty, they contribute to his broader call for the education of sentiments, or as he puts it more provocatively "sentimental education." Such education has the very serious and eminently practical aim of expanding "the reference of the terms 'our kind of people' and 'people like us.'" The purpose, Rorty continues, is to "sufficiently acquaint people of different kinds with one another so that they are less tempted to think of those different from themselves as only quasi-human."[50] Empathic knowledge in this way opens the door to constructive communication and possible joint action. It may, of course, also facilitate manipulation or other such less positive interactions. In any case, a complete mapping of the inner thoughts and feelings of potential partners is not needed. To talk and act in concert with someone for practical ends, whether positive or negative, we need not think and feel exactly as he or she does; all that is required is that we think and feel *with* him or her on behalf of some common, real-world project.

Grounded pragmatic accounts of the experiences of others cannot escape from the need for generalization and abstraction. For the purpose of communication and joint action with Islamic centrists about their democratic aspirations and strivings to realize them, for example, we clearly need at a minimum some generalized concept of democracy to recognize their stories as relevant instances of the broader class of worldwide democratic efforts.

Dewey recognized this need but was wary of reified, pure forms like "democracy." He argued that the most useful generalizations would not be essentialized abstractions; rather, they would be cast in generic rather than essentialist terms. This distinction between the essential and the generic is critical to the pragmatic approach employed in this book. The essential characteristics of a phenomenon purport to identify those features that define its very essence—in other words, those whose absence would negate the phenomenon. Their specification requires piercing the veils of appearance to some pure form. Centrist Islamic thinkers, in common with pragmatists, doubt that such knowledge is possible. In midstream Islamic thought the notion of piercing realities to essences is knowledge reserved to God. Humanity has limitations that preclude the grasp of such absolute certainties. In Islam it is only God who knows such things. In contrast, generic features are simply those whose repeated occurrence is noted empirically in a variety of contexts. Unlike essential features, which require a God-like grasp of the unchanging essence of a given phenomenon, generic features simply refer to traits recognized as common to more than one example of the phenomenon. Islamic centrists are confident that knowledge of this kind is within reach of a limited humanity.

If two parties on different sides of an important cultural divide seek to talk to each other and even cooperate to achieve a common goal such as democracy or the realization of human rights held in common, each must find the resources in his or her respective cultural contexts to make that collaboration possible in practical ways. However, there is absolutely no necessity that they do so in the same or even parallel ways. We may, after all, arrive at a common destination coming from very different directions.[51]

We may do so by taking our cues from cultural landscapes that offer more in the way of striking contrasts than similarities. This insight represents some very good news: It removes a barrier that often seems daunting, notably the false assumption that achievement of a common goal requires traversing essentially the same pathways to its realization.

It is probably inevitable that the West, having achieved impressive, although still incomplete, advances in realizing a democratic politics, would assert a kind of cultural patent on democratic outcomes. The claim that the West's pathway to democracy is *the* pathway permeates the literature on democratic transitions. It takes the form of assertions that those who lack certain elements of Western culture or historical experience are unlikely to make a successful transition to democracy. For example, it is frequently asserted that real progress is impossible without a culturally sanctioned separation of church and state or the related historical imperative of a "reformation" of the dominant religious tradition or the development of economic liberalization in tandem with an expansion of democratic freedoms. Clearly, all three features did play a key role in the Western path to democracy. However, those facts of Western history tell us little or nothing about the history of others and about the shape their journey to democracy might take.

The alleged democratic deficit in *Dar al Islam* invites the remaking of Islamic societies. The invidious claim of a Western patent on democracy manifests itself in the dangerous assertion that since democracy is one of humanity's great attainments, the West as pioneer has a responsibility to remake the deficient cultures of others in order to bring the blessings of democracy to them from the outside. Now, critics of these views in the West have vigorously, although for the most part unsuccessfully, attacked the disastrous policies to which such views have led. The American official war for freedom and against terrorism in reality advances the imperial struggle for resources and strategic advantage abroad, even as it assaults democratic gains at home. The backlash of citizen resistance to the calls for endless war in the West did not come in time to avert the devastation of whole societies and the unleashing of deadly sectarian impulses that continue to wreak havoc throughout the area. While these policy critiques have increasingly taken hold, there has been far less attention to the underlying theoretical issue about which Western critics are usually silent. This silence may well explain at least part of the failure of the critics to put much of a dent in the dangerous and often violent policies that flow from this fundamental theoretical misunderstanding.

The pragmatists in general and Dewey in particular have addressed this fundamental issue of cultures and outcomes in constructive ways. To be sure, since the policies that originate from the flawed position of a Western cultural patent on democracy reflect not only flawed thinking but also deep-seated interests, they may well persist even after the intellectual basis for such thinking has been undermined. In truth, the West has shown little or no interest in actually supporting democracy in the Islamic world, despite the incessant rhetoric to that effect. But at least we can hope to clear away some of the fuzzy and unhelpful thinking that has helped to rationalize destructive policies and win support for them from often-reluctant publics.

A particular pattern of culture may be a sufficient condition for the shaping of human beings capable of a certain way of life, like democracy. However, it is groundless to extend that argument to the untenable claim that such a cultural pattern is the *necessary* condition for the way of life it produces. Those who know more than one culture in some depth repeatedly experience similar outcomes and experiences from very different cultural resources. I base this insight on the experience of a lifetime wandering through and staying for extended periods in cultures other than my own, not at all bothered by the title of *khawaga* (foreigner in long-term residence). I also rely on the work of the great political sociologist Barrington Moore, Jr., into whose seminar at Harvard I also wandered in much the same haphazard way. The seminar was over-enrolled and theoretically closed. However, I discovered that by just showing up and asking questions and offering comments that showed I had engaged the readings, Moore's cool graciousness took over; he never asked me to leave. For all the casualness of my access, there was nothing haphazard in what I discovered. In his indispensable study *The Social Origins of Dictatorship and Democracy*, on which he was working at the time, Moore provides exactly the kind of generic rather than essentialized characteristics that Dewey invoked.

What matters for the advancement of democratic struggles around the world is emphatically not that other experiences duplicate those of the relatively more successful democratic experiments like the American one. The difficulty of criticism, especially in the face of particularly inept policies like those pursued in the wake of the terrible 9/11 attacks, has made it easier for illusions about what we have accomplished to persist. I have never been quite clear about why people are so reluctant to air dirty laundry in public; the sun and open air, after all, have sanitizing advantages, as my mother, my first instructor in the nuances of pragmatism, repeatedly assured her seven children. All of us learned a reverence for soap and water, a very Islamic trait, I was later to learn! Isn't it wiser to concentrate on getting out the stains and the unpleasant smells rather than on what the neighbors think? My mother considered it important to acknowledge the messes you made and to figure out how they could possibly have happened. Simply moving forward, not looking back and not assessing the causes of mistakes, just was not something she tolerated. Nor should it be, whether in personal or public life. At a minimum, the notion that our path to democracy has not been without its share of stained sheets of our own doing would at least give us sufficient pause to allow others to find their own way to pursue, institute, and sustain a democratic way of life.

Barrington Moore, Jr., provides the practical insight necessary to recognize democratic experiences elsewhere and their possible contributions without turning the insight into an essentialized abstraction. According to Moore, "the development of democracy is a long and incomplete struggle to do three closely related things." Moore employs verbs rather than nouns. He nestles the generic struggle for democracy in three project verbs: checking arbitrary rulers, securing just and rational rules, and providing for participation in making the rules.[52] Democracy is something for which human communities strive in these generalized ways. It is not an object that America or Israel or any other state owns and with which it is entitled to bludgeon those "quasi-humans" who are judged less far along. When the issue of democracy is cast at this level of generality, it is possible to recognize that sustained efforts to pursue the democratic idea in Islam have taken place and to document them empirically.

Islamic Narratives and Theorizations of Democracy

Muslims have their own narrative of struggles for social justice. Its inspiration comes to them from the Qur'an. Lived experiences that curtail arbitrary power, generate just rules to govern the common life, and create broader opportunities for the people to take part in determining these rules, inspired by the Message, are an important part of the history of the *ummah*. These real-world experiences ground the narrative. Each of the core countries of the Islamic strategic triangle of Turkey, Iran, and Egypt has a proud history of battles for constitutional systems. They have all enjoyed mass support and have engaged trends across the political spectrum, always including Islamic trends.

Islamic democracy, the New Islamic school candidly acknowledges, is an unfinished project that challenges the *ummah* to bold thinking. They argue forthrightly that Islamic *fiqh* (legal reasoning, based on interpretation of the Qur'an and *Sunnah*) must appropriate the gains of Western political constitutional thought. Speaking with unembarrassed frankness, Muhammad al Ghazzali pronounced Islamic constitutional *fiqh* to be "severely underdeveloped." He urged Islamic thinkers to borrow freely from Western democratic concepts and mechanisms. More precisely, the thinkers of the New Islamic school have singled out the following notions as proven instruments of democratic rule that should be imitated: separation of powers, multiple parties and competitive elections, constitutional guarantees of basic political freedoms such as speech and assembly protected by an independent judiciary, equal civil and political rights for minorities, and limited terms for the highest offices. The intellectuals of the New Islamic trend have accepted the challenge of integrating these elements from the experience of others into a coherent theory and practice of Islamic democracy.[53]

The rich conception of democracy as a way of life goes farther still, demanding an attention to what Tareq al Bishri calls *al mujta'a al ahaly* (communal society). The concept for Bishri captures much of what is attractive about the Western civil society notion of a public space dominated neither by the market nor ruling power and committed to serving the common good. The distinguished Egyptian historian suggests this alternative term, however, because it avoids the secular bias against Islamic organizations that the civil society notion often carries, while preserving the positive features of a public arena where the general welfare can be defended.[54]

The New Islamic vision of communal society is far more inclusive than realized. As an intellectual school, these scholars have, for example, produced bold and innovative studies of the role of women in public life, with the lead taken by the late Muhammad al Ghazzali in advocating for an expansion of women's rights. New Islamic thinkers argue for the full inclusion as well of non-Muslims as citizens, a point of view boldly put forth in Fahmi Huwaidi's early book *Citizens, Not Zimmis*. Yusuf al Qaradawi and Tareq al Bishri have also written extensively on an inclusive role for non-Muslims. Their efforts have yielded a collective body of work that is widely regarded as the most enlightened on this critical issue.[55]

Their contributions provide a firm foundation for the equal participation of non-Muslims in the new political world that Islamic democracy would bring. However, these works by centrist Islamic groups are for the most part unread in the West, and the clear evidence of their value in combating extremism and preparing the ground for inclusive, democratic visions of Islamic community that draw on indigenous sources is completely ignored in mainstream Western commentary.

For decades New Islamic intellectuals have been engaged in collective efforts to theorize the Qur'anic narrative of justice and of the real-world struggles for democracy on Islamic ground that it informs. Their efforts to do so have repeatedly generated turbulence, as they raise controversial issues of great importance for the advancement of the *ummah*. They have registered critical gains in theory and practice on behalf of democratic objectives. On more than one occasion, democratic experiences judged antithetical to Western interests have been curtailed by repressive interventions and domestic tyrannies. In the face of these formidable obstacles, intellectuals of the New Islamic trend have developed ways of thinking and acting as part of the Islamic Renewal that can be validly and persuasively described as contributing to efforts to limit arbitrary ruling power, yield more just laws, and enhance participation in rule making. It matters little how their pathways to these positions compare to our own.[56] Their efforts merit serious attention. Such practical and theoretical work over several decades gives the lie to unfounded yet endlessly repeated Western assertions that Islamic culture cannot nurture the values of justice, equality, and freedom that democracy requires and all of the great monotheistic traditions advance.

8

The Islamist Imaginary

They (the hypocrites) have made their oaths a screen (for their misdeeds):
Thus they obstruct (men) from the path of God: truly evil are their deeds.

QUR'AN 63:2

WHEN AN IDEA is elusive, it is appropriate to give it an ambiguous label.
The ambiguity avoids misleading concreteness and suggests something
of the complexities that can be blamed for the clarity not quite achieved.
Such is the character of the "Islamist Imaginary," the core analytical concept deployed here to characterize the intimate connection between Islam
and empire. "Imaginary" refers to something imagined, in this case the
powerful conjured Islam of the American imperial project. The challenge
is to make such a hyper-real conception of Islam tangible. The Islam of
empire must be powerful. Its usefulness resides in its capacity to screen
from view the real-world influence that Islam as a faith and way of life
has on the world's 1.6 billion Muslims. The Islamist Imaginary must
overshadow these experienced realities to project the imagined Islam that
empire requires. How can one distinguish between the usefully imagined and the simply real?

At Trinity College, a small and very old New England liberal arts college where I teach, a measure of clarity was given to me, in a quite unexpected way. During graduation week in the spring of 2006 at Trinity,
a small drama in two acts unfolded. A Muslim student of mixed Indian-
European parentage, whose thesis I supervised, boarded an evening bus
provided by the college for attendance at senior week activities. He would
graduate the next day with honors in international studies and as the re-
cipient of a distinguished Japanese prize for fostering international understanding. The student next to him noticed only his "Middle Eastern"
looks and announced in a loud voice his anxiety at "sitting next to Osama
bin Laden who might have a bomb." At graduation the next day, the same
student heard the cautionary words of our president, addressed at the end

of the ceremony to all graduating seniors about the dangerous world they were entering. To illustrate the dangers, the president singled out "those Muslims who danced in the streets on 9/11/2001 when the twin towers collapsed and the Pentagon burned." What makes this scene noteworthy is not just the presence of our small contingent of Muslim students, including my honors student, but on the stage, seated right next to our president, of Shirin Ebadi, the Iranian Nobel laureate. Ebadi is one of the best-known Muslim women in the world today. She is an honored champion of human rights in Iran and worldwide. She had just been awarded an honorary doctorate of humane letters by our president. Yet the imagined Islam of terror and violence that justifies the War on Terror obscured the very real Muslim, committed to peace and justice, there in flesh and blood within arm's reach.

The Islamist Imaginary is that compelling.[1] It is that powerful. When this glaring and hurtful contradiction was pointed out, our president responded with genuine surprise. After some reflection, he apologized to our distinguished guest and others offended by the unintended hurt of his remarks. The Islamist Imaginary has deeply penetrated the American psyche. There should be no cause for surprise that the American media firmly believed that, just behind the people's movement that swept through the Islamic world in the spring of 2011, there lurked a terrible Islamic menace.

Understanding the conjured Islam of empire has nothing at all to do with the religion of the world's multitude of Muslims. Nor does it originate in a psychological malady of those who guide the American empire. The extensive work by Western scholars and journalists on Islamophobia is well intentioned.[2] However, it obscures more than it illuminates. It is ultimately distracting. The notion of Islamophobia asks that we think of the Islam of empire as the result of a failure of understanding. The misrepresentations of Islam are presumed to result from ignorance compounded by psychological imbalances, parallel to other instances of phobic behavior. The approach has two negative consequences. First, Islam itself, the faith of some 1.6 billion persons, is put in a defensive and apologetic position. Articles and books pour forth to counter the "misunderstandings" about Islam's attitude toward such issues as democracy, women, or violence. The Islam that emerges in such studies is an Islam in the dock, defined and distorted by the necessity to respond to the false charges made against it by the "Islamophobes." A second consequence of the Islamophobia approach is to point to educative and psychological remedies for the phobia. In fact, America has imperial interests rather than a knowledge deficit or a psychological problem. Neither education nor psychology has much to do with the generation of the Islamist Imaginary.

The Islam of empire must be confronted on the rough political terrain from which it emerges. The collapse of the Soviet Union meant that the American empire had no real adversary. An imperial project cannot tolerate such a void. The War on Terror filled the void and continues to do so today. Ridding the world of terror is a metaphysical notion. Terror is just another word for evil. President George W. Bush, and Ronald Reagan before him, did in fact use them interchangeably. Those formulations cast the net so widely that both are essentially meaningless. Yet there is a difference. A war against evil makes no intuitive sense. Terror, on the other hand, can be rendered more particular and less metaphysical. The Islamist Imaginary gives evil Muslim features.

Evil with Islamic Features

Against the background of the Islamist Imaginary, a War on Terror becomes plausible. The existence of networks of dangerous Islamic extremists, and their deadly criminal actions, contributes in invaluable ways to make the formula work. The beheadings of Western captives stage-managed by ISIS provide an instructive instance. Violent extremists do pose a threat, most of all to the Muslims whom they oppress. The march toward Baghdad and Erbil of the militants of ISIS in the summer of 2015 is a particularly ominous example. They are undoubtedly also a deadly challenge for America and the West. However, the threat they pose is very far from an existential one for the United States or Europe. A perfectly reasonable strategy of surveillance and targeted police and security action is available to deal with infiltrators. Should extremists succeed in consolidating a state, then containment represents a proven strategy for managing even that risk.[3] The War on Terror represents a policy decision to reject these measured and modest alternatives in favor of an imperial American foreign policy. Such a policy is driven by the standard imperial interest in dominance and control of vital global resources. Unlike other justifications for intervention abroad, such as the abstract notion of protecting human rights, "terrorism" allows for violent intervention against a militarized enemy, personalized by ominous-looking men with long beards and guns over their shoulders, flying black flags.

The approach to exposing the Islamist Imaginary must be blunt and direct. Neither accurate information about Islam nor psychological therapy to counter a phobia will be of much use. Islam itself needs no defense because the Islamist Imaginary has nothing to do with it. Let us recognize at the outset that the imagined Islam of empire is conjured from a tissue of outright lies, endlessly and deliberately repeated. Big lies are the most difficult to identify as such, especially when they are repeated by great powers with all the media resources at their command. The Egyptian journalist Fahmi Huwaidi describes himself as mystified by the spectacle of the American leaders reacting to the 9/11 attacks in what can only be described as highly irrational ways. Huwaidi fails to find an explanation for the American "fondness for the process of simplifying that focuses on the process of describing rather than the description itself that aims to personify the reality of evil and not the evil reality." He pronounces himself unable to understand how an advanced and highly complex society with "great minds, great institutions, and a record of achievements in science and technology can accept unreasonable matters that can't be accepted by human reason such as relating evil to one person and fundamentalism and terrorism to one religion or ethnic group."[4]

The terrible crime of 9/11 committed by Islamic extremists created an opportunity to advance the imperial project. President George W. Bush launched the American War on Terror. In fact, at issue was control over oil and the advancement of Israeli aims, not the containment of terror. The battle to control the oil of that great Arab people was launched and the blood, overwhelmingly Iraqi blood, flowed. All key decision makers, from the president on down, avoided mention of Israel. They insisted that the war had nothing at all to do with oil. They lied. To screen the lies, one alternative rationale after the other was trotted out to justify the unjustified and unprovoked war. The war aimed to rid the Iraqi people of a terrible tyrant on a par with Hitler. Saddam Hussein had weapons of mass destruction. A nuclear-armed Iraqi regime would inevitably pass those weapons on to al Qaeda, to which the regime was linked.

Even before the assault began, the common sense of ordinary people in key Western cities refused one false justification after another. The lies could not have been more obvious, ridiculous, and easy to refute. Millions filled the streets with the astute demand of "no more blood for oil." They knew the truth. With so many of the key American decision makers linked directly to the oil giants and their subsidiaries, it was really not that hard to see through the lies. We now have the documents that reveal in excruciating detail the official planning that had targeted Iraq and control of its oil long before 9/11. It is important to add that secondary gains would flow from this primary objective. Advocates for Israeli interests would secure their goal of "ending" a major Arab state and dividing it into continuously fighting religious and ethnic factions. The United States would have a wonderful stage to put on display its terrifying technologies of war. To secure Iraqi oil the United States would establish military bases right in the heart of the Middle East. The bases would immeasurably enhance American economic, political, and cultural leverage in the region. The question that hangs over this criminal violation of international law is less "why we did it" than what made the American architects of war believe they could pull it off and keep their citizens in line.

Arrogance of power and inordinate confidence in military means to secure imperial ends set the course to war. The invasion would be a "cakewalk" and Iraq itself would be remade without great difficulty. Still, there remained the problem of ordinary citizens who saw through the lies. They were willing to put their bodies on the streets to disrupt the plans of the war-makers. The war-makers had a solution. Manipulated apprehensions would overcome this dilemma. Fear would silence truth.

War requires a fearsome adversary. Enter the Islamist Imaginary. The level of Western hostility to Islam reaches extraordinary proportions. It generates anxieties to match. From Europe, America inherited and fostered a rich vein of animus toward all things Islamic. Falsehoods about Islam lace the Western civilization heritage. They are dangerous and distressing. They are also useful for imperial purposes. They feed the Islamist Imaginary. At times, they do so in indirect ways. Westerners through the centuries have heard that Muslims do not worship "God." Rather, they worship a quite different, alien "Allah." Yet Allah is simply the Arabic word for "God." The Arabic term is related to the word for God, Alaha, in Aramaic. It is the language that Jesus spoke. It is still spoken today.

More often, the calumnies are less subtle, more direct, and far more aggressive. The American public is subjected to particularly vulgar variants. Jerry Vines, former head of the Southern Baptist Convention, has described the Prophet Muhammad as a "demon-obsessed pedophile." Franklin Graham, son of Billy Graham and the minister who gave the invocation at President Bush's inauguration, describes Islam as "a very evil and false religion." Jerry Falwell of the Moral Majority pronounced Islam "a terrorist religion."[5]

Muslims do not trade in such degrading insults. Both Moses and Jesus are revered as prophets in Islam. The Qur'an refers to Jesus quite simply as the Messiah. In Islam, Jesus is born of Mary "purified above all women." Reverential descriptions of Mary in the Qur'an exceed the space accorded to her in the New Testament. An entire *surah* entitled "Mariam" tells the story of Mary and Jesus. Muslims simply cannot denigrate Moses or Jesus without repudiating core beliefs of their own faith and most sacred teachings. In the almost five decades I have lived and traveled among Muslims on four continents, I have not one single time heard a practicing Muslim insult Jesus, not even in the wake of the most virulent and degrading attacks on the Prophet Muhammad.

The endlessly repeated allegation that Islam fosters violence and war is the most vile and damaging of the lies out of which the Islamist Imaginary is spun. It should be a fact of great interest and importance that the more than a billion and a half Muslims believe that they are divinely ordained both to refrain from aggression themselves and to resist attacks and oppression by others.[6] The Muslim daily greeting is "as salamu 'alaikum," or peace be upon you. Such understanding has yet to make its way into public consciousness and discussion of Islam.

On war, Islam takes a middle position. Judaism preaches an eye for an eye. Christianity instructs its adherents to turn the other cheek, although Christians "marching as to war" have historically paid little attention to that pacifist injunction. Islam condemns aggression but defends rightful resistance. It is a moral view. It seem eminently reasonable to me and echoes the words I heard as a child on how to deal with violence in a rough neighborhood. The first Islamic community suffered assaults by its enemies. Revelations addressed this peril directly. In the Qur'an failure to resist when attacked is tantamount to supporting oppression, and oppression is something God hates. "And fight in the way of God those who fight against you, but begin not hostilities. Surely God loves not the aggressors."[7] In Islam, the permissible resort to force is also sharply circumscribed. A threatened community is authorized to strike its enemies when religion itself is endangered. "If God did not repel some people by others, then monasteries, churches, synagogues, and mosques wherein God's name is abundantly remembered, would have been destroyed. God will certainly aid those who aid his cause for surely God is strong and mighty."[8] The Qur'an urges confrontation of those who deliberately break their pacts and treaties and attack religion and the culture it generates. An important verse cautions against "those with whom you make an agreement, who then break their agreement every time, and honor not their word . . ." The verse continues "if they break their oaths after their agreements and revile your religion, then fight the leaders of unbelief because surely their oaths mean nothing and will not restrain them."[9] Resort to force is also not only permissible but fully expected when Muslims suffer oppression: "And why would you not fight in the way of God and of those who because they are weak are ill-treated and oppressed? Men, women, and children whose cry is: Our Lord, rescue us from this city whose people are oppressors and raise for us from Thee one who will protect; raise for us from Thee one who will assist."[10] In particular, the Qur'an clearly spells out the right of defense when Muslims are driven from their lands. At the same time, the Qur'an warns against excesses and urges that responses be proportional. A verse quite clearly states that "whoever retaliates with the like of that with which they are injured and are again oppressed, God will surely help him."[11] It is important to remember that, in modern times, Muslims have fought in defense of their own lands and on their own territory, such as the Algerians in Algeria and the Palestinians in Palestine. Muslim armies were not sent thousands of miles away to invade Western lands.

It requires no great effort of the moral imagination to understand that many Muslims—Algerians in an earlier age; Palestinians, Afghans, and Iraqis today—believe themselves to have been placed in a situation where they must resist, most often against overwhelming odds and even at the cost of forfeiting their own lives. Islam does not condone suicide; it is, in fact, rare in Islamic societies. However, the sacrifice of one's own life to safeguard the faith and free others from terrible repression is regarded in most religions as heroic action. Epidemics of collective embrace of death swept through early Christian communities faced with persecution and the forced renunciation of their faith. Martyrs occupy a large space in the Christian religious imagination.

Judaism, too, has its history and myths of martyrdom. In the story of Masada the Jewish people have contributed perhaps their most dramatic story of self-inflicted death as a form of resistance. To those with a sense of history, to visit Israel today is to go first to the old city of Jerusalem and then to the ancient fortress of Masada. The fortress sits atop a cliff at the western end of the Judean Desert, overlooking the Dead Sea. It is a place of stark and majestic beauty. It is also the site of what many regard as one of the greatest stories of collective resistance unto death in Jewish history. At Masada hundreds of Jews fought in the year 73 the last, losing battles against Roman invasion. After three years, they could no longer keep the

Romans at bay. Elazar ben Yair, the leader of the fighters, argued for death rather than capture. Elazar's final speech provided a clear and eloquent defense of these acts as a form of honorable resistance:

> Since we long ago resolved never to be servants to the Romans, nor to any other than to God Himself, Who alone is the true and just Lord of mankind, the time is now come that obliges us to make that resolution true in practice . . . We were the very first that revolted, and we are the last to fight against them; and I cannot but esteem it as a favor that God has granted us, that it is still in our power to die bravely, and in a state of freedom.[12]

Historians, archaeologists, sociologists, and anthropologists, led by Israeli scholars, have all chipped away at important elements of the Masada story, questioning some of the elaborate details that have been woven into Masada to enhance its utility as an Israeli national myth.[13] Yet, for all the shadings, there seems to be no doubt that of the hundreds of Jews who died at Masada, substantial numbers did so at the hands of their families or themselves. Christians and Jews have both had a worldly experience that provides abundant materials to reflect seriously on questions of suicide and resistance. It is puzzling, therefore, that so many in the West find it difficult to understand the reasoning of Islamic martyrs, and to recognize the moral complexities of acts of suicide that have both religious and political significance for those who commit them.

There is in the Qur'an no celebration of violence, per se, as a cleansing force. However, the Qur'an is clear about regarding just struggles as a religious obligation. In a knowing way, God asks, "Did you suppose that you would enter Paradise without God knowing who among you have striven and are patient?"[14] However, Muslims are instructed that all acts of war by them must cease immediately if their enemies sue for peace, pledge to end persecution and oppression, and sincerely undertake to abide by their oaths and covenants. A verse clearly admonishes that "if they incline to peace, then incline thou also to it, and trust in God. Surely He is All-Hearing, All-Knowing."[15] The Qur'an also discusses the issue of deterrence as a preferred way to circumvent war. "And make ready for them whatever force you can, and [have] horses tied at the frontier, to frighten thereby the enemy of God, and your enemy, and others beside them, whom you know not. God knows them."[16] Muslims are ordered to be ready for war, not in order to start it but to deter their enemies. The widely accepted Western notion of Islam as a religion of the sword has made it easy for Westerners to imagine that war is enjoined in Islam for the propagation of the faith, but nowhere in the Qur'an is such an idea to be found.

The Entanglements of Islam and Empire

The United States is at war with a very different, mythic Islam of its own making that has nothing at all to do with this Islam of the Qur'an. To make sense of that conjured threat, scholarly studies of Islam or Islamic movements are of no help at all. Even the examination of the real-world history and practice of empire has limited value, unless the *perceived* Islamic dimension is considered. The American imperial project cannot be brought into clear view without assessment of the distinctive rationale that the Islamist Imaginary provides. The task is not an easy one. The Islamist Imaginary has no simple and unitary existence. Rather, it is a complex amalgam that shapes both the delusions of empire and a conjured threat to imperial power into a co-evolving composite. It is a "difficult whole," in the helpful language of complexity theory. The Islamist Imaginary, unlike Islam itself and political movements of Islamic inspiration, does not exist outside of the imperial interests that shape it. It has no independent cultural or historical reality, outside its role as predatory threat to Western global interests. The American empire, in turn, requires a hostile and threatening enemy, which today takes the form of Islam of its imagination, to realize and rationalize its expansionist project that must remain unacknowledged and unspoken. The two elements of the imaginary and empire co-evolve. The needs of a threatened empire as vulnerable victim change over time. The Islamist Imaginary transforms itself to meet those needs. Imaginary and empire circle one another in a dance of predator and prey. Their roles are interchangeable, a clear sign that they are not entirely real. The predator is prey; the prey is predator. They develop in tandem in a complex process of mutual adaptation. Boundaries give way between the real and the imagined. In the end it is the imagined that haunts our imaginations and drives our policies.[17]

The idea of the co-evolution of Islam and empire in the Islamist Imaginary is not as strange as it might at first seem. Scholars know that the entanglement of Islam and empire has an intricate chain of precedents.

Edward Said provided a useful starting point for analyzing these complex linkages with his frequently quoted assertion that ours is an age of "many Islams." It is also the time of the singular American empire. He pointed out that Islam and empire have an intricate history of connections.[18]

The dominant notion of civilizational conflict between the Islamic world and the West rightly highlights the Islamic ideological roots of the most persistent resistances to American global dominance, provided that we recognize that the conflict has political and economic causes. However, this same notion obscures an important history of instrumental cooperation between Islam and the United States. American assertions of imperial power have had a consistent and often compliant Islamic dimension. It is now rarely acknowledged, though, that the cooperative dimension is at least as important for understanding the relationship today of the Islamic world and the West as the contrary record of oppositions to American hegemony of Islamic inspiration.

Of the "many Islams," America has for decades actively fostered and manipulated its own useful preferences. These "preferred Islams" of earlier periods are part of the story of the Islamist Imaginary of our own. The consequences of the manipulations of these preferred Islams have not always been those intended, at least not in the long run. They have often entailed violence that in the end was turned back first on U.S. clients and then on the United States itself. Yet, for all these qualifications, it remains true that the preferred Islams, cultivated and shaped by the United States, have been critical to the post–World War II projections of American power.

At the end of World War II, President Roosevelt made an historic agreement with the house of Saud in Saudi Arabia. In exchange for privileged access to oil, the United States guaranteed the royal family's hold on power, declaring the defense of Saudi Arabia a vital U.S. interest. The eighteenth-century origins of the current Saudi regime in the alliance between Muhammad Ibn Sa'ud, a local chieftain, and Ibn Abdul Wahhab, a puritanical and ultraconservative Islamic reformer, proved no obstacle. U.S. material support for all the usual instruments of repression enabled the Saudi royals to impose themselves on "their" people, despite Islam's deeply rooted antipathy to monarchy. It also allowed the interpretation of Islam to take firm hold in Saudi Arabia and, through Saudi oil revenue funding, make itself felt worldwide as a powerful reactionary tradition. The royal family's self-appointed role as guardian of Islam's most holy sites, Mecca and Medina, provided the requisite religious cover for the U.S.-backed repression that secured their hold on power. This critical

Saudi connection ensured American triumph over its European rivals for control of Middle Eastern oil. It also ensured a linkage between American empire and one of the most reactionary forces in the Islamic world, if not the world at large.

Complicit Saudi Islam played a critical role in the subsequent geopolitical competition with the Soviet Union in the 1950s and 1960s. The United States knowingly used the retrograde Wahhabi Islam of the Saudis as a counterweight to progressive Arab nationalisms. These nationalisms had shown themselves willing to open doors to the Soviets in exchange for support for their projects of independent national development. By doing so, they threatened to challenge American hegemony over the Middle East and its precious oil resources.

Personified most effectively by Gamal Abdul Nasser of Egypt, Arab nationalists threatened to chart the kind of independent path of development that is intrinsically anathema to any imperial power. A combination of external blows and internal manipulations brought these nationalist assertions to an end by the late 1960s. In the wake of the collapse of the nationalist project, the United States saw no problems when a state-controlled Islam provided ideological cover for the compliant Egyptian successor military regimes. Egypt after Nasser was effectively brought within the American orbit and voided of all genuine nationalist content. For such regimes, the threat to their hold on power came from the left and the memories among the masses of the material and social advances registered under progressive Arab nationalist banners. Such successor regimes were no less repressive in pursuing their regressive aims than their predecessors had been in advancing more progressive objectives of autonomous development and improvement of mass welfare. Once again, Egypt provided the prototype, with Anwar al Sadat as the "believing President" who expelled the "Godless" Soviets, opened Egypt to American penetration, and welcomed disciplined Islamists back into public life as a counter to the "atheist left." The Americans embraced both Sadat and the domesticated Islam in which he draped himself. In the end, however, Sadat's cynical manipulation of Islamic symbols as a cover for policies of alignment with America and capitulation to Israel on the issue of Palestine incited the anger of Islamic extremists. Khalid al Islambouli assassinated Sadat on October 6, 1981, shouting "Death to Pharaoh!"

When an already weakened Soviet Union blundered into Afghanistan in 1979, the United States turned to yet another variety of politicized Islam to hasten Soviet defeat. U.S. intelligence services, with assistance from their regional counterparts, actively and effectively mobilized the resources of Islamic militants, drawn from all over the Islamic world and including the Saudi Osama bin Laden. Enormous levels of funding were provided from American and Saudi sources, variously estimated but certainly in the billions. They aimed to take advantage of Soviet vulnerability in occupied Afghanistan. The strategy worked: Defeat in Afghanistan helped precipitate the demise of the Soviet Union.

That direct contribution to unchallenged American hegemony was neither the last nor the most significant by the violent transnational Islamic networks the United States helped finance and train for work in Afghanistan. As a result of the successful American-sponsored guerrilla war against the Soviet Union, violent extremist groups proliferated. They created havoc, everywhere not least in New York City on September 11, 2001. These terrible events were reprisals for American Middle East policies and the work of assassins, whom the United States initially encouraged and even in some cases trained.

The crime against humanity committed on September 11, 2001, had the unintended consequence of serving the breathtaking expansionist plans of the neoconservatives who dominated the Bush administration. Only a plausible enemy was lacking to make their execution possible. From the storehouse of the Western historical imagination, age-old images of a hostile Islam were retrieved. Islamic terrorists conjured up in a believable form for a frightened America the "threat to civilization" that every empire requires to justify its own violent acts of domination.

The Islamist Imaginary in the service of the neoconservative version of empire was born. The administration used all the resources of media control at its disposal to make sure that no links were made between the 9/11 crime and unjust U.S. Middle Eastern policies and the bloody instrumentalities the United States forged to enforce them. Plans for the United States to topple the Taliban and occupy Iraq, and for the Israelis to "resolve" the Palestinian issue by force, were all in place before 9/11. The most expansive version of the neoconservative agenda to advance U.S. and Israeli interests found forthright expression in a position paper written for the newly elected Israeli Prime Minister Benjamin Netanyahu of the Likud party in 1996. It is entitled "Clean Break: A New Strategy for Securing the Realm" and was published by the Institute for Advanced Strategic and Political Studies. The document calls for a "clean break from the peace process," the annexation of the West Bank and Gaza, and the elimination of Saddam's regime in Iraq, as prelude to regime changes in

Syria, Lebanon, Saudi Arabia, and Iran. The authors all became influential players in the second Bush administration.

President Bush's elaboration of a more comprehensive strategy of global hegemony came in the fall of 2002 in a document called "National Security Strategy of the United States."[19] The United States would never again allow a hostile power to approach parity with U.S. military capabilities. The United States would take the offensive to ensure its continued "full spectrum" dominance. Endlessly repeated images of 9/11 provided the backdrop for a doctrine of "preventive" wars that would give a defensive coloration to what were, in reality, projections of American imperial power. The president rallied a cowed Congress to a strategy of endless wars to ensure global hegemony under the cover of a worldwide War on Terrorism whose features, while murky, were still recognizably Islamic.

An innocent and wounded America recast its public role in the Middle East as the champion of democracy and the bulwark against the Islamic wellsprings of irrationalism that ostensibly fed global terrorism. The stage was set for the full-blown evocation of the Islamist Imaginary. There was already an established American practice of manipulating Islam, including the most backward-looking and violent versions, for imperial ends. This time, however, strategic planners for the Bush administration departed from the established pattern with a breathtaking innovation.

At each prior critical strategic moment, America had made use of an existing form of Islam that could be reshaped to serve its needs. The Saudi connection yielded a royal, reactionary, and repressive Islam with which America cooperated without complaints for decades. The American-backed *jihad* against the Soviets in Afghanistan, in contrast, called forth an assertively violent rather than simply repressive Islam. America enthusiastically assembled, funded, and trained its transnational advocates. At the same time, the subservient successor regime in Egypt needed a domesticated "house Islam" that would support the right-leaning, authoritarian government. The Sadat regime would preside over the deindustrialization of Egypt and facilitate the ruthless pacification of the Palestinians. The United States had little good to say about Nasser and his Arab socialist policies. It did, however, welcome his efforts to "modernize" the venerable mosque-university of al Azhar. Nasser pursued a strategy of enhancing the role of Islam in Egyptian life while at the same time bringing al Azhar under firm state control.[20] The number of mosques doubled and Islamic broadcasts from Cairo, supported by the government, reached to countries across *Dar al Islam*.

Sadat, for his part, sought to manipulate official Islamic figures and institutions to support his right-wing domestic policies and global re-alignment into the American orbit. The Americans welcomed Sadat's self-interested efforts to wrap his pro-American policies with whatever legitimacy a domesticated Islam could provide.

In each of these instances, the Islamic dimension derives from a "found Islam" that originated to meet the needs of local actors. It had its own independent roots in the soil of the Islamic world and served, in the first instance, identifiable aims of already existing regimes or movements. The Bush administration sought to pioneer a distinctive variant on this general pattern, in ways that would clarify the new cultural and intellec-tual dimensions of its exercise of global power. Iraq was made the case in point.

The Islamist Imaginary: America's Preferred Islam

The preferred Islam of the Bush administration comes into view most clearly and authoritatively in a Rand Corporation study. For that reason, rather than any scholarly value, Cheryl Benard's work merits very close attention. I know of no other source as revealing about the way Islam was understood by the circle of neoconservative intellectuals to which Benard belonged in these critical years of assertions of American imperial power. The book carries the engaging title *Civil, Democratic Islam: Partners, Re-sources, and Strategies*. It was prepared with the imprimatur of Rand's Na-tional Security Research Division in 2003. Benard's assessment of the Islamic world quiets the apprehensions that resistance in the name of Islam raised for America's neoconservative strategic planners.

The worries of the Bush team were not entirely misplaced. There was an Islamic threat, not to America per se but rather to American empire. There still is. To be sure, American propaganda exaggerates both the power and moral depravity of the Islamic enemy. The idea that hostility toward America in the Islamic world springs from frustration with the obvious and inherent failings of the Islamic world and envy at the equally obvious success and innate superiority of the West is sheer nonsense, no matter how frequently and portentously repeated. It parrots the message of every expansionist imperial power that history has known. It does so for all the obvious reasons. The colonized are at fault and their failings invite, even demand, colonization. There is no better way to exculpate the

West for the consequences of its historical record of violent occupation and exploitation of Islamic lands. Attention is shifted from any serious evaluation of American dominance of the Middle East and its destructive policies in Palestine, Afghanistan, and most dramatically Iraq.

Benard takes the reality of an Islamic threat as a premise of her argument. Her analysis begins with a presentation of the self-imposed predicaments of the Arab Islamic world that threaten to spill over and endanger others. In Benard's formulation the entire world, and not just the United States, is the innocent and vulnerable witness to the tumultuous internal disorders in the Islamic world. "What role," she asks, "can the rest of the world, *threatened* and affected as it is by this struggle, play in bringing about a more peaceful and positive outcome?" Benard states clearly that these dangerous predicaments of the Islamic world are entirely self-imposed. She writes that "Islam's current crisis has two main components: a failure to thrive and a loss of connection to the global mainstream. The Islamic world has been marked by a long period of backwardness and comparative powerlessness; many different solutions, such as nationalism, pan-Arabism, Arab socialism, and Islamic revolution, have been attempted without success, and this has led to frustration and anger." To conclude, Benard gravely notes that "at the same time, the Islamic world has fallen out of step with contemporary global culture, an uncomfortable situation for both sides."[21]

Benard's assessment eliminates any reference to the West's colonization of the Islamic world, and of the physical and psychological damage those violent assaults caused. There are no hints at all of an American imperial presence in the Islamic world through an impressive and constantly expanding network of bases. There is no consideration of the ways that presence constrains autonomous development. There are no references to the awkward facts of consistent American political and economic interventions, often violent and consistently aimed at undermining economic and political autonomy. Israel, heavily armed with all forms of weapons of mass destruction, a cruel occupying force, and the regional superpower, mysteriously disappears from view. These awkward realities are overshadowed by the Islamist Imaginary.

Only with these erasures can Benard take for granted the irrational grounding of the Islamic threat. Her analysis highlights the ways that the usual state-based threats to the national security exemplified by the Soviet Union in the era of the Cold War have been replaced by the challenge of nonstate actors, operating below the nation-state horizon. To face this threat, she argues that American strategic planners must make Islam itself a resource. In short, like her predecessors Benard is in the business of strategic manipulations of Islam to serve American economic and political ends. She evokes a malleable Islam that can be turned into an instrument to confront the Islams of resistance, while obediently serving America's ends. However, Benard does so with a difference.

The Challenge of Religion-Building

What is new in Benard's work is abandonment of the old strategy of reliance on a "found" Islam that can be turned to American ends. It may well be that Benard is right to urge this radical departure. The American invasion of Afghanistan in the wake of 9/11 represented the first *direct* American assault on an Islamic country and its Muslim citizens. In the wake of the devastation and appalling loss of civilian lives in that shattered land, America may indeed no longer be capable of finding effective allies on Islamic ground, especially given subsequent depredations in Palestine and Iraq. In place of an Islam that can be reshaped, Benard counsels that imperial America should create de novo the Islam it requires. What is needed, she implicitly argues, is an Islam made in America and then exported to the Islamic world. The language to describe the remaking of one of humanity's greatest religious and cultural traditions is particularly blunt and vulgar. "It is no easy matter to transform a major world religion," writes Benard. "If 'nation-building' is a daunting task, 'religion-building' is immeasurably more perilous and complex."[22] For such a project of remaking Islam, almost unbearable in its arrogance and cultural disdain, Benard recognizes that the intellectual resources will have to be imported from the West.

Surveying Western scholarship and media coverage periodically throughout his career, Edward Said at times came close to despair that humanistic knowledge of Islam was even possible.[23] Benard has no such misgivings about her own quest to know Islam. The kind of knowledge she seeks is within easy reach. Benard is untroubled by any barriers at all to understanding Islam for the purposes of empire. Muslims themselves may be confused by their internal struggles to determine their own nature and values. They are, nevertheless, transparently available to Benard for "sorting out" along a spectrum defined by "critical markers" that make it possible to "locate them correctly." "It is then possible," Benard continues confidently, "to see which part of the spectrum is generally compatible with our values, and which is fundamentally inimical. On this basis," she concludes, "this report identifies components of a specific strategy."[24]

Benard's confident methodology as an analyst of Islam merits a closer look, before considering the strategy she proposes. In fairness, it should be noted upfront that she herself puts forward no claims of disinterested scholarship for her work. She has written a policy paper, and the policy to be served is unapologetically American, as befits a Rand Corporation study. Nevertheless, even in the Bush era, it was still considered good form to wrap those interests in soothing lies, although the effort to do so here is casual and not sustained for long. Benard does describe American aims in the terms required for public consumption, detached as usual from the actual historical record. Benard explains that "the United States has three goals in regard to politicized Islam. First, it wants to prevent the spread of extremism and violence. Second, in doing so, it needs to avoid the impression that the United States is 'opposed to Islam.' And third, in the longer run, it must find ways to help address the deeper economic, social, and political causes feeding Islamic radicalism and to encourage a move toward development and democratization."[25]

At critical points in her essay, however, Benard does go beyond these hollow formulations with a candor befitting thinking intended to guide an assertive imperial power. When describing the "positive changes" America seeks in the Islamic world, Benard invokes not only "greater democracy and modernity" but also "compatibility with the contemporary international world order."[26] The wording is revealing. The accommodation urged is not with international law or international organizations. Such an argument would be difficult for intellectuals tied to the Bush administration to make, given the prevailing contempt for both that is characteristic of American foreign policy. Rather, compliance is to be fostered with the contemporary world order—in other words, a global system of American hegemony.

The magic in Benard's scheme clearly does not reside in the categories themselves. What she proposes is a rather mundane typology of secularists, fundamentalists, traditionalists, and modernists, loosely defined in terms that do not depart much from standard categories in the literature. Nor is there anything particularly inventive about the markers that define each of these slots. In line with the strand of Orientalist scholarship represented by Bernard Lewis and the late Fouad Ajami with which she explicitly identifies, Benard derives her distinguishing markers essentially from cultural and lifestyle issues.

What makes Benard's typology appear so comprehensive and effective is that it has nothing at all to do with the realities on the ground in the Islamic world. Everything falls so neatly into place, precisely because recalcitrant realities impose no constraints. The typology is self-consciously and triumphantly part of an effort not to understand the messy complexities of the Islamic world but rather to replace those undesirable realities with new ones, more in line with American interests. Benard's book is about power and its rightful exercise to remake Islam. It has nothing at all to do with the scholar's quest for knowledge of Islam itself.

Benard's typology aims to identify which partners and what resources exist among Islamic actors to serve American interests. Benard's answer is: None. She is not quite that direct, of course. However, in the end the boxes her typology identifies as containing potential allies and helpful assets are empty. Once this determination is made, the logic is inexorable: America, she counsels forthrightly, will have to manufacture the Islam it needs. It will be necessary to formulate the preferred Islam in the West and then export it to the Middle East.

Benard's analysis has prepared the ground for the execution of her strategy in two ways. First, all traces of the historical record of previous American manipulations of Islamic regimes and movements have been obscured. Second, her analysis reverses the power relationship between the weak and vulnerable Islamic world and a globally dominant America. The United States is presented as threatened by a virulent Islam that is inherently opposed to the most cherished American values. Benard accomplished these linked objectives by arguing that cultural factors, rather than politics or economics, are at the heart of the American conflict with the Islamic world. To understand Muslims, she reasons, primary attention must be given to cultural issues. Benard patiently explains that only the cultural categories she identifies will allow the analyst to differentiate among Islamic actors and place them in the appropriate boxes, as fundamentalists, traditionalists, modernists, or secularists. The lifestyles approach has clear advantages for Benard's purposes. If the questions asked are who is occupying whose land, who has appropriated whose resources, and who has inflicted massive violence on whom, the notion of a vulnerable America would be hard to sustain. Yet, since Benard's entire argument is premised on the alleged threat that Islam represents to the West, particularly the United States, these awkward questions must be avoided. The move to culture and away from economics and politics makes this possible.

Using the cultural prism, Benard can argue that Islamists of all kinds threaten American values and principles, notably democracy and freedom. Their animus has nothing to do with American economic and political policies. Rather, their own self-inflicted failures, Benard explains, have produced an explosion of irrational rage among Muslims that targets the United States out of envy for its success and rage at the democracy and freedom that have made it possible. Magically, this perspective directs attention to issues of women's dress and polygamy that, in cultural terms, trump such matters as whose resources have been appropriated, whose economies crippled, and whose politics violently manipulated. There is a message in the silenced questions. What Benard is really saying here is that all Islamists, whether moderate or extremist, now oppose the economic and political depredations of the United States, when those are brought into view. This judgment is exactly right. She recognizes that it extends to most secularists as well. This conclusion guides the strategy Benard proposes, although for obvious reasons she leaves it unstated.

To fill the void created by her erasures of actual U.S. economic and political policies, Benard invokes a mythic quest for democracy that the Bush administration aims to revitalize. This high-minded quest "covers" the historical record of U.S. manipulations of retrograde and violent Islamic movements. What is brought into view is a purely imaginary project to foster democracy in the face of unpromising and recalcitrant Islamic realities. "The notion that the outside world should try to encourage a moderate, democratic interpretation and presentation of Islam," Benard comments, "has been in circulation some decades but gained greater urgency after September 11, 2001." In line with this vision and in view of the dangers to global stability that certain Islamic ideologies and actions represent, she suggests that "it therefore seems sensible to foster the strains within it that call for a more moderate, democratic, peaceful, and tolerant social order." Benard casts her own work as part of this quest. "The question," she remarks, "is how best to do this. This report," she concludes, "proposes a strategy."[27]

In fact, Benard offers more than a strategy. Most importantly, she has defined the nature of the problem, and the problem is ultimately Islam. What requires attention to alleviate the terrible violence that scars our world is nothing short of remaking Islam. Benard's remaking has nothing at all to do with efforts under way by centrist Islamic intellectuals and activists, who argue that midstream Islam and democracy are fully compatible and that Islam poses no intrinsic barriers to social and economic development. Thinkers such as the Egyptian Tareq al Bishri, the Tunisian Rashid al Ghannouchi, and the Qatar-based Yusuf al Qaradawi have laid the intellectual groundwork for such an elaboration. They have done so in bold and creative interpretive and historical studies that are read widely throughout the Islamic world but almost never engaged in the West. Benard, too, pays no attention at all to such works of the Islamic midstream and the significant advance in Islamic thinking they represent. They are not among the thinkers she considers.

The use to which Benard puts her typology explains how she could "miss" such important developments. At first glance, Benard appears to have created a classification that takes for granted a diverse, even vibrant universe of Islamic thinkers and activists. Indeed, some in the Islamic world have misread the report precisely in this way. The Islamic thinker and journalist Fahmi Huwaidi in *al Ahram* of August 10, 2004, for example, writes approvingly of Benard's report to the extent that it recognizes the diversity of Islamic actors and does not place them all, moderates as well as extremists, in the same basket, as many secular intellectuals do. In fact, Benard has made no such advance, as becomes clear when close attention is paid to the examples she uses to people each of her categories.

Huwaidi, for example, would most likely see his own work and the work of the New Islamic trend to which he belongs as closest to the Islamic modernism to which one of Benard's categories refers. To be sure, his school uses the culturally authentic and more accurate term *Wassatteyya* as a self-description. Nevertheless, the general outlines of the modernist position that Benard describes would not be alien to him. Unfortunately, Benard's version of the required understanding of the ongoing ideological struggle within Islam misses Huwaidi's own work on democracy and development, as well as equally important contributions of such figures as the late Shaikh Muhammad al Ghazzali, Kamal Abul Magd, Muhammad Selim al Awa, and Tareq al Bishri. The only figure from the New Islamist school mentioned by Benard is Yusuf al Qaradawi.

Benard's treatment of Qaradawi is instructive. First, he is classified as a traditionalist despite his consistent and well-documented opposition to traditionalist positions on a whole range of social issues, notably the role of women. To be fair, Benard does recognize those progressive elements in Qaradawi's work, placing him in a "reform traditionalist" subcategory. But then, in a rare instance of complete candor, she comments forthrightly that Qaradawi is ineligible as a partner because he is, as Benard puts it, "aggressive on the issue of an Islamic foreign policy."[28] The logical contradiction passes unnoticed. Despite an explicit insistence that her categories are generated on the basis of cultural and lifestyle considerations, politics has found its way back into her analysis when the issue is a political orientation that does not serve American interests.

In Benard's scheme, fundamentalists are of course hopelessly beyond the pale. They are judged without hesitation to be incapable of producing partners for the United States. The traditionalists present the greatest dilemmas for Benard. For one thing, her definition produces unacceptable absurdities in classification, as we find al Azhar and the oppositional Muslim Brothers in the same box. Even more problematic are the close interactions across categories. To the degree that the distinctions do hold, Benard urges that they be used to foster conflict between the two groups, particularly highlighting traditionalist criticisms of the more virulent fundamentalist positions. However, the distinctions between the fundamentalists and the traditionalists, as Benard understands them, prove so fluid and the interactions so frequent that the categories collapse. In the end, all differentiations blur and all the Islamic thinkers and activists are in one box. Moreover, it is a box with which real cooperation is impossible.

Thus, for Benard fundamentalists and traditionalists not only overlap significantly but, more to her point, are both beyond the pale. At the same time, the modernist category, as Benard understands it, contains none of the important mainstream Islamic figures who actually are at work for reform. Who, then, does occupy that place in Benard's scheme? All of the figures she mentions are émigrés living abroad, who have settled outside the Islamic world. They have no discernible connection to Islamic activists on the ground, nor has their work generated any significant following in the Islamic world. So, when we take a closer look at those in that box of potential partners, they turn out to be individuals working as lone scholars in the West. Their task is a difficult and essentially textual one. They start from scratch. They go back to the sacred texts to "uncover" neglected truths. The clear implication is that Islamic intellectuals on the ground in the Arab Islamic world have uniformly gotten it wrong. By this calculus, there is a great deal of work to be done to remake Islam, and in Benard's view, it can only be done by émigré scholars, rooted in Western culture.

Some important secularist thinkers, their heads apparently turned by the notion that Benard describes secularists as the natural partners for the project of civil and democratic Islam, have missed the essential point of Benard's analysis. In the end, for Benard the Arab Islamic world contains no suitable partners for the American project. Sayyid Yassine, the

Egyptian political analyst who is a major voice for secularism, praises Benard's study for its "comprehensive methodology." He characterizes her typology as "attuned to the current era in ways that improve on more traditional approaches."[29] Yassine's own views echo Benard's introductory remark that the secularists should be America's logical partners in any effort to encourage a civil and democratic Islam. However, Yassine fails to notice that Benard in the end quite explicitly rejects such a partnership.[30] Despite her recognition of the theoretical compatibility of the secularists with such a project, Benard categorically refuses such a partnership. She raises two objections to the secularists as partners for America's transformation of the Middle East. First, the secularists have in her view a checkered relationship with the democratic ideal, presumably unlike such "moderate" allies as the Saudis. But, more to the point, Benard says bluntly that the increasingly apparent opposition of the secularists to American foreign policy makes them ineligible for any collaborative role. Once again, although Benard ostensibly builds her classification scheme on cultural issues, political considerations prove decisive in identifying U.S. allies rather than the compatibility of their views on issues like the headscarf. Benard's study points to the inescapable conclusion that there are no natural partners to be found in Islamic lands to carry out the required remaking of Islam.

Although bereft of partners, American policy should not abandon its sweeping objectives. Benard argues that a major policy aim should be the fostering of distracting conflict among Muslim thinkers and activists. In her view, it will be most useful to heighten the conflicts between secularists and Islamic activists. American policy, Benard is arguing, should actively work to enlarge the secular–Islamic divide. However, the Islamic camp itself should be divided, by drawing attention to the differences between fundamentalists and traditionalists. Benard announces bluntly "the aim of weakening them all and preventing their unification since none are suitable partners for the U.S. project." She continues that "under the guise of democratic reform," it will be essential to "propagate notions of a 'modernist' Islam, developed by émigré Muslim scholars living in the West, politically neutered and effectively divorced from all social and intellectual trends active in the Islamic world."

At this point Benard brings the most sweeping goal of her study into view. The objective of American policy, she argues, should be nothing short of weakening and diluting Islamic identity "so that it has little or nothing to contribute to a unifying politics of identity." In the end Islam itself is the target. Benard understands that indirection will be necessary. She quotes with approval Ibn Warraq, perhaps best known for his essay "Why I Am Not a Muslim." In a footnote, Benard remarks that "in my interview with him, Mr. Warraq conceded that a frontal critique of Islam was not realistic at this time" and that "efforts to promote a kinder, gentler, 'defanged' Islam were likely to achieve better results."[31] As a complementary strategy Benard urges that assistance be given to those who represent non-Islamic identities. She seeks backing to heighten awareness of pre- and non-Islamic history and culture in the media, and in government-imposed school curricula. Finally, Benard calls for media and educational efforts to win popular support for the politically neutered Islam that is envisioned. She concludes by recommending encouragement of Sufism, presumably because of what she mistakenly takes to be its inherently apolitical character.[32]

The project Benard outlines necessitates, as she puts it, America's lead role in nothing less than "religion-building." Her work represents currently existing Islam as no longer amenable to the kinds of manipulations that had been possible at U.S. hands in the past. Islamic movements are now in the forefront of active revolt against the projections of American power. More daunting still from an imperial perspective, the moderate midstream of the world's Muslims also stands for resistance to American empire, as peaceful as conditions allow. Remaking Islam, Benard concedes, will not be an "easy matter" in that "many extraneous issues and problems have become entangled with Islam."[33] While Benard refrains from naming them, the thrust of her "cultural" focus indicates that she is delicately alluding to such intrusive and unmentionable political and economic questions as American domination of the Middle East through its network of bases and client regimes, Israel's systematic appropriation of Palestinian land and water, and the U.S. use of military force to secure its interests in Islamic lands.

To counter the troublesome Islamic inspiration for resistance to these depredations, Islam must be remade. Benard's study makes it clear that the neoconservative intellectuals who played so large a role in the Bush administration's Middle East policy believed that American imperial objectives required Islam to be effectively remade. Islam was understood to be the enemy of empire, and it still is. American support for the repression of the Muslim Brotherhood in Egypt in the wake of the coup of July 3, 2013, makes that clear. Efforts by the new military regime to exert near-total control over mosques and generally to discipline all Islamic institutions also make it clear that the notion of a remade Islam still has a role to play. The Egyptian generals are fully engaged in their own project of manufacturing a "good" Islam. They are actively waging their own war on terror after declaring the Muslim Brothers to be a terrorist organization. Undoubtedly, these efforts are part of the explanation for the support the dictatorial regime has received from the United States.

Iraq and the Global Screening of the Islamist Imaginary

The binary opposition of a "good" Islam yet to be "made" and an established "recalcitrant" Islam that refused manipulations reflected perfectly the Manichaean ideological worldview of George W. Bush's Washington, DC. What is surprising is just how resilient the formulation has proved to be.

Religion-building, as outlined by Benard, proved difficult to achieve. The "good" Islam that was envisioned never quite made it into the real world in the service of American imperial needs. Ironically, "bad" Islam precisely filled the bill. Perhaps even more than allies, a war on a global scale would require an implacable enemy against which the power of empire could be arrayed. For an expansionist, unilateral global project like the new American empire, the right enemy was indispensable to rally domestic support for the militarization of society and to justify worldwide assertions of imperial power. The Islamist Imaginary has also proved durable and a marker of the continuity between Bush and his successor. Today, as Barack Obama's two-term presidency draws to a close, it is instructive that America is still fighting the War on Terror. Terrorist Islam, now in the form of a wildly exaggerated threat of ISIS, remains the implacable and threatening adversary that rationalizes the new forms that Obama has given the unending war.

Critics of the American imperial project have too easily settled into the argument that Islam, the green threat, has replaced communism, the red threat, as the requisite American enemy. In broad outline, the argument is correct, but the analogy can also obscure some of the distinctive features of the new definition of the enemy that came so clearly into view in the Bush years and remains in place to this day.

The Islam that is imagined as a threat to empire has only the most tenuous connection to realities on the ground. Its mythic character is far more pronounced than that of communism. Terrorist Islam has no fixed address. There is no single nation-state or even cluster of states that stand with any consistency as the analogue of the Soviet Union or other communist powers. The new threat has little in the way of actual history either of ideas or movements that can match the sophistication of Marxism as the seedbed for communist ideology. Nor has it engendered the same kind of mass movements of support, giving the United States greater flexibility in identifying its "terrorist" enemies.

Unbound by the realities of time or space, terrorism with vague but menacing Islamic features is the perfect enemy for an empire that itself has taken shape in the new age of globalization. The incarnations of the Islamist Imaginary take on a useful yet deceptive solidity. The terrible image of the turbaned Ayatollah Khomeini performed its task in screening a mass revolution from view. It then transformed itself into the mustached and even more threatening figure of Saddam Hussein, conjured first as an ally and then a mortal enemy poised to hand over nuclear weapons to Islamic extremists. Those images then dissolved and reform as the tentacled Muslim Brothers who not only hijacked Egypt's revolution of January 25, 2011, but effortlessly infiltrated the highest reaches of the American government itself. On the horizon looms the refurbished threat of the Neo-Ottomans, personified by Recep Tayyip Erdogan, who recaptures for the "Turk" the status of the threatening Muslim "other." Most threatening of all is the caliphate declared by the extremist movement ISIS that has arisen from the wreckage of Iraq and the destruction that has spilled over into Syria. It is easy enough to exaggerate the menace they pose. The idea of an ISIS "caliphate," capable of threatening Europe and America, is sheer fantasy. The brutality of the group has been very real and very graphic. The antidote may well be to remind ourselves that our Saudi "friend" regularly beheads criminals for such offenses as blasphemy, drug smuggling, sedition, and "sorcery." Most recently four hapless brothers were beheaded for marijuana sales.

The horrific spectacle of American journalists murdered in such a cruel way is heart-wrenching, but it does not justify the launch of yet another war. It should now not be hard to see that each of our military interventions in the Islamic world has had more disastrous results than the last. Always the unintended consequences have been more destructive than the dangers of the precipitating condition. It is easy enough to exaggerate dangers and threats. It is always impossible to know what disasters will come next from efforts to counter such exaggerated threats with military power. Without the American military destruction of Iraq and the imposition of a sectarian government in Baghdad, there would be no ISIS.

The Islamist Imaginary is always about manufactured and manipulated fears and is quite impervious to facts on the ground; the American experience in Iraq should have taught us that much. Iraq, led with unspeakable tyranny by Saddam Hussein, presented itself as the perfect screen for the global projection of the Islamist Imaginary as the preeminent rationale for American empire. The screening of the Islamist Imaginary in Iraq had a dual function. First, it allowed projection of this image of the enemy of the American empire in the most terrifying way in order to present it as a threat to civilization itself. As is often the case with such projections, there was an element of truth, greatly distorted, to the projection. Saddam, an absolute secularist, had nevertheless portrayed himself as an Islamic leader, likening his struggle with the West to the legendary 636 Islamic battle of Qadisayyah in which the Muslims faced Sassanid Persia. Equally important to the American imperial project was the opportunity provided to use the horrific image of Saddam Hussein poised to hand over nuclear weapons to Islamist extremists as a way to screen from view the actual sources of legitimate resistance in Islam to foreign occupation.

Battered by decades of domestic tyranny, war, and the brutal regime of sanctions, the Iraqi regime on the eve of invasion was little more than a hollow shell. Yet it was a shell that retained considerable importance. As a regional Arab actor, Iraq lent support to the Palestinian resistance and in other ways represented an obstacle to total Israeli hegemony in the Middle East. Moreover, Iraq was an Arab state with cultural and historical weight, unlike the emerging new Arab centers of influence in the Gulf. Finally, Iraq was the site of impressive oil resources. In global perspective, American control of Iraqi oil was judged critical to the potential great power rivals just over the horizon, notably China with its disturbing economic vitality and Russia with its resurgent nationalism. Should the American economy continue its decline, it was judged that Iraqi oil in American hands would be an extremely helpful lever in facing the Chinese, Russians, and other threats to American dominance.

For all it had suffered, Iraq still mattered. The Bush team understood that on this important Iraqi screen could be projected both the conjured Islamist Imaginary and "the shock and awe" of U.S. military power to contain it and protect Western civilization. Neither serious military opposition nor any real media attention to the wanton destruction of infrastructure and the catastrophic loss of civilian life marred the display. The destruction carried the message of just how unforgiving American displeasure could be. The message was especially pointed since Iraq had once been a compliant American ally. Day after day, night after night, the world watched as America displayed its impressive arsenal with the appreciative commentary of security experts and breathless "embedded" journalists. The intended message was clear: America's power was beyond challenge. The Islamic threat would be buried once and for all in the rubble of a shattered country. Only American power could rise to the challenge of remaking the Middle East and the world beyond as the cleansing sword of the civilized world.

There were, of course, obstinate realities on the ground that would have called into question the relevance of the Islamist Imaginary to the Iraqi situation. Saddam, at the end of the day, was essentially a secular ruler who brutally repressed Iraqi Islamic movements and systematically opposed those abroad. Iraq, in Saddam's day, was hardly an extremist playground. These inconsistencies mattered little: The neoconservatives were really uninterested in existing or historical Iraqi realities that were, in the end, irrelevant to their overt project of state-ending in Iraq. Media manipulation, bullying, and all manner of pressures made power, rather than logic or reason or even common sense, the driving force of policy. The mechanisms are now well known: Executive pressures on the intelligence community, the sidelining of the State Department, the concentration of power in the Department of Defense, and the abdication of responsibility by Congress all helped to generate the stream of "secrets and lies" that generated a succession of phony rationales, from the Iraqi possession of weapons of mass destruction to direct links to al Qaeda.[34] Iraq would turn over its weapons of mass destruction to the terrorists. By the end of the day, Americans came to believe that the Iraqi regime had a hand in September 11 and Saddam Hussein was really Osama bin Laden in disguise. Unintended consequences also played a role. The destruction of a dictatorship and the failure to replace it with any viable system left Iraq open to infiltration by militants across the Islamic world. The poisonous viruses of sectarianism and corruption moved easily into devastated Iraq. Shadowy figures inevitably emerged to exploit the new possibilities that the chaos in the wake of the American invasions created. Reality was transformed, but not in line with the fantasies of unimpeded access to oil and the transformation of Iraq as a whole into a base of imperial operations. Iraq was transformed instead into a factory for producing new extremists and a magnet for those already in the field.

The Islamist Imaginary and the Needs of Empire

Neither the study of language and culture nor decades of experience living in Islamic countries has any great relevance to the imagined Islam of American empire. The Islamist Imaginary as a subject of inquiry belongs in American rather than Islamic studies. If anything, humanistic knowledge of the lives of Muslims and of Islam is an obstacle and a diversion. Certain assumptions are in place when the subject of inquiry is the Islamist Imaginary. It is quite simply a waste of time to learn Arabic or Farsi or Turkish or any of the myriad of other languages spoken by Muslims when we already know what Islamic actors say is mostly an expression of irrational hatred and envy. Moreover, it makes little sense to pay careful attention to their words when we know that those words do not convey what they really mean. Since we anticipate that Islamic religion and culture are destined to be remade by models derived from our own history, there is little point to their study.

Barack Obama has struggled to distance himself from the militarization of foreign policy that he inherited from his predecessor, although without success. At the same time, he has retained and even enhanced the messianic sense of American exceptionalism. Obama, with a more believable professorial tone, projected the very clear attitude that there is little incentive to observe and listen when you have so much to teach the rest of the world. Just below the surface of this projected educative attitude lies the totalitarian impulse, still very much intact, to remake *Dar al Islam* in the West's own image. Through a string of recent presidents, the sense of the United States as "the indispensable nation" lives on.[35] These inherited and deeply entrenched attitudes provide the backdrop against which the Islamist Imaginary makes its appearance, in endlessly renewed forms.

America of selfless goodness requires a contrasting pole of predatory evil. That pole must not be fixed. It must be flexible and malleable in the details of its features, although always an existential threat, ready to engulf us and overwhelm our improbable goodness. What we have in the Islamist Imaginary is a moving swarm of hostile, disembodied particulates. They are all products of the Western imagination. They are generated not only by hostile contemporary misrepresentations of Islam but also from centuries-old religious and cultural hostility to Islam. The particulates are all in constant formation and reformation. Any specific incarnation of the Islamist Imaginary draws on these elements to project a plausible enemy that meets the needs at that moment. The swarm of particulates shapes itself as a mirror of imperial needs. It can deconstruct and reform in an instant. It did so with the death of Khomeini and again with the assassination of bin Laden. When those images lost their usefulness, the swarm moved on. It reconfigured itself to meet the ever-changing imperatives of empire.

New incarnations are always taking shape right before our eyes. None of these new incarnations, like those that preceded them, have much to do with sober reality. Yet, intuitively, for Western publics the successive incarnations do seem real. The constituent particulates are familiar. Each mirrors unacknowledged, but dimly understood, traits of empire. They are recognizable on a subconscious level. Jungian "projection" explains how these toxic elements are generated. The qualities of the dark side of empire are attributed to a threatening Islamic enemy that can appear in a variety of nightmarish guises. The American empire wraps its actions in high-minded campaigns for freedom and democracy. In its practices, however, empire is undeterred by moral scruples, legal restraints, or the opinion of mankind. Preventive war, torture, black holes, and kill lists: The Islamist Imaginary feeds on them all. Profits were not the only product of the criminal invasion, of course. The supreme war crime has also been a producer of violent extremists, coming to life out of the death, destruction, and disorder brought on by the invasion and the "creative chaos" deliberately cultivated by the invaders. The terrorist yield ensures that the process of criminal war-making is transformed into an autocatalytic one. More extremists fuel more wars on terror, with each group of violent militants worse than the last.

Terrible in themselves, the successive waves of extremists are projections as well of the evil of the American war-makers and the greed and brutalities of the successor sectarian Iraqi regime the invaders put in place. They are, as Chris Hedges has explained, "the ghoulish face of empire." Of ISIS, he explains that "they are the specters of the hundreds of thousands of people we murdered in our deluded quest to remake the Middle East. They are ghosts from the innumerable roadsides and villages where U.S. soldiers and Marines, jolted by explosions of improvised explosive devices, responded with indiscriminate fire." Hedges continues that "they are the risen remains of the dismembered Iraqis left behind by blasts of Hellfire and cruise missiles, howitzers, grenade launchers and drone strikes. They are the avengers of the gruesome torture and the sexual debasement that often came with being detained by American troops." Hedges concludes that "they are the final answer to the collective humiliation of an occupied country, the logical outcome of Shock and

Awe, the Frankenstein monster stitched together from the body parts we left scattered on the ground."[36]

Mirroring these traits, the Islamist Imaginary emerges as a strangely familiar incarnation of absolute evil that takes on new forms, in response to the needs of empire. In the fall of 2014 the Imaginary briefly took center stage in yet another guise. As President Obama geared up for entry into the Syrian civil war, justification for the extension of the air war to Syria was needed. The president's problem arose when U.S. intelligence reported that ISIS focused its violent energies on expansion in the Levant and did not pose a threat to the United States. Enter the Khorasan Group. Suddenly the name, previously completely unknown, was everywhere in the media. Unlike ISIS, this new embodiment of the Islamist Imaginary was poised to strike America with "sleeper cells" already at work and planning terror strikes. The president had his threat to the homeland, and the bombs began to rain down on both Syria and Iraq. Miraculously, or so it seemed to those unacquainted with the strange but persistent history of the Islamist Imaginary, the Khorasan Group simply vanished, even more rapidly than it appeared.[37]

In all such incarnations, the Imaginary acts at once as prey and predator. As *prey*, it justifies massive American military spending, so crucial for the American military machine. All manner of surveillance at home and abroad is required to hunt and keep the Islamist Imaginary at bay. As *predator*, the Islamist Imaginary lies in wait around every corner of the globe and at our borders to make our fears real.

The tight embrace of prey and predator imparts to the Imaginary a stunning generative power. Any incident of violence or threatened violence against empire takes on exaggerated importance as the product of the predatory Islamist Imaginary. It is not that real threats do not exist; they do, but, framed by the Imaginary, they are systematically blown out of proportion. The Islamist Imaginary lurks behind them all. Against such an outsized predator, all manner of retaliatory actions are justified. Those punishing actions, which include invasions, occupations, and drone attacks, in turn inspire reprisals. They help immeasurably to populate the violent networks of extremists who challenge the imperial presence and the threat to Islam it is judged to pose. The excesses of empire in this way provide the primary recruitment agency for the most violent and extreme of the anti-imperialist militants.

These real-world militants do make the imagined real, although never on the scale projected. In turn, the Islamist Imaginary continues to provide the most compelling justification for empire and the most useful screen for its misdeeds. Even the terrible cruelties and criminalities of empire pale before the absolute evil of the Islamist Imaginary. The violence of empire is always purely defensive and always fully justified. The death of half-a-million children is a price worth paying in wars with an illusion. Entire cities must be demolished to be saved. An Afghan wedding party, massacred by a drone strike, just might have been a band of terrorists.

The Islamist Imaginary and the intense fears it evokes, unconstrained by reason or logic and quite unrelated to facts on the ground, are now more important to empire than ever before. Ours is an age when the American assertion of global hegemony relies on an empire of roughly a thousand bases that dot the globe. From these bases, terrible new technologies of war, symbolized by the pilotless drones, enable both surveillance and the projection of deadly and often indiscriminate violence to all corners of the globe. Astronomical American military budgets that routinely surpass the next ten highest country defense budgets combined must be justified. We should expect that the Islam imagined by empire will be with us for some time to come, haunting, among other things, our graduation ceremonies. Americans, especially young Americans whose futures have been mortgaged to the military–industrial–congressional complex, must be told on all such occasions just how dangerous the Islamist Imaginary has made their world.

9

The Epochal Story of Islam and the Common People

And verily, We shall recount their whole story with knowledge,
For We were never absent (at any time or place).

QUR'AN 7:7

THROUGH HIS PROPHETS, God spoke to all of humanity (*al Nas*). The Qur'an tells the Prophet: "Oh Prophet, We have indeed dispatched you as a witness, a healer, and a warner."[1] The Prophet in his life and in his example was to assume specific responsibilities for all of humankind, but especially for the common people. Today, Islam is telling an epochal story, scripted from the lives of millions across *Dar al Islam*. For all those who have contributed their personal narratives, no matter their other differences, it is a grand chronicle of Qur'anic inspiration, recounted with the "witness" of the Prophet. It tells of the cosmic human struggle for justice in the face of evil. It sounds a call to spiritual renewal as the way to find strength for this most daunting of battles. It is, at the same time, a very human story of the struggles of ordinary people against tyrants, social injustice, extremists, and invaders.

Muslims are not alone in their battles. The Qur'an tells us that the core message conveyed by the prophets to people everywhere is the same. Muslims stand with all other human beings in their dreams and highest aspirations. They are called, like all of humanity, to recognize and embrace in their lives the values of justice, love, peace, and freedom, all of which have a spiritual dimension. The details of the revelations and the nuances of prescribed forms of worship and ways of living inevitably varied. Yet the higher spiritual purposes of the charge to humanity of the great religious faiths transcended all differences.

All prophets sought to inspire *al Nas* to live good and just lives, lifted up by spirituality. Repeatedly throughout human history, a flawed humanity has stumbled on that path, only to find in God's "signs" ways to regain secure footing and guidance for the way forward. Muslims, the Qur'an makes clear, can rightfully look, alongside their Holy Book and the example of the Prophet, to communities outside their own for ways to attain desired goals and for allies in their worldly struggles. God's world, by design, is a plural world.

In a fourth great surge of renewal that swept through all of *Dar al Islam*, Muslims have called themselves to *al Tagdid al Islami* (the Islamic Renewal). They seek to renew their sense of the meaning of God's final message to humanity. Reverberations of that energizing wave have been felt most recently with particular effect in Tunisia and Egypt. Organized movements of politicized Islam have made themselves a presence in public life in both countries, acting as visible reminders of the spirit of Islamic Renewal afoot in the land. However, the response that matters most in these sites, and others like them, has come not from particular movements, charismatic figures, or parties. It originates from the spiritual power generated by common people, acting together in massive numbers. Politicized Islam and the movements it generates at times actually weaken the Renewal by overemphasizing its political dimension. It is the spontaneous collective action of *al Nas* on behalf of freedom and justice that has done most to advance the Islamic Renewal, however limited particular achievements might be.

The Qur'an, all Muslims know, was sent to humanity by God. Throughout *Dar al Islam*, the Qur'an is everywhere a presence to guide humanity's spiritual and worldly struggles. The first verse of the Qur'an commands Muslims to "read, recite."[2] They are not called to worship the Qur'an or to treat their Holy Book as a religious relic. Rather, believers are summoned to use their minds and to respond to the promptings of their hearts to understand the guidance the Qur'an provides. In this difficult work of *ijtihad* (interpretation), they find assistance in the *hadiths* (prophetic traditions that record the sayings and actions of the Prophet Muhammad). The Prophet acts as an exemplar of how to live in accord with Islam. For all the challenges through the centuries of interpretation and evaluation, the *Sunnah* (all the deeds and words of the Prophet) of the Prophet Muhammad has retained its place in the minds and hearts of Muslims as the second source for understanding Islam.

The *Sunnah* of the Prophet preserves a record of his leadership of the first community of Muslims. An important verse instructs the Prophet to act in his role as a guide but not a governor: "So revive their memories!

You are but a reminder! Not their dominating governor."[3] The Prophet is to be a presence in the lives of Muslims as an inspiration for the creation of communities that will enable people to live as God intended in ways that make sense, given their own particular circumstances. The Prophet is not, however, the advocate of any particular societal order. Neither the Qur'an nor the *Sunnah* provides a rigid template for the building of community. That task must be the work of *al Nas*, inspired by the Message.

God's confidence in humanity is reflected in the fact that the imperative to create communities of believers is central to the message of Islam. It is as members of the *ummah* that Muslims tell their worldly stories. Like Jews and Christians, Muslims are a people of the Book. They, too, have received their holy book from God. For Muslims, to practice Islam is to be reminded not only of the sacred texts but also of community bonds that create a way of life centered on the truths those texts convey. The doctrine of Islam reassures Muslims that they are not alone in the world. The *ummah* gives them brothers and sisters in Islam. However dispersed they may be, the *ummah* links them to a worldwide community. Islam, expressed in their beliefs and behaviors, instructs them in what should be the larger purposes of their collective lives. Some fifty verses in the Qur'an remind believers of the necessity of *acting* on belief. Qur'anic descriptions of true believers refer to them as "those who believed and were righteous in deeds."[4] Passive belief alone does not suffice: Righteous actions and behavior are essential parts of a good Muslim life.

Worldly Islam, as understood by the *Wassatteyya* (the Islamic midstream), today calls ordinary Muslims to reform and spiritual renewal, as well as resistance where circumstances require. Those who have responded by the millions include Sunnis, who represent some 85 percent or more of the world's Muslims; Shi'a, who represent somewhat less than 15 percent; as well as those from both main branches who have turned to Sufism, Islamic mysticism. The division in the *ummah* between Sunni and Shi'a arose shortly after the death of the Prophet Muhammad. At issue were pressing questions of political succession, rather than doctrine. The great Sufi orders (*turuq*) spread throughout Islamic lands, including such far-flung places as India, central Asia, and Africa as well as the Arab, Turkish, and Iranian heartland areas. In earlier waves of Islamic Renewal in the eighteenth and nineteenth centuries, the Sufis had a substantial role. Today, the Sufis remain of great importance, although often in complex and sometimes contradictory ways.[5] *Dar al Islam* (the Islamic world) is suffused by a rich and pervasive Sufi influence that all those who traverse Islamic lands cannot help but feel. The Islamic midstream embraces all of these communities of Muslims, whatever tensions and even conflicts that arise among them and however distinctive their traditions become. Midstream religious scholars see them simply as communities of Muslims, part of the *ummah*. For the midstream, what matters most are not the surface differences but the core beliefs that are shared. They all recognize that there is but one God and that he is one (*tawhid*).[6] Sunni, Shi'a, and Sufis are joined in their reverence for the Prophet Muhammad. They all pray in the direction of Mecca.

These diverse communities of Muslims have all been touched by the Renewal. All have contributed to it. The Renewal cannot be labeled Sunni, Shi'a, or Sufi. It bears no exclusively Arab, Iranian, Turkish, or any other ethnic imprint. The Renewal takes on all of these characteristics and more besides. It is an *Islamic* Renewal (*al Tagdid al Islami*) that resonates around the world, wherever communities of Muslims are found. Today, the realities of bitter splits in the *ummah*, often created and manipulated by authoritarian and hostile outside powers, challenge this precious unity. However, the *Wassatteyya* clings to the ideal of *tawhid* and works to strengthen it.

For all its power and critical importance, this epochal story of Islamic Renewal in our time has yet to be heard in the West. The West has not listened. The idea that something of global importance is happening in Islamic lands, but independent of Western influence, simply cannot be entertained. For decades, the Arab heartlands of the Islamic world have been in the American sphere of influence as a strategic reserve. Inevitably, American dominance has meant that reasons of empire have taken priority over all else. Every American global initiative has had a special place for a dominated and subordinated Middle East. Local elites, whatever their character, are bent to those ends. Everywhere, the needs of ordinary people are sacrificed. The Renewal inherently challenges that dominance; for that reason, resistance is at the heart of this latest wave of Islamic assertiveness.

The United States has its own, all-consuming agenda. The details have varied but the same sweeping vision of *global hegemony* has consistently animated American policies and obliterated all else from view. That imperial vision came with the onset of the Cold War, while World War II was still raging. The guiding principle from the first has been "full-spectrum world dominance." The means to achieve it all flow from overwhelming military capability and the political will to wield it. Opposition to the American imperium assumes a variety of guises. In essence, however, it is always the same. Essentially, any independent force with any capability at all to challenge the American imperial vision earns that status, whether a rising challenger nation, like China or Russia, or any of a variety of mass movements, from leftists and communists to Islamic resistance parties and groups. Genuine mass movements with popular support, in particular, are always and everywhere treated as a threat to American empire. When possible, they are brutally repressed. At other times, they are manipulated and controlled. However, such management strategies do not always work and, even when they do, they do not last forever. The elusive potential for resistance is always there.

The Islamic Renewal for decades has represented just such a potential threat, although its relative importance has fluctuated. When it cannot be controlled and manipulated, it is demonized. Today in the Western media and scholarly work, all attention is riveted on the extremists as the face of Islam. They provide the essential justification for the brutalization of Islamic societies and the rationalization of empire for domestic publics.

For these durable reasons of empire, the self-directed and defensive work of the autonomous Islamic midstream to renew and protect Islam receives almost no attention at all in the West. Such massive inattention has occurred before. In the late 1960s and early 1970s Western scholars and policymakers, convinced of their own vision of the secular future of *Dar al Islam*, failed to hear the announcements of Islamic intellectuals and activists of the emergence of the contemporary *al Tagdid al Islami*. The Renewal, heralded by intellectuals and activists across *Dar al Islam*, penetrated deeply into Muslim societies throughout the region in subsequent decades. It did so in ways that confounded Western expectations and stock understanding of the future of Islam and the Islamic world.

Today, the most important story from Islamic lands tells how the Islamic Renewal has taken hold in the lives of millions of common people, making it a powerful force not only among Islamic intellectuals and movements but on a mass level.[7] Exaggerated attention to the extremists and their narrative of distortion of the faith and violence is misplaced. The *Wassatteyya* of centrist intellectuals and diverse groupings has succeeded as no other Islamic grouping in giving voice to the everyday dreams of ordinary people for a better life as Muslims. In doing so, the *Wassatteyya* strives to guide the Islamic Renewal. It looks to its worldly as well as spiritual success.[8]

The extraordinary energy of the Renewal comes from the response of the masses. This impressive wave of Islamic Renewal is inclusive, although not without definition. It is not owned by particular individuals or movements, nor can it be hijacked by any of them. Rather, the contemporary Islamic Renewal speaks for the oldest, midstream trend in modern Islamic thought, with its roots in the works of the pioneering figures of Muhammad Abduh (1849–1905) and Gamal Eddine al Afghani (1838/9–1897). The Islamic scholars of the *Wassatteyya* take as their most fundamental sources the Qur'an and the *Sunnah*, enriched further by the insights of Sufism and the rich body of *fiqh* (understandings of Qur'an and *Sunnah*, the work of specialists). *Fiqh*, Yusuf al Qaradawi has pronounced, provides a virtual "ocean" of interpretive scholarship as a resource to guide the *ummah*.[9] For each generation of Muslims, the *Wassatteyya* has taken new forms and drawn diverse individuals and groupings to its banner. Today, it is a diffuse, mass trend with tributaries throughout the Islamic world.

The rigid typologies and "bucket thinking" typical of so much of Western social science can contribute little to the characterization of so fluid and adaptive a phenomenon as the *Wassatteyya*.[10] In our age of Islamic Renewal, the *Wassatteyya* raises the banner of reform of Islamic thought. At the same time, it calls for legitimate resistance to imperialism, colonialism, and domestic tyranny. In doing so, it opens a space between midstream Islamic scholars and movements, on the one hand, and traditionalists who cling to rigid and inflexible understandings of the heritage, on the other. The *Wassatteyya* holds itself apart even more emphatically from extremists, who have little regard for the heritage of learning on which the *Wassatteyya* draws for its creative adaptations to rapidly changing global conditions. The extremists, in contrast, either adhere to literalist and outmoded views or innovate with radical distortions of Islamic thought. They translate these distortions of the faith into violent actions that tarnish legitimate struggles of resistance. Midstream scholars have not hesitated to condemn their indiscriminate actions as *haraba* (war on civilization).[11]

Characterizations of the midstream must be kept flexible to be useful. The center itself is always moving. What is midstream in one context may well not be in another. Moreover, particular individuals and groupings may well move between these typifications. They may also take on the markers of more than one type. All categorizations of Islamic groupings should be thought of as eddies in a river rather than islands, fixed and set apart.

No one scholar or public figure can speak for the *Wassatteyya* in all its variety, nor can any single grouping of activists. The contemporary Islamic midstream has at times found leadership in diverse figures such as the Egyptian Yusuf al Qaradawi, who heads the Union of Islamic Scholars and is a prominent member of the New Islamic school of Egyptian centrists.[12] In addition, mention should be made of Turkish Prime Minister Recep Tayyip Erdogan with his Islamic roots, former Iranian President Muhammad Khatami, and the Tunisian leader of the Renaissance Party, Rashid al Ghannouchi. However, a simple catalogue of centrist Islamic scholars, collectives, and public figures across *Dar al Islam* would overwhelm this brief chapter. Yet, because they are invariably overlooked by Western pundits and scholars who focus on extremists, some representative examples can usefully be mentioned. In the Arab world, for example, the venerable and now violently persecuted Muslim Brothers in Egypt do not stand alone. There are other centrist Islamic actors, rarely given much attention, from a variety of sites in the Arab Islamic world. They include the now-banned Wassat Party in Egypt, the Justice and Development Party in Morocco, the Reform Party in Algeria, the Renaissance Party in Tunisia, the Jordanian Islamic Action Front, the Ummah Party in Kuwait, and the Yemeni Reformist Union. Each of these parties of politicized Islam has contributed experience and theoretical understanding to the development of Islamic centrism.

Midstream Islamic intellectuals, from these and other similar groupings, have taken the lead in an innovative transnational Islamic project of radical rethinking and renewal to advance the relevance and cogency of contemporary Islamic discourse and practice. They balance their attention to adaptations to contemporary conditions with insistence on thoughtfully drawing strength from the heritage. The three great demographic and cultural reservoirs at the heart of the Islamic world, Egypt, Turkey, and Iran, have each played important, complementary roles in the Renewal. Outside this Islamic strategic triangle, developments to the west in North Africa, to the north in central Asia, and to the east in southwest Asia have made the Renewal a presence in the lives of the immense communities of Muslims in these areas. In each of these cases, and others like them, including growing Muslim minority communities in the East and West, the Islamic Renewal takes at times strikingly varied forms. Yet "they are all Muslims," to echo the words of Ibn Battuta from the fourteenth century.[13]

America and the Islamic Renewal

For a brief moment, it appeared that a new American president had grasped the importance of these momentous developments and sought accommodation with midstream Islam. In July 2009, Barack Hussein Obama traveled to Cairo, the intellectual and cultural capital of centrist Islam.[14] He addressed an audience of students, intellectuals, and public figures at Cairo University. Obama seemed poised to turn a page in America's relationships with the Islamic world. The speech did open with some stunning new language of respect and appreciation for Islam and for Islamic civilization. From his highly visible platform in Cairo, Obama addressed the Muslim world as a man of color with a middle name and family roots that connect him to the Islamic world. The new American president translated the symbolism of his person into an historic call for a transformed relationship between the West and Islam. The speech was remarkable in many ways: No American president had ever before spoken with such respect for the contributions of the Islamic heritage for humankind. The Qur'anic passages cited by the president captured the most uplifting dimensions of Islam's universal message for the moral and material progress of humanity. The president quoted them with an aptness that was captivating.

The magic of the moment dissipated, however, when President Obama turned in his Cairo speech from generalities about Islam to actual policies at the heart of American tensions with the Islamic world. The thread of the old narrative that justified limitless support for the militarism of the War on Terror and one-sided support for Israel ran through all his remarks.

Yet again, the world was told the fabulous tale of America as a caring colossus, tiptoeing in innocence and good intentions across the globe, uninterested in resources or bases, although notably tarrying in the oil-rich and strategically important Middle East region. The colossus moves protectively, hand in hand with a tiny, frightened ward with a tragic past and a future at risk. His plucky companion acts only in self-defense, although with a "terrible, swift sword" when threatened.[15]

The inhabitants of distant lands, notably the Muslims among them, find it difficult to fathom such a powerful yet selfless and well-intentioned force for good. They are unable to comprehend all the gifts the colossus and his tiny companion seek to bring to one of the most troubled regions in the world. They see only "an interested empire" and its regional junior partner. Blinded by jealousy and envy, some from these misguided peoples respond to the presence of the colossus in the region with deadly strikes on the symbols of its power back home, killing several thousand innocents. They do so by sending fanatic murderers from sanctuaries in a distant, mountain land. The colossus must respond to these wanton and irrational acts of violence. The betrayal of such innocent benevolence fully justifies the death and destruction the colossus must rain on that distant refuge for the evildoers.

Once the mist of the warm rhetoric about Islam had cleared, one could not fail to see all these misguided self-delusions of the Bush years. Obama's underlying narrative in Cairo reaffirmed the basic arguments that rationalized the endless War on Terror, initially centered on Afghanistan and Iraq and extended by the new president to Pakistan and Yemen. The president intoned ominously that the Afghani people are better off without the Taliban, the Iraqi people are better off without Saddam, and so the wars must continue, not just for self-defense but also so the troops can come home from these pacified, secured lands. This unchanged narrative makes it clear that the violence begins with 9/11 and the irrational and unwarranted attack that brought the twin towers down. Obama identified the core problem of the area as the violent extremism of Islamic movements.

There was no mention at all of the provocative work of imperialism or the repressive client regimes that America backed. There was no strong position against the expansion of Israeli settlement of the remnants of historic Palestine. Obama let it be known one more time that America was no "interested empire." America, he averred, seeks neither oil nor bases. The U.S. aim is rather the transformation of the tumultuous Middle East region into an oasis of peace and prosperity, open to global investment and trade. Israel exercised only its right to defend itself from the existential threats it faces. Violence had other wellsprings. The Islamic world remained dangerously mired in age-old conflicts and irrational hatreds. These irrational hatreds make the realization of the disinterested and benign vision of the colossus unattainable. They also necessitate the cleansing assertions of American and Israeli power. Terrorist states must be "ended," terrorist groups wiped out to provide security for Israel and to protect the American homeland from an infiltration of terror to its shores. Ironically, in Cairo Barack Hussein Obama announced quite clearly that the American War on Terror was henceforth a bipartisan war, as fully embraced by Democrats as by Republicans.

Obama's retelling of the narrative left no space for even a hint that U.S. intrusions, often violent, have been the main motivation for the various forces, and not just the extremists, that feed the resistance to American policies in the Islamic world. A reasonably fair accounting of the sources of American tensions with the Islamic world would include, as a Central Intelligence Agency (CIA) analyst has forthrightly explained, U.S. and Western exploitation of the region's energy resources; unlimited support for Israel and its expansionist actions; U.S. backing for the brutal police states that rule in much of the Arab and Islamic world; compliant acquiescence by the United States in the oppression of Muslims by other great powers, like Russia, China, and India; and, perhaps most damaging of all, the U.S. military presence in Afghanistan, Iraq, and other Muslim countries.[16]

The unchanged narrative gives no space for even an acknowledgment of the horrific price paid for the false gifts of "freedom and progress" by the Muslim peoples of Afghanistan and Iraq, not to mention Palestine. Little wonder that the Democratic president with the anomalous middle name preferred to see only the Islamist Imaginary rather than these very real policies as the root cause of American policies.[17] There was no repudiation of the disastrous and explicitly imperial policies of the Bush years that took the lives of hundreds of thousands of Muslim civilians, as well as over four thousand young Americans. The president failed to even mention the terrible and totally disproportionate violence unleashed on the essentially defenseless people of Gaza just six months before his address, nor the "separation" wall, nor the widespread Israeli settler violence against the occupied Palestinians on the West Bank.[18] Obama repeated the American mantra that the only violence that must be stopped was Palestinian resistance. In Cairo, the president unveiled no new thinking to make sense of the terrible moral and political failures of U.S. policy in the region. Hopes were dashed that the president would find a way to chart a more rational and modest foreign-policy course. Instead, the president's words simply reinforced the rationale for the violence of empire and colonization. The message only sounded new because it was delivered by a charismatic president with a warm smile and a talent for ringing phrases. It was not new in any significant way. What President Obama offered in Cairo was nothing more than an elegant retelling of the old story that had brought Muslims such endless suffering.

The record is now clear that the initial assault on Afghanistan on October 7, 2001, the subsequent invasion of Iraq on March 20, 2003, and then Obama's war in the border regions between Afghanistan and Pakistan (the so-called Af-Pak theater) and the president's unrestrained impulse to "send in the drones" have all deepened the enmity toward the United States of ordinary people throughout the Islamic world. They have also proved a recruitment boon for extremists, including both al Qaeda and its Islamic State of Iraq and Syria (ISIS) offshoot. Bloody military interventions, and the civilian deaths and maiming in large numbers that they inevitably inflict, are a stimulus rather than a cure for extremism.

The president's Cairo narrative, for those with ears to hear, made it perfectly clear that the man who urged Americans not to look back had ensured two things about the future: There would be endless American wars in Islamic lands, and, at home, there would be a corrupting and unaccountable surveillance state that guaranteed those wars would be waged in secrecy and at the cost of self-inflicted wounds to American democracy.

The Extremist Challenge

Imperial wars and their inevitable civilian casualties provide the core explanation for the rise of ever-more-militant extremisms. However, it is no contradiction to recognize the Islamic rationalization of the murderous logic that leveled the twin towers. Criminal political acts were thought out in a radicalized Islamic vocabulary, with distorted understandings of *jihad* (struggle for the faith) and *jahilliyya* (condemnation as un-Islamic, atheist, or pagan), traceable to Islamic thinkers such as the Pakistani Maulana Abul Ala Maududi (1903–1979) and the Egyptian Sayyid Qutb (1906–1966). ISIS calls itself the Islamic state for a reason. Such Islamic labels and rationalizations are intended to tap into the Islamic Renewal to win recruits, against the background of American and Israeli depredations. For that reason, it is all the more important to take note of the quite distinctive, distorted, and idiosyncratic character of these readings of the sacred texts by the extremists who draw on the work of these scholars in tendentious ways. The conclusions that contemporary extremists reach have only the most distant connection to the work of figures like Maududi and Qutb. The *Wassatteyya* has offered consistent, critical assessments of these radical thinkers. At the same time, they see clearly that the terrifying and indiscriminate violence of extremist groups like al Qaeda and ISIS cannot reasonably be attributed to these Islamic scholars, despite their disagreement with some of their views. As the midstream scholars see it, what we have are double distortions that heighten the potential damage to Islam. The midstream has criticized as distortions the interpretations of Qutb and Maududi of such concepts as *jihad* and *jahilli-yya*. With far greater forcefulness, they have rejected out of hand their extensions to rationalizations of the sheer barbarism by groups like ISIS. Midstream Islamic scholars have been making both sets of arguments for years. Moreover, the fact that extremist ideology does not offer the major explanation for the rise of increasingly successful groups does not mean it plays no role at all.

With equal clarity, the midstream unapologetically endorses the legitimate violence of Islamic resistance movements that confront foreign occupation with bravery and impressive inventiveness, most often against overwhelming odds. New Islamic intellectuals argue forcefully that there is an *obligation* in Islam to actively resist occupation and colonization. It falls on both the collective shoulders of Muslim communities wherever Muslims are attacked (*fard kifaya*) and on the individual shoulders of all Muslims who directly suffer such injustices in their own homeland (*fard al 'ain*). They insist that resort to armed resistance, as understood by leading centrist Islamic scholars like Ayatollah Fadlallah and Yusuf al Qaradawi, must always be *both* principled and practical. Violence is never defended theoretically as an end in itself or as a means to ease the pain of past wrongs. Resistance is not revenge. Campaigns of resistance must be conducted with a clear calculus of their likely effectiveness in achieving liberation, as weighed against their costs to the *ummah* in lives and treasure. Legitimate violence is also constrained by commitments to proportionality and to close examination of the morality of the actual means used to realize just ends. Certain groups, such as children, women, the aged, farmers, religious figures, and other innocent civilians, can never be deliberate targets. International law recognizes such a right of resistance for peoples under foreign occupation, subject to parallel restraints. These principles of Islamic legal reasoning and international law have force, whatever interested and arbitrary laws and motions the U.S. Congress or the Israeli Knesset enact.[19]

Extremism inevitably becomes the face of Islam for alarmed Westerner publics and wins their support for further military interventions. It also means that almost all of our efforts in the West to understand the Islamic world go into assessments of this Islamic threat. In this way, even the best Western work on Islam risks reinforcing a narrow security perspective that leaves the midstream in the shadows. The spotlight is cast on the extremists rather than the midstream intellectuals and activists who consistently and successfully contest their influence on the majority of Muslims. Scholarly efforts to lean against this unfortunate outcome have been far too modest in number and impact, although there are important exceptions.[20]

Overlooking the Dreams of Ordinary Muslims

The aspirations of ordinary Muslims center on the prospect of living decent lives with adequate means, a measure of freedom, and a cultural environment of their own making. National battles for basic rights and freedoms across the region now draw inspiration from Islam. Islam, with its call to a righteous life in awareness of God, becomes an active participant in struggles against domestic tyrannies. Islam also enables millions to embrace modernity without the necessity of accepting Westernization. Islam inspires ordinary people to courageous and unpredictable actions in accord with these ways of thinking. Today, very little understanding of these shifts in attitude, inspired by Islam, is reaching the West, and not for the first time.

My generation of graduate students who began their careers in the early 1970s was trained by social science scholars convinced that history's direction was set.[21] Western secular experience was understood to provide a mapping of the future of the Islamic world. Ahistorical models were drawn from the West's secular experience. Pathways to modernity on the Western model were mapped. The results were labeled economic and political development theory. With their gaze fixed on an imported and secular future for Muslim societies, most scholars missed the importance of the Islamic surge that was then just gathering strength. At that time, the very notion of Islam defining an alternative future was simply inconceivable. Today the Islamic Renewal shapes politics in much of the Islamic world. Unfortunately, Western analysts are fixated on the criminal, marginal Islamic minorities represented by al Qaeda and ISIS and on the mayhem they periodically cause. We are led to ignore the normalcy and decency of ordinary lives, lived in the embrace of Islam. We pay no attention to the everyday dreams of common people in the Islamic world who make faith central to their lives.

The area studies programs of the 1960s were motivated by the certitude that the United States had established itself as a superpower with worldwide responsibilities. The vastly overexaggerated challenge from the Soviet Union rationalized an unprecedented national effort to secure

America's "rightful" role in the world. These new, self-imposed burdens extended to the Islamic world. They required specialists with language and cultural competence. The competitive aim was to facilitate transformations along the modern lines that we, rather than the Soviets, had pioneered. We considered ourselves the vanguard of "the great global ascent," to borrow Robert L. Heilbroner's celebrated phrase.[22] To be sure, the language of global responsibility provided nothing more than a screen for imperial assertiveness. Moreover, talk of underdeveloped Islamic societies slid easily into condescending assumptions about underdeveloped peoples. Very few at Harvard, or elsewhere, paid any mind to these unsavory implications of prevailing views.

Today, things are far worse. Now, the call is for terror specialists, fluent in Arabic, Farsi, and other regional languages, and with an understanding of asymmetrical warfare. The terror specialists, with their special focus on the Arab world and Iran, are preparing themselves to face a vast and nameless army of Islamic extremists that must be confronted abroad, we are told, with as much violence as is needed in order to avoid another 9/11 at home. The rhetoric defining America's aim has shifted from the need to develop backward societies. Now, efforts are focused on demolishing conjured enemies and protecting the "homeland," whatever the cost to peoples in the Islamic world. Little attention is given to the quite clear evidence that precisely such military efforts have been a major stimulus for the violent antipathies to the West that are a tremendous recruitment advantage for extremist groups. To make matters worse, the War on Terror has become extremely profitable for a whole complex of interests, centered on powerful corporations whose profits have come to depend on war, as well as the army of contractors and security consultants who circle around them. The complex is awash with taxpayer dollars. In the West, the old centers for development and modernization now take a back seat to a new wave of institutes for terror and security studies at some of the West's most prestigious universities. When the corporate media look for experts to explain events in the Islamic world, they turn overwhelmingly to the terror and security specialists, who themselves are a part of the ever-expanding complex that profits from the War on Terror.

The Most Important Story from Islamic Lands

During all the decades of my life in Cairo, hardly a day has gone by without front-page coverage of two or three events, usually violent, in the

Islamic world by the major global news outlets. American family, friends, and students repeatedly have commented on what a fascinating time it must be to live and work in the Middle East, referencing the latest disaster, upheaval, or war. They are responding less to what is happening in the Islamic world and more to the way it is imagined in the West. In fact, the most important story in the Arab Islamic world today makes no impression at all.

From my vantage point in Cairo, where I first settled into a personal and professional home some forty years ago, I would tell that epochal story something like this. Ordinary people throughout the region are struggling resolutely every day with whatever means available to them to create better lives for themselves and their children. They actively yearn for more just economic and political systems for their sons and daughters. They dream of making a decent and honest living that provides food, shelter, health, and education for their families. They seek to create just societies grounded in Islamic values and higher purposes but also more connected to the larger world, more secure, and with greater freedom and more justly shared prosperity. As the Lebanese journalist Rami al Khouri has pointed out, this is the "big story" yet to be told.[23]

Circumstances of domestic tyranny and foreign invasions frame these everyday struggles and give them a truly remarkable character. In many parts of the Arab Islamic world, peoples are subject to the tyranny of authoritarian rulers, extremist terror, and periodic violent interventions from the West. The struggles for ordinary lives are waged under these quite extraordinary conditions. It is these exceptional circumstances, and not the very human dreams themselves, that make the lives of the peoples of the Islamic world seem so different. Perfectly understandable battles for normalcy foster resistance, including the forceful resistance that so many in the West find impossible to fathom. In these struggles there is little room for nonviolence. There is no constitution or even shared values to appeal to, as the occupiers, the extremists, and the local despots routinely ignore international human rights law and universal moral codes. Dreams of a normal life are all too often framed by crippling oppression and the constant threat of violence. It makes little sense to fault Arab citizens and the movements they support for the dualities of their commitments. They act at once to fulfill everyday dreams for themselves and their families, while at the same time supporting, when they can, resistance to local tyrants, violent extremists, and foreign occupiers, using force as circumstances require.

Nevertheless, these terrible complications do not mean that the short-comings of Islamic resistance movements should be overlooked. The human rights violations by both Hizbullah and Hamas have been ful-somely documented by the most respected regional and international human rights organizations.[24] So, too, have the at times horrific viola-tions by the Israeli and American occupation forces. The right of resist-ance, legitimated by international law, does not guarantee that the forms resistance takes will themselves always be legitimate. Those disadvan-taged by a power imbalance often engage themselves in brutalities. They should not be rationalized away. Clearly, there have been excesses, at times criminal, by both Hamas and Hizbullah. The more recent decision of Hassan Nasrallah to send Hizbullah fighters into Syria to help defend the murderous Assad regime has brought all such criticisms to a new level. Definitive evaluative judgments, however, remain difficult. Clearly, the Western opposition to Bashar Assad has far less to do with the tyran-nical nature of his rule and more to do with this unwillingness to comply with Western demands. A factor, too, is the Western desire to "end" yet another recalcitrant Arab state. Still, Hizbullah fighters battling to save a corrupt and tyrannical minority regime tarnish the cause of resistance that Hizbullah had come to embody. Yet, for all of these failings, both Hizbullah in Lebanon and Hamas in Palestine have played historic roles as legitimate movements of national resistance, however their adversaries seek to label them.

These unlikely and unforeseen resistance movements, and the sup-port they have won from ordinary people, have contributed to making Muslims once again independent players in world history. Unequal con-tests against local tyrants and foreign invaders have become part of the meaning of the Islamic Renewal, although they are by no means the heart of it. Its core lies elsewhere. The historic rethinking of Islam that has been under way since the early 1970s deserves greater weight and will have a longer-term impact on *Dar al Islam*. While resistance is part of the Awak-ening, its essence is rather renewal. The serious work to renew Islam and reform Islamic thinking and practices aims to shape the expanded role that Islam will play in the years to come of the twenty-first century, as the Islamic body continues to grow. Resistance movements of Islamic in-spiration against occupation are a source of well-deserved pride through-out Islamic lands. Yet the advancement of the centrist agenda of reform and renewal of the heritage as a resource to address the challenges of the global has a still greater historic importance. The calculated exaggeration of the bloody work of the extremists obscures a very important truth for our time. The overwhelming majority of the world's immense Muslim community has rejected the extremist ideology. The heart of Islam remains with the center.

The distinctive neoconservative tactical vision that drove the disastrous assertions of the Bush version of imperial America is now in ruins. However, it is crucial to remember that it represented simply an extremist variant of the underlying drive for full-spectrum dominance already in place as the Cold War got under way. These continuities explain the ease with which a president committed to ending wars could find himself in the fall of 2014 engaging America in yet another war in an Iraqi theater, now expanded to Syria.

By not looking back, America learned little from the disaster in Iraq. It is simply untrue that there were no signs that the invasion of Iraq would have horrific consequences, and not just for Iraqis. Nor is the assertion that we should have known better an instance of Monday-morning quarterbacking, although I must add that I have never quite understood this phrase as a way of blocking the criticism of misguided strategies. It has been my good fortune over the years to have professional coaches with world-class standing as close friends. I know from them that good coaches, even when they win, spend hours endlessly watching clips of the last game or match to understand mistakes made, even when those mistakes did not cost them the game. When they lose, the clips just don't stop—and well past Monday morning. It is self-serving claptrap when elite policymakers and pundits whine that in the buildup to war "we were all fooled." Demonstrators who took to the streets to protest the criminal invasion *before* it took place were not fooled.

Islam and the Alchemy of Resistance

The overwhelming military strength and technological advantage of the United States and Israel have not translated into unchallenged dominance of Islamic lands. Battles for dominance are regularly won, but not the war. That simple fact is the source of endless frustration for both Israeli and American planners. It also prompts an irrational commitment to the mindless repetition of failed policies. Strategic planners appear to reason that one more bout of repression or one more war will finally make the difference.

The Lebanese succeeded in expelling the Israeli army after an eighteen-year occupation of southern Lebanon. The Palestinians, in the face of the stunning brutalities of the American-armed Israeli army, continue their refusal to accept the status of a defeated people. They are occupied, but they are not defeated in spirit. Postinvasion Iraq could not be as easily molded and reshaped as American planners imagined. There is a strange alchemy at work in these anomalous outcomes. Islam translates the evident weaknesses of Muslims into the surprising and formidable strengths of Islamic resistance. How does this happen? The simple answer is the power of Islamic identity. It is a power enhanced by the spiritual awakening of *al Tagdid al Islami*. It is expressed in a resilience that cannot be defeated by military means.

At just this point, Western scholarship averts its eyes. Islam is always a proximate and never an ultimate explanation for Western analysts. Neoconservative theorists of Islam, for example, argue that the forces that drive Islamic movements are rage and envy. Islamic movements in their view are purely reactive. The reactions always come in instinctual and nonthinking ways. The liberal midstream of Western opinion agrees, although the rise of what is called Islamism is attributed to uneven development, the disruptions of oil wealth, or simple poverty. Islamic movements are always understood in terms of some other more fundamental driver; Islam itself is never the prime mover.

Midstream Islamic scholars of the global order and its impact on the Middle East, in sharp contrast, place Islam itself at the center of their analyses. In their view, no event or movement in the Islamic world can possibly be understood without careful attention to the ways it reflects larger, inherited patterns of Islamic thought and action. Understandably, perhaps, Western scholars turn to Western social theory that is presumed to be secular and to have universal application. To explain the surprising resilience and strength of Islamic movements, most now lean heavily on the flourishing literature on social movements to make sense of these developments. They most often miss the very simple fact, clear to Islamic historians and social theorists, that resistance is best understood as part of a far more expansive and durable historical pattern whereby the *ummah* as a whole defends itself. In *Dar al Islam* such resistance to external intrusions is always tied to more fundamental internal efforts to rethink the heritage for new times and places. Resistance is part of the larger patterns of adaptation and absorption that have served the survival of the Islamic *ummah* through the centuries.

The Power of Islamic Identity in the Global Age

Islam has thrived in the new conditions of the post–Cold War period. This remarkable adaptation belies the persistent myth of Islam as "stubbornly resistant to change, except on its own terms."[25] Even an incisive critic of U.S. imperial policies in the Islamic world, such as Andrew Bacevich, cannot shake this all-pervasive stereotype. Neither the assertion nor even the qualification is accurate. In fact, since the late eighteenth century Islam has undergone four successive waves of sweeping reform.[26] It has been in a constant state of change, often adopting ideas, concepts, and useful terms for understanding the world from others, always adapting them with great flexibility to its own environment and its own needs.

Both Israelis and Americans have, on occasion, made the painful discovery that Islam is not a force to be lightly dismissed. The power that flows from Islamic Renewal cannot be measured in the standard ways, they have learned. Nor is that power irrevocably linked to any particular individual, movement, organization, or state, although the Islamic midstream represents its deepest reservoir of strength. When assaulted, Islam is unpredictable in both locus and timing for riposte. When and where the Islamic response will come cannot easily be anticipated.

Islamic theorists explain Islam in the world as a living, rather than mechanical, entity. As a living organism, Islam has a remarkable capacity for self-organization, even in the absence of clear leadership or even a stable hierarchy. Islam has the capacity to take on extraordinarily variable forms. Yet, for all the variety of its colors, it remains recognizably Islam. Variable forms emerge from inventive adaptations to very different and changing circumstances that include domestic authoritarianism hostile to Islam, foreign occupation, and the special challenges of minority status in Western, Chinese, or Indian societies. Yet the imprint of these diverse circumstances never eclipses the Islamic character of what emerges. Islam reacts to but remains apart for all such environments to preserve the essentials of its own distinctive identity.

Islamic scholars see little that is new in these contemporary patterns of effective resistance. The 1,400-year history of Islam, as interpreted by midstream Islamic thinkers, demonstrates precisely these modalities of adaptation and absorption that, strangely, in no way diminish authenticity. Islam acts as a living organism to make sure, whatever the environment, that its essential needs are met. Only the Qur'an, the *Sunnah*, and a community are necessary to sustain Islam in any setting, no matter how hostile. As self-generated entities, Islamic communities always take on distinct colorations that blend into their environment. Islamic communities are self-generated and self-organized. Therefore, they inevitably have different features. All such communities consider themselves and are considered by others as part of the Islamic *ummah*. Struck in one place, Islam may well respond in another, physically quite far from the initial assault. The inability to predict where the response will come makes it all the more efficacious. Flexible timing adds to this advantage. The response may not be immediate, but there will be a response.

To explain these strengths, Western analysts have been reluctant to look at Islam itself. Avoidance of attention to Islam itself takes several forms. Some seek to read the character of a movement from the environment in which it arises. Others focus on the nature of the struggles in which the group engages. Both strategies fail. There is always an excess of meaning that transcends the environment and the struggles. Only Islam itself can explain that meaning.

Understanding of the Islamic world requires the study of Islam. The starting point for such understanding is always the Islamic midstream. Extremism commands the lion's share of attention. Yet the simple reality is that it is the vital and living forms of Islam, inspired by the midstream, that have already reshaped the Islamic world in essential dimensions. By focusing on the extremists on the margins, the West has missed the momentous success that the midstream has registered in restricting Islamic extremism to the margins of the life of the world's 1.6 billion Muslims. The various extremist ideologies have not captured the vast majority of Muslims. Islam's 1,400-year history reveals a consistent pattern of the triumph of centrism. Through the centuries, when extremist movements are not supported by outside forces and manipulated as agents, they are in the end reabsorbed into the mainstream. Outside support can only delay the enactment of that historical pattern that has always defeated extremism.

The alternative of military means used against Islamic extremists by outside powers simply does not work. Not even the unmatched power of the world's sole superpower, recklessly and brutally deployed under the last two American administrations, has succeeded in defeating extremism. The effect of the wars, particularly the wars against Iraq, has been the exact opposite: The more deeply American power is drawn into the contest, the more extremism flourishes. Islam of the center is really the only antidote to Islamic extremism.

By not paying attention to the Islamic Renewal and to Islam's epoch story for our own time, we deny ourselves the opportunity to make better sense of the one Islam and the many worlds of Muslims. We also lose potential partners in the Islamic world. We cannot create them. We can, however, recognize them. We have consistently failed to do so, even when clear and explicit overtures are made, as in the case earlier of Iran under President Mohammad Khatami. The current opening under President Hassan Rouhani remains on hold. Our record, rather than the Iranian record, is not encouraging. To the limited degree that we have faced our own most recent failings, the focus has been on the shortfalls of the military and the intelligence efforts in the context of inept, ideologically driven political leadership.[27] These are all important beginnings. Yet it seems deeply regrettable that so little attention has been paid to the colossal intellectual failure to develop a reasonable understanding of Islam and the Islamic world that might actually guide our broad policy toward the world's Muslims.

The Myth of the Moderates

The president's denial notwithstanding, America is quite clearly "an interested empire." Our interests, above all oil and Israel, draw us deeply into developments in the Islamic world in the most damaging ways. The United States has shown pernicious skill in developing ways of looking at the Islamic world that allow us to escape from any responsibility for our actions, through either demonizing Muslims or morphing them into incomplete copies of ourselves. These efforts have had painful consequences for the Islamic world and for America as well. Fears of Islamic terrorism channel American passions into the drive for cruel and unfeeling wars. It cannot be that hard to understand that the American destruction of Iraq, bombing cities, killing civilians by the uncounted hundreds of thousands, and failing to prevent the theft of its cultural treasures, has convinced ordinary people in the Islamic world that no place in *Dar al Islam* is safe from American self-righteous and always self-interested anger.

Endlessly, the United States searches for mythic Islamic "moderates" as local partners for the interested transformations it seeks to engineer.[28] Dialogues quickly become invidious indictments of putative moderates who inevitably fail to live up to the images we conjure for them. The efforts to "train" local partners really aim to remake them in the Western image. For the most part, such efforts fail miserably. Even when some success is registered, such clones of ourselves will be at best marginal in their own societies. They will be simply counterfeits, suitable only for the role of agents of a foreign power.

The greatest damage of such approaches to the question of Islam and the West is the way they steer us away from a critical look at what has gone wrong with our own policies. The evils of our adversaries overwhelm any impulse to self-reflection and criticism of American policies. Even more damaging is the way that both approaches blind us to the existence of genuine, autonomous Islamic centrists with whom we do share some important commitments, such as democracy and development, even though they may well consistently oppose American interventions and blind support for any and all Israeli policies. Such independent figures, when viewed realistically, do represent potential partners for joint projects of mutual interest.

The United States has only very rarely shown the maturity that such an orientation would require. Astonishingly, the calamities of the Bush and Obama years have not provoked massive inquiries, robust congressional hearings, painful Truth and Reconciliation commissions as to just how we got so much wrong in Palestine, Afghanistan, Iraq, Yemen, and beyond in *Dar al Islam*. Bombing Iraq back to the Stone Age killed hundreds of thousands and destroyed a state. It also created an environment in which an estimated $11.7 billion in assistance could go missing, presumably to myriad forms of corruption and not all of it Iraqi. The U.S. destruction of the Iraqi state created a fertile field for a plethora of extremist groups, and not just ISIS. One would also expect some consideration of reparation for the damage done, massive assistance, and, at a minimum, recognition of the war crimes committed. Ordinary people in the West are ready to face these terrible realities of what America has done, although the political elite and their publicists in the media are not.

Everyday citizens have already registered their realism about the workings of empire. Millions of Americans and others around the world recognized that the unprovoked war on Iraq was a supreme war crime. They were unmoved by Colin Powell's charade at the United Nations in presenting the "evidence" for Saddam's link to al Qaeda terrorism and possession of weapons of mass destruction. They understood that they were being asked to pay for oil with the blood of their sons and daughters. They understood that those calling for war were bent on renting the children of the poor to do the dirty work and suffer the appalling wounds of war for those who made fortunes off the endless wars. They knew that war is *never* a cakewalk and that there would be neither flowers nor jobs nor even adequate health care for the returning troops.

When confidence in America and the West more generally falters, we should not forget that the world had never seen anything like it. America is not monolithic. Massive antiwar protests took place in Western capitals *before* the war was launched. In the end, ordinary citizens could not restrain an imperial president, an outsized American military machine, and a compliant "coalition of the willing." Still, a great debt is owed to those millions of demonstrators for reminding the world that not all Westerners, not all Americans, are "warriors" and that, for many ordinary citizens, America still represents more than a besieged "homeland." Neither the American punditry nor the political class has yet to express its gratitude for that message of truth from the demonstrators. Prominent Islamic intellectuals of the center have.[29]

Despite the Soviet-style embedding of journalists with the American military and the deadening hand of the corporate news conglomerates, enough investigative journalism and real scholarship have been produced that we can now prove a good deal of what ordinary people in the West already knew. The American public was, indeed, systematically lied to in the buildup to the war of choice against Iraq. The arrogant architects of that catastrophe had no grasp of the realities of the world into which they recklessly plunged. Such ignorance of the powerful is no small matter. Clearly, the United States failed in the most flagrant ways to understand the Islamic world into which America blundered with such deadly violence. Yet there has been no radical rethinking of the underlying causes for our massive failings.

In summer of 2015 the American airwaves were flooded by the usual security and military analysts with their instant analyses of the fresh and always dire threats from Islamic extremists. It is always all about them and never about American and Western policies. Instead of a consideration of why American policies went so tragically wrong in the Islamic world, the United States has simply increased our "special ops" military budget, launched planning and weapons development programs for the new wars of counter-insurgency, ordered more weapons, and hired more consultants. Endless wars remain on the horizon. They will continue to target Islamic lands. We dare not look at Iraq in the rearview mirror. It is hard to see how things will turn out differently.

Humanistic Scholarship and the Promise of Cooperation

We can do better in both understanding and policies, although national political institutions have shown themselves to be incapable of generating any such new understanding and new ways of relating to the Islamic world.[30] It is time for the progressive movements that animate civil society and have been responsible for the most important democratic advances America has achieved to make the intellectual, moral, and political effort themselves to rethink America's global role. Particular attention must be paid to the Islamic world, for it is there that our actions have done the greatest damage, both to others and to ourselves. Our returning troops and their families are shell-shocked by what they have seen and what they have done. Antiseptic, clinical terminology for what they have suffered only increases the harm. The only reasonable name for their "stress" is *war*. From the psychological wounds of war, there is no easy path to normalcy. America needs to face the reality that we sent them to war on a long train of secrets and lies. We sent them into a reality we did not bother to understand. In doing so, we did intolerable damage in the world. We did great damage to ourselves as well.

The fully developed intellectual and human resources for such a reorientation are not yet at hand. Empires inevitably generate some version of "the white man's burden." They also inevitably conjure up some horrific threat to the homeland, emanating from the irrational "natives." There is no other way to understand the 24/7 hyping of the threat of ISIS. The combination of an appeal to high principle and fear is designed to bring home populations into line. It justifies the terrible violence, for the most part against civilians, empires use to achieve their ends. Yet, just as inevitably, empires also create waves of domestic critics. The rate of their appearance increases as losses in treasure and lives mount. Eventually, imperial overreach is understood to be the real threat to the nation, and opposition to war takes root first in nationalist soil. Invariably, however, there are also some from imperial capitals who see further. They come to recognize a common human interest in resistance to imperial and colonial expansions and the terrible material and human toll they take.

Such individuals and groups have succeeded in making themselves a presence in the West. They are open, in theory at least, to cooperation in resistance to empire and in common projects to build a somewhat more just world. Recent years, despite the failures to restrain imperial and colonial policies, have seen precisely such developments. There have been important beginnings in the United States and Israel. At the same time, in Islamic lands under assault, there have appeared individuals and groups who recognize that, while empire and colonization must be resisted, there are potential allies for those resistance struggles within the imperial and colonial centers. Not all Americans support endless war-making; not all Israelis support colonization of Palestinian lands. Possibilities of joint effort are less distant than they might appear.

Humanistic scholarship must aim to document these unlikely developments and to provide the knowledge base to help turn them into cooperative, activist efforts in the human interest. The creation of a body of positive, humanistic learning that can underwrite principled acts of cooperation across the separating walls that imperialism and colonialism build has hardly begun. A critical dimension of the work ahead is seeing more clearly how existing transnational movements that seek to transcend narrow nationalisms can find common ground and cooperative projects on behalf of a more just world system. The massive antiwar movements in the West represent one such resource. The *Wassatteyya* in the Islamic world is another. The growing number of critics within Israel and in Jewish diaspora communities of occupation is yet another. Anti-imperial and anticolonial commitments, often at variance with the diverse national settings out of which they each grow, are shared. At the same time, they confront critical differences, notably on social and cultural issues. Progressives in the West find Islamic notions of the unity of politics and faith difficult to fathom, although the midstream Islamic view of such matters is not nearly as far from progressive Western understandings as many imagine. Western humanists are also troubled by questions of the role of women and minorities in Islamic lands, although they recognize that much work remains to be done in the West on precisely these issues. What they often do not know is that Islamic centrist scholars have made important advances on Islamic ground on behalf of precisely these questions. For their part, Islamic intellectuals find rampant consumerism, and excesses of sexual freedom at variance with their convictions. Jewish activists confront nagging fears that somehow their criticisms of Israeli state policies may foster anti-Semitism. More damaging still to genuine cooperation is a generalized Western cultural arrogance that refuses to believe that advancements on issues in the human interest can be made on Islamic ground. Difficulties on both sides are compounded by the lack of a refined understanding of the respective positions on all sides of the prospective partnerships, as well as a limited understanding of the forgiving sophistication of their own traditions.

These barriers are not insurmountable. Not all differences have to be leveled; some can simply be dealt with at another time. What is needed is a pragmatic openness to cooperation on issues where the possibility of cooperation is real. There can then be agreement to simply set other contentious matters aside in the interest of what *can* be accomplished. Activists for global peace and justice have for many years cooperated with diverse groups across the globe on specific campaigns for social progress and against war, while fully aware that principled differences would almost certainly preclude joint action in other arenas. Midstream Islamic movements have a parallel tradition of overcoming conflicts on secondary matters while cooperating on primary issues. Centrist Islamic intellectuals have developed a sophisticated *fiqh* of priorities, which allows them to pay less attention to divisive and less important matters in the interest of the advancement of such large questions as spiritual renewal, peace, and social justice. If anything, the midstream Islamic moral universe has a far more highly developed notion of the importance of tolerating difference.

At times such possibilities of mutual understanding and cooperation flash before us. Yusuf al Qaradawi created one such moment when he addressed his audience of shaikhs, callers to Islam, and the massive Muslim publics that respond to his words. Qaradawi said not only that he rejected the unjust and illegitimate war of aggression against Iraq but that he did so with the recognition that millions of protestors on the streets of European and American capitals called for the same. He signaled that they deserved appreciative recognition.[31] To underwrite such possibilities, only dimly glimpsed and almost never acted on, there is serious work ahead for that treasured tradition of humanistic scholarship to which both Islamic and Western civilization have contributed.

God at the Beginning and al Nas *at the End*

The Holy Qur'an begins with God and ends with *al Nas*. The first verse of the first *surah* opens: "In the name of God, Most Gracious, Most Merciful."[32] God in that verse is spoken of as "the Cherisher" of *al Nas*. The last *surah* of the Qur'an, entitled *al Nas*, completes its final verse with the word "*al Nas.*" The very last word in the Qur'an invokes the common people, just as the first invokes God.

The Islamic midstream knows that God did not bring Islam to the world to serve as a cloak for criminal extremism. Nor do midstream Islamic intellectuals and activists accept the notion that Islam should serve as an adornment for powerful royal families, the wealthy, or absolute rulers. Only by radical distortion can Islam be used to enhance the power of regimes or opposition forces that seek aggrandizement by draping themselves in the externalities of religion. Islam is not destined by God to serve authoritarian rulers or *amirs* who pronounce themselves the infallible interpreters of the Message and founders of a new caliphate. Islam is no plaything of empire, to be distorted and manipulated. Nor is it meant to be an adjunct for states that declare themselves the guardians of the faith. Islam has no need of such garrisons that in the end always turn their weapons against *al Nas.* It is to the people, ordinary people, that Islam is addressed, very clearly including the wretched of the Earth. Islam belongs to them. In Islam, the very poorest and the most vulnerable find refuge. Islam gives them not only dignity and comfort but also the opportunity to earn a place among the righteous.

Surely, Muhammad al Ghazzali was right to declare in book after book and sermon after sermon that those bent on capturing Islam for their own purposes, whether of power, wealth, or status, defile the faith and make Islam itself an orphan in the lands of *Dar al Islam* they dominate. Muslims who today willingly cooperate with tyrants, empire, and criminal extremists give Islam's message a hollow ring. They gain only false identities and shallow values. As to the imperial American project for the Islamic world, with its total disregard for the needs of ordinary people in Islamic lands, it is enough to note that those with knowledge of Islam and the lands where it flourishes agree that today American influence stands at an all-time nadir. Those who manipulate and exploit Islam fall from grace. Tyrants are under siege. The empire weakens. The overwhelming majority of Muslims abhors and rejects the extremists. Islam itself continues to rise.

There is a startling simplicity to that which Islam asks of true believers. In a beautiful and greatly loved *surah*, God explains that the essence of righteousness has to do with more than the ritual practices of the faith, such as the body movements followed in prayer, more than the public display of religiosity. God placed "righteousness" within the reach of very ordinary people in their everyday lives, but they must not only believe but act to do good deeds in the world:

> It is not righteousness that ye turn your faces Towards East or West; but it is righteousness to believe in God and the Last Day, and the Angels, and the Book, and the Messengers; to spend of your substance, out of love for Him, for your kin, for orphans, for the needy, for the wayfarer, for those who ask, and for the ransom of slaves; to be steadfast in prayer, and practice regular *zakat*; to fulfil the contracts which ye have made; and to be firm and patient, in pain (or suffering) and adversity, and throughout all periods of panic. Such are the people of truth, the God-fearing.[33]

The promise of righteousness is the opportunity for *al Nas* to live a good life in consciousness of God. *Al Nas* in the Qur'an refers to all people, not just to Muslims. The promise of righteousness is a promise within reach for all humanity.

10

The *"River of Life"*

But those who believe and do deeds of righteousness,
We shall soon admit them to gardens,
With rivers flowing beneath, to dwell therein forever.

QUR'AN 4:122

A RIVER WENDS its way through this book. The river is Islam, the "River of Life."[1] Its waters bring extraordinary generative powers. Midstream Islamic intellectuals report on the progress of the river, as it cuts innumerous channels through Islamic lands and to territories beyond. These openings enable *al Tagdid al Islami* (the Islamic Renewal) to work its worldly effects on a global scale. The great nineteenth-century Islamic reformer Muhammad Abduh (1849–1905) first formulated this compelling representation of Islam. Today, the metaphor for Islam's spiritual and temporal power has even greater resonance than when Abduh first offered it. In our time, the lifegiving force of Islam is apparent around the world. Twenty-first-century Muslims have established flourishing communities of believers on all continents. *Al Nas* (the common people) come to the "River of Life" from a myriad of ethnicities and cultures, bringing with them astonishing diversity. They come in ever-increasing numbers. People of all ages, including the Arab youth who played so large a role in the revolutionary upheavals of the spring of 2011, all act within a cultural context shaped by Islam. Islam is in the air in all those places *al Nas* gather.

The triumph of Islam of *al Nas* offers a compelling narrative. Islam has a serious claim as the world's fastest-growing religion.[2] More impressive than this surge in numbers has been the success of Islamic communities around the world in creating loyalties that commend to their members sacrifice of their most precious possessions to protect the *ummah* (community of Muslims). The human warmth of Islamic communities is especially attractive in a global age dominated by a Western, neoliberal order, which is experienced as cold and unfeeling. The market obsession of Western societies has taken a toll on all values, other than the competitive individualism and possessive consumerism it fosters. In such a barren global climate, Islamic ideas and values exert great appeal, creating what Rashid al Ghannouchi has called "the largest religious base in the world."[3]

All of that, and more, could be read from my long-term vantage point in Cairo. Quite by chance, Tunisia, then as now, framed my experience of Egypt. It was in Tunis, rather than Cairo, where I first stayed put long enough in those early years of travels to actually experience Islam as a lived social presence. Even in the heyday of President Habib Bourguiba's secularization drive, when I first visited in the mid-1960s, the deep roots of Islam in Tunisia preserved the country's Islamic character. Elaine, my partner, loved the sea. I loved the villages. In August 1968 we married in Tunis. French bureaucrats foiled our original plan of a Paris elopement before proceeding to Tunis to study Arabic. Once we were in Tunisia, the old city in Tunis captured our imaginations. We had our small wedding party there. The City of Lights was eclipsed. We honeymooned in Sidi Bou Said, a village on the sea north of Tunis that is far too beautiful to be real.

The experience of Tunisia played the role of prelude to a lifetime love affair with Egypt. Still, some part of my heart has always belonged to Tunisia. I find myself frequently looking over my shoulder to catch a glimpse of what is going on there. However, for over forty years, it has been Cairo that has afforded me the most privileged vantage point and base for witnessing the unfolding of the Islamic Renewal. As it flows through Egypt, the waters of the "River of Life" have mingled from the first with Christianity, already firmly established along the Nile. Those confluent waters have flooded the land. The people have all drunk deeply from them. Inescapably, the river passed through Tahrir Square in January 2011, nurturing the souls who gathered there. It made its impact felt on all that happened in the square.

Worldly Miracles

I am often asked now why I continue to return to live in Egypt when the country is in such turmoil. Given the world-shattering events in Tahrir Square and across Egypt, the question always seems odd to me. How often in our lives do we have the chance to see a worldly miracle up close?

The Earth moved in Tahrir Square on January 25, 2011.⁴ Only *al Nas* and the spiritual power of Egypt's people, both Muslims and Christians, brought with them to the square could accomplish that. As the masses moved toward Tahrir, the "River of Life" moved with them. Subsequent events and the reversals they have brought do not change that reality, any more than the Great Terror erased the historic importance to the entire world of the battles for "liberty, equality, fraternity" that defined the French in 1789. The whole world watched mesmerized in 2011 as the ordinary people of Egypt made spiritual power a force in Egypt's public squares. It was that power, drawn from both Islam and Christianity, that made possible their extraordinary revolutionary moment when they demanded "bread, freedom, and social justice." No planning, no calculus of politics or economics, no abstract speculations of "tipping points" that tally accumulating causes or "swans" of any color telling us to expect the unexpected can diminish the wonder of so momentous an event. It is not surprising that at the time Egypt's revolutionary upheaval confounded the policy pundits and academic experts, the Mossad and Central Intelligence Agency (CIA) operatives who swarm all over Cairo, and even the countless brave souls who themselves acted as the carriers of the revolutionary spirit. With spies and the best intelligence agents in the world everywhere, no one expected a revolutionary upheaval.

Those averse to metaphysical explanations have no hope of understanding what actually transpired. A genuine revolutionary upheaval in Egypt was impossible. The greatest power on the planet had spared no expense to keep America's man in Cairo in power. The United States stood by the dictator until his very last days, clinging to power and to the extraordinary wealth and privilege it had made possible for him and his family. Mubarak's Egypt boasted a gulag of prisons and concentration camps with torture machines second to none. Cairo was for years a destination of choice for the notorious American renditions program that sent prisoners to be tortured. The useful dictator and his cronies were protected by a military of half a million and an even larger force of a million and a quarter security police. The hated central security police swarmed all over the land, dressed in their black uniforms and with shields and truncheons in hand. They had as their sole responsibility the elimination of "enemies"—that is, the brutal repression of any who might be tempted to act on the mildest criticism of the regime. In Cairo and the major cities, the security forces were always just around the corner, packed into transport trucks in side alleys or left standing to bake in the sun for hours on end. They were poor, undernourished, and abused young men from the villages and slums, tormented themselves by a regime that trained them as torturers of their own brothers and sisters.

Like all miracles framed culturally by Islam, this momentous event was spiritual in its wondrous improbability. Yet it was practical in its causes and effects. Islam's miracles, like the faith itself, are worldly. The Qur'an tells humanity less about seas parting and bushes burning and more about the wonders of the human mind and heart. At the core of the Qur'anic Message is the call to all human beings to live decent lives and build good societies. Ordinary men and women, and not just their shaikhs, imams, and religious scholars, are called to use their reason to guide efforts to establish just communities. Islam, no less than the other great monotheisms, belongs to no one group. The Islam that fed the revolutionary spirit that took hold of Egypt's people was too beautifully spontaneous to be owned. It was the Islam of *al Nas*, the Islam that flows directly from the Qur'an and *Sunnah*. It is the "River of Life." Justice is the word the Qur'an gives to freedom. It evokes economic and social fairness, political freedom, dignity, and divinely sanctioned rights for all of humanity. In this sense, the call to justice in Islam is a demanding one. Worldly miracles are expected of those whose lives are framed by Islam. Repression, foreign interference, poverty, and sheer exhaustion from the struggles of everyday life delayed their arrival. But on January 25, 2011, the miracle-makers did find their way to Tahrir. There were, as Žižek observed, "sublime moments" when the spiritual was right before our eyes. Christian Egyptians on Fridays surrounded their Muslim brothers and sisters as they bowed to pray and made themselves vulnerable to the security forces. Muslims returned the protective gesture on Sundays as the demonstrations continued.[5] Even those Egyptians who rarely if ever pray joined in the massive collective prayers in the square. When I asked my friend Moustafa why, he replied simply that he was overwhelmed by the feeling of Islam's presence in Tahrir. Prayer was the only possible response.

Facing revolution in Islamic lands, only the philosophers have dared to call things by their right name. In Western societies that we pretend are secular, we are not comfortable acknowledging that other people's faith can play so large and positive a role in their affairs. When the philosophers have spoken this simple truth, they have paid a price. At no point in his career was the French thinker Michel Foucault more ridiculed and scorned than when he allowed himself to see the "the political spirituality" afoot in the land, when Iranians rose to overthrow the shah in their great mass revolution of 1979.[6] Surveying the revolutions in Tunisia and Egypt in 2011, the Slovenian philosopher Slavoj Žižek pronounced them a "miracle."[7] Both philosophers got it right, but both paid the price for being wrong by conventional lights. When the spiritual touches ground, as it always does in Islam, acknowledging its presence causes discomfort. Foucault stopped writing of Iran and all he learned there. Žižek began to back away from his description almost immediately.

It seemed clear to everyone that Egypt's revolutionary moment could not be sustained. That message was on everyone's lips. Everyone, that is, except for the hundreds of thousands of Egyptians who showed a skeptical world that the revolutionary flame could be kept burning. The military, with the blessings of the Americans, put a despised figure of the old regime forward as the strongman to end the chaos. Then, in response to a call for yet another march of a million, the authors of the impossible returned to Tahrir Square. The images from the square of the second revolutionary wave were terrible: the body of a youth dumped onto a pile of garbage, a young woman pulled across the ground by her hair, soldiers firing on unarmed demonstrators, armored trucks driving into peaceful demonstrators. The call went out that all was at risk. Incredibly, the people did respond. Unbowed and in massive numbers, the people came again to the square to rescue not just the demonstrators but the revolution itself. *Al Nas* with their voices and their bodies, not laptops or cellphones, made themselves the primary movers in Tahrir.

Tunisia was the site where the spark was first struck. Events in Tunisia consistently over the years have spoken to my life in Cairo. The narrative that would move the world started with the police harassment of a Tunisian son of *al Nas*. Muhammad Bouazizi, a street vendor from a poor village in central Tunisia, suffered the seizure of his unlicensed vegetable cart. Muhammad appealed to the municipal authorities—"How will I earn a living?"—but to no avail. He simply could not bear this final indignity. In protest, he set on fire his one possession of value, his own body. It was an act that spoke to the humiliation and frustrations of a generation of young people across the Arab world, not least in Egypt. It was their response that gave Muhammad's desperate and tragic act historic importance.

Not long after, from the Egyptian city of Alexandria came the unbearable image of Khaled Said, a very ordinary middle-class young man, beaten to death by the security forces who pulled him from an Internet café.

Khaled, like so many of his generation, had become ensnared in recreational drugs and impossible dreams of immigrating to America. To be a martyr, one need not be a political or religious activist. Nor does it really matter why the police dragged him from the café and beat him to death. It was Khaled's face after the beating that mattered. Khaled's brother rescued him from oblivion as just another anonymous victim of Mubarak's tyranny. He took the terrible picture of what the police had done to his brother and projected it to the world.

Just barely recognizable, Khaled's broken face was intended as a lesson to Egypt's rebellious youth. It was—but not the one imagined. The Arab youth of Egypt and beyond refused to look away from the inhuman brutality inscribed on Khaled Said's face. Instead, the image was posted on Facebook and it immediately went viral: "We are all Khaled Said." With that embrace, Egypt's young people in massive numbers restored Khaled's human dignity. They made him a symbol of their own. The youth said quite simply that they were ready to die for their freedom. Khaled Said passed into history alongside Muhammad Bouazizi. It is hard to imagine that the youth, so empowered by their self-generated revolutionary roles, will ever return quietly into the night of tyranny. Large numbers of young Tunisians and Egyptians lost their fear of ruling power, whether bearded or dressed in khaki. The understanding that change is possible registered.

In January 2011 Egypt's youthful rebels issued the call to revolution. They presented themselves to the world as the Facebook Generation, young, educated, principled, tech-savvy, and fearless. They adhered to no one party. They announced no religious program other than unity and tolerance, with both cross and the crescent in hand. Theirs was neither a narrow political nor a religious revolution, with party bosses or clerics in the lead. Instead, they created a mass revolutionary moment for the social justice, human dignity, and freedom that Muhammad Bouazizi and Khaled Said had come to symbolize. Acts of desperation and unspeakable cruelty had all happened before. Over the years Egyptians and Tunisians had displayed similar flashes of the will to resist, but always the tyrants remained in place. This time was different, although no rational calculus can tell us why. The youth movement, holding the hands of the martyrs Muhammad and Khaled, had somehow sent a message to the people that broke through the wall of fear that had kept odious dictators in power for decades. Ordinary Tunisians and Egyptians by the millions took to the streets in a numberless stream. *Al Nas* ended the terrible dictatorships, to the astonishment of the world.

Entranced by the fearless, young, and educated revolutionary youth in Tunisia and Egypt, it has been all too easy to forget the other faces of the revolutions. From the outset, it was the common people of Tunisia and Egypt who were far more important in grounding the revolutions and enhancing their prospects for success. The cellphones, laptops, and satellite channels did matter, but their importance should not be overstated. Fahmi Huwaidi got it exactly right when he wrote that "yes, Facebook played a role but not the essential one. The entire people moved. The Tunisian example stirred the people of Egypt—it was the beginning of real movement."[8]

My apartment is a few minutes' walk from Tahrir Square, and over the next several years, I experienced those tumultuous events most directly in Cairo, going frequently to the square. I did so with reflexive side glances to Tunisia. For me, Cairo was the big screen, while Tunis was the smaller, yet at times more intense, embedded screen. More than once, critical events would first crystallize on the small screen and then project onto the large one. Tunisians were in no sense secondary players. Tunisia launched the first uprising. Tunisians held the first democratic elections, with an astonishingly high 90 percent turnout of the country's four million-plus voters. In January 2014, Tunisia crowned these achievements by crafting an exemplary constitution with provisions both for democratic elections and protections for public freedoms, notably for women and minorities. The landmark Tunisian charter may well be the most liberal and democratic ever produced in the Islamic world. Civil liberties are protected. Legislative, executive, and judicial powers are separated. There are unprecedented guarantees for the parity of women in political bodies. The constitution recognizes Islam as Tunisia's official religion but also provides explicit guarantees of religious freedom. These Tunisian achievements and their impact in Egypt and across the Arab world should be kept in mind, although the primary focus in this account will be on Egypt.

Revolutionary Uprisings

Western analysts, enamored with social media and susceptible to trendy talk of "millennials," have led Western audiences to understand these massive events in Tunisia, Egypt, and beyond as merely derivative reflections of their own experiences. The uprisings are all about the technology and social media and "youth bulge" that came with it; human agency and the Islamic cultural context disappear in these renditions. The human meaning of the historic events of 2011 is then further vitiated by labels like the "Arab Spring," that originate with Western commentators and are then picked up in the echo chamber of regional media. The French and the Americans have revolutions; the Arabs have seasonal changes.

No, these were revolutionary uprisings in the Arab heartland by purposeful human actors with large dreams of freedom, equality, and justice. No single trend dominated events. However, in all cases Islamic intellectuals and activists played an important role, ensuring that these universal values were pronounced with Islamic shadings. It is generally recognized that the Kefaya movement that took shape in 2004 was the most important precursor to the groups such as the April 6 movement that issued the call to action in 2011. Less frequently noted is the critical role played by centrist Islamists, greatly influenced by the guidance of the New Islamic trend, in bringing together the multiple political forces that formed Kefaya. Key activists and intellectuals of the centrist Islamic Wassat Party, notably Abul Ela Mady and Essam Sultan, hosted an *iftar* gathering to break the Ramadan fast. The diverse intellectuals and activists who attended coalesced to form the core of the new movement. The highly respected jurist Tareq al Bishri, one of the most important of the New Islamic scholars, wrote the first manifesto of Kefaya in October 2004. Bishri forthrightly called Egyptians to "withdraw their long-abused consent to be governed."[9] Kefaya's embrace of democracy and reform and this explicit call for civil disobedience hung in the air until 2011.

The Tunisian people took to the streets first in December 2010 and drove Ben Ali, their ruler for some twenty-three years, into exile in just twenty-eight days. Egyptians responded and within eighteen days accomplished the upending of Hosni Mubarak and his dreary and corrupt dictatorship of almost thirty years. These momentous events rippled through Arab lands with reverberations in street protests by hundreds of thousands in nearby Libya and Morocco, but reaching to Jordan and as far as Yemen and Bahrain. These massive uprisings all articulated values and aspirations that drew on a shared Islamic cultural context. Everywhere, the cries of the people invoked Islam for inspiration.

It was the faces of ordinary Egyptians in revolution that I saw close up. They bore the traces of accumulated anguish and humiliation. Egypt's people were the victims of the cruel neoliberal economic order, imposed by the West and enforced by Mubarak. "Structural adjustment" programs made Egypt the darling of the International Monetary Fund (IMF) for its impressive rise in gross domestic product, while the conditions of ordinary Egyptians deteriorated. Regime cronies amassed fortunes in the billions of pounds. Income inequalities reached staggering proportions. Meanwhile, common people were routinely brutalized by the police and security forces. In such a context, the preeminent Islamic value of social justice has revolutionary potential. Ordinary Egyptians were forced to work themselves to an early death, literally, in order to survive day to day and feed their families.

It was not always so for Egypt's people. The poor and the working class have memories of other times, shared with them by their parents. They have not forgotten that their families were once treated as human beings by their government. The invitation to revolution was indeed issued by the liberal middle-class youth. We should not forget, however, that workers in Mahalla, an industrial center known for its activist labor base, and labor elsewhere had already undertaken a series of brave strikes. Egypt has a proud history of independent initiatives by informally organized workers that is routinely overlooked. Women often played a prominent role among the striking workers. It was the workers' strikes that first inspired the youth, not the other way around. Simple people, including those from the villages around Cairo, had also committed spontaneous acts of resistance, blocking highways to signal their local hardships. Periodically, anomic and seemingly chaotic disturbances erupted in the poorest neighborhoods of Cairo, Alexandria, and other large cities. Political oppression, economic grievances, and the endless humiliations of daily life of the mass of Egyptians drew them to the squares and to the improbable sense of hope the young people had stimulated. Hope became a historic force when al Nas embraced it. Suddenly, people believed that it just might be possible to end the tyranny. Those public squares, above all Tahrir Square, became sacred ground.

Egypt's revolution in January 2011 was not an Islamic revolution in the Iranian sense, nor did politicized Islam in Egypt play the role it did in Lebanon or Palestine. The religious establishment in Egypt provided neither the leadership nor cadres to make the revolution happen. The Muslim Brothers came late to the square. They clearly did not speak for Islam in Tahrir Square. Nor did the Brothers hijack the Egyptian revolution. Egypt's revolutionary moment was the work of al Nas, and the people spoke for Islam. It was that simple fact that bleached out the influence of Western political ideologies and strengthened its Islamic character.

Western scholars and pundits write all too often of Egypt's revolution as though they believe that the West has a patent on core revolutionary values. If you call for bread (i.e., social justice), then you must be a socialist. If you call for dignity (i.e., the right to your own identity), then you are clearly a nationalist. If you call for freedom (i.e., liberation from a foreign-backed tyrant), then obviously you are a liberal. Therefore, the ideologies afoot in Tahrir were Western; they had nothing to do with Islam. Such absurdities pass without comment, even though a moment's reflection by anyone with the slightest familiarity with Islam would make it clear that the Qur'an speaks clearly to humanity of social justice, human dignity, and freedom. These values are universal human values, and they have for 1,400 years been expressed in an Islamic idiom. No modern civilization, not even the powerful West, holds their patent. *Al Nas* quite clearly brought the spiritual into Tahrir Square from their own rich Islamic heritage. Islam was pervasive in the square, although, given these ideological blinders, not everyone could see it. *Al Nas* did not have to see it. They felt it. They experienced it directly.

With their gaze fixed on movements or mosques, observers have missed the real spirit of Islam that was pervasive in the square. Some have seen Islam only in the fiery Friday sermons in mosques that undoubtedly did galvanize some of the demonstrators who poured into the streets when the prayers ended. Others felt Islam's presence only when the bearded Brothers raised their chants and veiled women called out the greatness of God. It is not that such perspectives are wrong, but rather that they understate and diminish the spiritual character of the uprising. In the end, Islam required neither the government-controlled mosques nor politicized movements. Its capacities exceeded both. Islam came to the squares with *al Nas* in the millions. They brought it with them as naturally as their prayers. It came as Islam itself. It came as Islam of the Qur'an and *Sunnah* that eclipses both mosques and movements.[10]

Few could see beyond the pain and suffering of the mass of Egyptians to their incredible reserves of resilience and undiminished capacity for hope, both nourished by their deep religious faith. For the largest numbers of Egyptians that meant Islam; for others it meant Christianity. The deep reserves of inner strength of Egyptians find reflection in their legendary sense of humor and the warmth of their family and personal relationships. Very few observers thought a revolutionary upheaval was possible in Egypt, precisely because they had little understanding of these reserves of strength. The Egyptian writer Belal Fadl, known as the author of "the have-nots," was one figure with such awareness. For years, he has been telling the stories of the long-suffering but always resilient Egyptian people with insightful humor, compassion, and a balanced sense of the role of religion in their lives. His extraordinary work, although unknown in the West, reveals the hidden sources of impressive strength of Egypt's common people. Fadl celebrated the centrist Islam of figures like the late Muhammad al Ghazzali, who comforted and inspired ordinary Egyptians.[11] Readers of Fadl and others like him were prepared to see the spirits of ordinary Egyptians soar in those historic days in January 2011. No plausible explanation for the success of the January 25 revolution can sideline the role of the religious faith of Egyptians and the spirituality it made manifest in Tahrir Square. *Al Nas* in that sacred square reminded the world that the voice of God can still be heard in the cries of common people for justice.

Tunisia's Rashid al Ghannouchi has spoken of Islam's "overall upward curve" to characterize the trajectory of the Islamic Renewal.[12] This global narrative of Islam's rise provides the backdrop against which all developments across Islamic societies in the last decades of the twentieth century and the first decades of the twenty-first century must be assessed. To be sure, not all developments mirror the ascending arc. Great spiritual moments do not last forever. The pressing concerns of everyday life and more mundane politics, including the politics of Islamic movements, always reassert themselves. In recent years, important political movements that raise an Islamic banner have suffered serious blows. They include the Muslim Brothers in Egypt but also Hamas in Palestine and Hizbullah in Lebanon. The terrible assault on the Egyptian Brotherhood has attracted the greatest attention. It has also occasioned the most serious misreadings of Islam's future.

The Muslim Brothers in Power

In the wake of their revolution, Egyptians directly experienced democracy. A presidential election was held in two rounds in May and June 2012, and Muhammad Mursi, the candidate of the Muslim Brotherhood, was elected by a slender majority. Among international monitors, the most prominent was the Carter Center, whose delegation was headed by the former president himself. Carter later reported in a press release that the center "confirms the integrity of Egypt's latest parliamentary elections and its compliance with international standards of fairness."[13] A year later, on July 3, 2013, President Mursi was ousted by the military.

The record of governance by Egypt's fifth president, and the first elected democratically, was decidedly mixed. Despite the weak record when once in power, it remains true that the Muslim Brothers had performed remarkably well in the electoral space the Egyptian revolution opened up. In the two years immediately following Mubarak's ouster, Egyptians voted for the Islamic political alternative in reasonably free elections and monitored referenda at least six times. Not once did the secular and liberal parties mount a serious challenge to the Islamic parties. In March 2011 there was a referendum on the political path to be followed. There were votes in November 2011 and January 2012 for the two chambers of parliament. Finally, in May and June 2012, presidential elections were held in two rounds. In December 2012 there was a referendum to ratify the new constitution. The parties of politicized Islam triumphed in all these contests.

The electoral successes of the Brothers and the lightening of repression during the year when Egypt had a Muslim Brother president make the story of the military action and the subsequent all-out violent assault on the Brothers all the more disturbing. With the active support of the secular trends, a military junta seized power on July 3, 2013, and removed the elected Brotherhood president. The new regime then launched a massive and brutal repression of Brotherhood members, their supporters, and all others who challenged their dictatorship.

Islam One Thing, Islamic Movements Another

The devastating losses suffered by the Brothers and their supporters have led to the misleading judgment that Islam itself is somehow losing strength. That line of reasoning is not surprising: Western analysts routinely mistake Islamic political and social movements such as the Muslim Brotherhood for Islam itself. Loose talk of the "end of Islamism" has resurfaced with a vengeance. In the international corporate media especially, stock obituaries for Islam by Western experts have reappeared.[14] We are alerted with playful but pointed irony to the possibility of "a world without Islam."[15] Portentous talk of "post-Islamism," whatever the odd expression may mean, has become pervasive.[16] This standard Western rhetoric has little to do with realities on the ground. The simple truth is that no attractive alternative has arisen to replace the inspiring promise of *al Tagdid al Islami* to bring justice to *al Nas*. A military dictatorship can crush a movement and destroy the individual lives of its members, but in the long run, it cannot easily eradicate a vision and a movement with deep historical roots and an impressive mass following, no matter how much power and American weaponry are at its command.

Safely ensconced in the hearts and minds of ordinary Muslims, the "River of Life" continues to flow through landscapes where movements that claim the Islamic banner have suffered reversals. Midstream Islam does not recognize divisions such as those that pit the Muslims who support the Brothers against those who do not, secular Muslims against Islamic activists, Sunnis against Shi'a, and Arabs against Iranians. The misguided and often manipulated struggles of these factions, sects, and nationalities do not alter the fact that they are all Muslims, no matter how they may be labeled and mistreated on political grounds. The "River of Life" passes through them all, nurturing improbable Islamic communities on both sides of these artificial divides.

It is impossible to know whether the Brothers will rise again, although their history suggests such a long-term outcome is likely. It is more difficult to hope for the repair of Egypt's secular trends. The painful reality is that although liberal youth were in the forefront of those who launched the January 25 revolution, the secular camp has from the first been far weaker than both the Brothers and the military and far less connected to ordinary people. In five free elections in the wake of Mubarak's deposition, the liberals consistently polled miserably among the mass of poor Egyptians, whether those in crowded neighborhoods on the margins of the big cities or in rural areas. Unable to defeat the Brothers by democratic means, the secular opposition embraced the military junta. Their actions tell a calamitous story of a signal betrayal of human rights and democratic commitments by Egypt's secular political class. Leading advocates of human rights and democracy threw themselves into the arms of the generals. Their sole objective became elimination of the Muslim Brothers. They showed themselves willing to sacrifice all values and commitments on that altar. Their betrayals have clearly dimmed Egypt's prospects. Khalil al Anani, an independent Egyptian analyst, notes that they did not "read the history of similar experiences, where the military reached power and the price was decades of authoritarianism, corruption and tyranny."[17]

Removing the Muslim Brotherhood President

The removal from power of President Mursi was not a simple military action: It had substantial mass support. *Tamarod* (Revolt), a movement of young activists that only appeared to be spontaneous, had organized a signature campaign for early elections to remove Mursi and reinvigorate the democratic spirit of January 25. Any account that leaves out the events of June 30, 2013, is seriously misleading. On that day hundreds of thousands of Egyptians poured into the streets, totaling in the millions in Cairo alone. Those who marched believed themselves to number ten, twenty, or even thirty million. They judged that they achieved the largest mass demonstration in Egyptian history. Standard objective measures of crowd assessment suggest far lower numbers, although definitive results have not been possible.

Whatever their exact numbers, it is clear that a rainbow of social forces, missing only the Islamic groups, had lost confidence in the president. Revolutionary youth groups had a strong presence, expressing their resentment at being marginalized, with their demands unmet. The voices of ordinary citizens expressed deep disappointment that so little had been done to meet their pressing needs. Secularists, having failed to defeat Islamic candidates in elections, seized on the demonstrations as a way to remove the discredited and hated Muslim Brothers. The majority of Christians echoed these sentiments and expressed even greater fears about what continued Muslim Brother rule would mean for their communities.

The demonstrators were divided between advocates of two very different pathways to ending the Mursi presidency. Many, most likely the majority, demanded Mursi's resignation and early elections. They saw their movement as congruent with the democratic aspirations of the January 2011 revolutionary uprising. Others called on the military to remove the president, and thereby embraced a return to military rule.

Within three days of the onset of the mass demonstrations, the democratic experience had been terminated. Behind the screen of a hand-picked civil government, Egypt was once again ruled directly by a military strongman. Such a move could not have been made without an American nod. Susan Rice, President Obama's national security advisor, was out front in subverting Egypt's democracy. Rice called the generals just before July 3 to assure them that there would be no consequences to removing Mursi. Rice then called Mursi's advisers to tell them bluntly, "You're over. The generals are coming." No great efforts were made to conceal U.S. complicity. The Israelis, for their part, had reportedly made Mursi's removal a condition for their resumption of the sham talks with Palestinians to keep the smoke of a "peace process" coming. Within days, the meaningless negotiations did in fact resume. Inane talk from Washington of a "democratic transition" in Egypt once again clogged the airwaves of the corporate media.[18]

The spectacle of huge crowds imploring generals to depose democratically elected leaders has been repeated frequently in places like Buenos Aires and Bangkok, among others. Nowhere have they set the stage for a democratic transition. Those familiar with the history of the last half-century cannot be blamed for cautioning that the results of military takeovers and manipulated mass demonstrations have uniformly entailed violence, repression, and human rights violations. There was no real reason to think that things would be different in Egypt. What happened in Egypt in the wake of Mursi's removal from power and arrest has little to tell us about Islam. That story must be told in a strictly political register.

The Political Narrative

Egypt's current regime has been quite clear that the development of the country will take generations, not years. Meanwhile, to justify its authoritarianism the regime has been eager to wrap itself in a Nasserist mantle. The aura of a faux Nasserism that surrounds the new military dictator will be the most difficult to sustain. Tunisia's Rashid al Ghannouchi incisively explained why. No admirer of Nasserism, Ghannouchi nevertheless recognized that, in addition to Nasser's record of suppression of the Brothers and stifling of political freedoms more generally, his regime successfully advanced a bold and progressive agenda for Egypt. Ghannouchi comments that "the security and political oppression was obscured by a vast number of promising and very attractive cultural and political projects, such as land reform, the spread of education, the expansion of al Azhar, the liberation of Palestine, the unification of the Arab nation, anti-imperialism, and leadership in the non-allied movement." In contrast, Ghannouchi asks, what project does the new ruler "carry for his people and nation, other than a pseudo-intellectual cover for brutal repression that has reached such low levels as to accuse the legitimate president of the 'crime' of collaborating with Hamas"?[19] For all of these reasons, the new ruler's improbable and poorly conceived recent attempts to drape his regime in an Islamic mantle have even less chance of success.

The presidential elections of May 2013 suggested that Ghannouchi's assessment resonated in Egypt. The general had called for a massive turnout of some forty million or an ambitious 80 percent of the electorate. He didn't get it. Made desperate by the shockingly low turnout on the first day of voting, the interim government extended the voting period by a full vacation day and threatened to fine nonvoters. The Muslim Brothers were not alone in boycotting the elections; the April 6 youth movement, their staunch opponent, echoed that call. In the end, outside observers estimate that the general won support from approximately 25 percent of the electorate. Even the official figure of 46 percent, challenged as inflated from all quarters, was a galling six points less than the 52 percent turnout that Mursi had received.

Assessing the Brotherhood's Record

Clear-eyed and fair assessments of Muslim Brotherhood governance are now becoming possible. They include incisive critiques by prominent Islamic intellectuals.[20] The Brothers did narrowly win an internationally monitored election for the Egyptian presidency. *They did not win the right to speak in Islam's name*, but the Brothers in power acted as though they did. It also appears certain that some in the Brotherhood leadership came to see their movement as the driving and defining force behind the success of the 2011 revolutionary uprising. These patently false claims may well explain the arrogance that ultimately contributed to their downfall. The Brothers in the presidential palace made too little progress in restoring security, giving substance to their calls for social justice, and sharing power in meaningful ways with other political trends. They knew how to run mosques, social service projects, and entrepreneurial business enterprises, but administering state structures and engaging in the political give-and-take that governance requires was another matter. No transition from a thirty-year dictatorship to a democratic political system could realistically be dominated by one trend. No constitution written without the *effective* participation of a representative range of the nation's political forces could hope to command legitimacy across the political spectrum. No majority party could display insensitivity to the legitimate concerns of women and Egyptian Christians and still claim to speak for the nation. The Brothers committed all these sins. They were self-inflicted, costly, and unnecessary. To be sure, Muhammad Mursi was only given a year. Moreover, there were important development projects in the works. They ranged from an ambitious development project for the Suez Canal Zone to enhancements of the food subsidies program. Unfortunately, time ran out. Miscalculations and plots overwhelmed the presidency.

President Mursi made his most egregious political miscalculation when in November 2012 he issued a constitutional decree that placed his presidential power above that of all other government branches, most notably the judiciary. From a presidential perspective, there was good cause for the decree that set off a firestorm of protest. The judiciary in place from the Mubarak era had set about systematically undercutting the president's ability to govern. Nevertheless, his action looked very much like a power grab that would have placed the president above the law. The outcry was deafening: It included critical assessments by prominent New Islamic intellectuals, including Tareq al Bishri.[21] The president reversed the order under intense pressure, but it was too late: Mursi had handed his political enemies the smoking gun. The dam broke. In the eyes of too many Egyptians, the president had completely lost the legitimacy his electoral victory had conferred. A wise and experienced political leader would have recognized that political reality, resigned, and established procedures for early elections. Egyptians in more than sufficient numbers had given Mursi a ringing vote of no confidence. For the sake of Egypt and for the sake of democracy, Mursi should have accepted that decision.

These were all political miscalculations that have nothing at all to do with Islam. There was nothing inevitable about the course of action Mursi actually took in the face of the massive demonstrations of June 30. The Muslim Brotherhood was never a monolithic bloc with a fixed authoritarian and theocratic trajectory dictated by its Islamic roots. Decisions emerged in the context of power struggles at the highest leadership levels that reflected competing policy orientations within the Brotherhood. Different factions had quite distinctive policy preferences. Outcomes were in no way predetermined.

The Islamic background of the movement did not preclude a more flexible and accommodating politics. Islamic critics of Mursi's decisions make this case by contrasting the rigidity of the Brothers in Egypt with the flexibility of the Islamic Ennahda party in Tunisia. Egypt's Muslim Brothers must be one of the most studied movements on the planet. At the highest organizational levels of the Brotherhood two factions were locked in a dispute over grand strategy for the society. A useful simplification would identify one group as reformers. They sought a less rigidly hierarchical organization, more inclusive of younger Brothers, and more open to contemporary influences of a globalized world. At the same time, they claimed continuity with that aspect of al Banna's legacy that emphasized the proselytizing "call" rather than politics. Their goal was to work at the societal level to strengthen Islamic values and create effective Islamic social institutions. This faction was represented by some of the more sophisticated thinkers in the Brothers who also had closer relationships with the younger generation of Brothers. A second, conservative faction embraced these proselytizing goals but subordinated them to a drive for political power. The conservatives are sometimes referred to as Qutbists, although the label is misleading. This group did accept the political thrust of Sayyid Qutb's later work. They did tend to have elitist attitudes. However, the conservatives, like the reformers, accepted peaceful, democratic change. They sought to come to power through the ballot box. The conservatives triumphed. They succeeded in driving deeper thinkers and politically more savvy and progressive figures like Abdel Moneim Abul Futuh out of the society.

Muhammad Mursi represented the second tier of the conservative wing. Nevertheless, during his year in office he did not make assertive efforts to use the presidency to Islamize Egyptian society. There was no concerted drive for the implementation of *Shari'ah*, although the issue did come up in discussions on the new constitution. There were numerous Brotherhood appointments to important governmental posts. Yet such a practice is standard everywhere when a new administration assumes power, although a government with only a very slim mandate should have exercised more restraint. Despite reasonable concerns about the placement of Brotherhood figures in key media and educational organizations, the national press and higher education under the Brothers were freer than under Mubarak, and infinitely more so than what the return of military rule would bring.

From the outset, Mursi worked within very strict constraints. The president was locked into both Camp David and the neoliberal economic order underwritten by the United States. American dominance of the Middle East region ensured that these economic and political frameworks would remain in place no matter who occupied the Egyptian presidency. The Brothers immediately signaled their compliance on both scores. Change that would benefit the mass of Egyptians would be difficult. In lieu of an alternative economic vision, the Mursi government concentrated, although without success, on finalizing an IMF loan as a passport for additional loans for investment and to plug the budget gap. The mass of Egyptians would have found their suffering increased even farther under such a solution, as Mursi realized. He therefore prolonged the negotiations by refusing to make concessions to the IMF that would have severely damaged the subsidy programs.

Even within these constraints, Mursi did find some room for maneuver. He was able to signal that a new orientation might just be possible. His earliest initiatives suggested that he might try to bring Egypt closer to the Islamic world. The president's first trip abroad took him to China, and not to the West, and he made a point to visit Teheran early in his presidency. Mursi actively courted the best possible relations with Turkey. He relaxed to the maximum degree the border pressures on the Palestinians. None of these gestures represented a substantial reorientation of Egyptian foreign policy, but they did signal that a change might well be possible over the longer term.

Domestically, Mursi never effectively controlled the army, the police, or the security apparatus. As with the Americans and Israelis in the foreign policy arena, he had little choice but to bow to superior power. The president signaled that the privileges of all of Egypt's military and security institutions would remain intact. Abuses of power by all three had long been an established part of Egyptian life. The abuses continued under Mursi, although at a lower level of intensity. Most egregious was the violence in Port Said during three days of protests that left forty-five dead, due to the disproportionate lethal force used by security forces.[22] Overall, the government hand, especially on freedom of expression, was somewhat lighter during that one year of Brotherhood governance than in the thirty years before.

Opportunities were missed. The president could have exposed the mystifying nonsense of an Egyptian "deep state." Deconstruct the concept of the deep state and you have a predatory and corrupt military, with massive and secret economic holdings, and a brutal police and security apparatus, supported by a bloated bureaucracy. An authoritarian ideology that the Egyptian people must be ruled by the rod justified this debilitating complex of structures. Mursi could have appealed directly to the people and explained honestly and openly just how retrograde these structures had become. At a minimum, he could have made clear in frank language just how little room for new initiatives he had. Many of his early supporters wondered what had become of the Mursi who, in a dramatic moment at the time of his inauguration celebration in Tahrir Square, had defied the assassins and opened his jacket to give his enemies a better target.[23] What happened to that creative spirit of defiance that knew instinctively how to express itself in a way the people could understand? What had become of the bold leader who, in one dramatic swoop, replaced the Mubarak-era generals with a new cohort? Mursi could have acted to do something, *anything* for the mass of poor Egyptians so that they could see signs that the president stood with them. There were some gestures to the lower middle class, notably some salary and minimum wage increases. There were also efforts to protect and even enhance the subsidies for bread, critical to the masses on the edge. They were simply not enough. Moreover, on the macro level, the economy suffered. Foreign currency reserves dropped precipitously and the government was unable to defend the Egyptian pound. It steadily lost value. Since Egypt now depends on imported food, including the wheat staple for bread, the poor suffered disproportionately as the prices of imports rose. So, too, did public sector companies and the workers they employed.

The president's hold on the people was slipping. Mursi was told all of these things by the wider array of Islamic and nationalist figures around him who were more in touch with society than his narrow inner circle of top Brotherhood figures. Mursi always listened politely, but he never acted. Even as his power slipped away, the president showed a complete lack of realism about just how tenuous his grip on the presidency really was. Instead of facing this reality and reaching out, he seemed to address himself more and more to the Brotherhood and less and less to *al Nas*.

All of these mistakes and missed opportunities took their toll. Any fair accounting of the Brotherhood experience must also acknowledge the dark forces of counter-revolution and reaction arrayed against Egypt's first democratically elected president. The army, the police, and the security structures actively conspired against the president. The business elite that had thrived under Mubarak and had gravitated to his son Gamal joined their efforts. Elements of the old statist regime welcomed any and all opportunities to obstruct the president. The oligarchs who financed the destabilization campaigns and supported the efforts of the mobilized young people of *Tamarod* have been only too glad to tell the world of their hand in deposing the Brotherhood president.[24]

Throughout Mursi's rule, the attacks by the opposition media on the Muslim Brothers were unrelenting, lacking in minimal journalistic standards and remarkably innocent of any factual basis. Mursi confronted a truly astounding range of conspirators, eager to bring him and the Brotherhood down. There was more. The judiciary, led by the Mubarak-era Supreme Constitutional Court, systematically reversed and undermined all attempts to build democratic institutions to fill the void created by the dark years of Mubarak's dictatorship. Finally, the very fact that Mursi came to power via the ballot box alarmed regional states, notably including the Emirates, Saudi Arabia, and Israel. They all feared a democratic contagion, although they masked that fear of democracy with useful but unfounded talk of the Brothers as terrorists.

From my Cairo apartment just outside of Tahrir Square, I got a look at garden-variety conspiracies close at hand. Years ago, I learned that the great Egyptian novelist Naguib Mahfouz walked each morning very early through the streets of the city while most Egyptians slept. I have followed suit, convinced that the morning walk stimulated Mahfouz's enormous talent. I concluded that a brisk morning walk held great hope for the improvement of my own writing; the logic seemed airtight. By the time I realized that it wasn't, and that no noticeable improvement in my writing had occurred, it was too late: I was hooked on very early morning meanderings through the streets of central Cairo. Through all the tumultuous events of the last several years, I have walked just about every morning when in Egypt. In the months before Mursi's ouster, the lines at gas stations seemed to start earlier each day and grow longer and longer by the time I doubled back to my apartment near the square. Then something wondrous happened for those beleaguered drivers: Within just a few days of Mursi's removal, gasoline deliveries resumed and gas returned to the stations in Cairo. The lines disappeared. In parallel fashion, my investment in a huge electrical surge protector for my apartment was rendered unnecessary, thanks again to unknown forces. The electricity that had shut down periodically and fluctuated dangerously during Mursi's year in power suddenly stabilized at a time when the military regime was cultivating popular support. Egypt's new military rulers brought with them the blessings of gasoline and electricity—although I have noticed that the lines started forming again in the early summer of 2014 and cuts in electricity have become more frequent as well.

Dark Days of August 2013

In the wake of the military action against the elected president on July 3, 2013, the Muslim Brothers and their supporters turned their demonstrations in public squares into occupations. They created Islamic communities of nonviolent resistance of men, women, and children, displaying generosity and compassionate care for each other. These were assemblies of ordinary Muslims. Food was prepared for hundreds, a respectful security system was created, crude sanitation facilities were set up, and makeshift medical clinics were established. The occupation continued for some fifty-five days, extending through Ramadan with communal *iftars*, prayers, and various celebratory programs, highlighting the talents of children.

The military responded on August 14, 2013 with utter brutality, slaughtering approximately nine hundred in Rabaa al Adawiyya and another eighty-seven in al Nahda squares. Whatever the final count of men, women, and children killed and maimed, the massacre is quite clearly, as Human Rights Watch proclaimed, the worst mass killing in Egypt's modern history. The regime had quite clearly committed a crime against humanity.[25] In their investigations, Human Rights Watch found less than twenty weapons among the some thirty thousand demonstrators. When the merciless onslaught came, the demonstrators were unable to defend themselves. Their defenselessness gives the lie to the stories of armed terrorists threatening the public order. Not surprisingly, official Egyptian and Arab human rights organizations in the wake of Mursi's deposing have lined up with the regime estimates of far fewer deaths and charges of crimes by the Brothers. They also put emphasis on the human rights violations that had occurred during Mursi's year in power. However, subsequent charges against the Brothers and the trials of members have been flagrantly evidence-free and scandalously unmindful of the most fundamental legal procedures. In the face of the vicious repression, the Brotherhood and a growing number of diverse supporters, on democracy and legitimacy grounds, continued to demonstrate across Cairo and around the country in the aftermath of the slaughter, demanding the end of military rule and the restoration of the legitimately elected president.

At the heart of all these events stands the battered, deeply flawed, yet resilient and nonviolent Muslim Brothers. All agree that the Brothers displayed a damaging unwillingness to work constructively with other trends. There is not, however, the slightest justification in the best academic studies for the persecution of the Brothers as terrorists.[26] Muhammad Mursi's presidency lasted only one year, undermined by mass dissatisfactions, serious mistakes by the inexperienced president, quite real plots, and the shallow commitment to democracy of secular elites. However, without the help of an arrogant and close-minded Brotherhood leadership and an inexperienced and poorly supported president, it is hard to believe that Egypt's democratic experiment could have been ended so easily. The Tunisian experience suggests as much and more.

Obstructions in Egypt, Openings in Tunisia

Outcomes in Tunisia are awkward for those who seek to read the end of politicized Islam into the disasters that have engulfed Egypt's Muslim Brothers. The overall upward ascent of the Islamic wave has created impressive alternative reserves. In its fourteen-century history, Islam has consistently displayed the capacity to respond to a setback in one context by creative initiatives in another, more favorable to those who raise the Islamic banner.

This broad pattern can be seen most recently in the context of the historic fourth surge of Islamic Renewal that began in the 1970s and continues to this day. Comparisons between the experiences of Tunisia and Egypt are illustrative. Constructive developments in Tunisia respond to the serious setbacks in Egypt. This complementarity should occasion no surprise. The connections between the two peoples and the two Islamic movements are multiple and longstanding. From the outset, experiences have been shared as well as awareness of the dangers confronting political parties with Islamic roots from powerful secular forces.[27] In October 2011, following the Tahrir revolution, a workshop was held in Istanbul for revolutionary activists, including representation from the Egyptian Muslim Brothers and the Tunisian Ennahda party. Discussing prospects for the transition to democracy, the participants identified two worrisome obstacles. They feared that remnants of the old regimes in both countries that remained entrenched in the military, police, judiciary, and bureaucracy would work to block revolutionary advances and undermine the democratically elected government. They also expressed apprehension that despite democratic rhetoric, the Obama administration and the EU would place their longstanding ties with authoritarian elites above the interests of the advocates for democracy. The military action against Mursi with American complicity and European vacillation confirmed the worst of these common fears.

In the face of these adversities, the Tunisian revolutionaries have quite remarkably managed to keep alive the promise of a democratic revolution and transition with a major role for the Islamic trend. Once again, diminutive Tunisia, with some ten million inhabitants and a mere 64,000 square miles, has made itself the source of outsized inspiration for all of *Dar al Islam*. Comparisons between Tunisia and Egypt are most often cast as the contrast between the Egyptian failure and the Tunisian success, but that framing distorts both experiences.

The January revolution in Egypt has historic importance worldwide. The Iranians produced the first mass revolution in the modern era that was not based on Western ideologies. Their achievement bore a distinctive Islamic stamp. It had its greatest impact in the Islamic world. Egyptians also drew in profound ways on their religious traditions, both Islamic and Christian, to give their January 25 revolutionary uprising spiritual depth. That meaning expressed itself in ways that transcended civilizational definitions. A revolution for "bread, freedom, and justice" could draw deeply on Islamic sources, but it could also speak for unbounded human aspirations. The Iranians in the end moved Muslims. The Egyptians, with their Tahrir Square revolutionary uprising, were widely seen to speak for human aspirations. Despite all the blood and pain of subsequent developments, Egyptians succeeded in making Tahrir Square in the heart of their beloved Cairo a symbol of an enlarged horizon of freedom for people everywhere. Only a short-sighted view would label such an experience a failure.

The paired notion of a Tunisian "success" also has problems. Unintentionally, it understates the difficulties of the struggles of the Tunisians. In Tunisia, there was no easy walk to freedom. There was nothing facile about the Tunisian story of a self-immolation that moved a small nation to seize its freedom from a corrupt tyrant. Daunting parallels, rather than simplified contrasts, should dominate comparative reflection on the revolutionary experiences of Egypt and Tunisia. For decades both countries were ruled by dictators who amassed overwhelming powers. Those repressive rulers enjoyed the unfailing support of major Western powers. Both created oppressive police states. Both the Egyptian and Tunisian public suffered from the effects of the neoliberal economic order the dictators enforced. The economic suffering of ordinary Tunisians bears comparison to that of the Egyptians. The Tunisians experienced as well political betrayals as opposition forces failed to coalesce and engaged in destructive infighting. Tunisians suffered the murders of key national political figures. In short, Tunisians, like Egyptians, faced barriers that should have been impassable.

At the same time, there were certain key differences. They went beyond Tunisia's small size and homogeneous population and proved decisive in shaping the very distinctive outcomes of these parallel freedom struggles. Most important was the political legacy of the strongman rulers and the character of the contending Islamic and secular successor trends. While both Mubarak and Ben Ali ruled dictatorially, their political legacies differ markedly. Mubarak presided over the systematic deconstruction of the Egyptian state and the purposeful elimination of any independent political life. By the end of his tenure, the progressive achievements of the Nasser era had been totally vitiated. The feeble openings to a more democratic order under Sadat were summarily ended as well. During the Mubarak era, national political structures like the parliament were systematically hollowed out. Elections were voided of any meaning. The press was corrupted and manipulated. The independent judiciary was brought to heel by the appointment of subservient judges. Tamed opposition political parties, with their aging and discredited leaderships, all but disappeared in the shadow of the ruling party. Two classes of oligarchs ruled the country. First were the top-ranked military and security officers, with their monopoly of force and huge stake in the economy. Second in line stood the extraordinarily wealthy and flagrantly corrupt businessmen who flourished under the American and IMF neoliberal economic regime that Mubarak enforced.

The Tunisian political inheritance was much richer. It owed a great deal to Habib Bourguiba. Although a dictator, Bourguiba combined authoritarian rule with genuinely progressive developments. Studying in Bourguiba's Tunisia in the 1960s, my wife and I were very aware of the pervasive presence of secret police and informers who numbered in the tens of thousands. They cast an unmistakable pall over public life. Political speech of even the mildest kind was criminalized. Yet we were also aware that authoritarianism did not tell the complete Bourguiba story. Under Bourguiba, Tunisia retained its Islamic character and Tunisians tenaciously preserved their Islamic identity. However, the government was insistently secular. The military was kept relatively small and placed firmly under civilian control. Tunisian secularists were unburdened by the cult of the "deep state" that cast a debilitating shadow over Egyptian political life. The Bourguiba regime accommodated a strong and independent labor movement with an organizational independence denied its Egyptian counterpart. It survived through the Ben Ali years. On the critical social fronts of women's rights, education, and health, Bourguiba built the foundations for a substantial middle class and resilient political institutions. Particularly noteworthy is the 1956 Charter of Personal Status. This remarkable document enhanced women's personal rights by abolishing polygamy, establishing a minimum age for marriage, and enabling women to initiate divorce proceedings. Beyond these matters of family law, the charter advanced women's legal equality with men and explicitly ensured their right to education. These achievements survived the efforts of Bourguiba's successor, Ben Ali, to dismantle them. Tunisians were able to mount their 2011 revolution on more solid social and political ground.

Revolutionary politics in both Egypt and Tunisia was dominated by a core clash of Islamic and secular trends. Yet again important differences marked the two experiences. There were important contrasts in both the context for action and the character of the respective political actors. Egypt is a major country that borders Israel. The West, particularly the United States, has consistently blocked or undermined its development and regional power aspirations. The aim, as with Iraq and Iran, is to keep such potentially influential states as weak and divided as possible. Tunisia, in contrast, is small, with far less impact on and importance to regional power politics, so it can safely be left alone to develop an independent political model, with no perceived risks for the United States or Israel.

In Tunisia, the actors on both sides of the Islamic–secular confrontation were also in some ways more experienced and sophisticated as political players. Tunisia's Islamic trend was dominated by the Ennahda party and its impressive leader, Rashid al Ghannouchi, rightly regarded as a herald of the Islamic Renewal. Ghannouchi's party was originally inspired by the Muslim Brothers, and Ghannouchi has consistently recognized the major historical contributions of the Brotherhood. However, Ghannouchi's understanding of Islam has evolved in ways more progressive than the Brothers and closer to the thinking of Egypt's New Islamic trend. Ghannouchi has maintained multiple ties with New Islamic thinkers, notably including Yusuf al Qaradawi and Salim al Awa. Although Ghannouchi is not an Islamic scholar by training, he is a member of the International Union of Muslim Scholars headed by Qaradawi. In more recent years, Ghannouchi has been impressed as well by the advances in democratic practice and economic development by Turkey's ruling Justice and Development Party (AKP) of Prime Minister Recep Tayyip Erdogan, although his enthusiasm has cooled with the signs of authoritarianism in Turkey. Ennahda has displayed an impressive capacity to act effectively on the ground. The party has also demonstrated the wisdom not to push that advantage to humiliate and alarm other political forces.

Under Ghannouchi's leadership the party has demonstrated an understanding of democracy that entails more than the elemental principles of majority rule and transfer of power through the ballot box. To win broad support, a democratic order also has to guarantee fundamental freedoms that make the political rights and political participation meaningful. Most importantly, democrats must find ways to respond creatively to the historic strength of the civilian secular trend in Tunisia. Tunisian secularists had confidence in their weight and popular support, sufficient to deal with the Islamic movement, even in the face of the substantial electoral strength the movement immediately showed. In this regard, the contrast with the Egyptian secularists is striking. Despite the long years of persecution and the exile of its leading figures, Ennahda had rebuilt its ground organization in the wake of Ben Ali's overthrow. Almost immediately, Ennahda demonstrated great strength in electoral contests at all levels. Tunisia's secularists monitored every move of the Islamists that might infringe on the character of Tunisian society. They responded quickly and forcefully when the Islamists raised the slogan of the implementation of Shari'ah or questioned the advances that women had made. Secular forces retained confidence that they could respond effectively to any excesses of the Islamic party and act to correct their infringements on the delicate balance between Islamic and secular influences that Tunisia had achieved.

When the Islamic movement came to power in Tunisia, there were miscalculations. The party did not take adequate steps to signal that power would be shared. Ennahda, as governing party, should have included more leftists in its first cabinet to reflect leftist strength in parliament. The party also failed to take adequate steps to rein in the Salafis and extremist militias at the neighborhood level who were prone to violence. At times, Ennahda politicians themselves indulged in rhetorical excesses against secularist political actors. Meanwhile, economic conditions deteriorated with Ennahda in power, and the party leadership showed no great skill in managing the economy. Most devastating for the stability of the country was the assassination of two popular secular political figures by extremists. Secularists responded with anger and determination not to tolerate such violence. There were large demonstrations and clashes in the streets. Tunisia appeared to be moving in the dismal direction that had almost destroyed neighboring Algeria in the long years of its bloody civil war between 1991 and 2000.

Then, the completely unexpected happened: Political leaders on both sides compromised. Most dramatic was a series of unprecedented concessions by the Islamic movement under Ghannouchi's leadership. Early efforts to change the language of "equality" of men and women to "complementarity" were abandoned. During the discussions to draft the constitution, Ennahda dropped the drive for the inclusion of references to Shari'ah as the source for Tunisian law. In the new constitution, Tunisia was described as a free state, with Arabic its language and Islam its religion. There was to be no mention of *Shari'ah*. The Ennahda leadership accepted this formulation, despite the opposition of much of its base.

In the wake of the widespread disturbances caused by a second political assassination, Ghannouchi went still further. He did the unthinkable: Ennahda turned over power peacefully to a technocratic government and returned to the status of the loyal Islamic opposition. Clearly, the movement leadership had placed the well-being of Tunisia above that of the Islamic movement. While Mursi had seemed to turn from the Egyptian people to the Brotherhood in the face of such controversies, Ghannouchi moved in exactly the opposite direction with a stunning show of pragmatic wisdom. Militants in the Tunisian Islamic movement mounted their most serious assault on Ghannouchi for these compromises, accusing him of "trading in religion" to retain a leadership role in the power game. In the end, Ghannouchi's long years of persecution and decades of exile under Ben Ali gave him the stature to withstand the attacks. He carried the party with him.

The spirit of the grand compromise enabled the constitutional process to go forward. Debates were tumultuous, and memories of political violence that took the lives of two secular leaders were fresh. The possibility that the entire constitutional project would collapse remained very real—but it did not. Ghannouchi was crystal clear in his analysis of what had, in the end, been accomplished and how. "Tunisians," he explained, "have committed to the establishment of a pioneering model of political partnership between moderate secularists and moderate Islamists." He identified the key to the success, noting that "bringing together the center in this way helped us adopt a constitution in January [2014] with the backing of an astounding 94% of the national assembly." Ghannouchi, rightly, described the constitution as "among the most progressive in the Arab world."

In Egypt, these same issues of the role of *Shari'ah*, the rights of women, and the character of state and society had driven a fateful wedge between the Brothers and Salafis, on the one hand, and their secular opponents on the other. The Egyptian Islamic journalist Fahmi Huwaidi bluntly pronounced that Ennahda was paying attention to the unity of the nation, whereas in Egypt the Islamic movement gave priority to the gains of the Brotherhood. Forthrightly, Huwaidi pronounced that the Muslim Brothers "should have been smart enough" to see the danger to the nation, admit their mistake, and treat other trends in a more inclusive and less divisive way.[28] Concessions should have been made, Huwaidi argued. Instead, the Brotherhood leadership focused on clinging to power gains at the expense of the unity of the nation. In his reflection on the astuteness of Ghannouchi's unprecedented compromise, Huwaidi invoked Qur'anic values. Contrasting developments in Tunisia and Egypt, he told his readers, reminded him of the Qur'anic story of Moses and the Golden Calf, recounted in *surah* Ta Ha. This *surah* raises the difficult issues of compromise and priorities. Islam's worldly character, in the view of New Islamist thinkers like Huwaidi, means unavoidable confrontation of the dilemma faced when values are in conflict yet decisions must be made. As human beings go about the business of "building the world," the issues they confront are not all about the clear conflict between good and evil; at times, choices must be made between two goods or between lesser evils. Yusuf al Qaradawi, whom Huwaidi cites, has written extensively of such value conflicts and the pragmatic, situational wisdom they demand. Muslims, Qaradawi insists, need a *fiqh* of priorities to help them navigate such dilemmas.

Huwaidi retells the relevant Qur'anic story in some detail. Moses was called by God to leave his people, the Israelites, in the care of his brother, Harun, to receive guidance from God. He was ordered by God to fast for thirty days. He advised his people accordingly. At the end of the thirty days, Moses broke his fast by eating the leaves of a plant to sweeten his breath. God then ordered him to fast for an additional ten days. When he returned to his people, Moses found that the Israelites had lost patience due to his delayed return to them. They had turned away from worshipping God and began worshipping the Golden Calf.

A deeply angered Moses chastised Harun for breaking his trust and failing to safeguard his word to God. Harun responded that he tried to persuade the people to desist but could persuade only a small number. Although he was aware of the seriousness of their transgression, Harun feared that if he pushed the matter and caused a split among the people, he would be subject to the reproach of his brother for dividing the Israelites. Harun had given priority to the unity of the Israelites. Huwaidi judged that in his "deeds of righteousness" that avoided civil war in Tunisia and preserved the unity of the Tunisians, Ghannouchi too had understood the pragmatic importance of the *fiqh* of priorities.[29] He put the unity of Tunisia first.

Tunisia's secularists managed to reach agreement on the basis of Ghannouchi's compromise. They cooperated with the Islamic trend in producing a model constitution, thus laying the groundwork for a successful political transition to a democratic Tunisia. The secularists demonstrated their own political maturity by accepting activists of the Islamic movement as legitimate political actors. They did not press for a ban on their political participation, or worse, as happened in Egypt with such disastrous results. Ghannouchi could find in Islam the basis for principled compromise. The Tunisian secularists, for their part, reaffirmed a strong commitment to democratic principles that they extended to the Islamic movement. In a major address to the United Nations General Assembly in the fall of 2014 on terrorism and the means to counter it effectively, the American president singled out this historic success of Tunisians. Obama stated clearly and simply that Tunisia had given the world an example of the kind of positive change "where secular and Islamist parties worked together through a political process to produce a new constitution."[30]

As remarkable as this constitutional achievement was, it did not mark the end of Tunisia's historic achievements. In October 2014, with a democratic constitution in place, Tunisians held their second free and fair elections. For the first time, an Arab Muslim people had executed a successful democratic transition. Tunisians registered a political triumph that should be considered the single most important political event in the Arab Islamic world in the modern era. In Tunisia, in the context of intense citizen involvement, *al Nas* and a political leadership formed by both Islamic and secular trends achieved a successful democratic transition. The promise of freedom of the Arab uprising was not illusory after all.

The contrast with Egypt could not have been more painful. The Ennahda compromise had spared Tunisians the hysteria and despair that had gripped Egyptians who, in large numbers, had turned to the military to remove their democratically elected Muslim Brotherhood president and install yet another Arab military dictatorship. The Tunisian triumph did not, of course, belong to the Islamic trend alone: The disparate secular forces in Tunisia, including leftist nationalists, progressives of various stripes, and former officials, had coalesced for the elections to form the successful Nidaa Tounes party. Ennahda assumed the role of democratic opposition and normalized the democratic transition. Ghannouchi drew the obvious and most important lesson from the Tunisian experience: "Despite what some believe, there is no 'Arab exception' to democracy, nor is there any inherent contradiction between democracy and Islam." To be sure, Tunisia's young democracy still faced daunting challenges, not least those of a failing economy and massive unemployment among the young. Both the Islamic and secular trends recognized these daunting challenges and the need for support to meet them. Ghannouchi, for his part, expressed appreciation for "President Obama's positive citation of Tunisia in his speech before the United Nations in September." However, with the American role in Egypt clearly in mind, Ghannouchi added pointedly that "support for our democracy must come both in words and action. The West cannot return," he added for emphasis, "to the era when it perceived an illusory trade-off between stability and democracy." The leader of the loyal democratic opposition in Tunisia concluded "that long-term stability cannot exist if our people are disenfranchised, our institutions monopolized and our youth disempowered. The choice between stability and democracy is false."[31]

Islam, the "River of Life," had found its way to both countries in turmoil. Islam had made itself a presence in both Egypt and Tunisia. Still, it was up to the "the builders of the world" to make the most of the opportunities Islam created. Neither success nor failure was preordained. We know little about how this "River of Life" works its effect. The only thing we do know with some certainty is that the "River of Life" is not running dry. Clearly, any effort to gauge its effects must do so with a broad lens. Perhaps the greatest mistake of observers is to narrow the focus for the sake of detailed studies. However, the interconnections that give *Dar al Islam* coherence may mean that the real drivers or inspiration of events in one site may well originate in some more distant part of *Dar al Islam*. No one incarnation can encompass the "River of Life." Multiple incarnations coexist, and they may be complementary or contradictory. Islamic civilization, Muhammad al Ghazzali pronounced, invented pluralism and has thrived because of it. This multiplicity of expressions, all recognized as authentic, provides the resources for Islam's extraordinary powers of absorption and adaptation.[32] It exercises those powers while remaining everywhere and always Islam. Such was the lesson of the contrasting outcomes of Islamic parties in power in Egypt and Tunisia.

Humility in Knowledge of Islam

We should avoid making easy generalizations about the fate of politicized Islam and about the character of Islam itself. Clearly, we should write and speak of Islam with humility. Goethe, that Western sage and mystic, may have overstated the case when he pronounced that "a man doesn't learn to understand anything unless he loves it."[33] There is something to the notion: Without at least empathy, understanding others different from ourselves will remain out of reach. To the degree that Goethe is right, the quest for understanding of Islam should pass through those who have come to love Islam and have made it a presence in their lives. Only in this way can we hope to catch a glimpse of what the faith means to those believers who act for Islam. It is only Muslims and others who love Islam who can feel what the "River of Life" means for any age. There is no pathway around believing Muslims or behind their backs to direct knowledge of Islam. Their experiences, their observations, and their representations of the faith cannot be ignored in any serious attempt to understand Islam in God's world.

Islamic scholars know that God has spoken only once for Islam with the Word of the Holy Qur'an. Determination of the meaning of that Word for particular Muslims is always the demanding work of the human mind and the heart. As the Qur'an makes clear, such has always been God's high expectation of humanity. Scholars also know that God sent the Prophet Muhammad as an exemplar of what it can mean to live the way that the "River of Life" makes possible. However, the Prophet's struggles and resolutions of the challenges he faced cannot substitute for the strivings of other Muslims in other times and places to bring Islam into their lives and communities in ways suited to their own circumstances. The "River of Life" did not divulge the secrets of its life-giving, uplifting powers once and for all through the Prophet's example. The Qur'an instructs that, by God's design, there are no such secrets. The closest we can come are the diverse stories and distinctive reflections of those who have drunk deeply from the waters of the "River of Life" and learned to love the life its generative powers make possible.

Those who look to the river with the hubris to think they will learn its secrets risk falling into the trap of seeing only their own reflection on the surface of its waters. A great deal of what is taken to be knowledge of Islam in the West has this character of seductive self-reflection. Misplaced certainties about the nature of Islam more often than not represent little more than revelations of self. The Greek myth of Narcissus should be required reading for the army of Western commentators on Islam. Narcissus was a hunter of striking beauty, but his exorbitant pride in his appearance expressed itself in utter disdain for all those who loved him. He spurned the love of a gentle nymph who did not survive his insensitive rejection. As divine punishment, Narcissus was made to fall in love with his own reflection in a pool. He was so smitten by what he saw that he did not realize that he was merely looking at his own image. Unable either to consummate this love or to leave the perfection of his own image, Narcissus wasted away to death.[34] The myth conveys a haunting warning against the perils of deadly self-absorption.

A seductive thread runs through a great deal of the Western work on Islam. It has little to do with commonalities and everything to do with scarcely concealed hostility. So much of the literature is simply an excuse for invidious comparison and mindless preening. The struggle to know more about Islam means abandoning the narcissistic pleasure of "mirror" literature that is really all about us. We pretend to be writing about Islam, but in reality we lovingly search out every flaw and every inequity in *Dar al Islam* and use it as a background to show up the absolute perfection of our own culture and historical trajectory, turning studies of Islam into the most flattering of mirrors.

To gain even a modicum of understanding of Islam and of the momentous events in *Dar al Islam* we need windows and doors, not beguiling mirrors. Astonishingly, the most important such windows and doors are willfully kept closed. Islam cannot give interviews or have conversations. Only Muslims can talk to us. Yet the assumption is pervasive that what Muslims say has little to do with what they mean and what they will do. There is no point in listening. Nor is reading what Islamic scholars write worth the effort. The educated Muslim classes know our most important thinkers. They read the books of our most distinguished intellectuals. Only rarely do even Western scholars who are specialized in the Middle East return the gesture of intellectual respect. The very notion is unthinkable to pundits and instant media experts. Of course, neither a single Muslim nor even a group of Muslims can speak for all of the world's billion and a half Muslims. However, individual Muslims can tell us of their own direct experience of Islam. Experiences will vary widely. Some will have drunk deeply from the "River of Life" and Islam will have found its way to the very core of who they are. Others simply live on lands watered by the "River of Life." For them Islam is simply one thread among the many that define their life patterns. Their story of Islam will be quite different, but it will be no less important for that.

To gain knowledge of Islam, we must interact with Muslims. Those who would know them need to come to such interactions with an open responsiveness and with a clear sense that brothers and sisters who have taken a different path are worthy of our respect and attention. Ibn Battuta, for all his personal indulgences and hyperbole, provides a far more instructive model than our own Christopher Columbus. Admittedly, exchanges in a spirit of open responsiveness to what others can teach us are difficult, especially for those who come from a country that considers itself "the indispensable nation." It is hard to look beyond such a splendid self, but the myth of Narcissus warns of the dangers of losing the capacity to love others and learn from their experiences.

Yet perhaps Goethe demands too much. Love is not easy; it does not come by command, and the responsive openness to others that love requires proves especially difficult for the powerful. Michel Foucault has offered a useful minimalist strategy. It is more within reach but actually would accomplish a great deal. Foucault remarks that "the question of Islam as a political force is an essential question for our time and will be for many years to come." With the utmost reasonableness, he then adds that "the first condition for treating it with a minimum of intelligence is that one not begin with hatred."[35]

Today, the landscape in key parts of *Dar al Islam* is bleak, characterized by violence and ignorance. Circumstances are so dire that frequent speculation arises about Islam's end. There are investigations of what would come after Islam, about what a world without Islam would look like. In such dark days, it might help to recall that those who give us authoritative characterizations of that landscape of despair and those who seek to monitor Islam's fate in the world by the usual military, political, and economic measures have always missed the real sources of its strength. They have always gotten it wrong. Islam's improbable and elusive power resides in the capacity to foster deep commitments from ordinary people. Those commitments are woven into the sense ordinary Muslims develop of who they are and what they can do.

These profound attachments of ordinary Muslims in the millions give Islam its startling capacity for reform and renewal, even in the face of devastating reversals. Ordinary Muslims rise from the ruins to make themselves the authors of extraordinary things. Islam itself demonstrates over and over its remarkable resilience.

The River Moves On

The narrative of Islam in God's world opens in this book with the observation that in the modern era Muslim peoples have endured a period of relative weakness and decline by all the usual measures of power and prosperity. Yet Islam itself has gone from strength to strength. For decades this great contradiction has loomed with no resolution or even understanding of its import. The Islamic world did not experience the death of God. Islamic intellectuals did not share the pervasive sense in the West that the grand narratives of human history had come to an end. Quite the contrary, a fourth great surge of Islamic Renewal has been sweeping through Islamic lands since the 1970s, although the West has barely taken notice. In contrast, the response across *Dar al Islam* has been electrifying: Hundreds of millions are feeling anew the power of God's Word and a heightened sense of connection to the *ummah* it had created.

Al Nas understands that Islam's fate cannot be read from outcomes of the political history of Muslims, whether assembled in empires, states, or movements. The successes and failures of such groupings of Muslims tell precious little about the future of Islam itself. They are worldly chronicles whose denouements have most to do with leadership, strategic vision, and political capacities, as the recent experience of the Muslim Brothers in Egypt indicates. They are best understood in those circumscribed political and social terms.

Islam's story unfolds in a very different register. It is always and everywhere the story of the values and higher purposes of the Qur'an. Jesus, the Savior of Christianity, returned to his Father in heaven. The Holy Qur'an, however, remained on Earth to provide guidance for humanity's spiritual and worldly struggles. This difference is crucial for all that has come from the Message of Islam. Islam inspires humanity, articulates values and purposes, and sets limits. It is not implicated in outcomes. The story of Islam in the world has no predetermined ending. Islam carries no authoritarian or theocratic gene. The manner in which Islam itself manifests itself is always open-ended and pluralistic.

The Qur'an alone speaks in Islam's name. Mosques and movements can contribute in extraordinary ways to the life of the *ummah*. They can also be captured and corrupted. The Message is secure only when safely ensconced in the hearts and minds of millions of ordinary Muslims. Addressed to *al Nas*, the Qur'an gives divine voice to values and higher purposes to guide an imperfect humanity. Islamic thought differs from philosophical thought in that its first premises originate from God rather than human reason or imagination. However, it is similar in that, like any system of thought, its elements are all related and developed from its first premises. Islam in God's world is understood to come to humanity from the general to give meaning to the particular, from the absolute to guide the relative, from the fixed to govern the changeable, from the permanent to rule the temporary.[36]

Carried by the "River of Life," the contemporary Islamic Renewal relies on the spiritual power of Islam itself to guide humanity in these ways. Islam made its first worldly appearance in a bleak landscape in seventh-century Arabia characterized by ignorance, violence, and war. The Message came from God. It addressed *al Nas* of Arabia and beyond. Through fourteen centuries a flawed humanity has responded. At best, there have been partial realizations of the Call to justice, equality, and freedom. There is always more work to be done, always yet another channel to widen, and always one more course to open. Today the obstacles to Islamic Renewal include daunting repression and destructive foreign interventions. The challenges include as well the terrible distortions by criminal extremist groups. The misdeeds of this minority are used to justify the campaigns of hatred and demonization that are regularly mounted against Islam itself.

Today the "River of Life" is making its way through a tumultuous landscape that is scarred yet again by ignorance, violence, and war. Yet not all the tumult generates despair. Against the odds, *al Nas* in Tunisia have bravely spoken and acted effectively for justice, equality, and freedom. Their success stands, however, against the powerful negative trends that dominate in *Dar al Islam*. Hope for the future resides in the knowledge that Islam made its first appearance in the world in just such difficult circumstances. The adversity of those initial circumstances paradoxically served to highlight Islam's inherent strength and promise. Nascent Islam's ability to rise above those circumstances and create an advanced and creative civilization continues today to inspire Muslims everywhere. As Muhammad Abduh explained: "How splendid is the wisdom of God in revealing the nature of Islam. Islam appeared as a River of Life, welling up in the barren desert of Arabia."[37]

Glossary

'adl justice

'alim (pl. *'ulema*) Islamic scholar

amir leader of a politicized and often militant Islamic group

'aqida doctrine; the Arabic word connotes that which is held onto, binds, knots, fixes firmly

'aql mind

asabiyya high energy and group cohesiveness

Ashura day of mourning in Shi'i Islam for the martyrdom of Hussein, the Prophet's grandson

ayah sign from God; verse of the Qur'an

Dar al Islam the Islamic world

da'wah the call to Islam

faqih (pl. *faqihs*) an Islamic scholar, specially trained and recognized by peers as qualified to contribute to *fiqh*; commonly but misleading translated as "jurisprudent"

fatwa (pl. *fatwas*) religious opinion by an Islamic scholar

fiqh Islamic legal reasoning, based on interpretation of Qur'an and *Sunnah*; the work of trained specialists known as *faqihs* (q.v.); subject to challenge and correction as a fully human endeavor. In Western scholarship, this is commonly translated as "Islamic law"; however, centrist Islamic scholars would likely regard this translation as misleading and an understatement of its scope.

gallabeyya a traditional long and loose garment, native to the Nile Valley

gariya (pl. *gawari*) bonded female servant who could be bought and sold

ghulam bonded male servant who could be bought and sold

gizya the tax on non-Muslims, provided for by a contract according to which they were exempted from military service and received protection and legal rights

hadith (pl. *hadiths*) sayings of the Prophet that illuminate his thoughts and actions, accompanied by their sources; term is interchangeable with *Sunnah*, although some scholars argue there are fine distinctions in usage

hajj pilgrimage to Mecca, held annually and prescribed for all Muslims once in their lifetime *hakemeyya or hakemeyyet Allah* God's rule

halal religiously permitted

haraba war against civilization

haram religiously forbidden

hegab headscarf

hikma wisdom

hudud punishments provided for in *Shari'ah*

iftar (pl. *iftars*) 'breakfast' meal to break Ramadan fast

ijtihad interpretation (i.e., an effort of interpretation of the sacred texts)

islah reform

istikhlaf the divine call to humanity to act as God's regent on Earth

ittisalat connectedness

jahilliyya the pre-Islamic age of ignorance

jihad struggle for the faith in both spiritual and physical senses

al jihad al kabir the great jihad or personal struggle to be a better person

al jihad al sughayir the lesser struggle to defend the community

khalifa man as God's regent on Earth

khawaga foreigner in long-term residence

khums payment of one fifth of acquired wealth

ma'asum infallible

marja' (pl. *maraji'*) the highest rank of authority among Shi'a religious scholars

marja' al-taqlid the "source of emulation" to which the faithful turn for guidance on religious and other matters

marja'iyya collective of *maraji*

maslaha 'amma the common good

mufti an Islamic scholar qualified to issue a religious opinion or *fatwa*

mugadid an Islamic scholar who is thought to appear every century to renew Islam

al mujta'a al ahaly communal society

mustakhlifun those charged to act as God's regent on Earth

naqba presence

al Nas humanity, the common people

niqab face veil

qadi judge who decides cases in accord with *Shari'ah*

rahal (pl. *rahala*) traveler

riba usury

sadaqa divine reward

shaikh a trained religious teacher or guide; entitled, for example, to give the Friday sermon

Shari'ah the provisions from Qur'an and *Sunnah* to regulate human behavior. In Western scholarship, this is commonly translated as "Islamic law," but midstream Islamic scholars would likely regard this translation as misleading.

sherif (pl. *sherifs*) descendant of the Prophet Muhammad

shumeleyya comprehensiveness

shura consultation

sillat connectedness

Sunnah all the deeds and words of the Prophet; the second source of Islam after the Qur'an; term is interchangeable with *hadiths*, although some scholars argue there are fine distinctions in usage

surah (pl. *surahs*) chapter of the Qur'an

al Tagdid al Islami the Islamic Renewal

takfir declaring Muslims to be unbelievers

takhlif the divine trust to humanity to live life in accordance with God's laws, calling for righteous deeds and action against evil

talab al 'ilm travel in search of knowledge

ta'lim formal schooling

taqiyya dissimulation

tarbeyya proper upbringing

tariqa (pl. *turuq*) a school or order of Sufism

tarshid guidance

tawhid the Islamic belief in the oneness of God

ummah Islamic community

'umra recommended but not prescribed pilgrimage to Mecca at times other than the *hajj*

waqf (pl. *awqaf*) Islamic endowment

Wassatteyya the centrist Islamic midstream

wilaya a historical and therefore not binding concept of rule that precludes the rule of women and non-Muslims

wilayet al faqih rule of the *faqih*; the Iranian system of government in which a leading Shi'i religious leader exercises absolute authority

wusuli opportunistic

zakat religious obligation owed to support those in need

zawiya a small, informal mosque

zhikr Sufi ritual of remembrance of God, marked by collective chanting and swaying body movements

zimmi "protected" non-Muslim people subject to a covenant according to which they were exempted from military service and received protection and legal rights, in return for which they paid a special tax called the *gizya*

Notes

CHAPTER I

1. For earlier treatments of some of the themes that drew on this chapter, see "The Paradox of Islam's Future," ed. Daniel Byman and Marlena Mantas, *Religion, Democracy, and Politics in the Middle East* (New York: The Academy of Political Science, 2012), 197–239.

2. Tareq al Bishri, *The General Features of Contemporary Islamic Political Thought* (Cairo: Dar al Sharuq, 1996), 11, 60, and 61. (Arabic)

3. Max Weber, *The Protestant Ethic and the Spirit of Capitalism*, trans. Talcott Parsons (New York: Charles Scribner, 1958), 47.

4. Ahmed Fuad Negm endlessly affirmed his love of colloquial Arabic and pronounced it the finest expression of the spirit of the Egyptian people and one of their greatest cultural achievements.

5. Alija Ali Izetbegovic, *Islam between East and West* (Indianapolis, IN: American Trust Publications, 1993). See especially Chapter 11, 271–286. Fahmi Huwaidi frequently drew attention to Izetbegovic's work; see, for example, *al Ahram*, February 7, 1995, and *al Ahram*, September 17, 1996.

6. Chapter 5 of this book provides a study of Ibn Battuta's revealing travels through Islamic networks in the fourteenth century.

7. "Love and Insight." [Online]. Available: https://notes.utk.edu/Bio/greenberg .nsf/f5b2cbf2a827c0198525624b00057d30/4a623ac9eba9e88685257aa90083 ce10?OpenDocument. [September 12, 2014].

8. Fahmi Huwaidi has done the most to familiarize his readers with the parallels between midstream Islam and philosophical American pragmatism. See *al Ahram*, September 17, 1996, for an illustrative example.

9. Qur'an 49:13, 2:3.

10. See Ali Shariati, *Religion vs. Religion*, trans. Laleh Bakhtiar (Chicago: ABC International Group, 2000).

11. The most detailed treatment can be found in Chapter 8.
12. Mark Taylor, *The Moment of Complexity: Emerging Network Culture* (Chicago: University of Chicago Press, 2001).
13. Angel Rabasa et al., *Building Moderate Muslim Networks* (Santa Monica, CA: Rand Corporation, 2007).
14. Albert Hourani, *Arabic Thought in the Liberal Age, 1798–1939* (Cambridge: Cambridge University Press, 1962), 33.
15. The Tahrir Revolution is treated in Chapter 10.
16. Muhammad al Ghazzali, *Women's Issues between Rigid and Alien Traditions* (Cairo: Dar al Shuruq, 1994). (Arabic)

CHAPTER 2

1. Muhammad al Ghazzali, *The Bombshell of the Truth* (Damascus: Dar al Dustur, 2002), 9. (Arabic)
2. Imam Muslim, *Sahih Muslim, The Book of Faith*, trans. Abdul Hamid Siddiqui. [Online]. Available: http://theonlyquran.com/hadith/Sahih-Muslim/?volume=1&chapter=66 [September 26, 2014].
3. The phrase "Islam itself" is used frequently by Muhammad al Ghazzali in various Arabic formulations. See, for example, *Renew Your Life*, ninth edition (Cairo: Nahdit Masr, 2005), 8, 10. (Arabic)
4. For a literary exploration of the Western culture of violence and its impact on the Arab world, see Tayeb Saleh, *Season of Migration to the North* (Boulder, CO: Lynne Rienner, 1997), 3.
5. See Peter Nichols, "The Struggle to Ban Chemical Weaponry: Lessons from World War I to the Present." [Online]. Available: http://globalresearch.ca/articles/CHU407A.html [September 11, 2014].
6. *Famous Quotes*. [Online]. Available: http://www.famousquotes.com/author/winston-churchill/5 [September 11, 2014].
7. See Nichols, "The Struggle."
8. Cited by Eqbal Ahmad, *The Selected Writings of Eqbal Ahmad* (New York: Columbia University Press, 2006), 54.
9. Historical background from E. San Juan, *US Imperialism and Revolution in the Philippines* (New York: Palgrave, 2007); see also quotation from Nima Shirazi, "Bleak News, but Vital for Us to Understand: American Morlocks: Another Civilian Massacre and the Savagery of Our Soldiers" [Online]. Available: http://fabiusmaximus.com/2012/03/17/36583// [September 26, 2014].
10. "The Benevolent Assimilation Proclamation." [Online]. Available: http://www.historywiz.com/primarysources/benevolentassimilation [July 3, 2013].
11. General James Rusling, "Interview with President William McKinley," *The Christian Advocate*, January 22, 1903.

12. Cited in John Bellamy Foster and Robert W. McChesney, "Review: *Kipling, the "White Man's Burden," and U.S. Imperialism.*" Rev. November 2003. [Online]. Available: http://monthlyreview.org/2003/11/01/kipling-the-white-mans-burden-and-u-s-imperialism/ [October 17, 2014].

13. Norman Soloman, "Mark Twain Speaks to Us: 'I Am an Anti-Imperialist,'" *Common Dreams*, April 15, 2003. [Online]. Available: http://www.iefd.org/manifestos/anti_imperialist_twain.php [September 26, 2014].

14. See the succinct treatment, with quotation, in David Waines, *An Introduction to Islam* (Cambridge: Cambridge University Press, 2003), 214.

15. See Theodore H. Von Laue, *The World Revolution of Westernization: The Twentieth Century in Global Perspective* (Oxford: Oxford University Press, 1987), 160–164.

16. Ghazzali, *Bombshell*, 6. (Arabic)

17. See Tareq al Bishri, *The General Features of Contemporary Islamic Political Thought* (Cairo: Dar al Sharuq, 1996), 52–58. (Arabic)

18. For a discussion of these groups as a reaction to the traumatic abolition of the caliphate, see Muhammad al Ghazzali, *The Bitter Truth* (Cairo: Ahram, 1993), 63. (Arabic)

19. Richard Mitchell, *The Society of the Muslim Brothers* (Oxford: Oxford University Press, 1993), 8.

20. Cited in Mitchell, *The Society*, 1.

21. Cited in Mitchell, *The Society*, 6.

22. Cited in Mitchell, *The Society*, 30.

23. Cited in Roger Hardy, "Islamism: Why the West Gets It Wrong," *The Guardian*. Rev. March 20, 2010. Online: http://www.theguardian.com/commentisfree/belief/2010/mar/16/islamism-west-muslim-brotherhood [October 16, 2014].

24. Muhammad al Ghazzali, *Culture among the Muslims* (Cairo: Dar al Sharuq, 2010), 223. (Arabic)

25. See, for example, Hassan al Banna, "Tract of the Fifth Conference," *Collected Tracts of the Imam Martyr Hasan al-Banna* (Cairo: Dar al-Shihab, n.d.), 169; cited by Roel Meijer, "The Muslim Brotherhood and the Political: An Exercise in Ambiguity." [Online]. Rev. January 7.

26. Cited in Ammar Ali Hassan, "Rising to the Occasion," *Al-Ahram Weekly*, December 19, 2012.

27. Sayyid Qutb, *Milestones* (Damascus: Dar al Ilm, n.d.).

28. Tareq al Bishri provided a nuanced view of Qutb as a serious Islamic intellectual who made important contributions. At the same time, he contrasted Qutb's attitude of withdrawing from, condemning, and attacking society unfavorably to Banna's work to connect with and strengthen society. See Bishri, *General Features*, 31–33 and 40–41.

29. An appreciation for the necessity of force and "physical power" to build the Islamic society runs through Qutb's later work. See especially *Milestones*, 55, 63, 96, and 80.

30. A General Guide of the Muslim Brotherhood is given as the author of a book intended to discredit the thinking of Sayyid Qutb, although the book is clearly a collective effort. See Hassan al Hudeibi, *Callers Not Judges* (Cairo: Dar al tauzir wa al Nashr al Islammiyya, 1977). (Arabic)

31. Qutb, *Milestones*, 11–12.

32. On opposition to theocracy, see Qutb, *Milestones*, 58, 85; on servitude to man-made systems, 45.

33. Cited in Paul Berman, *Terror and Liberalism* (New York: W. W. Norton & Co., 2003), 75.

34. Sayyid Qutb, *In the Shade of the Qur'an* (Cairo: Dar al Sharuq, 1992), vol. 3, p. 282.

35. Sayyid Qutb, *Social Justice in Islam*, trans. B. Hardie and Hami Algar (New York: Islamic Publications International, 2000), 83.

36. The fullest discussion of Qutb's mentorship of the military figures who spearheaded the 1952 coup comes in an al Jazeera documentary of Qutb's life. [Online]. Available: https://www.youtube.com/watch?v=CwcJ_n0F7uE [October 2, 2014].

37. Qutb, *In the Shade of the Qur'an.*

38. See John Calvert, *Sayyid Qutb and the Origins of Radical Islamism* (New York: Columbia University Press, 2010); James Toth, *Sayyid Qutb: The Life and Legacy of a Radical Islamic Intellectual* (New York: Oxford University Press, 2013).

39. Sayyid Qutb, *Artistic Representation in the Qur'an* (Cairo: Dar al Sharuq, 1949).

40. Over the years, I have been struck by the number of postings of Qutb's *In the Shade of the Qur'an* by ordinary citizens during the month of Ramadan on a Facebook "What are you reading?" page.

41. Cited in *History Controversy in the News*, 2009. "Syed Qutb—Muslim Brotherhood Origins." Rev. October 11, 2009. Online. Available: http://history controversy.blogspot.com/2009/10/syed-qutb-muslim-brotherhood-origins .html. [February 9, 2015].

42. See Bediuzzaman Said Nursi, "Nursi, Discourse, and Narrative." [Online]. Available: http://www.bediuzzamansaidnursi.org/en/icerik/nursi-discourse-and-narrative [October 16, 2014].

43. Bediuzzaman Said Nursi, *Syqal al-Islam* (Istanbul: Sozler Publication, 1998), 22. His students wrote him a letter expressing the same notion: "Our revered Master, who through the effulgence of the Qurán and truths of the *Risale-I Nur* and aspirations of his loyal students, weeps tears of blood for the well-being of the Islamic world in this world and the next." Said Nursi, *The Rays Collection* (Istanbul: Sozler Publications, 1998), 293.

44. Nursi, *The Rays*, 167.

45. Bediuzzaman Said Nursi, *Al-Mathnawai al Nuri: Seedbed of the Light*, trans. Huseyin Akarsu (New Jersey: Nur, n.d.), 297.

46. This story circulates widely among Nursi followers. A typical account can be found at Questions on Islam, *"Who is Bediuzzaman Said Nursi?"* Online. Available: http://www.questionsonislam.com/article/who-bediuzzaman-said-nursi. [February 9, 2015].

CHAPTER 3

1. Cited in "Johann Wolfgang von Goethe (b. 1749 - d. 1832)." [Online]. Available: http://www.whale.to/a/goethe_q.html. [October 15, 2014].

2. John Esposito has made notable contributions to correcting Western misunderstandings about Islam. From his voluminous writings, see John L. Esposito and Dalia Mogahed, *Who Speaks for Islam: What a Billion Muslims Really Think* (New York: Gallup Press, 2007). Edward Said's *Orientalism* revolutionized Middle East studies in the West, although his contributions remain controversial to this day. See Edward Said, *Orientalism* (New York: Knopf Publishing Group, 1979).

3. Qur'an 2:143.

4. See Manuel Castells, *The Rise of the Network Society* (Cambridge, MA: Blackwell, 1996).

5. Mark Taylor, *The Moment of Complexity: Emerging Network Culture* (Chicago: University of Chicago Press, 2001), 47–72.

6. Taylor, *Moment*, 36.

7. Taylor, *Moment*, 65. Taylor shows how "important work now being done in complexity studies suggests that such systems and structures are not merely theoretically conceivable but are actually at work in natural, social and cultural networks."

8. For a fuller treatment of complexity theory and midstream Islamic thinking, see Raymond William Baker, "'Building the World' in a Global Age," ed. Armando Salvatore and Mark Levine, *Religion, Social Practice, and Contested Hegemonies: Reconstructing the Public Sphere in Muslim Majority Societies* (New York: Palgrave Macmillan, 2005), 109–132.

9. This account draws from Youssef H. Aboul-Enein, *Iraq in Turmoil: Historical Perspectives of Dr. Ali Wardi* (Annapolis, MD: Naval Institute Press, 2002), 27.

10. The idea of complex semantic connections comes naturally to the speaker of Arabic. Arabic vocabulary is built from three-syllable verbs in the past tense, like ka-ta-ba or katab, "he wrote." From this root comes a plethora of semantically linked words, easily recognized as such by native speakers. They include kitab (book), maktab (desk), maktaba (library), or katib (author). In English, these derivatives appear as quite separate and unconnected words. In Arabic, their semantic connection to the root "katab" remains apparent to the Arabic

speaker, although they are lost in translation. Arabic spontaneously creates
these complex, interactive semantic webs.

11. Yusuf al Qaradawi emphasizes a broad reform platform in all his voluminous
writings; for a representative work, see Yusuf al Qaradawi, *Our Islamic Community between Two Centuries* (Cairo: Dar al Sharuq, 2002). (Arabic)

12. Fahmi Huwaidi writes perceptively of the Western opposition to the civilizational project itself, as the heart of Western enmity. In his view, it goes
much deeper than the parallel anti-Western feelings in the Islamic world.
"The Western position surpasses the rejection of Islam as a belief and ideology to the rejection of the Islamic civilizational project. Therefore, the call of
civilizational and cultural independence by Islamists or non-Islamists is perceived in the West as an enmity discourse." See Fahmi Huwaidi, *al Ahram*,
July 17, 1990.

13. Fahmi Huwaidi frequently invokes Abduh to make this point. See, for example, *al Ahram*, October 17, 1989, and *al Ahram*, July 28, 1992.

14. Kamal Abul Magd, *A Contemporary Islamic Vision: Statement of Principles*
(Cairo: Dar al Sharuq, 1991), 8. (Arabic)

15. To this day, Abduh's remark is frequently quoted, as in this recent article by
Essam Dessouqi, "Islam without Muslims, Muslims without Islam," *The Sev-
enth Day*, August 23, 2010. [Online.] Available: http://www1.youm7.com/News
.asp?NewsID=764,105. [August 9, 2014].

16. Selim al Awa, *al Ahrar*, March 23, 1992.

17. Muhammad al Ghazzali, *The Bitter Truth* (Cairo: al Ahram, 1993), 18. (Arabic)

18. Manuel Castells, *The Power of Identity: The Information Age: Economy, Society,
and Culture, Volume II* (Malden, MA: Blackwell Publishing, 2010).

19. Muhammad al Ghazzali, *Toward a Substantive Interpretation of the Surahs of the
Holy Qur'an* (Cairo: Dar al Sharuq, 1955), 5. (Arabic)

20. As Fahmi Huwaidi expressed it, "each book for Ghazzali was a battle . . . and
he never dismounted from his horse." Fahmi Huwaidi, *al Ahram*, March 26,
1996.

21. Muhammad al Ghazzali, *The Bombshell of the Truth* (Damascus: Dar al Dustur,
2002), 5. (Arabic)

22. Qur'an 13:11.

23. This account and the citations that follow draw from the report on the site by
Fahmi Huwaidi in *al Ahram*, October 28, 1996.

24. For an extended discussion of Egyptian New Islamic scholarship in education,
culture, social life, and politics, see Raymond William Baker, *Islam without
Fear: Egypt and the New Islamists* (Cambridge, MA: Harvard University Press,
2003).

25. Fahmi Huwaidi, *al Ahram*, March 24, 1992.

26. Fahmi Huwaidi, *Iran from Within* (Cairo: Markaz al Ahram lil Targama wa
Nashr, 1987), 12. (Arabic)

27. Kamal Abul Magd, *A Contemporary Islamic Vision: Declaration of Principles* (Cairo: Dar al Sharuq, 1991). (Arabic)

28. All of the major thinkers of the New Islamic school contributed to the elaboration of the centrist vision for broad cooperation across political trends. For a detailed study of this new thinking, see Baker, *Islam without Fear*, especially 27, 42, 69, 76, 109, 124, 126, 131.

29. For this conception of the *Wassatteyya*, see Yusuf al Qaradawi, *The Islamic Awakening: The Concerns of the Arab and Islamic Homeland* (Cairo: Dar al Sahwa, 1988), 13.

30. Taylor, *Moment*, 11–12.

31. Qaradawi, *Islamic Awakening*, 13.

32. Tareq al Bishri, *The General Features of Contemporary Islamic Political Thought* (Cairo: Dar al Sharuq, 1996), 17.

33. Bishri, *General Features*, 17.

34. For a comprehensive review of that role, including the New Islamic view of *ijtihad*, see Baker, *Islam without Fear*, 83–126.

35. Becket Fund for Religious Liberty, *New York Times*, October 17, 2001.

36. Thomas L. Friedman made this point repeatedly in his influential *New York Times* columns in the wake of September 11.

37. See Tareq al Bishri, *Arabs in the Face of Aggression* (Cairo: Dar al Sharuq, 2002).

38. This theme runs through Bishri's *Arabs in the Face of Aggression*; see especially his assessment of the popular reaction to the official "peace" agreements with Israel, pp. 66–67.

39. See Seymour Hersh, "The Missiles of August," *The New Yorker*, October 12, 1998.

40. For an informative and fair evaluation of this Pulitzer Prize–winning journalist's reporting, see Thomas E. Ricks, "Shameful Side of the War on Terror," *New York Times*, October 12, 2014. [Online]. Available: http://www.nytimes .com/2014/10/13/arts/in-pay-any-price-james-risen-examines-the-war-on-terror.html?_r=0. [October 18, 2014.]

41. See the discussion by Chris Hedges, a former *New York Times* journalist, also a Pulitzer Prize–winning investigative reporter, in a debate between Hedges and University of Chicago law professor Geoffry Stone. [Online]. Rev. June 12, 2013. Available: http://www.truthdig.com/avbooth/item/chris_hedges_on_ edward_snowden_hero_or_traitor_20130612. [October 7, 2014.]

42. Yusuf al Qaradawi, *Nurturance of the Environment in Islamic Shari'a* (Cairo: Dar al Sharuq, 2001), 258.

43. See, for example, Tareq al Bishri's assessment of the impact of the events of September 11 on American official thinking. Bishri, *Arabs in the Face of Aggression*, 55–57.

44. Tareq al Bishri, *Islam Online*, February 5, 2003.

45. Taylor, *Moment*, 273.

46. Cited by Fahmi Huwaidi, *al Ahram*, October 10, 1995.

47. Qur'an 30:11, 39:21, 11:120. In such verses the Message is presented as a message of remembrance of truths already known.

CHAPTER 4

1. The phrase is from Muhammad Abduh and serves as the epigraph for this book. Muhammad Abduh, *The Theology of Unity* (London: George Allen & Unwin, 1966), 148. (Translation modified, based on the Arabic original)

2. Alija Izetbegovic, *Notes from Prison, 1983–1988*. [Online]. Available: http://www.muslimtorrents.net/ [April 8, 2013].

3. The ayatollah recites his poem in Arabic with English subtitles in this YouTube video. [Online.] Available: http://www.youtube.com/watch?v=iKgDr01kIfk [September 12, 2014]. (Arabic with English subtitles)

4. Omayma Abdel-Latif, "Death of a Legend." [Online]. Available: http://weekly .ahram.org.eg/2010/1006/re06.htm [September 27, 2013].

5. Fadlallah provided the most cogent justification for armed resistance for the Lebanese, combined with genuine attention to a range of social issues. For a useful discussion of Fadlallah's important *Islam and the Logic of Force*, see Shimon Shapira, "Lebanon: Ayatollah Fadlallah's Death and the Expansion of Iranian Hegemony." [Online]. Rev. July 20, 2010. Available: http://jcpa .org/article/lebanon-ayatollah-fadlallahs-death-and-the-expansion-of-iranian-hegemony/ [October 27, 2014].

6. Qur'an 22:40–41.

7. Thanassis Cambanis, "Grand Ayatollah Fadlallah, Shiite Cleric, Dies at 75," *New York Times*, July 4, 2010.

8. For Fadlallah on "martyrdom operations," see Shapira, "Lebanon."

9. Quoted in Graham Fuller, "We Could Provide a Million Suicide Bombers in 24 Hours," *The Telegraph*, December 4, 2001. [Online]. Available: http://www .telegraph.co.uk/news/worldnews/middleeast/lebanon/1400406/We-could-provide-a-million-suicide-bombers-in-24-hours.html [October 27, 2014].

10. Zaid Al-Mosawi and Muhammad Habash, *Sayyid Muhammad Husayn Fadlallah, A Lifetime in the Call for Unity*. [Online]. Rev. April 2011. Available: http://www.taqrib.info/books/Taqrib%20Journal%208.pdf, 125-156 [September 13, 2014].

11. The ayatollah took strong critical positions against a number of Shi'i traditions that he regarded as excessive. Al-Mosawi and Habash, *Fadlallah*.

12. Al-Mosawi and Habash, *Fadlallah*.

13. Martin Child, "Grand Ayatollah Mohammed Hussein Fadlallah: Prominent Shiite Cleric Who Survived Several Assassination Attempts," *The Independent*, July 9, 2010.

14. See Robert Fisk, "CNN Was Wrong about Ayatollah Fadlallah," *The Independent*, July 10, 2010.

15. See the account of this incident in Abbas Milani, *Eminent Persians: The Men and Women Who Made Modern Iran, 1941–1979* (Syracuse, NY: Syracuse University Press, 2008), 350–357.

16. Quotations are from Muhammad Sahimi, "Grand Ayatollah Hossein Ali Montazeri: 1922–2009." [Online]. Rev. December 21, 2009. Available: http://www.pbs.org/wgbh/pages/frontline/tehranbureau/2009/12/grand-ayatollah-hossein-ali-montazeri-1922-2009.html [September 28, 2013].

17. See Bager Moin, "Dissident Cleric Becomes a Hero to the Reform Movement," *The Guardian*, December 20, 2009.

18. Moin, "Dissident Cleric."

19. Quoted by Sahimi, "Grand Montazeri."

20. Cited in Roschanack Shaery-Eisenlohr, "Imagining Shi'ite Iran: Transnationalism and Religious Authenticity in the Muslim World," *Iranian Studies*, volume 40, issue 1, 2007, 22.

21. See http://www.aljazeera.com/news/middleeast/%202010/07/201073542402 49363.html.

22. Cited in Robert Deemer Lee, *Overcoming Tradition and Modernity: The Search for Islamic Authenticity* (Boulder, CO: Westview Press, 1997), 127.

23. Ali Shariati, "Where Shall We Begin: Part 1." [Online]. Available: http://www.shariati.com/english/begin/begin1.html [October 4, 2014].

24. Ali Shariati, "Reflections of a Concerned Muslim on the Plight of Oppressed People." [Online]. Available: http://www.shariati.com/english/reflect/reflect1.html [October 18, 2014].

25. For an insightful discussion of this point, see Farzin Vahdat, *God and the Juggernaut: Iran's Intellectual Encounter with Modernity* (Syracuse, NY: Syracuse University Press, 2002), 147.

26. Reza Khojasteh-Rahim, "An Interview with Abdulkarim Soroush: 'We Should Pursue Shariati's Path but We Shouldn't Be Mere Followers.'" [Online]. Rev. June 2008. Available: http://www.drsoroush.com/English/Interviews/E-INT-Shariati_June2008.html [March 31, 2013].

27. Samuel Huntington, *The Clash of Civilizations and the Remaking of World Order* (New York: Simon & Schuster, 1996), 144–149.

28. Fatma Dislizibak, "Erbakan's Re-Election," *Today's Zaman*, October 19, 2010.

29. Richard Falk, "Ten Years of AKP Leadership in Turkey," *World Press*. [Online]. Rev. August 25, 2012. Available: http://richardfalk.wordpress.com/2012/08/25/ten-years-of-akp-leadership-in-turkey [October 4, 2013].

30. Fahmi Huwaidi, *al Ahram*, December 19, 1995.

31. Alija Izetbegovic, *Inescapable Question—Autobiographical Notes* (Leicestershire, United Kingdom, 2003), 13.

32. Quoted as an epigraph in Stephen Schwartz, *The Two Faces of Islam* (New York: Doubleday, 2001).

33. Alija Izetbegovic, *The Islamic Declaration: A Program for the Islamization of Muslims and the Muslim Peoples* (Sarajevo: n.p., 1990).

34. Izetbegovic, *Islamic Declaration*, 51.

35. Izetbegovic, *Islamic Declaration*, 30.

36. Izetbegovic, *Islamic Declaration*, 3.

37. Izetbegovic, *Islamic Declaration*, 36.

38. Izetbegovic, *Islamic Declaration*, 43.

39. Izetbegovic, *Islamic Declaration*, 64.

40. Alija Izetbegovic, *Notes from Prison* (Santa Barbara, CA: Praeger, 2001), Chapter 6, "Prison."

41. Izetbegovic, *Notes*, 50.

42. Izetbegovic, *Notes*, 11.

43. Quoted as an epigraph in Schwartz, *The Two Faces*.

44. Izetbegovic, *Islamic Declaration*, 6.

45. Izetbegovic, *Islamic Declaration*, 13.

46. Izetbegovic, *Islamic Declaration*, 53.

47. Muhammad al Ghazali [*sic*], "Islam between East and West: The Magnum Opus of Alija Izetbegovic," *Islamic Studies*, 36: 2, 3, 1997. Available: http://www.jstor.org/discover/10.2307/23076210?uid=3739256&uid=2129&uid=2&uid=70&uid=4&sid=21104744743487 [October 4, 2014].

48. Ghazali, "Islam Between," 526.

49. Ghazali, "Islam Between," 529.

50. Ghazali, "Islam Between," 529.

51. Ghazali, "Islam Between," 526.

52. Qur'an 28:77.

53. Alija Ali Izetbegovic, *Islam between East and West* (Indianapolis, IN: American Trust Publications, 1993), 271–279.

54. Ghazali, "Islam Between," 529.

55. "Erdogan Visits Former Bosnian President Izetbegovic in Hospital," *Hurriyet Daily News*, October 20, 2003. [Online]. Available: http://www.hurriyet dailynews.com/default.aspx?pageid=438&n=erdogan-visits-former-bosnian-president-izetbegovic-in-hospital-2003-10-20 [October 4, 2014].

56. "And among His Signs is the creation of the heavens and the earth, and the *variations* in your languages and your colours: verily in that are Signs for those who know." Qur'an 30:22 (emphasis added to translation).

CHAPTER 5

1. Qur'an 2:213.

2. Qur'an 109:6.

3. Qur'an 33:40.

4. This famous saying is often described as a *hadith* of the Prophet Muhammad. It is not, but rather simply a kind of folk wisdom that Muslims across *Dar al Islam* cherish.

5. Qur'an 11:118.

6. Fahmi Huwaidi, *al Ahram*, April 25, 1989.

7. David Waines, *An Introduction to Islam* (Cambridge: Cambridge University Press, 1995), 175–176.

8. See Paul Bloom, "What We Miss," *New York Times*, June 4, 2010, for a lucid explanation of the theory developed by Christopher Chabris and Daniel Simons in *The Invisible Gorilla and Other Ways Our Intuitions Deceive Us* (New York: Random House, 2009). [Online]. Rev. June 4, 2010. Available: http://www.nytimes.com/2010/06/06/books/review/Bloom-t.html [September 20, 2014].

9. There is a burgeoning, at times hyperventilating, literature on these networks. A helpful and reliable introduction remains the classic by Manuel Castells, *The Rise of the Network Society* (Cambridge, MA: Blackwell, 1996).

10. Olivier Roy, *Globalized Islam: The Search for a New Ummah* (New York: Columbia University Press, 2004).

11. Qur'an 49:13.

12. Cited in Muhammad Ali Khalidi, *Medieval Islamic Philosophical Writings* (Cambridge: Cambridge University Press, 2005), 157.

13. For a listing of works by al Suyuti, see Talib Ghaffari, "Writing of Jalaluddin al-Suyuti." [Online]. Rev. January 7, 2011. Available: http://www.maktabah.org/en/item/1839-writings-of-imam-jalaluddin-al-suyuti [October 10, 2014].

14. Sarah Abdul Mohsin, "Belal Fadl Defends the Work of Naguib Mahfuz from the Attack of the Salafis," *Day 7*. Rev. December 9, 2011. [Online]. Available: http://www.youm7.com/News.asp?NewsID=550,898&#.Un5umeJiz59 [September 28, 2014]. (Arabic)

15. [Online]. Available: http://www.sunnipath.com/Library/Articles/AR00000214.aspx [August 15, 2014].

16. Al Suyuti, *The Citron Halves: or, the Daintiness of Women* (Damascus: Dar al Kitab al Arabi, n.d)., 31. (Arabic)

17. Cited in Sachiko Murata, *The Tao of Islam: A Sourcebook on Gender Relationships in Islamic Thought* (Albany: SUNY Press, 1992).

18. Homage to Ibn Battuta now suffuses the field of anthropology with programs and prizes named in his honor. My favorite is the Ibn Battuta prize at Kansas State University that includes a tribute to the great *rahal*. The prize description can be read at "Ibn Battuta Award." [Online]. Available: http://www.k-state.edu/sasw/anth/ibn-battuta-award.html [October 10, 2014].

19. Edward C. Banfield, *The Moral Basis of a Backward Society* (New York: The Free Press, 1968).

20. After this first superficial encounter, I did grow to appreciate the breadth and complexity of his thought on a stunning range of issues. For a good bibliography in English, see Aziz al-Azmeh, *Ibn Khaldun in Modern Scholarship: A Study in Orientalism* (London: Third World Centre, 1981).

21. Ibn Battuta, *Travels of Ibn Battuta* (Beirut: Dar al Nafais, 2004), 36. (Arabic)

22. Ibn Battuta, *Travels*, 36–37.

23. Ibn Battuta, *Travels*, 33. This extraordinary phenomenon is mentioned several times in the Qur'an; see Qur'an 55:19–20 and 25:53.

24. Qur'an 25:53.

25. I am grateful to my senior researcher, Mostafa Mohamed, for accompanying me on that voyage through *Travels* and for the hours of stimulating discussion of what we found along the way.

26. Ibn Battuta, *Travels*, 610.

27. Ibn Battuta, *Travels*, 357–358; a second, more complicated story of a missing male servant is at 420.

28. Ibn Battuta, *Travels*, 572, 677.

29. Ibn Battuta, *Travels*, 548.

30. Ibn Battuta, *Travels*, 335.

31. Ibn Battuta, *Travels*, 329.

32. Ibn Battuta, *Travels*, 330.

33. Ibn Battuta, *Travels*, 334–335; translation in Ross Dunn, *The Adventures of Ibn Battuta: A Muslim Traveler of the 14th Century* (Berkeley: University of California Press, 1989), 168.

34. Ibn Battuta, *Travels*, 577.

35. Ibn Battuta, *Travels*, 578.

36. Ibn Battuta, *Travels*, 574.

37. Ibn Battuta, *Travels*, 413.

38. Ibn Battuta, *Travels*, 638.

39. Cited in Dunn, *Adventures*, 316.

40. Ibn Battuta, *Travels*, 279.

41. Ibn Battuta, *Travels*, 592.

42. Ibn Battuta, *Travels*, 573.

CHAPTER 6

1. I am grateful to the cultural anthropologist Marcene Marcoux for a critical reading of this chapter and for her many insightful suggestions on substance and style.

2. Ghazzali expresses these fears for Islam in the most extensive way in Muhammad al Ghazzali, *Between Reason and the Heart* (Cairo: Dar al I'tisam, 1973). (Arabic)

3. Fahmi Huwaidi, *Iran from Within* (Cairo: Markaz al Ahram lil Targama wa Nashr, 1987). (Arabic)

4. See, for example, Huwaidi, *Iran*, 11–12. Huwaidi writes forthrightly that "I am present in any place where the banner of Islam is raised and I move with Islam whenever it is on the march."

5. Huwaidi, *Iran*, 11–12. Huwaidi explains further that, when it comes to Islamic matters, "I may have criticisms, there may be differences, and even battles but in the end all of that comes from within the Islamic family."

6. See Olivier Roy, *Globalized Islam: The Search for a New Ummah* (New York: Columbia University Press, 2004), 6.

7. Roy, *Globalized Islam*, 8.

8. The English speaker can sample that literature in reliable translations in Muhammad Ali Khalidi, *Medieval Islamic Philosophical Writings* (Cambridge: Cambridge University Press, 2005).

9. Khalidi, *Medieval Islamic Writings*, 81.

10. Clifford Geertz, *Islam Observed: Religious Development in Morocco and Indonesia* (Chicago: University of Chicago Press, 1971).

11. Paul Rabinow, *Reflections on Fieldwork in Morocco* (Berkeley: University of California Press, 1977), 121.

12. Rabinow, *Reflections*, 50.

13. Rabinow, *Reflections*, 91.

14. Rabinow, *Reflections*, 91.

15. See Gabriele Marranci, *The Anthropology of Islam* (New York: Routledge, 2013). Also excellent and engaging is Daniel Martin Varisco, *Islam Obscured: The Rhetoric of Anthropological Representation* (New York: Palgrave Macmillan, 2005).

16. Michael Gilsenan, *Recognizing Islam: Religion and Society in the Modern Middle East* (London: I. B. Taurus, 1992).

17. Gilsenan, *Recognizing Islam*, 9.

18. Gilsenan, *Recognizing Islam*, 10.

19. Gilsenan, *Recognizing Islam*, 10.

20. Gilsenan, *Recognizing Islam*, 10–11.

21. Gilsenan, *Recognizing Islam*, 11.

22. Gilsenan, *Recognizing Islam*, 270 (emphasis added).

23. Gilsenan, *Recognizing Islam*, 266.

24. A good place to start in surveying network studies of this kind is Angel Rabasa et al., *Building Moderate Muslim Networks* (Santa Monica, CA: Rand Corporation, 2007). Critical reactions of Muslim scholars are summarized in "Muslim Scholars Respond to Rand Report." Rev April 27, 2007. [Online] Available: http://www.ikhwanweb.com/article.php?id=1735 [October 4, 2014].

25. Collaborative work by three distinguished scholars of Islam, Bruce Lawrence, Miriam Cooke, and Carl W. Ernst, has yielded a treasure trove of work on network analysis from the perspective of Islamic or, more broadly, religious studies. The place to begin exploring this literature is Bruce Lawrence and Carl

Ernst, eds., *Muslim Networks from Hajj to Hip Hop* (Chapel Hill: University of North Carolina Press, 2005).

26. See Andrew Gardner, *City of Strangers: Gulf Migration and the Indian Community in Bahrain* (Ithaca, NY: Cornell University Press, 2010), ix.

27. Tareq al Bishri, "Introduction," ed. Seif 'Abdul Fatah and Nadia Mustafa, *My Nation in the World* (Cairo: Civilization Center for Political Studies, 1999), 11. (Arabic)

28. Bishri, "Introduction," 7.

29. The notion of "scorekeeping" is adapted from the social practice theory of the pragmatist Robert Brandom and used here for the work of intercultural understanding. See Brandom, *Making It Explicit: Reasoning, Representing, and Discursive Commitment* (Cambridge, MA: Harvard University Press, 1994); for an elaboration on this methodology, see Raymond Baker and Alexander Henry, "We *Can* Do Better: Understanding Muslims and Ourselves," in Tareq Y. Ismael and Andrew Rippin, *Islam in Eyes of the West: Images and Realities in an Age of Terror* (New York: Routledge, 2010), 177–201.

30. The notion of "primary structuring ideas" is borrowed in modified form from the work of Adda Boseman, *Strategic Intelligence and Statecraft* (Washington, DC: Brazey's), 26.

31. See the analysis by Huwaidi in *al Ahram*, August 28, 2008. Huwaidi traces the influence of the Egyptian geographer Gamal Hamdan in developing the strategic triangle idea; see *al Ahram*, August 28, 2008. See also the parallel analysis of "the big three" by Hassan Hanafi, in *al Arabi*, April 8, 2001.

32. See the classic formulation of this insight in Tareq al Bishri, *On the Contemporary Islamic Question: The General Features of Contemporary Political Thought* (Cairo: Dar al Sharuq, 1996), 40–44. (Arabic)

33. Bahgat's references to Rumi were always numerous during Ramadan. See, for multiple examples, *al Ahram*, December 21, 1999, 11, 14, 16, 21.

34. Bahgat, *al Ahram*, July 26, 2007.

35. Bahgat, *al Ahram*, July 26, 2007.

36. Huwaidi, *Iran*.

37. Huwaidi, *Iran*, 141.

38. Huwaidi, *Iran*, 111.

39. Huwaidi, *Iran*, 137–140.

40. Huwaidi, *Iran*, 114.

41. Huwaidi, *Iran*, 135.

42. Huwaidi, *Iran*, 116.

43. Fahmi Huwaidi, *al Ahram*, December 19, 1995.

44. Huwaidi, *Islam in China*, 8 (Kuwait: 'Alim al Ma'rifa. 1998). (Arabic)

45. Huwaidi, *Islam in China*, 143.

46. Huwaidi, *Iran*, 78.

47. Huwaidi, *Iran*, 204.
48. Huwaidi, *Iran*, 194.
49. Huwaidi, *Iran*, 194–204.
50. Qur'an 22:46.

CHAPTER 7

1. The Qur'an is organized in chapters and verses. The verses, in Arabic, are called *ayahs*. The word *"aya"* actually means sign, evidence, or indicator. Thus, the Qur'an itself is understood to provide humanity with "signs" from God.

2. Israel has been labeled an ethnocracy by a substantial number of Israeli scholars over the past decade and a half. See, for an excellent beginning, Oren Yiftachel, *Ethnocracy: Land and Identity Politics in Israel/Palestine* (Philadelphia: University of Pennsylvania Press, 2000).

3. Qur'an 5:89, 24:33.

4. Qur'an 2:229.

5. For a clear and forceful discussion of apostasy, addressing all the interpretive complexities, such as the Islamic notion of discretionary punishment, see Mohamed S. El-Awa, *Punishment in Islamic Law* (Indianapolis, IN: American Trust Publications, 1982), 49–52, 96–97.

6. Qur'an 2:256.

7. Qur'an 2:256.

8. Qur'an 18:29.

9. Qur'an 88:21–22.

10. Fahmi Huwaidi, *The Qur'an and the Sultan* (Cairo: Dar al Sharuq, 1999), 20–21. (Arabic)

11. Imam Bukhari, *Sahih Bukhari*, volume 9, book 89, judgments 255 and 258. See, for example, judgment 255: "Allah's Apostle said: 'You should listen to and obey your ruler even if he was an Ethiopian (black) slave whose head looks like a raisin.'" Important for the limits to obedience is judgment 258: "There is no submission in matters involving God's disobedience or displeasure. Submission is obligatory only in what is good (and reasonable)." [Online]. Available: http://www.ahlalhdeeth.com/vbe/showthread.php?t=3704 [May 20, 2014].

12. *Al Shaab*, January 24, 1997.

13. These themes are developed throughout Safran's classic and still-influential *Egypt in Search of Political Community: An Analysis of the Intellectual and Political Evolution of Egypt, 1804–1952* (Cambridge, MA: Harvard University Press, 1969).

14. See Michelle M. Hu and Radhika Jain, *The Harvard Crimson*, May 25, 2011.

15. Kamal Abul Magd, *A Contemporary Islamic Vision: Declaration of Principles* (Cairo: Dar al Sharuq), 31. (Arabic)

16. Kamal Abul Magd, *Dialogue Not Confrontation* (Cairo: Dar al Sharuq, 1988), 29. (Arabic)

17. Fahmi Huwaidi, *al Ahram*, October 8, 1985. (Emphasis added)

18. *October*, July 8, 1990.

19. Samuel Huntington, *The Clash of Civilizations and the Remaking of World Order* (New York: Simon & Schuster, 1996), 97.

20. Huntington, *The Clash*, 121.

21. Huntington, *The Clash*, 217.

22. Theology, as Mark Taylor has observed, is "most often most influential where it is least obvious." Mark Taylor, *The Moment of Complexity: Emerging Network Culture* (Chicago: University of Chicago Press, 2001), 180.

23. Qur'an 17:70.

24. Qur'an 4:75.

25. Qur'an 15:19.

26. Muhammad al Ghazzali, *al Ahram*, March 17, 1991. The discussion here is a close paraphrase of Ghazzali's address in Cairo to a symposium called to discuss his study of the Islamic intellectual heritage between logic and *Shari'ah*. The *al Aram* coverage includes a summary of his findings as well as of the subsequent discussion session that was chaired by Dr. Muhammad Emara.

27. The Qur'anic notion of *ma'asum* (infallibility) refers to God and by extension to the Message that God sent to the Prophet Muhammad. It does not refer to the other spheres of the Prophet's time on Earth, as a fully human figure.

28. Qur'an 80:1–12.

29. Imam Muslim, *Hadith Sahih Muslim*, "Book of Virtues, chapter 2363." [Online]. Available: http://hadithmuslimonline.blogspot.com/search/label/Index%20 Hadith%20Sahih%20Muslim%20Online [May 30, 2014].

30. The discussion that follows relies heavily on the important but neglected article of Tareq al Bishri, where these critical interpretations are elaborated. See Tareq al Bishri, "About Religion and Knowledge," *Weghat Nathar*, April 2004.

31. See the discussion of this deep influence that is recognized throughout the best biography of Ghannouchi that we have: Azzam S. Tamimi, *Rachid Ghannouchi: A Democrat within Islamism* (Oxford: Oxford University Press, 2010).

32. The most insightful discussion of those inhibiting structures comes from Muhammad al Ghazzali, *The Bitter Truth* (Beirut: Dar al Qalam, 2002), 81. (Arabic)

33. See, for example, Yusuf al Qaradawi, *Fiqh of Jihad: A Comparative Study of Its Rulings and Philosophy*, vol. I (Cairo: Dar al Wahba, 2009), 394–403, 601. (Arabic)

34. Qur'an 20:126.

35. It should be no surprise that the American pragmatists, given the affinities between that American philosophy and Islam, use parallel categories to make sense of reason and culture in human thought and social action. My own

familiarity with the works of leading pragmatists helped in understanding the diverse ways that New Islamic thinkers elaborated both concepts. See, for example, Richard Rorty, *Truth and Progress* (Cambridge: Cambridge University Press, 1998), 176.

36. Qur'an 96:1–5.

37. For a representative discussion and elaboration of his thinking, see Yusuf al Qaradawi, *The Fiqh of Jihad: A Comparative Study of Its Rulings and Philosophy in Light of the Quran and Sunnah*, vol. *II* (Cairo: Dar al Wahba, 2009). (Arabic)

38. Fahmi Huwaidi, *al Ahram*, January 12, 19, 26, 1999; February 2, 1999; August 10, 1999.

39. Qur'an 50:22–23. See also Qaradawi, *Fiqh of Jihad*, vol. *I*, 143–173.

40. See the perceptive discussion of creativity in all its dimensions in Kamal Abul Magd in *Iza' a wal Television*, March 7, 1992.

41. John Dewey, *Democracy and Education* (Mineola, NY: Dover Publications, 1915; 2004), 83. (Emphasis added)

42. For an incisive and pointed discussion, see Andrew J. Bacevich, *The Limits of Power: The End of American Exceptionalism* (New York: Metropolitan Books, 2008), 18–19.

43. See especially Alija Ali Izetbegovic, *Islam between East and West* (Indianapolis, IN: American Trust Publications, 1993), 129, 179, and 212.

44. My understanding of the implications of American pragmatism for social research, spelled out in this section, has developed through collaborative research work and conversations over several years with Alex Henry, now of the Yale School of Management.

45. I have taken some of this language from private communications with Alex Henry of the Yale School of Management.

46. Bruce Lawrence, *Shattering of the Myth: Islam beyond Violence* (Princeton, NJ: Princeton University Press, 1998), 41.

47. Lawrence, *Shattering*, 11. (Emphasis added)

48. This striking phrasing, and the conceptualization of pragmatism it captures, took shape in conversations with Alex Henry of the Yale School of Management.

49. See Max Rodenbeck, "The Promised Land." [Online]. Rev. June 13, 1999. *New York Times*. Available: http://www.nytimes.com/books/99/06/13/reviews/990613.13rodenbt.html [October 10, 2014].

50. Rorty, *Truth and Progress*, 176.

51. Awa made this observation in a public discussion at the Cairo Center for Human Rights on October 17, 1994. I attended and took notes.

52. Barrington Moore, Jr., *The Social Origins of Dictatorship and Democracy; Lord and Peasant in the Making of the Modern World* (Boston, MA: Beacon Press, 1966), 144.

53. For a more extensive elaboration of these views, see the discussion in my *Islam without Fear*, from which this analysis and citations are taken. *Islam without*

Fear: Egypt and the New Islamists (Cambridge, MA: Harvard University Press, 2004), 170–181.

54. Tareq al Bishri gave the clearest explanation of the concept of "communal society" in his paper presented at the Thirteenth Annual Political Science Research Conference at Cairo University, December 4–6, 1999. This summary comes from notes taken at that event.

55. See Baker, *Islam without Fear*, 106–110. Key works in Arabic by New Islamic trend intellectuals include Yusuf al Qaradawi, *Non-Muslims in Islamic Society* (Beirut: Muasassat al Risala, 1983); Fahmi Huwaidi, *Citizens, Not Zimmis* (Cairo: Dar al Sharuq, 1985); and Muhammad Selim al Awa, *Copts and Islam* (Cairo: Dar al Sharuq, 1987). (All three in Arabic)

56. For the work of the New Islamic trend on democracy in Islam, see Baker, *Islam without Fear*, 165–211.

CHAPTER 8

1. I first worked out the concept of the "Imaginary" in Raymond William Baker, "The Islamist Imaginary: Islam, Iraq, and the Projections of Empire," *International Journal of Contemporary Iraqi Studies*, vol. 1, issue 1, January 2007.

2. The literature on Islamophobia is now extensive. A reliable introduction is still John L. Esposito and Ibrahim Kalin, eds., *Islamophobia: The Challenge of Pluralism in the 21st Century* (New York: Oxford University Press, 2011).

3. See the assessments along these lines by the military historian Andrew Bacevich and the realist political scientist Stephen Walt. Andrew J. Bacevich, *The Limits of Power: The End of American Exceptionalism* (New York: Metropolitan Books, 2008), 176–177; and Stephen M. Walt, "Do No (More) Harm," *Foreign Policy*. [Online]. Rev. August 7, 2014. Available: http://www.foreignpolicy .com/articles/2014/08/07/let_it_bleed_iraq_isis_syria_airstrikes_israel_ palestine_gaza_iran' [September 27, 2014].

4. Fahmi Huwaidi, *al Ahram*, September 21, 2001.

5. These hostile characterizations are cited by John Alden Williams. See Williams, "Misunderstanding Islam." [Online]. Available: http://www.israelshamir.net/ Contributors/islamW.htm [September 28, 2014].

6. See Williams, "Misunderstanding Islam."

7. Qur'an 2:190.

8. Qur'an 22:40.

9. Qur'an 9:12.

10. Qur'an 4:75.

11. Qur'an 22:60.

12. For background, see "Archaeology in Israel: Masada Desert Fortress." [Online]. Available: http://www.jewishvirtuallibrary.org/jsource/Archaeology/Masada1. html [March 12, 2014].

13. See Nachman Ben-Yehuda, "The Masada Myth." [Online]. Rev. May 14, 2008. Available: http://www.bibliotecapleyades.net/biblianazar/esp_biblianazar_55 .htm [March 12, 2014].
14. Qur'an 3:142.
15. Qur'an 8:61.
16. Qur'an 8:60.
17. For an insightful fictional depiction of such a dance, informed by complexity theory, see Michael Crichton, *Prey* (New York: HarperCollins Publishers, 2002).
18. For Muslim believers, of course, there is only one Islam. Its singular Message was given to the Prophet Muhammad by God for all humanity. With his evocative phrase, Said was drawing attention to the multiple human understandings of this message. These interpretations are the products of historical Muslim communities of interpretation. They represent fully human and diverse efforts to understand the universal divine Message. These interpretive efforts are inevitably flawed by the traces of the particular times and places from which they originate. See Edward Said, "There Are Many Islams," *CounterPunch*, September 16, 2001.
19. For the full text, see the *New York Times*, September 20, 2002.
20. The current military rulers of Egypt, in the wake of the July 3, 2013, seizure of power, have gone even further. Al Azhar scholars are reduced to state functionaries with ever more blatantly propagandistic functions of the most vulgar kind. They are regularly called on to rationalize in Islamic terms the regime's brutal politics of repression. They do so with dismaying subservience.
21. Cheryl Benard, *Civil, Democratic Islam: Partners, Resources, and Strategies* (Santa Monica, CA: Rand Corporation, 2003), iii. (Emphasis added)
22. Benard, *Civil, Democratic Islam*, 3.
23. See Edward Said, *Covering Islam: How the Media and the Experts Determine How We See the Rest of the World* (New York: First Vintage Books, 1997), xi–2.
24. Benard, *Civil, Democratic Islam*, iii.
25. Benard, *Civil, Democratic Islam*, x.
26. Benard, *Civil, Democratic Islam*, x.
27. Benard, *Civil, Democratic Islam*, 1.
28. Benard, *Civil, Democratic Islam*, 30 n5.
29. Sayyid Yassine, *al Ahram*, July 22, 2004.
30. Yassine, *al Ahram*, July 22, 2004.
31. Benard, *Civil, Democratic Islam*, 49 n1.
32. Sufi orders often provided the indispensable leadership for battles against colonialism in Algeria, Libya, the Caucasus, and China.
33. Benard, *Civil, Democratic Islam*, 3.
34. Dilip Hiro, *Secrets and Lies: Operation Iraqi Freedom and After* (New York: Nation Books, 2004).

35. The phrase is from former Secretary of State Madeleine Albright, who commented that "if we have to use force, it is because we are America; we are the indispensable nation. We stand tall and we see further than other countries into the future, and we see the danger here to all of us." Albright was interviewed on *The Today Show* with Matt Lauer, and the statement was released by the U.S. Department of State. [Online]. Rev. February 19, 1998. Available: http://www.state.gov/1997-2001-NOPDFS/statements/1998/980219a.html [September 27, 2014].

36. Chris Hedges, "The Ghoulish Face of Empire." [Online] Rev. June 22, 2014. Available: http://www.truthdig.com/report/item/the_ghoulish_face_of_empire_20,140,623 [September 7, 2014].

37. See Murtaza Hussain and Glen Greenwald, "The Fake Terror Threat Used to Justify Bombing Syria." [Online]. Available: https://firstlook.org/theintercept/2014/09/28/u-s-officials-invented-terror-group-justify-bombing-syria/ [October 5, 2014].

CHAPTER 9

1. Qur'an 33:45.

2. Qur'an 96:1.

3. Qur'an 88:21–22.

4. See Qur'an 2:25, 82; 4:57, 122, 124, 5:9; 10:9; and 95:6.

5. See, in particular, John O. Voll, "Foreword," in J. Spencer Trimingham, *Sufi Orders in Islam* (Oxford: Clarendon Press, 1971), vii–xviii.

6. Qur'an 112:1–3. "Say; He is Allah, The One and Only; All, the Eternal, Absolute. He begetteth not. Nor is He begotten."

7. See Tareq al Bishri, "The Islamic Revival Added Much to Our Lives," Rev. July 26, 2006. [Online]. Available: http://www.islammemo.cc/Wassatteyya [July 29, 2007]; and Yusuf al Qaradawi, *The Islamic Renewal* (Cairo: Dar al Sharuq, 1997). (Arabic)

8. For a discussion of the importance of the popular expressions of the Renewal, as well as of the guiding role of the *Wassatteyya*, see Bishri, "The Islamic Revival."

9. See the striking, midstream characterization of the role for contemporary thinkers of the "ocean" of *fiqh* from all schools in Yusuf al Qaradawi, *Fiqh of Jihad: A Comparative Study of Its Rulings and Philosophy*, vol. 1 (Cairo: Dar al Wahba, 2009), 20–29. (Arabic)

10. The phrase, with the meaning intended here, was coined by Robert M. Sapolsky, an advocate for interdisciplinary learning, in his *Great Course Lecture Series*, 2nd edition. [Online]. Available: http://www.thegreatcourses.com/courses/biology-and-human-behavior-the-neurological-origins-of-individuality-2nd-edition.html [October 4, 2014].

11. Yusuf al Qaradawi's statement is available on Charles Kurzman, "Islamic State-
    ments against Terrorism." [Online]. Rev. September 27, 2001. Available: http://
    kurzman.unc.edu/islamic-statements-against-terrorism/ [October 5, 2014].

12. See the detailed discussion in Chapter 3.

13. Ibn Battuta, *Travels of Ibn Battuta* (Beirut: Dar al Nafais, 2004), 572, 677.
    (Arabic)

14. For a more detailed treatment of President Obama's Cairo speech and some
    of the other related themes treated here, see Raymond William Baker, "The
    Islamic Awakening," in *Interpreting the Middle East*, ed. David S. Sorenson,
    (Boulder, CO: Westview, 2010), 252–258.

15. The biblical phrase is best known to Americans from the "Battle Hymn of
    the Republic" by Julia Ward Howe. The historian Barbara Tuckman borrowed
    it to characterize the periodic "chastening" of Arab aggressors by Israel. See
    Edward Said, *Orientalism* (New York: Knopf Publishing Group, 1979), 286.

16. Michael Scheuer, Statement before the House Armed Services Subcommit-
    tee on Terrorism, Unconventional Threats and Capabilities, presented Sep-
    tember 18, 2008. [Online]. Rev. September 18, 2008. Available: http://armed
    services.house.gov/pdfs/TUTC091808/Scheuer_Testimony091808.pdf [Octo-
    ber 15, 2008].

17. For a detailed discussion of the Islamist Imaginary, see Chapter 8.

18. See Ira Chernus, "Palestinian Violence Overstated, Jewish Violence Under-
    stated. Time to Change the Story." [Online]. Rev. June 25, 2009. Available:
    http://www.tomdispatch.com/post/175088 [July 30, 2009].

19. For a pointed representative discussion of such purposive violence and the
    rules that circumscribe its use, see Yusuf al Qaradawi, *Islam and Violence*
    (Cairo: Dar al Sharuq, 2004), 26. (Arabic)

20. An important early contribution along the lines needed is John L. Esposito
    and Dalia Mogahed, *Who Speaks for Islam: What a Billion Muslims Really Think*
    (New York: Gallup Press, 2007). More attention should be given as well to
    the English-language work of such diverse scholars as François Burgat, Samer
    Shehata, Graham Fuller, Emad Chahine, Alastair Crooke, Khalil al Anany, and
    Michael Vlahos.

21. The ideas presented here were first worked out and presented in greater detail
    as a critique of the West's failure to give adequate attention to the Islamic mid-
    stream in Raymond William Baker, "Possible Partners, Probable Enemies:
    Why the US is Losing the Islamic Mainstream," Special Issue of *Arab Studies
    Quarterly*, January 2009, 81–103.

22. Robert L. Heilbroner, *The Great Ascent* (New York: Harper & Row, 1965).

23. See Rami al Khouri, "The Arab Story: The Big One Waiting to Be Told," *Daily
    Star*, July 21, 2007.

24. On Hizbullah and Hamas human rights violations, there is a fulsome and
    regularly updated record in the periodic reports of Human Rights Watch and

Amnesty International. The same respected international organizations regularly record the human rights violations of the Israeli state.

25. See Andrew J. Bacevich, "9/11 Plus Seven." [Online]. Rev. September 9, 2008. Available: http://www.tomdispatch.com/post/174974 [August 16, 2009].

26. See Tareq al Bishri, *The General Features of Contemporary Islamic Political Thought* (Cairo: Dar al Sharuq, 1996), 58–59. (Arabic)

27. This broad generalization that sums up the midstream Islamic explanation is, ironically, argued by Michael Scheuer, the former CIA official charged with tracking Osama bin Laden. See Scheuer, *Imperial Hubris: Why the West Is Losing the War on Terror* (Dulles, VA: Potomac Books, 2004).

28. For an extensive treatment of the "search for the moderates" and the question of democracy, see Raymond William Baker, "Degrading Democracy: American Empire, Islam, and Struggles for Freedom in the Arab Islamic World," in *Islamist Politics in the Middle East*, ed. Samer S. Shehata (New York: Routledge, 2012).

29. Some of the most prominent Islamic centrist intellectuals, with standing throughout the Islamic world, have done precisely that. See, for just two examples, Tareq al Bishri, *Islam Online*, February 5, 2003, and Qaradawi, *Fiqh of Jihad*, 717.

30. For an elaboration on the intersection of scholarship and policy, see Raymond William Baker, "Getting It Wrong, Yet Again," and Raymond Baker and Alex Henry, "We Can Do Better: Understanding Muslims and Ourselves," both in *Islam in the Eyes of the West: Images and Realities in an Age of Terror*, ed. Tareq Y. Ismael and Andrew Rippin (New York: Routledge, 2010).

31. Qaradawi, *Fiqh of Jihad*, 717.

32. Qur'an 1:1. The first verse opens with God; Qur'an 114:1–6. *Surah* 114 is titled *"al Nas."*

33. Qur'an 2:177.

CHAPTER 10

1. Muhammad Abduh, *The Theology of Unity* (London: George Allen & Unwin, 1966), 148.

2. Philip Jenkins, "The World's Fastest Growing Religion," *Real Clear Religion*. [Online] Rev. November 13, 2013. Available: http://www.realclearreligion .org/articles/2012/11/13/the_worlds_fastest_growing_religion.html[August11, 2014].

3. See Rashid Ghannouchi, "How Credible Is the Claim of the Failure of Political Islam?" [Online]. Rev. October 31, 2013. Available: https://www.middleeast-monitor.com/articles/africa/8087-how-credible-is-the-claim-of-the-failure-of-political-islam#top [February 26, 2014].

4. For a discussion of the January 25 revolutionary uprising and an earlier treatment of some of the themes developed here, against the backdrop of a review

of nine recent books on Egypt, see Raymond William Baker, "Understanding Egypt's Worldly Miracles," *The Middle East Journal*, vol. 66, no 1, winter 2012.

5. Slavoj Žižek, "For Egypt This Is the Miracle of Tahrir Square," *The Guardian*. [Online]. Rev. February 10, 2011. Available: http://www.theguardian.com/global/2011/feb/10/egypt-miracle-tahrir-square [September 28, 2014].

6. See Janet Afary and Kevin B. Anderson, *Foucault and the Iranian Revolution: Gender and the Seductions of Islamism* (Chicago: University of Chicago Press, 2005); see especially the introduction, 1–11. [Online]. Rev. May 19, 2005. Available: http://iranian.com/Books/2005/May/Foucault/index.html [September 27, 2014].

7. Žižek, "For Egypt This Is the Miracle."

8. Fahmi Huwaidi, *al Sharuq*, February 15, 2011.

9. Cited in Mona El-Ghobashy, "Egypt Looks Ahead to a Portentous Year," *Middle East Report*, February 2, 2005.

10. For the most part social scientists have not taken note of the meaning of spirituality in the revolutionary uprising. Foucault did, although his assessment has been received critically. See Michael Hoffman and Amaney Jamal, *Religion in the Arab Spring: Between Two Competing Narratives*. [Online]. Rev. March 20, 2013. Available: http://aalims.org/uploads/Hoffman_and_Jamal_AALIMS .pdf [September 27, 2014].

11. For a particularly evocative discussion of the influence of the New Islamic thinkers, especially Muhammad al Ghazzali, see Belal Fadl, *al Sharuq*, April 14, 2013.

12. Rashid Ghannouchi makes this broad argument to great effect. See Ghannouchi, "How Credible."

13. Jimmy Carter, "Egyptian Elections Have Been Fair and There Is an International Consensus on Recognizing Their Results," *Middle East Monitor*. [Online]. Rev. January 13, 2012. Available: https://www.middleeastmonitor.com/news/ middle-east/3273-jimmy-carter-egyptian-elections-have-been-fair-and-there-is-an-international-consensus-on-recognizing-their-results [October 23, 2014].

14. The "Endist" literature that predicts the end of Islamism and/or Islam itself is now almost three decades old, yet Islam still flourishes alongside the luxuriant commentary that predicts its end. Olivier Roy has been the most celebrated promoter, establishing his position with *The End of Political Islam* (New York: I. B. Taurus, 1994), which declared the end of political Islam in the 1990s. Roy has periodically renewed his position with predictions of endings after 9/11 and most recently in the wake of the Arab uprising in the spring of 2011. The works in the same vein are too numerous to mention and do not add much to Roy. A variant has appeared with the "post-Islamist" school, most persistently advanced by Asef Bayat in works such as *Post-Islamism: The Changing Faces of Islamism* (New York: Oxford University Press, 2013). A conceptual problem plagues this offshoot of the "endist" discourse since many Islamic scholars

would be hard pressed to see any break or any need for a hyphen in an approach that appears to fuse formal religiousness with societal rights, faith with freedom, Islam with liberty, and seeks to focus on the rights of believers rather than obligations alone, pluralism rather than unitary authoritarianism, interpretation of texts rather than a literalist approach to fixed texts, and the future rather than the past. Major intellectuals of the Islamic midstream, such as Shaikh Muhammad al Ghazzali, Tareq al Bishri, and many others too numerous to name have made such interpretations a part of their scholarly work for some five decades.

15. See Graham Fuller's provocatively titled *A World without Islam* (New York: Little, Brown, and Company, 2010). Fuller argues that if the death wish for the "end of Islam" were granted, little of substance to Western policy dilemmas would change and that the most intractable problems are mostly of the West's own creation.

16. See Note 1 of this chapter.

17. Khalil al Anani, "El-Sisi and Egypt's Bankrupt Civil Elite," *AhramonLine* [Online]. Rev. October 19, 2014. Available: http://english.ahram.org.eg/ NewsContent/4/0/84231/Opinion/ElSisi-and-Egypts-bankrupt-civil-elite.aspx [July 15, 2014].

18. For the Rice quotation, see Patrick L. Smith, "*New York Times*: Complicit in the Destruction of Egyptian Democracy." [Online]. Rev. August 18, 2013. Available: http://www.salon.com/2013/08/18/new_york_times_complicit_in_the_ destruction_of_egyptian_democracy/ [October 6, 2014].

19. Ghannouchi, "How Credible."

20. For an ongoing critique from a leading Islamic intellectual of the Brothers in power and their subsequent removal by the military, see the weekly Fahmi Huwaidi columns in *al Sharuq*. Rashid Ghannouchi has also offered a valuable critical commentary from an Islamic perspective, most notably in Ghannouchi, "How Credible."

21. Tareq al Bishri argued forthrightly that the decree exceeded the president's legitimate authority. Bishri, *al Sharuq*, November 24, 2012.

22. See the January 28, 2013, press release from Amnesty International. [Online]. Rev. January 28, 2013. Available: http://www.amnesty.org/en/for-media/press-releases/egypt-uprising-commemoration-unleashes-death-and-destruction-2013-01-28 [August 1, 2014].

23. That telling moment was captured on video. See https://www.youtube.com/ watch?v=MPva9Lv9PFU [October 12, 2014].

24. The movement was financed and supported by wealthy business figures, such as Naguib Sawiris, as well as the elements in the military that overthrew the regime. Details are hard to pin down, but the general outlines of the manipulated demonstrations and inflation of the number of participants have become clear. For a start, see Max Blumenthal, "People Power or Propaganda:

Unraveling the Egyptian Opposition." [Online]. Rev. July 19, 2013. Available: http://m.aljazeera.com/story/201371711575641o917 [October 12, 2014].

25. Human Rights Watch, "Egypt: Security Forces Used Excessive Lethal Force." [Online]. Rev. August 19, 2013. Available: http://www.hrw.org/news/2013/08/19/ egypt-security-forces-used-excessive-lethal-force [July 11, 2014].

26. See, among others, Carrie Rosefsky Wickham, *The Muslim Brotherhood: Evolution of an Islamist Movement* (Princeton, NJ: Princeton University Press, 2013), 247–288; and Abdullah al-Arian, *Answering the Call: Popular Islamic Activism in Sadat's Egypt* (Oxford: Oxford University Press, 2014), 215–240.

27. See John L. Esposito, "Egyptian Reform: A Coup and Presidential Election to Restore Authoritarianism?" [Online]. Rev. June, 23, 2014. Available: http://www .huffingtonpost.com/john-l-esposito/egyptian-reform-a-coup-pr_b_5518364 .html [July 4, 2014].

28. Fahmi Huwaidi, March 31, 2012.

29. Qur'an 4:122.

30. Remarks as Prepared for Delivery by President Barack Obama, Address to the United Nations General Assembly. [Online]. Rev. September 24, 2014. Available: http://www.whitehouse.gov/the-press-office/2014/09/24/remarks-prepared-delivery-president-barack-obama-address-united-nations- [October 29, 2014].

31. Rashid Ghannouchi, "There Is No Contradiction between Democracy and Islam," *Washington Post*, October 24, 2014.

32. For a brilliant exposition of these broad themes of "absorption and adaptation," see David Waines, *An Introduction to Islam* (Cambridge: Cambridge University Press, 1995), 59.

33. "Art Quotes." [Online]. Available: http://artquotes.robertgenn.com/auth_ search.php?authid=9 [March 20, 2014].

34. The myth is recounted with innumerable variations. See the useful survey of interpretation at "Greek Myths and Greek Mythology: The Myth of Narcissus." [Online]. Available: http://www.greekmyths-greekmythology.com/narcissus-myth-echo/ [October 2, 2014].

35. Cited and translated by François Burgat, "Islam and Islamist Politics in the Arab World: Old Theories and New Facts." In *Islamist Politics in the Middle East*, ed. Samer S. Shehata (London: Routledge, 2012), 23.

36. See Tareq al Bishri, "About Religion and Knowledge," *Weghat Nathar*, April 2004.

37. Abduh, *The Theology of Unity*, 148.

Index